Deep-sea challenge

Deep-sea challenge

The John Murray/Mabahiss
Expedition to the Indian Ocean,
1933–34

Edited by A. L. Rice

Unesco

FRONTISPIECE. The *Mabahiss* in the Western Harbour, Alexandria, with participants in the Fiftieth Anniversary Symposium, September 1983. (*Photo:* M. V. Angel.)

Published in 1986 by the United Nations Educational,
Scientific and Cultural Organization
7 place de Fontenoy, 75700 Paris

Printed by Richard Clay (The Chaucer Press) Ltd, Bungay

ISBN 92-3-102400-0
© Unesco 1986
Printed in the United Kingdom

PREFACE

In response to the wishes of its Member States, Unesco has made commitments to the strengthening of national and regional marine science and technology infrastructures and research programmes on the world ocean and its environment, and to the dissemination of oceanographic research results and scientific information in the marine sciences.

One of the means employed by the Organization in the pursuit of these commitments has been the publication of information on historic oceanographic expeditions. As the date approached marking the fiftieth anniversary of the joint Anglo-Egyptian John Murray Expedition which took place in 1933–34 on board the Egyptian research vessel *Mabahiss*, the University of Alexandria approached Unesco, the Royal Society of the United Kingdom and several senior oceanographers, inviting their assistance in celebrating the historic event.

The ensuing collaboration resulted in, firstly, the organization of an international symposium entitled 'Marine Science in the North-West Indian Ocean and Adjacent Waters', held at the University of Alexandria, Egypt, on 3–7 September 1983; and, secondly, the production of this book, which Unesco agreed to publish.

The first draft of the manuscript was distributed at the symposium in Alexandria. A number of individuals, especially those having knowledge of the Expedition, its participants and its impact, were invited to review the text and make comments to the editor. Unesco appreciates the enthusiastic collaboration of these people, especially the tireless efforts and dedication of A. L. Rice, the editor. Recognition is also due to the co-operative spirit of officials of the University of Alexandria, the Royal Society and the Institute of Oceanographic Sciences, United Kingdom, and to the various people and institutions involved in all the activities connected with the 50th anniversary celebration.

The author is responsible for the choice and the presentation of the facts contained in this book and for the opinions expressed therein, which are not necessarily those of Unesco, and do not commit the Organization.

The original painting for the dust jacket was donated by a private source in memory of Geraldine Wendy Wright, who in her career typed many Unesco texts, but enjoyed none better than the manuscript of this book.

CONTENTS

11 List of illustrations

13 Foreword

17 Part 1. The John Murray bequest and the organization of the Expedition
    A. L. Rice

33 Part 2. Narrative of the John Murray Expedition to the Arabian Sea
    Lt.-Col. R. B. Seymour Sewell

269 Part 3. Biographical notes on the principal participants
    R. B. Seymour Sewell   *A. L. Rice*
    K. N. MacKenzie   *K. M. MacKenzie*
    W. I. Farquharson   *J. Farquharson*
    E. F. Thompson   *D. Merriman*
    H. Faouzi   *A. L. Rice*
    A. F. Mohamed   *S. A. Morcos*
    H. C. Gilson   *H. C. Gilson*
    T. T. Macan   *T. T. Macan*
    Four Egyptian officers:
    Ahmed Badr, Ahmad
    Sarwat, Mahmoud Mukhtar
    and Edward Morcos   *S. A. Morcos*

299 Part 4. *Mababiss*—the story of the ship
    A. L. Rice

307 Part 5. The significance of the Expedition
    G. E. R. Deacon and A. L. Rice

325 Appendix. John Murray Expedition Scientific Reports published by the
    British Museum (Natural History)

329 Index

LIST OF
ILLUSTRATIONS

FRONTISPIECE—The *Mabahiss* in the Western Harbour, Alexandria, with participants in the Fiftieth Anniversary Symposium, September 1983

FIG. 1. Sir John Murray with the German zoologist Ernst Haeckel and the *Challenger* Expedition chemist John Young Buchanan 23

FIG. 2. The *Mabahiss* loading gear in Alexandria, August 1933 43

FIG. 3. The Expedition burgee 45

FIG. 4. The otter trawl 51

FIG. 5. The large triangular dredge 55

FIG. 6. The Harvey phyto-plankton net 56

FIG. 7. Ekman water-bottles in their rack on deck 63

FIG. 8. The central part of the chemical laboratory 65

FIG. 9. The Priestman grab, open, is hoisted over the side 67

FIG. 10. Hauling in the full grab 69

FIG. 11. The ship's complement 70

FIG. 12. Track chart, Cruise 1 74

FIG. 13. Track chart, Cruise 2 96

FIG. 14. Getting the Agassiz trawl over the side 103

FIG. 15. *Chaetodon gardineri* 105

FIG. 16. Track chart, Cruise 3 110

FIG. 17. A pause in paying out the trawl warp 118

FIG. 18. Washing a dredge haul on deck 126

FIG. 19. Track chart, Cruise 4 134

FIG. 20. Muscat waterfront 141

FIG. 21. The sailors ashore in Muscat 143

FIG. 22. *Plesionika minor* 147

FIG. 23. The scientific staff in working dress 151

FIG. 24. Track chart, Cruise 5 156

FIG. 25. Looking aft from the forecastle of the *Mabahiss* 165

FIG. 26. Track chart, Cruise 6 174

FIG. 27. *Glyphocrangon mabahissae* 182

FIG. 28. Track chart, Cruise 7 192

FIG. 29. Track chart, Cruise 8 208

FIG. 30. In the Maldives: visitors alongside 222

FIG. 31. Track chart, Cruise 9 236

FIG. 32. *Bathymicrops sewelli* 245

FIG. 33. The Agassiz trawl bent on a rocky bottom 247

FIG. 34. *Puerulus sewelli* 255

FIG. 35. Track chart, Cruise 10 258

FIG. 36. Sewell in IMS uniform 264

FIG. 37. The John Murray Expedition Medal 266

FIG. 38. Scientific staff of the Expedition 272

FIG. 39. Title page of Faouzi's
account of the
Expedition   282
FIG. 40. Officers of the
Mabahiss   292

FIG. 41. The launch of the
Mabahiss, 11 September
1930   302
FIG. 42. The *Mabahiss* undergoing trials   303

FOREWORD

At 7 a.m. on Sunday, 3 September 1933, His Egyptian Majesty's Ship (HEMS) *Mabahiss* weighed anchor in the Outer Harbour at Alexandria to begin the John Murray Expedition, a joint Anglo-Egyptian venture which was to take her through the Red Sea, the Gulf of Aden, the north-western Indian Ocean and the Gulf of Oman. By the time the ship returned to Alexandria almost nine months later, she had worked 209 scientific stations and had brought back data and preserved material which were to form the basis of a long series of scientific reports published by the Natural History section of the British Museum over a period of more than thirty years.

The Expedition not only laid the foundation of modern knowledge of marine science in the region but, by stimulating interest in the subject in Egypt, contributed indirectly to the establishment of the Department of Oceanography at the University of Alexandria and to the further development of what is now the Egyptian Institute of Oceanography and Fisheries. Accordingly, as the 50th anniversary of the Expedition approached, several senior Egyptian oceanographers felt that the event should be celebrated in some way; they therefore contacted Unesco, the Royal Society and a number of individual colleagues in the United Kingdom for help and collaboration. One result was a symposium on the Arabian Sea and the adjacent regions, held in Alexandria in September 1983, the proceedings of which are published as a special volume of *Deep-Sea Research* under the editorship of Dr M. V. Angel.[1] A second result is the publication of the present volume.

In the Introduction to the Scientific Reports (published in 1935), the Expedition Leader, Lieutenant-Colonel R. B. Seymour Sewell, provided a brief narrative of the voyage, but referred to a much fuller account which was to be published elsewhere. During his lifetime Sewell tried, unsuccessfully, to find a publisher for this extended narrative. After his death in

---

1. *Deep-Sea Research*, Vol. 31 (6–8A), 1984, pp. 571–1035. The formal report of the Alexandria symposium was issued as Unesco Report in Marine Science No. 31 (123 pp).

1964 the manuscript passed to the British Museum (Natural History), where it is still held. The text of the manuscript forms the basis of this book.

When, late in 1982, I was asked by Unesco to examine Sewell's narrative with a view to its ultimate publication, I felt that while it provides a fascinating impression of a privately funded oceanographic expedition in the inter-war years, it did not, alone, warrant publication. I have accordingly tried to assemble a range of ancillary information which will hopefully fill some of the gaps left by the narrative and provide the modern reader with a clearer view of the context in which the Expedition took place and of its significance. This additional material consists principally of an historical introduction summarizing the background to the voyage, biographical notes on the main participants, an assessment of the significance of the scientific results, and a brief history of the *Mabahiss* from her launch in 1930 to her possible imminent rebirth as an oceanographic museum in Alexandria. For the accuracy or otherwise of much of this information I take full responsibility, though several sections have been provided by other contributors who are identified in the text and to whom I am very grateful.

In addition, my thanks are due to several other individuals and organizations for their help and co-operation. First, I must thank Dr E. Sewell for her permission to edit and publish her father's typescript and the Trustees of the British Museum (Natural History) for allowing me access to Sewell's narrative and to other relevant documentary material in their care. The staff of the British Museum libraries, especially the Zoological Library, were always helpful during my frequent visits to examine this material. Mr K. M. MacKenzie not only provided an excellent biography of his father, but also allowed me to quote from the journal which Captain MacKenzie kept during the Expedition and to obtain photographs of the ship's burgee and the Expedition Medal in his possession. Similarly, Dr H. C. Gilson allowed me to select most of the photographs reproduced in this volume from those which he took during the cruise, while both he and T. T. Macan gave me the benefit of their personal recollections by commenting on parts of an early draft and answering my many queries. Mr N. Gilchrist of Swan Hunter Shipbuilders provided me with details of the *Mabahiss* when she was built, photographs of the launch ceremony and of the ship's trials. Ann Shirley of the National Maritime Museum, London, also made many valuable comments on an early draft and Mr F. W. Manders of the Central Library, Newcastle upon Tyne, identified members of the *Mabahiss* launch party for me. Captain A. M. Tewfik of Alexandria Shipyard contributed much of the information on the history of the *Mabahiss* after the war, particularly what has happened to her since she was laid up in Alexandria in 1965.

I have received much help from my colleagues at the Institute of Oceanographic Sciences, in particular from the staff of the library and of the photographic studio. Finally, my thanks are due to Mrs C. E. Darter for drawing the track charts, to Mrs P. H. Talbot and Mrs B. D. Allen for typing the various drafts from almost illegible originals, and to Mrs G. W. Wright of Unesco who typed the final manuscript.

A. L. Rice
Institute of Oceanographic Sciences
February 1984

PART 1

The John Murray bequest and the organization of the Expedition

By A. L. Rice

THE John Murray Expedition is rather unusual, compared with similar oceanographic voyages, in that it is rarely referred to under the name of the vessel employed. Indeed, outside Egypt the name *Mabahiss*[1] is not widely known and some references to the Expedition clearly assume that the ship used was called the *John Murray*. In fact, the Expedition took its name from the celebrated oceanographer whose bequest, made almost twenty years earlier, largely financed the venture,[2] whereas the use of the *Mabahiss* was a late choice made only after a series of other possibilities had failed to materialize.

John Murray was the son of a Scottish accountant who had emigrated to Canada in 1834. Born at Coburg, Ontario, in 1841, Murray came to Scotland at the age of 15 to live with his maternal grandfather at Bridge of Allan. He studied at the High School in Stirling and eventually attended classes at the University of Edinburgh. In 1868 he began medical studies, but probably never intended to take any examinations. In any case, after only a few weeks as a medical student, he obtained a position as surgeon on a Peterhead whaler and spent seven months in the Arctic during which time he visited Spitsbergen and Jan Mayen Island.

Murray returned to the University of Edinburgh and was working in the laboratory of P. G. Tait, the Professor of Physics, when Sir Charles Wyville Thomson was organizing the *Challenger* Expedition. All of the scientific staff had been appointed when, at the last moment, one of the assistants resigned and Murray was offered the vacant post.

During the cruise, from 1872 to 1876, Murray paid special attention to the plankton, to the sea-bed deposits and to the origin and formation of coral reefs. Although he made important contributions in all of these areas, it was this early interest in sediments and coral reefs that, in a curious way, was to prove particularly significant as far as the John Murray Expedition was concerned.

1. The name *Mabahiss* is a transliteration of the Arabic word for 'researches'. A more correct transliteration would actually be '*Mabahith*' but the other version continues to be used because of long tradition and because the ship herself carries this form. See S. A. Morcos, 'The Egyptian Expedition to the Red Sea 1934/35', *Deep-Sea Research*, Vol. 31 (6–8A), 1984, pp. 599–616.

2. There are many published accounts of the life of Sir John Murray, of which perhaps the best known is that of W. A. Herdman, *Founders of Oceanography and their Work*, London, Edward Arnold, 1923, 340 pp. There are also numerous accounts of John Murray's involvement with the Christmas Island Phosphate Company, which brought him considerable wealth and enabled him to make the bequest which ultimately led to the John Murray Expedition. By far the best is H. Burstyn, 'Science Pays Off: Sir John Murray and the Christmas Island Phosphate Industry 1886–1914, *Social Studies of Science*, No. 5, 1975, pp. 5–34.

After the *Challenger* Expedition Murray returned to his studies in Edinburgh, but in 1877 he joined Sir Charles Wyville Thomson in the 'Challenger Office', established in a small house near the university, to oversee the study of the expedition collections and the publication of the results. Initially Murray was responsible mainly for the documentation and despatch of the collections, but with his colleague's failing health he assumed more and more responsibility, taking over the editorial task completely after Wyville Thomson's death in 1882.

The final two volumes of the Report, containing Murray's own Summary of Results, did not appear until 1895, and the story of the long-standing battle against the parsimony of the Treasury in the publication of the *Challenger* Reports has been told many times. In the meantime, Murray continued his researches begun during the *Challenger* voyage, the first of a series of papers on coral reefs, challenging Darwin's theory of their origin, being read to the Royal Society of Edinburgh in 1880, while his classic monograph with the Abbé Renard on the deep-sea deposits collected during the Expedition was published in 1891.

To further his researches into coral reefs, Murray needed geological samples from as many mid-oceanic islands as possible. One such locality was Christmas Island, lying some 300 kilometres off the coast of Java in the Indian Ocean, and for help in obtaining samples from the island Murray turned to the hydrographer, Captain W. J. L. Wharton. Anxious to assist, Wharton ordered Captain J. F. L. P. Maclear, who had been second-in-command to Captain G. S. Nares during the *Challenger* Expedition and was now in command of HMS *Flying Fish* in the Far East, to call at Christmas Island on his return voyage to England. Accordingly, in January 1887 Maclear collected samples of beach rocks and coral reefs from Christmas Island and when the ship arrived home these were sent to Murray in Edinburgh. Among the specimens he found a reef sample within which was embedded a pebble of pure calcium phosphate—previously unknown from coral islands.

Murray asked Wharton to arrange a more thorough exploration, including the collection of rocks from the highest parts of the island as well as from the shore. This time another former officer from the *Challenger*, Captain Pelham Aldrich, in command of HMS *Egeria*, was ordered to visit the island during a sounding survey that he was to undertake from Malaya to Mauritius. During October 1887 a ten-day exploration of Christmas Island was undertaken and twenty-one geological specimens were collected for Murray. He again identified calcium phosphate and became convinced that rich beds of this rock were to be found on Christmas Island.

The demand for superphosphate, the most widely used artificial fertilizer in the increasingly intensive British agriculture, was growing enormously in the 1880s and Murray was quick to see the economic significance of the initially purely scientific investigation. As soon as his examination of the *Egeria* samples was completed in February 1888, he contacted the Duke of Argyll, the father of yet another *Challenger* officer, who in turn wrote to the Prime Minister, Lord Salisbury, recommending the annexation of Christmas Island as a matter of urgency. Salisbury accepted this recommendation and the relevant government departments acted with consummate speed. Christmas Island was taken into British possession on 6 June 1888, only about six months after Murray had received the *Egeria* specimens; Murray had a much longer battle to obtain permission to explore (and exploit) the island's mineral resources!

The main obstacle was a rival claimant to Christmas Island—George Clunies Ross, whose family occupied and controlled the nearby Cocos and Keeling Islands under a lease from the British Government. The Colonial Office had the task of adjudicating between the claimants and, after a series of vicissitudes in which first one and then the other was favoured, finally awarded a joint lease which took effect at the beginning of 1891. Murray and Ross were to occupy the island jointly for 99 years and were to pay a royalty of 5 per cent on all timber and phosphate exports.

The Ross family organized the initial colonization of Christmas Island, but during the first few years of the joint lease Murray was unable to get them to make any effort to exploit the phosphate resources, for they preferred the activities with which they were already familiar—agriculture and lumbering. Finally, however, the Rosses gave in to Murray's persistent pressure to form a mining company and in January 1897 the Christmas Island Phosphate Company was registered, with Murray as Chairman.

Mining began in earnest in 1899, and by 1911 1 million tons of phosphate had been removed from the island, bringing very considerable financial rewards to the company's shareholders, including Murray and the Rosses, and to the British Government. Writing in 1913, Murray claimed that the government had already received more revenue from the Christmas Island venture in the form of rents, royalties and taxes than the £170,000 which had been the total cost of the *Challenger* Expedition. He may have anticipated this event by a few years, particularly in view of the disastrous effect of the First World War on the Phosphate Company, but there is no doubt that the British Treasury ultimately received much more from Christmas Island than it spent on the Expedition. Moreover, there is a strong case to be made for Murray's other claim that the Christmas Island phosphate industry was a direct result of the *Challenger* Expedition and that, but for this connection, the phosphate resources might either never have been exploited or the revenues might have gone to another country.

Accepting this relationship, Murray's private gains resulting from knowledge obtained in the public service seem curious by modern standards, but he ploughed much of his personal fortune back into oceanography. During his lifetime he paid the costs of producing the *Challenger* Medal on completion of the Expedition Reports, when the Treasury refused to pay; he maintained a research laboratory near his home at Challenger Lodge; he endowed the Alexander Agassiz Medal of the United States Academy of Sciences; and, in 1910, he covered all the expenses, other than those normally incurred by the vessel, of the four-month cruise in the North Atlantic on the *Michael Sars*, which was lent by the Norwegian Government.

Murray's support for oceanography continued after his death in a motor accident near Edinburgh in 1914: under the terms of his will, 250 shares in the Christmas Island Phosphate Company were to be set aside and the dividends received from them were to be applied, under the direction of his children, to 'scientific research or investigations or exploration which are likely to lead to an increase of natural knowledge and especially in the science of oceanography and limnology'.

Initially, Murray had hoped that his children, especially his sons, might carry on his scientific work. However, shortly before his death he had apparently 'been made aware that his sons' tastes and feelings lay in other directions'[1] and in his will he therefore suggested that, though his children were to administer the bequest, if more than £300 were to be spent on an individual project they should consult the Royal Society, the Challenger Society or the Royal Society of Edinburgh.[2] Murray's younger son, Thomas Henderson Murray, emigrated to Northern Rhodesia shortly after the end of the First World War and although, as Seymour Sewell's narrative records, he travelled to Egypt to welcome the *Mabahiss* home at the end of the Expedition, the main responsibility for administering the bequest was left to his elder brother, John Challenger Murray.

By mid-1931 a considerable sum had accumulated in the bequest. It was decided that £20,000 should be used to finance a major oceanographic Expedition and J. C. Murray enlisted the help and advice of Professor J. Stanley Gardiner, Professor of Zoology at the University of Cambridge, Dr E. J. Allen, Director of the Marine Biological Laboratory at Plymouth, and Dr W. T. Calman, Keeper of Zoology at the British Museum (Natural History). These scientists consulted their colleagues worldwide and concluded that the Ex-

1. Report of the Keeper of Zoology, Natural History section of the British Museum, dated 21 January 1920, on the contents of Villa Medusa, Edinburgh, where the John Murray collections were then housed. (British Museum (Natural History) Mineralogy Library, pamphlet box 187.)
2. Sir John Murray's will, General Register House, Edinburgh, 4197–238.

Fig. 1. Sir John Murray (left), with the German zoologist Ernst Haeckel (centre) and the *Challenger* Expedition chemist John Young Buchanan, in front of the Musée Océanographique, Monaco, during its construction in April 1904. (*Photo:* courtesy of the Musée Océanographique.)

pedition should investigate the western Indian Ocean region and that the Scientific Leader should be Lieutenant-Colonel R. B. Seymour and Dr W. T. Sewell.[1]

1. Letter from J. Stanley Gardiner to the Chairman of the Trustees of the British Museum dated 19 May 1932. According to this letter Gardiner 'circularized the leading authorities of every country on this matter' and received thirty-seven replies.

The choice of the Indian Ocean was especially apt, for Sir John Murray had himself felt that this region was particularly deserving of attention, since it had not been visited by the *Challenger* and, except for a series of cruises by the Royal Indian Marine Ship (RIMS) *Investigator* from 1881 onwards, had hardly been studied during his lifetime. The Danish research vessel *Dana* had crossed the western Indian Ocean from Ceylon to Madagascar and Mombasa during her circumnavigation from 1928 to 1930 and, in doing so, had discovered the Carlsberg Ridge, but there had otherwise been little work in the area since John Murray's death. Moreover, the relatively enclosed nature of this part of the ocean, being landlocked on all but its southern boundary, together with the lack of major rivers emptying into it, suggested that the chemistry and physics might be easier to understand than in more complex regions.

It is not clear whether the choice of Sewell as Scientific Leader preceded or followed the decision to investigate the north-western Indian Ocean, though he was certainly one of the correspondents who had recommended the study of this region.[1] His experience as Surgeon Naturalist on the *Investigator* was highly appropriate, while his imminent retirement from the Directorship of the Zoological Survey of India was particularly timely.[2] In any event, he was deeply involved in the preliminary planning of the Expedition, some months before the John Murray Committee was formally established.

This Committee met for the first time on 15 June 1932.[3] It consisted of J. C. Murray (Chairman), Stanley Gardiner (Secretary), Allen and Calman, all representing the Sir John Murray Trustees, C. Tate Regan representing the Trustees of the British Museum, G. I. Taylor representing the Royal Society, Vice-Admiral H. P. Douglas, the previous Hydrographer to the Admiralty, and Sewell.

Having reviewed the decisions already made and having approved Sewell's general plan of work, the most important item discussed was the ship.[4] The possibility of using the *William Scoresby*,[5] which had been

1. J. Stanley Gardiner, 'The John Murray Expedition', *Nature* (London), No. 131, May 1933, pp. 64–641.
2. See biographical note on Sewell, Part 3, p. 271.
3. Committee papers, British Museum (Natural History) Zoology Library, 89.f.M.
4. Sewell's plan shows that E. F. Thompson's participation had already been decided upon but that the remainder of the scientific staff was determined only as 'two or three junior zoologists, the number depending on which ship is secured for the expedition'.
5. The *William Scoresby* was built by Messrs Cook, Welton & Gemmell Ltd and launched at Beverley, Yorkshire, on 31 December 1925. She was 134 feet in overall length and had engines of 1,050 h.p. Built on whalecatcher lines, she was larger and more powerful than most whalecatchers of the time, and was engaged in scientific investigations

specially built to join the RRS *Discovery* in the Antarctic investigations, had already been considered, but Sewell was more favourably inclined towards the *Dana* since it had 'forced ventilation suitable for a tropical climate and also more accommodation for the scientific staff'. However, the Committee was then, and for some time to come, hoping that a cruise sponsored by some other organization might be undertaken at the same time as the John Murray Expedition; it was possible that Johannes Schmidt might agree to conduct such a cruise in the *Dana*, in which case the Murray Committee would have had to be satisfied with the *William Scoresby*. The situation was to be clarified during a visit which Sewell was about to make to Copenhagen.

Following this visit an updated document by Sewell reported that as a result of discussion with Schmidt and with Mortensen, Director of Fisheries for Denmark, he had concluded that the *Dana* was not likely to be obtainable during the planned period of the John Murray Expedition, because of the heavy programme of work which the ship was expected to undertake for the fisheries department.

Accordingly, J. C. Murray, Sewell and Stanley Gardiner met on 30 August 1932 and produced a revised plan, based on the use of the fisheries research vessel *George Bligh*, owned by the British Ministry of Agriculture and Fisheries, which was circulated to the Committee. This plan called for a departure from England in August 1933 and a return voyage leaving Great Hanish Island in the southern Red Sea in April 1934.

The plan also reported that an approach to the Egyptian Government had been made to ask if HEMS *Mabahiss* could undertake a 'synchronous expedition . . . in the Red Sea', for the results of such an expedition, together with the echo-sounding work in the Red Sea to be accomplished from the *George Bligh*, would be 'likely to yield results of high value to science and would worthily initiate and greatly help the work of the fine Station for scientific research established by Egypt at Gardaga' (Al-Ghardaga).

As Sewell points out in his narrative, the Egyptian authorities decided that they alone did not have sufficient expertise available to organize such an expedition; instead, they offered the loan of the *Mabahiss* for the John Murray Expedition. In December 1932 Stanley Gardiner circulated the Committee members with a memorandum about the *Mabahiss* and a letter explaining that the loan offer had been accepted and that several outstanding decisions could now be made. He accordingly intended calling a second

---

from 1926 until 1950. See S. Kemp and A. C. Hardy, 'The *Discovery* Investigations: Objects, Equipment and Methods used in research', *Discovery Report*, No. 1, 1929, pp. 151–229.

meeting of the Committee in January 1933, after which Captain Marriott, RN, would travel to Egypt in order to organize the necessary alterations to the vessel.

Those attending this second committee meeting, on 26 January 1933, were somewhat different from those present at the first. Murray, Stanley Gardiner, Calman, Allen and Tate Regan were once again present, but Sewell had had to return to Calcutta to wind up his directorship of the Zoological Survey, while Douglas and Taylor both sent apologies for absence. In the meantime, Stanley Kemp, Director of the *Discovery* investigations, had been co-opted onto the Committee along with Captain J. A. Edgell, the current Hydrographer, who was accompanied by D. J. Matthews. Finally, Captain Marriott, RN, was present as a guest.

The Committee was clearly relieved that the Expedition at last had a ship and they gratefully accepted Marriott's offer to organize the vessel's refit in Alexandria. They went on to express gratification that Lieutenant-Commander W. I. Farquharson, RN, was to be seconded to the Expedition by the Admiralty. The allowances to which he would have been entitled during this period, had he been employed in the Hydrographic Service, were to be met from the Expedition funds; for a twelve-month period the cost was estimated at £180–£200!

The Committee were also told that the 'Surveyor General of India had agreed to send Major Glennie on one cruise of the *Mabahiss* to the Maldives, etc., with the object of making gravity observations as to the depth of the rocks underlying the carbonate of lime formation of coral reefs', surely a line of investigation which would have pleased Sir John Murray.

There followed a rather detailed discussion of the number, pay and duties of the scientific staff, though in addition to Sewell only one, E. F. Thompson, a chemist who was to act as second-in-command of the scientific team, was named in the minutes. Thompson was to 'hold himself at the disposal' of Sewell from 1 April 1933, in return for which he was to receive £25 per month until the start of the Expedition when, like the other scientists employed, he would receive an honorarium of £100 for his services during the voyage itself.

Curiously, the minutes contain no mention of the appointment of a Captain for the *Mabahiss*, though with only about seven months to the proposed start of the Expedition this problem must have greatly concerned the Committee.

On 4 April, however, Stanley Gardiner sent out a further circular detailing the deliberations of the Ship Subcommittee which had met on 30 March following Marriott's return from Egypt. This circular summarized the conditions under which the *Mabahiss* was to be loaned, including the need to appoint the Commanding Officer by 1 July.[1] Marriott had apparently tried without success to find a suitable captain during his visit to Egypt. The Subcommittee had therefore interviewed and appointed K. N. MacKenzie, who had had considerable experience of oceanographic research aboard the *Discovery* during Sir Douglas Mawson's British, Australian and New Zealand Antarctic Research Expedition of 1929–31.

Stanley Gardiner admitted in his circular that 'a few matters are still not as clear as might be desired', surely something of an understatement since, among other deficiencies, they had yet to appoint a Chief Engineer, only two of the British scientist participants had so far been settled upon, and the Scientific Leader was out of the country for a further two months! However, 'no serious difficulties were anticipated' and Stanley Gardiner intended to call a further meeting of the full Committee in June after Sewell's return to the United Kingdom from India, via Alexandria, where he was expected to spend some time during late May.

This third and final committee meeting before the *Mabahiss* sailed was held on 20 June, with all the members present except for Douglas, Allen and Taylor. Considerable progress had been made since Stanley Gardiner's memorandum of 4 April. Thus, on the question of staff, the Committee was able to confirm the appointments of W. J. Griggs as Chief Engineer, H. C. Gilson as Assistant Chemist and T. T. Macan as Assistant Naturalist, the latter two both from Stanley Gardiner's department in Cambridge.[2]

1. The 4 April 1933 memorandum lists the following conditions:
   1. The *Mabahiss* is at the disposal of the Committee from 1 July 1933 to 1 May 1934. She will be conditioned to go to sea by 1 September 1933. She will fly the Egyptian flag with the British ensign at the masthead; the Egyptian Government will through their diplomatic channels inform the countries where the *Mabahiss* will work of the purposes of her cruises.
   2. The *Mabahiss* will be handed over in perfect seagoing condition and the Committee turn her over in the same state with no demands 'due to wear and tear'. All alterations and fittings added by the Committee 'will be left for the future use'. The Committee will insure the *Mabahiss* in London. The Egyptian Government assure a free passage through the Canal.
   3. The general principle of carrying two Egyptian Deck Officers, two Egyptian Engineers, two Egyptian Scientists and a crew of seafaring men from the Egyptian ports is agreed. The Commanding Officer is to be appointed from 1 July 1933 and the Chief Engineer (British) from 1 August 1933.
2. Dr Macan suggests that although the possibility of participating in the cruise had been mentioned to him as early as 1931, the lateness of the official appointments of both Gilson and himself was due to Stanley Gardiner awaiting the results of the Part II examinations due out in June, so that he could select first-class awardees from among the unusually large number of students presenting themselves that year.

With the exception of the Wireless Operator (ultimately J. Lloyd Jones) the British staff was now more or less complete. Moreover, Thompson had spent some ten weeks studying chemical techniques at the Marine Biological Laboratory in Plymouth and was about to leave, together with one of the Egyptian participating scientists, Abdel Fattah Mohamed, for a period of further study with Scandinavian scientists including Helland Hansen, Sverdrup and Gaade.

Sewell presented a detailed proposed itinerary, very similar to the one which was actually followed, and the Committee was enabled to discuss the detailed plans for the scientific work and express its satisfaction with them. J. C. Murray, in his capacity as Treasurer, presented his Financial Report and an estimate of the total cost of the Expedition. These costs had increased beyond the earlier estimates, due mainly to increasing costs of coal, insurance[1] and wages, but they nevertheless seemed to be neatly covered by the £20,000 available and included the refrigerator plant for the ship which the Treasurer was authorized to order at a cost of about £425. Murray's estimate of June 1933 makes interesting reading when compared with present-day prices (Table 1).

Lastly, Stanley Gardiner presented what was in effect his final report as Secretary before the start of the Expedition, since he had by then 'completed the preliminary work and handed over all practical matters as to the *Mabahiss* and as to the scientific gear, apparatus and work of the Expedition'. One of his last tasks had been to write articles on the proposed Expedition for publication in *Nature*[2] and the *Geographical Journal*[3] to counter 'inaccurate reports in the press, especially in respect to the Egyptian participation', for, wrote Stanley Gardiner, 'the daily press seems particularly shy of saying anything nice about Egypt—I wish they would'.

There is no further documentation of the organization of the Expedition in the British Museum (Natural History), for the Committee was not convened again until its fourth and final meeting on 17 October 1934, after the Expedition was completed.

---

1. The *Mabahiss* was initially to be insured for E£25,000. The Egyptian Committee which, in March 1933, considered the conditions under which the vessel was to be loaned for the Expedition felt that this figure did not represent its true value. Instead, they recommended that the insurance cover should be increased to E£25,000 for the hull and E£11,000 for the engines. See H. Faouzi, *The Cruise of the Egyptian Vessel 'Mabahiss' to the Indian Ocean with the Sir John Murray Expedition: A Commemorative Book*, Cairo, Egyptian Printing House, 1939, 123 pp. (In Arabic.)
2. J. Stanley Gardiner, *Nature*, op. cit.
3. J. Stanley Gardiner, 'The *John Murray* Expedition to the Indian Ocean', *Geographical Journal*, Vol. 81, No. 6, June 1933, pp. 570–3.

TABLE 1. Estimated cost of the John Murray Oceanographical Expedition to the Arabian Sea, 1933–34

Mabahiss running costs per month

Wages (Captain, officers and crew)	£350	
Feeding	175	
Ship's stores	50	
Coal and water	425	
	1 000	
Agent's charge 2.5%	25	
	1 025	

Running costs for nine months		£9 225
Preliminary expenses		300
Alterations to ship (including refrigeration plant)		800
Echo-sounding set and expert's expenses		1 000
Docking and painting		100
Insurance		1 100
Scientific gear		2 500
Cost of travelling to Alexandria and return		
Four at £100	£400	
Three at £70	210	
		610
Allowance to four scientists		600
Preliminary expenses		
Thompson	£300	
Sewell	300	
Miscellaneous	600	
		1 200
		17 435
Research workers		2 000
Publication		565
		£20 000

After the June 1933 meeting there was clearly still much to be done in England, including the organization of the dispatch of equipment, and communications with institutions such as the Meteorological Office and

the Admiralty. Nevertheless, Stanley Gardiner had certainly handed over
the day-to-day arrangements of the final details of the Expedition participants and, while Sewell stayed on in England and did not finally reach
Alexandria until a week or so before the *Mabahiss* sailed, the focus of the
activities gradually shifted to Egypt.

The ship entered the Government Dockyard in Alexandria early in July
1933 and at about the same time MacKenzie and Griggs arrived in Egypt
to supervise the refit, together with Tyler, an expert from Hughes Bros,
who was to fit the echo-sounder and accompany the *Mabahiss* as far as
Aden to ensure that it was functioning properly. Over the succeeding two
months, the British team gradually gathered in Alexandria. Farquharson
and Thompson arrived in early August; Gilson, Macan and Lloyd Jones on
21 August, and Sewell finally reached Alexandria on the 24th.

During the few weeks before the ship sailed a series of minor calamities
overtook the *Mabahiss* including, as Sewell describes, problems with the
newly fitted refrigeration plant and the loss of one of the over-the-side
platforms. Ultimately, however, all these difficulties were overcome and,
with the exception of some items of equipment from England which had to
be picked up from Port Said, all was ready in early September and the
Mabahiss sailed on the 3rd, only two days later than Sewell's planned
departure date which had been presented to the John Murray Committee in
June.

Comment by S. A. Morcos,
Division of Marine Sciences, Unesco

The account given by Lieutenant-Colonel R. B. Seymour Sewell, referred
to on page 37, that the *Mabahiss* was offered by the Egyptian Government,
differs from that of Hussein Faouzi in his memorial book on the Expedition,
published in 1939.[1] According to Dr Faouzi, Professor Gardiner
talked to HE Dr Hafez Afify Pasha, the Plenipotentiary Minister in Great
Britain, on the importance of the Red Sea, and the desirability of carrying
out an Egyptian expedition to the Red Sea at the same time as the John

---

1. Faouzi, op. cit.

Murray Expedition to the Indian Ocean. However, one month after the discussion, Professor Gardiner wrote to the Egyptian Minister, putting forward a new proposal, which was the origin of the Egyptian Government's participation in the John Murray Expedition.

In summary, it was proposed that the John Murray Expedition borrow HEMS *Mabahiss* to carry out a study of the Indian Ocean and that the Egyptian Government follow with an expedition to the Red Sea. In setting out his proposal, Professor Gardiner elaborated on the various benefits to the Egyptian Government that would arise as a result of this undertaking. I believe that Dr Faouzi's account is more accurate, especially as it was more or less maintained in an official memorandum in August 1933 by the Vice-Minister of Finance to the Council of Ministers of Egypt.

PART 2

Narrative of the John Murray Expedition to the Arabian Sea

By the late Lt.-Col. R. B. Seymour Sewell,
Leader of the Expedition

Editor's note

Three versions of Sewell's typescript are held by the British Museum (Natural History): (1) an unbound incomplete version which is very heavily edited by Sewell and has many passages, which the author evidently felt were sensitive, crossed out; (2) an unbound almost complete version (with page 4 missing) apparently produced from (1) above, and with relatively minor additional changes; (3) a fair, bound copy of (2) above with very few corrections and accompanied by a bound volume of photographs. The version reproduced here is based on this final bound copy.

In editing Sewell's typescript I have endeavoured to keep as closely as possible to the original, only correcting obvious factual and typographical errors and (hopefully) improving the readability by changing the author's rather curious punctuation and word order. Although I believe that in so doing I have nowhere altered Sewell's sense, any changes of this sort which have crept in are, of course, entirely my responsibility.

A. L. Rice

Chapter 1

Background to the voyage, the ship, its equipment and personnel

Introduction

Iᴛ has been stated that students of the history of science may well date the birth of modern oceanography from December 21, 1872, the day on which HMS *Challenger* put to sea from Portsmouth, England, on her great voyage of discovery that lasted for nearly four years and during which she sailed round the world across the three great oceans: Atlantic, Pacific and South Indian. But just as there is a pre-natal period that precedes the actual birth of an animal, so too in the case of oceanography there was a period antecedent to the *Challenger* Expedition in which observations and researches on the conditions that are present in the deep sea were being pursued and as a result of which the belief that it was impossible for animals to live under the conditions that exist in the deeper water layers was gradually being replaced by uncertainty and doubt.

To zoologists who, like myself, have spent much time in India, one name among those of the earlier workers has a special interest: in 1813 the Hon. East India Company attacked and captured Seringapatam and among those who were made prisoner was a Danish scientist of the name of Nathaniel Wallich. Wallich had already made a reputation for himself and shortly after his capture he was admitted to the East India Company's service and was appointed Curator of the Botanical Gardens, Calcutta, while in his spare time he acted as Curator of the Natural History collections of the Asiatic Society of Bengal (or, as it was then known, the Asiatick Society). In 1815 a son, George Charles Wallich, was born and a few years later the boy was sent to Edinburgh to be educated and there qualified in medicine and passed into the Indian Medical Service. After his retirement from this service he was appointed in 1860 to be Naturalist on the *Bulldog* during her survey of the north Atlantic Ocean in connection with the laying of the submarine cable, and for over twenty years he studied marine biology, being one of the first zoologists to prove that animals actually existed in the deep waters of the ocean.[1] Wallich carefully preserved a number of animals that were obtained, and exhibited these to zoologists in England; at first it was maintained that these must have been caught in the upper levels, but gradually it came to be realized that they must have been obtained in depths beyond those known to be inhabited. Finally, Sir Wyville Thomson obtained from the Admiralty the services of first HMS *Lightning* and later of HMS *Porcupine* for the purpose of exploring the north Atlantic. The results obtained left no room for doubt that the deep sea was populated by animals that had been hitherto unknown and this led to a proposal to carry out a worldwide exploratory cruise to investigate all the great ocean beds. Again the Admiralty exhibited that readiness to co-operate with scientists in the advancement of knowledge that they have shown so consistently that it is nowadays almost taken for granted, and HMS *Challenger* was duly commissioned for her great scientific expedition.

While the plans for the *Challenger* Expedition were being drawn up, the Asiatick Society approached the Government of India and urged that it should carry out similar researches in the northern parts of the Indian Ocean. At this time the Government of India was considering the creation of a special Marine Survey of India and it agreed to the appointment to the new survey of an officer of the Indian Medical Service, whose duties would include those of Medical Officer to the survey ship and of Deep-sea Biologist. Whether it was the direct result of this action on the part of the Government of India that the decision was reached to omit the northern part of the Indian Ocean from the tour of the *Challenger* is not known, but at any rate the course of the expedition was laid far to the south past Crozet and Kerguelen Islands. The first appointment of a Surgeon–Naturalist to the Marine Survey of India was actually made in 1875, though the survey did not possess a sea-going vessel until 1880, when the RIMS *Investigator* was launched. Through the kindness of the Admiralty the *Investigator* was supplied with apparatus for deep-sea research by the presentation of a selection of gear that had actually been used by the *Challenger* during her world cruise. For nearly fifty years a succession of Surgeon–Naturalists have been carrying out the investigation of a deep fauna of the Indian waters, namely the Laccadive Sea, the Bay of Bengal and the Andaman Sea; and I had the privilege of holding the appointment, with an interval during the years of the Great War, from 1910 to 1925.

---

1. See A. L. Rice, H. L. Burstyn and A. G. E. Jones, 'G. C. Wallich M.D.—Megalomaniac or Mis-used Oceanographic Genius?', *J. Soc. Biblphy nat. Hist.*, No. 7, 1976, pp. 423–50.

Sir John Murray, who died in 1914, left by his will the sum of £20,000 to be devoted to oceanographic research and towards the end of 1931 his Trustees decided to spend this sum in equipping another oceanographic expedition, the John Murray Expedition, to explore the north-western part of the Indian Ocean, namely the Arabian Sea and its offshoots, the Gulf of Aden and the Gulf of Oman. It was in February 1932, that I was first approached by the Trustees and a few months later the post of Leader of the Expedition was offered to me; with the sanction of the Secretary of State for India, I accepted the appointment.

After my appointment as Leader, it was necessary for me to return to India in 1932 for a few months in order to complete my service under the Government. During my absence much of the work of making the necessary preparations fell on the shoulders of Mr J. C. Murray, the President and Treasurer, and Professor J. Stanley Gardiner, FRS, of Cambridge University, who was acting as Secretary to the John Murray Committee.

The first and most important arrangement to be made was the securing of a suitable ship. At first we tried to obtain the loan or charter of the Royal Danish Research Ship *Dana*, whose capabilities had already been thoroughly proved during a scientific cruise round the world, under the late Dr Johannes Schmidt, in 1928–30; but her service could not be secured. The Trustees then considered the possibility of getting a charter of either the *William Scoresby* from the *Discovery* Committee or of the Lowestoft fishery research vessel, *George Bligh*, from the Fisheries Department; but neither of these vessels was thought to be quite suitable. While discussions had been taking place regarding the John Murray Expedition, the Government of Egypt had been approached and an attempt had been made to persuade them to conduct, simultaneously with the John Murray Expedition, in their Coast-guard and Fishery Research vessel, HEMS *Mabahiss*, an investigation of the Red Sea. At first this proposal was favourably received, but later the Egyptian Government came to the conclusion that they did not possess either scientists or officers who had had sufficient training to give such an undertaking a prospect of success.

The best available vessel for the John Murray Expedition itself thus appeared to be HEMS *Mabahiss*, which had been built for fishery research work by the Egyptian Government in 1929.[1] The Committee therefore placed its dilemma before the Government of Egypt, King Fuad being well known for the interest that he takes in oceanography. In reply the Egyptian Government most generously proffered the loan of the *Mabahiss* for the winter of 1933/34 under certain conditions, the most important of

1. The *Mabahiss* was launched on 11 September 1930 (see page 301).

which were that we should take an Egyptian Government crew and officers and train them in the work and that the Expedition should be accompanied by two Egyptian scientists, one from the Fisheries Department of the Coast-guard Service and the other from Cairo University. A further condition was that everything in the shape of scientific gear that was put into the vessel should be left in her at the termination of the Expedition and become the property of the Egyptian Government. These conditions were accepted and in due course the *Mabahiss* was handed over to the Murray Committee.

The *Mabahiss* is of the Mersey Trawler type and was built by Swan Hunter and Wigham Richardson Ltd of Newcastle-on-Tyne, partly for coast-guard patrol work and partly for fishery research. She has a total displacement of 640 tons; her length measurement is 138 feet and she has a beam of 23 feet 6 inches, while she draws about 12 feet 6 inches of water forward and 14 feet 6 inches aft.[1] I first made her acquaintance in May, 1933, when I was on my way home from India. I had arrived at Port Said on Monday, 8 May, in the early hours of the morning, and had proceeded to Cairo to interview a number of government officials and officials of Cairo University in connection with the expedition and the loan of the vessel. On the following morning I was sitting in the office of Dr Bangham, the Dean of the Faculty of Science, when a telegram was handed to me. It read: 'Colonel Sewell can inspect *Mabahiss* at Port Said on Thursday morning at 9 o'clock'; so Wednesday evening saw me retracing my steps to Port Said. On the journey down I was comfortably seated in the corner of my compartment when the train stopped at Benha, the junction for Alexandria, and three people got in and occupied the other end; of the three, one was in civilian clothes, but two were in uniform and were clearly in government service. During the rest of the journey I idly wondered who they were and what their jobs might be. They were speaking Arabic, of which I didn't understand a word, but one of them was reading a recent issue of an engineering journal and I therefore, and as it subsequently turned out correctly, concluded that engineering was his profession, for one doesn't read an engineering journal for pleasure! It was late when I reached Port Said and I went straight to my hotel; the next morning at about 8.45 there was a knock on my door and I was informed that Dr Faouzi, the Director of Fishery Research, was waiting below. I immediately

---

1. Sewell mixes Imperial and metric units of length and weight indiscriminately. I have occasionally given the metric equivalents of depths given in fathoms in the original (1 fathom = 1.83 m) for clarity, but otherwise I have left the figures unchanged, since Sewell's disregard for uniformity was fairly typical of English texts of the time.

went down and there on the terrace were the identical three gentlemen who had travelled down in the compartment with me. They introduced themselves and I learnt that they were Dr Faouzi, Salama Bey, the Acting Director of the Coast-guard Administration, and Mr Albani, the Superintending Engineer to the Coast-guard Service. They had come over from Alexandria to meet me and show me round the *Mabahiss*, which they said would be arriving in port at 9 o'clock. A few minutes before the time a little grey ship flying the Egyptian Government flag steamed past the jetty and the statue of de Lesseps and anchored in the harbour, and a little later we were all in a motor launch making our way out to her.

Having inspected the *Mabahiss* and discussed the proposed arrangements and the conditions of loan, I returned to Cairo and again interviewed Dr Bangham and various officials and then left for Alexandria, where I met El Miralai Ahmed Fuad Bey, the Director General of the Egyptian Marine, Admiral Wells Pasha, RN, the Head of the Ports and Lights Department and again Salama Bey and Dr Faouzi, as well as several other officials, from all of whom I received the greatest kindness. Finally, I again inspected the *Mabahiss* and then sailed for England, arriving home on 28 May.

While negotiations regarding a vessel for the expedition were being conducted, the equally important subject of scientific personnel was under consideration. Owing to the comparatively recent birth of the science of oceanography, the number of trained oceanographers in England is but small, and those who were fully acquainted with the necessary techniques, and especially those which deal with the chemical and physical branches of the subject, were for the most part either permanently employed in the Fishery Department or in the various marine biological laboratories, so that their services were not available for a prolonged cruise. The post of Deputy Leader and Senior Chemist was offered to Dr E. F. Thompson of Cambridge University and he consented to take over the charge of the chemical and physical sides of our investigations;[1] two other appointments, a Biologist and a Chemist, were given to Mr T. T. Macan and Mr H. Cary Gilson respectively, both also from Cambridge. The very important post of Navigator and Surveyor was filled by the appointment of Lieutenant-Commander W. I. Farquharson, of the Hydrographic Department of the Royal Navy, whose services were very kindly lent to us by the Admiralty; he was also placed in charge of the samples to be obtained from the sea bottom. The two Egyptian scientists, who were to sail with us in accordance with our agreement with the Government of Egypt, were Dr

---

1. Thompson did not, in fact, obtain his Ph.D. until 1936, for his thesis was based on data obtained during the John Murray Expedition (see page 279).

Faouzi, who was appointed by the Coast-guard Department, and Abdel Fatteh Effendi Mohamed of Cairo University, whose special line of work had been physical chemistry and who was sent for a course of training to the Marine Biological Laboratory at Plymouth and later to Bergen for some months prior to the departure of the Expedition.

The question, and an exceedingly important one, that next arose was that of our Captain. Here we were fortunate in being able to secure the services of Captain K. N. MacKenzie who had served with Sir Douglas Mawson on two of his expeditions to the Antarctic, firstly as Chief Officer and then as Captain of the *Discovery*. The post of Chief Engineer was filled by the appointment of Mr W. J. Griggs, MIMarE, who had also been to the Antarctic with Mawson in the *Discovery* and thus was well-known to Captain MacKenzie. As our crew was drawn from the Egyptian Government Service it became necessary for his Egyptian Majesty to confer temporary commissions in the Coast-guard Service on both Captain MacKenzie and Chief Engineer Griggs, the former holding the rank of 'Bimbashi' and the latter that of 'Bash Mahandis'. The post of Wireless Operator was given to Mr Lloyd Jones and his duties very rapidly expanded until they included those of Ship's Clerk and Purser.

On my return to England in May 1933, I was able to take over from Professor J. Stanley Gardiner the work of collecting together and getting shipped out to Alexandria all the required scientific apparatus. Until one has had actual experience of this kind of work one can have no conception of the amount of gear that is necessary. The Murray Committee were fortunate in being able to secure from Australia House, London, much of the apparatus that had been got together by Sir Douglas Mawson for his Antarctic expedition. Very great assistance was obtained from the staff of the British Museum (Natural History) and especially from Dr W. T. Calman, FRS, the Keeper of Zoology, and from the Deputy Keeper, Dr G. C. Robson. Dr S. W. Kemp, FRS, the Director of the *Discovery* investigations and Mr Herdman, spared no time or trouble to help in every way that they could, while the Hydrographers to the Admiralty, first Rear-Admiral Sir Harry Douglas, CMG, RN, and later Captain Edgell, RN, gave us every assistance in their power. Finally, Dr J. Allen, FRS, and the staff of the Marine Biological Laboratory, Plymouth, assisted us with advice and with the supervision of the manufacture of some of our gear, especially of the trawls and dredges, and by putting all our chemists through a course of training.

The Director of the Hydrographic Department of the Admiralty had requested that during our visit to the Maldive Archipelago, Lieutenant-Commander Farquharson, RN, might be permitted to make observations on the lines of magnetism that run across the islands.

Moreover, the Director of the Survey of India asked us to carry on board Major Glennie, RE, during our cruise through the archipelago and put him on shore at suitable places when he could carry out observations on the pendulum to enable him to calculate the strength of gravity.

Among the various firms that made and supplied much of our gear, and who are deserving of our best thanks, were Messrs Munro Bros, who made several pieces of apparatus, often at short notice, in order to replace losses during the course of the Expedition; Messrs Kilner and Co., who made all our glass storage jars and water-sample bottles; the Telegraph Construction and Maintenance Co., who supplied us with a Lucas sounding machine and with several sounding tubes and leads; and Messrs Priestman Bros, who made a special grab for obtaining samples of the sea bottom. Messrs Hughes Bros supplied the ship with the latest model of echo-sounding apparatus and sent out one of their experts, Mr Tyler, to supervise its installation in the *Mabahiss* and to accompany us during our first cruise down the Red Sea in order to make sure that the apparatus was working satisfactorily; Messrs Negretti and Zambra installed a recording thermo-graph in the ship in connection with the engine-room intake and also made a number of thermometers for us; and Messrs Hall and Co. supplied us with a refrigerator.

When all the apparatus had been got together it became evident that there was such an accumulation that the question of getting it all shipped out to Alexandria in time was one of considerable difficulty and magnitude; here, thanks to the influence of Captain MacKenzie, Captain MacDonald of the Ellerman-City Line most kindly came to our assistance; he undertook on behalf of the Ellerman-City and associated Lines, especially Messrs Westcott and Laurance and the Ellerman-Wilson Line, to convey all of our gear out to Egypt.

Some of the gear left England on board the SS *Thurso* about the middle of July, while the greater part was dispatched on the SS *Gerano* that sailed on 29 July 1933. A few of the last articles to leave were sent out by the P and O and BI Co. in the SS *Kaiser-i-Hind* that reached Egypt on 23 August; but even up to the end of that month a few articles were still being received at Port Said, where they were kept for us by the English Coaling Co. Ltd. These were put on board the *Mabahiss* in the early hours of the morning of 4 September, when we passed through the Suez Canal on our way to the Arabian Sea.

In order that all arrangements for the Expedition might be made be-forehand in the various ports at which we were to call during the course of the Expedition, it was necessary that we should appoint an Agent, and the P and O Company very kindly undertook this duty for us. Furthermore, all the various Government and Port Authorities were notified through our Foreign and India Offices, of our intended visits and of the proposed itinerary and programme of work.

One very important necessity in an expedition such as this is the provision of a suitable reference library. Here the Expedition was much indebted to Dr Baini Prashad, the Hon. Director and Superintendent of the Zoological Survey of India, who very kindly presented to the Expedition a complete set of *Investigator* Reports on the fauna of the Indian Seas and copies of every part of the *Records* and *Memoirs of the Indian Museum* in which any paper dealing with marine biology had appeared. We were also much indebted to my old friends, the Authorities of the Royal Indian Marine, who kindly lent to the Expedition several volumes of the *Challenger* Reports and some of the gear formerly used on the *Investigator* by the Surgeon–Naturalist, as well as coming promptly to our assistance during the course of the Expedition when an accident had robbed us of much of our trawling wire. I think it may safely be asserted that very few scientific expeditions have been sent to sea better equipped for their work than was the *Mabahiss* when she left Alexandria.

In order that additional information regarding the character of the surface water of the Arabian Sea might be obtained, we were able, through the kind offices of Captain Brooke-Smith of the Meteorological Department of the Air Ministry, London, to arrange that a number of Merchant Marine vessels would take surface-water samples for us for a period of a year, at stated hours of the day, at the same time taking a record of the sea-and air-temperatures and of the strength of the wind. The lines along which these vessels were to take samples were from Aden to Karachi, Aden to Bombay, and Aden to Colombo or along this line as far as 80° E.; through the kindness of the BI Company an additional series of similar observations were taken between Bombay and Mombasa. For this work boxes of water-sample bottles had to be sent out to the Port Officer, Port Said, and to Messrs MacKinnon, MacKenzie and Co., Bombay, so that these might be put on board the various ships that were undertaking this work. It was arranged that these samples should be returned to Cairo University, where they were subsequently analysed for us by Dr Tourky, under the supervision of Dr Bangham, the Dean of the Faculty of Science.

Early in July 1933, the *Mabahiss* was placed in the hands of the staff of the Government Dockyard, Alexandria, for the purpose of refitting and alteration, and at the beginning of that month Captain MacKenzie, Chief Engineer Griggs and Mr Tyler arrived in Alexandria to supervise the work and to see to the installation of the echo-sounding apparatus and the recording thermograph. Lieutenant-Commander Farquharson and Dr

Thompson arrived at the beginning of August, while Mr Gilson, Mr Macan and Mr Lloyd Jones reached Egypt on the 21st of that month.

I reached Alexandria on 24 August, having spent a day in Port Said to arrange with the Port Captain regarding the supply of boxes of water-sample bottles to the Merchant Service ships and also to make the acquaintance of our Agents and hand over to them certain packages that had arrived with me on the P and O *Kaiser-i-Hind*; these were to be sent on board when we came through the port at the beginning of the next month.

FIG. 2. The *Mabahiss* loading gear in Alexandria, August 1933. (*Photo:* H. C. Gilson.)

By this time most of our scientific gear had arrived and when I made my way down to the Government Dockyard, where the *Mabahiss* was lying, I found it all stacked on the jetty alongside. There was such a pile of it that at first sight it looked as if we should never be able to get it all stowed away on board. Stacks of boxes of bottles and jars rose as high as the lower bridge and extended along nearly half the length of the little vessel; but as one day succeeded another the pile got steadily less and finally everything was in its place on board.

During July and August, while the *Mabahiss* was being refitted, three of the Expedition staff were attacked by a mild form of dysentery. Captain MacKenzie was the first to be attacked, and soon after he arrived Dr Thompson was also laid low by the disease, while on 29 August, only four days before we were due to sail, Mr Macan was similarly attacked. In spite of these difficulties, work on the vessel steadily progressed, though considerable difficulty was encountered in the work of installation of the refrigerator; in this case nearly everything that could go wrong did so, and it was not until the afternoon of 1 September, the *Mabahiss* being due to sail on the 2nd, that the machine was at last persuaded to work properly. During the process our Chief Engineer, Mr Tyler, and Mr Rey, one of Hall and Co.'s engineers who had been sent down from Cairo to install the machine, had all been nearly anaesthetized by the methyl chloride gas on which the machine works. Even up to the very end things continued to go wrong, and a few hours before we left our moorings alongside the jetty in the Arsenal one of the platforms, that our chemists were to stand on when carrying out their work of collecting water samples, was lost overboard. We had specially arranged for a second platform to be made so that two chemists could work simultaneously from the two sides of the ship, for originally the vessel possessed only one. A diver was sent down but he failed to recover the lost platform. However, the Khedevial Mail Co. Ltd. nobly came to our rescue and a new platform was actually made in their workshops in four hours and was sent out to us in the outer harbour later on the night of 2 September.

During the last week of our stay in Alexandria there were several court and social functions given in our honour. His Majesty King Fuad received Captain MacKenzie, Lieutenant-Commander Farquharson and myself in a private audience and wished the Expedition every success; and a large tea party was given by El Miralai Ahmed Fuad Bey, the Director General of the Egyptian Marine, and the officers of the Egyptian Coastguard Administration, on board HEMS *El Amira Fawzia* at which the Acting Prime Minister of Egypt and a number of other officials were present. In a speech, delivered first in Arabic and then in English, the Director General wished us every success on the Expedition and a safe return.

At 3 p.m. on 2 September 1933, the *Mabahiss*, flying the John Murray Expedition burgee, slipped her moorings and steamed out to an anchorage in the outer harbour, in preparation for a departure in the early hours of the morning of 3 September. There was a large crowd on the jetty to see us off and just before we left El Miralai Ahmed Fuad Bey and Admiral Wells Pasha came on board to say goodbye to us.

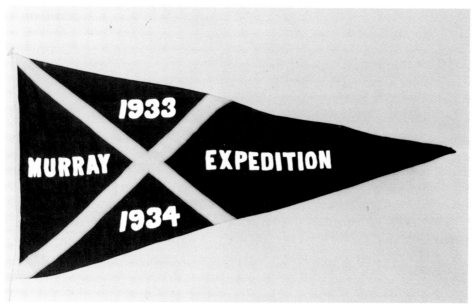

F<small>IG</small>. 3. The Expedition burgee, made by Mrs K. N. MacKenzie and now in the possession of her son, K. M. MacKenzie.

It was planned that the Expedition should, if possible, carry out a series of cruises, each lasting for approximately twenty days, in the following areas:

(a) the south end of the Red Sea and the head of the Gulf of Aden;

(b) the Gulf of Aden and the channel between Cape Guardafui and Socotra;

(c) the southern coast of Arabia and across to Karachi;

(d) the Gulf of Oman and down to Bombay;

(e) across the Arabian Sea from Bombay to Mombasa;

(f) the African coast in the region of Mombasa and Zanzibar;

(g) across the Arabian Sea from Zanzibar to Kardiva Channel in the Maldives, calling at the Seychelles;

(h) from Colombo through the Maldive Archipelago and back to Cochin in India;

(i) from Cochin across the Arabian Sea to Aden;

(j) the Gulf of Aden, repeating our previous observations;

(k) the south end of the Red Sea, repeating our previous observations, and back to Alexandria.

During the course of these various cruises, routine observations were to be carried out at intervals of every four hours, namely at 4, 8 and 12, morning and evening, on

(i)   the temperature of the surface water;
(ii) the salinity of the surface water;
(iii) the temperature of the air, as shown by both the wet and dry bulb thermometers;
(iv) the direction and force of the wind; and
(v)   the height of the barometer.

During each cruise stations were to be made at intervals, the distance between them depending largely on circumstances, but falling as far as possible in definite lines to enable sections to be drawn. It was hoped that it would be possible to carry out some 10–12 such stations in each of the main voyages so that the distance between each would be in the neighbourhood of a day's steaming, or some 200 miles. At each station a complete examination was to be made of the sea water at the following depths:

Surface	150 metres	1,500 metres
10 metres	200 ,,	2,000 ,,
20 ,,	300 ,,	2,500 ,,
30 ,,	400 ,,	3,000 ,,
40 ,,	600 ,,	etc.
50 ,,	800 ,,	
60 ,,	1,000 ,,	
80 ,,		
100 ,,		

and was to include the temperature, salinity, pH concentration (acidity or alkalinity), phosphate, nitrate, nitrite and silicate content, amount of dissolved oxygen and any other estimations as might be thought desirable. In certain areas, such as the Gulf of Aden, it was hoped to get stations at closer intervals so as to be able to trace the movements of deep water masses in more detail, while during our two visits it was expected that we should be able to detect seasonal changes in the general conditions. Also on each of the main cruises it was hoped that we should be able to carry out, on at least two occasions, 24-hour observations on the conditions present in the upper few hundred metres in order to detect the changes that occur in:

1. the level at which the floating plant population (phytoplankton) is concentrated;
2. the total quantity of this phytoplankton;
3. the level at which certain ingredients of the zooplankton are to be found by day and by night.

Certain areas of the continental slopes were selected for specially intensive study, namely:

1. the southern end of the Red Sea;
2. the Gulf of Aden;
3. the south and south-east coast of Arabia;
4. the Gulf of Oman and the entrance to the Persian Gulf;
5. the coast of Africa in the vicinity of Zanzibar; and
6. the western slopes of the Maldive Archipelago.

The actual selection of the areas had to be left to circumstances, since much would depend on the character of the sea-floor as revealed by the echo-sounding apparatus, the first necessity being a gradual slope so that the contour lines should lie as far apart as possible. In these areas a special study was to be made of the zonal distribution of the fauna according to depth between the levels of 50 and 1,000 fathoms; the general routine envisaged was as follows:

(a) the depth of water to be ascertained by the echo-sounding apparatus;
(b) a sample of the bottom to be obtained, this also serving as a check on the depth as given by the echo;
(c) a collection of the bottom fauna by means of a grab, dredge or trawl, the actual selection of the apparatus to be used being dependent on the character of the sea-floor.

The scientific equipment of the ship

For oceanographic research of this nature a very varied assortment of equipment is necessary, different types of apparatus being necessary for each branch of work. The first essential is the possession of winches that will accommodate on the winch-drums the requisite length of wire rope. The *Mabahiss* was already fitted out with two such winches: on the well deck was situated the large and powerful trawling winch, that had two drums, a large one capable of holding some 6,000 metres of trawl wire and a smaller drum that could be used for a length of about 1,000 metres of wire. This second drum is essential if one is trawling with two wires, each attached to one of the otter boards of the otter trawl. This method of trawling is in common use in shallow water, but for deep-sea work the use of two wires is impossible; instead one uses two bridles or wire ropes, each of about 25 fathoms in length, with one end attached to the otter board of the net, while the other is shackled on to the end of the single trawling wire. The main trawl wire is manufactured in such a way that its diameter gradually increases as it is paid out from the winch, the reason for this being that as more and more wire is paid out for trawling in deep water the strain on the wire gradually increases, since at any given point the wire has to take the strain of the net on the end of the wire plus the weight in water of the length of wire that has already been paid out. The wire on the *Mabahiss* was tapered from a circumference of 1 inch at the outboard end to $1\frac{1}{2}$ inches circumference at the inboard end, the strength of the wire increasing from a capability to stand a strain of 7 tons up to a strain of 12 tons.

When we left Alexandria we had on board a continuous wire rope of 3,800 fathoms in length but unfortunately we had been working for only a week or so when, as a result of an accident, the strain became too great and the wire parted very near the middle of its length, so that from then on we were compelled to use two wires that were shackled together: for this purpose we used a type of shackle that is made by Priestman Bros, in which there is no projecting lug, such as there is in most shackles, where the lug is perforated by a hole to enable the pin to be screwed tight home by a marlin spike. In the Priestman shackle the pin is screwed home by a key that fits into a sunken socket and no part of the shackle projects; this prevents the wire from getting caught when being paid out.

As the trawl wire left the winch drum it first passed through a fairlead, situated a little to the starboard side on the forward part of the well deck, and from there was led to the gallows on the port side over which it passed out and down into the sea. Between the fairlead and the gallows was placed the meter-wheel, which measured the length of wire that had been paid out, the wheel being attached by a block and tackle to the boom, which had to be swung out and topped up, in order to get the wheel in the right position and at the same time be in a position for hoisting the net in again at the end of the trawl if it was too heavy to be manhandled in over the bulwark.

As soon as the trawl wire had been paid out sufficiently to allow the trawl or dredge to reach the bottom, an additional length of wire, depending on the depth at which the trawl was to be carried out, was paid out and then the meter-wheel was taken off and a pair of nippers were attached to the wire. These in turn were attached to a dynamometer that measured the strain of the wire, the dynamometer itself being securely fastened to another fairlead firmly fixed to the deck. In order to prevent, so far as possible, the strain becoming too great, one end of the wire sling by which the dynamometer was attached to the nippers was not shackled directly on to the nippers but was attached by a rope becket, consisting of two turns of 1.25 inch rope, that was calculated to part when the strain rose to about 3 tons; if the strain becomes too great the parting of this rope becket immediately releases the wire nippers and thus allows the trawl wire to run out freely. One drawback to this arrangement was that before the wire was hauled in at the conclusion of a trawl the dynamometer had to be taken off and the meter-wheel again put on, so that one then had no means of judging the strain on the wire and in order to compensate for this we found it necessary carefully to adjust the amount of steam that was turned on to the winch, so that it wasn't working at its full strength but with only just sufficient power to haul in the wire and net. It was during the process of hauling in, when we had no indication of the strain of the wire, that our first accident happened and the wire parted.

A second winch, for the purpose of taking hydrographic observations, was situated on the front part of the lower bridge just forward of the chart room. This winch was of a regular type supplied by Messrs Elliot and Garrood and consisted of two drums, the smaller of which accommodated about 500 metres of hydrographic wire, having a diameter of 4 mm, while the larger drum accommodated about 6,000 metres of such wire. Either drum could be used independently when the wire was running out, but only one drum could be used at a time when hauling in, since both drums were attached to the same driving shaft. This would have necessitated frequent stoppages, since the Nansen-Pettersson water bottle on the short wire was used for taking water samples at small intervals in the upper layers of the ocean, whereas the second pattern water bottle, the Ekman reversing-bottle, was used at wide intervals on the long wire for obtaining samples from the greater depths. By careful co-operation between the two scientists in charge of these two different sets of observations on opposite sides of the ship, it was possible to avoid a considerable part of the delay. It would, however, have been preferable to have had two separate winches for each series of observations.

From our experience we reached the conclusion that the pattern of the larger drum in this type of winch was unsatisfactory; the drum was narrow and, therefore, to accommodate the length of wire required had to be deep. When a series of water bottles or the heavy Bigelow bottom-sampler were in use the strain on the wire was such that the drum rapidly developed a tendency to 'spread' and finally cracked. Twice during the course of the Expedition this happened, even though the second drum, that was made for us in Colombo, was stouter and stronger than the drum originally supplied with the winch. It seems desirable that the type of drum for this work, especially if heavy apparatus is to be used in great depths, should be long and shallow.

The hydrographic wires were led from the drum through blocks attached to the boom to a davit that was fixed on each side of the vessel and there passed over a meter-wheel that recorded the length of wire that had been paid out. The wire from the smaller drum passed over the starboard side, while that from the larger ran out on the port side of the vessel. When using the long wires for the deep observations it was found that the strain and the speed with which the wire passed through the block tended to cut through the revolving wheel of the block and a special ball-bearing block, with a pulley made of specially tough material, was manufactured for us by Munro Bros, after which we had no further trouble on this account.

In order to capture the fauna of the deep sea, several different types of nets are required, each adapted for different conditions of the sea-bottom etc. and for the different character of the animals that it was desired to collect.

Otter trawl

The size of this trawl that we used on the *Mabahiss* was a 40-foot one. In this trawl the net is made with a wide mouth, the upper or head rope of which is 40 feet in length, while the foot rope, which is much heavier and is protected by a binding of smaller rope, is much longer. Both the head rope and the foot rope are at the sides of the net connected together by wings and each wing is shackled on to one of the otter boards. The head rope is further raised off the ground by means of a number of glass balls that act as floats, and when the otter boards under the strain of towing act as kites and tend to diverge from each other, the head rope is pulled up by the floats and so the mouth of the net is kept open to its maximum extent. It is a matter of comparative simplicity to keep the mouth of the net open when each otter board is attached to a separate wire, but, as a matter of practical experience, we found it a somewhat difficult proposition to get the net to function to its fullest extent when the two bridles were shackled on to a single trawl wire.

As the strain comes on the bridle while trawling there is a very marked tendency for these bridles to twist and the combined effect of this twisting of the two bridles is to make them twine round each other, thus preventing the full opening of the mouth of the net since it prevents the two otter boards from separating to their fullest extent. In order to avoid this we attached each wire bridle to the corresponding otter board by means of a swivel shackle that was capable of standing a strain of 2 tons and this permitted the bridles to twist and untwist. The net itself tapers to what is called the cod-end and the underside of the net is protected by additional bits of netting against the rubbing on the sea-floor. The length of the net is

Fig. 4. The otter trawl, November 1933. (*Photo:* H. C. Gilson.)

about 40 feet and as the mesh is comparatively large we usually attached to the upper side of the net about halfway back small nets made of finer material, so that these might catch the smaller animals that had been stirred up by the passage of the foot rope and would otherwise pass through the meshes of the otter net and not be captured. To facilitate the hauling in-board of the net on the conclusion of the trawl, a rope, known as the bosom rope, was attached to the middle of the foot rope at one end and to one of the otter boards at the other, so that when the otter boards were hauled up to the gallows, hauling on the bosom rope would bring in the foot rope.

While quite successful in comparatively shallow depths, in deep water this net was difficult to manage and we then usually made use of some other type.

Agassiz trawl

In this type of trawl the net is attached to a fixed metal frame. In our nets this frame consisted of a stirrup at each end, between which ran two metal bars, one between the front ends of the stirrup and the other between the middle of the foot plate of the stirrup. At both ends of each foot plate was a ring through which was passed the endless chain to which the mouth of the net was attached: that part of the chain that ran along the two longer sides of the frame was bound with rope. This chain was kept slack so that when the net reached the bottom and one side began to take the strain of the drag on the sea-floor, the upper part of the chain would be pulled taut and thus act in much the same manner, though to a less extent, as the head rope in the otter trawl. The great advantage of this type of net is that both sides are the same and thus it makes no difference which side falls on the bottom; there is thus no trouble in shooting the net, as is the case in certain other types of net, such as the beam-trawl, which have to go down with one side always on the bottom. The width of the mouth in our Agassiz trawls was 10 feet. The net itself was of a small mesh, $\frac{3}{4}$ inch from knot to knot, and thus captured a number of small animals that would have passed through the wider meshes of the otter trawl. From each end of the frame a wire bridle passed to a shackle and this was attached to the end of the trawl wire. In order to permit the trawl wire to twist and turn without affecting the net, a swivel shackle, capable of taking a strain of 5 tons, was always shackled on between the trawl and the wire.

As a matter of experience we found that this frame was rather too light for work in regions where there was a strong undercurrent and on two occasions, after having sent the trawl down and towed it for an hour, we found, on hauling in, that the net had been caught by such a current and had been twirled round and round like a kite, so that the first 200 metres or so of wire were festooned round and round the trawl frame in great loops and all our time and trouble had been in vain since the net had not been fishing at all. After our second experience of this we attached two additional 50 lb weights to the frame and the net then seemed to work much more efficiently. In this type of net we also had a safety device in the shape of a rope becket between the end of one of the bridles and the frame of the net; this was calculated to take a strain of 2 tons, so that if the net got too full of mud or other material from the sea-floor or the frame got caught on rock, this rope becket would part and the trawl would then be dragged sideways and would no longer fish effectively or, if caught up on the bottom, might possibly be pulled clear.

For work on a rough bottom or in the greatest depths we used yet another type of trawl:

Monegasque trawl

This trawl has a much stronger frame, though constructed on much the same principle as the Agassiz trawl. The frame consists of two stirrup-like ends that are slightly curved so that any pull on them falls in the same line as the curve, and the mouth of the net is firmly attached to a rectangular frame of iron bars measuring 7 feet by 3 feet 6 inches, while a third supporting bar runs across the mouth of the net from side to side. At the front end of each stirrup a metal bar runs up to a single ring; one of these bars is directly attached to the stirrup, while between the bar and the stirrup on the other side is attached a rope becket, that would part under a strain of about 2 tons; here again, if the strain became too great, the rope becket would part and the net would be towed sideways and not fish. The net itself was of a graduated mesh of about 3 inches from knot to knot; then came a zone of 6 feet in which the mesh was about 2 inches and the last part of the net and the cod-end had a mesh of about an inch, this being as close as the knots could conveniently be tied in a material of the stoutness of which the net was composed. Judging from our experience, this type of net acted in a manner intermediate between a trawl and a true dredge, for although it did not have a definite cutting edge, such as one has in a true dredge, the solid metal bar of the frame at times seems to have acted as such and we obtained fragments of rock from the bottom. This was especially noticeable in a trawl at the depth of 3,385 metres on the Carlsberg Ridge (Station 133).

For work on a rough coral or rocky bottom dredges of various kinds were used. Of these, two in particular were of great use; the best of these was undoubtedly the:

Four-foot triangular dredge

In this there is a heavy frame of a triangular shape with a sloping cutting edge along each side. At each corner there is a projecting lug to which is attached a short length, about 4 feet, of chain. Two of these chains were shackled directly on to a stout iron ring, while the third was attached by the usual rope becket, that would part if the strain became too great. This ring was shackled by means of a swivel shackle to the end of the trawl warp. The net was conical in shape and was made of a multiple-strand material, the distance from knot to knot being about an inch. In our experience this type of net was extremely good for a rough bottom and it was wonderful the way in which it stood up to the rough usage and wear and tear on some of the reefs. Not infrequently this dredge collected so much of the bottom material, either mud, sand, shingle or even rock, that we had to leave the net over the side while the finer material was washed out before we could hoist the net inboard.

We were also provided with similar trawls of smaller sizes; these were 3-foot triangular dredges for use from the *Mabahiss* or 2-foot dredges for use from the motor boat; but it was found that these latter dredges were too heavy for the motor boat to drag over the bottom and when full they merely served to anchor the motor boat, and in their place we used a lighter rectangular net.

The second type of dredge was the:

Salpa dredge

In this the mouth is composed of a stout metal frame that is roughly oblong in shape but the two long sides are bowed out so that, as the dredge is dragged over the ground, this bowed part of the frame will dig into the bottom. Here again the net is of the bag type and is composed of stout twine with an inner bag of a finer and smaller meshed material.

One of the objects of the expedition, though of perhaps secondary importance, was the collection of those animals that live in the mid-depths

Fig. 5. The large triangular dredge, November 1933. (*Photo:* H. C. Gilson.)

FIG. 6. The Harvey phytoplankton net, incorporating a flow meter in the central section. (*Photo:* H. C. Gilson.)

and do not frequent either the surface or the bottom. For the purpose of capturing these animals we used a large net having a circular metal frame the diameter of which was 2 metres and the frame itself was streamlined so as to offer as little resistance as possible when it was being towed through the water.

Two-metre plankton net

The frame of this net is carried by three bridles that run up to a ring to which the trawl wire is attached.

At the cod-end of the net there is attached a metal bucket to contain the catch. The material of which the net itself is composed is graded so that near the mouth it is made of a net, with the distance between the knots of about $\frac{3}{4}$ inch; then comes a circular belt of stout canvas to which are sewn a number of brass rings that serve to take a rope with a sliding ring when the net is used in conjunction with the self-closing mechanism. This mechanism is so constructed that the trawl wire can be shackled on to it by means of a swivel shackle, while the ring of the net is held by a catch. When the net is to be released, a weight or 'messenger' is allowed to slide down the trawl wire and when this reaches the self-closing mechanism it impinges on a trigger that releases this catch and the net is then held by the throttling line that is attached to the mechanism and passed in a loop through the rings mentioned above; the centre part of the net is thus pulled tight by the rope and the circular frame and the cod-end hang down on either side of it. Unfortunately this closing mechanism never seemed to work very satisfactorily; first the length of the self-closing mechanism was too short to admit the swivel-shackle and the eye-splice at the end of the wire without considerable readjustment, and, secondly, the rope that had to be used as a throttle rope was too stout to act well. We at first tried a 1.25-inch rope but there was so great a strain on it when heaving in that I was afraid that at any moment it would part, in which case we should have lost the whole net, for there is nothing else holding the net to the trawl wire; we then tried a 2-inch rope, but this was so stout that it prevented the net from opening properly when the net was sent down and in consequence it didn't fish to its fullest extent. Another piece of mechanism that we used with this type of net was a depth recorder; the principle on which this mechanism works is that of a spiral tube that, as the pressure increases, tends to straighten out and this movement operates a lever that traces a line on a revolving disc of paper. The actual record is, of course, not the actual depth, but the pressure to which the apparatus has been subjected, and it is necessary to calibrate the instrument in order to obtain an estimate of the depth to which it has been sent. This was done by sending the depth recorder down vertically when samples of the sea-water were being taken. We thus knew to within a metre or two the depth to which it had gone and from the tracing could calculate the amount of movement of the lever that corresponded to a given depth.

In addition to the 2-metre-diameter plankton net we also made use of nets of 1-metre diameter, the net itself being made of a fine-meshed material known as stramine. The cod-end of this large plankton net was composed of fine-meshed material, strengthened by longitudinal bands of canvas and at its extreme end there was a sleeve of canvas to which a metal bucket was fastened. A series of these nets were usually attached to the trawl wire at intervals, so that when the nets were towed either horizontally or vertically they captured animals from a different stratum of water than the larger 2-metre net or each other. Of course, when these nets are used on the trawl wire it is not possible to use the self-closing mechanism, since the messenger could not slide down the wire.

Another important line of biological work is the determination of the plant life of phytoplankton and for this purpose the very finest silk nets have to be used. The *Mabahiss* was fitted out with the type of net devised by Mr Harvey of the Marine Biological Laboratory, Plymouth. This consisted of a conical bag of the finest silk fitted with a metal receiver at the cod-end, while at the front end of the net was a mechanism consisting of a revolving vane that turned a clockwork mechanism and recorded the total quantity of water that had passed through the silk net; by carefully noting the total number of organisms in the catch one can thus reach a fairly accurate estimate of the numbers present in a known volume of water, thus arriving at an indication of the paucity or otherwise of the population. This apparatus was worked at regular depths and we thus determined the vertical distribution of the phytoplankton.

Since the greater part of the phytoplankton consists of chlorophyll-bearing microscopic plants, such as diatoms, it is of course dependent for life and activity on the amount of sunlight that penetrates to the various levels and we had hoped to carry out a determination of the depth to which the various coloured rays of the sun's spectrum penetrated into the sea water. Unfortunately, however, we could never get the apparatus to work satisfactorily, so that no results were achieved. However, we frequently took a reading of the transparency of the water, that is to say the depth at which a white metal disc, known as a Secchi disc, can be seen from the deck of the ship and it seems probable that there must be at least some degree of correlation between this transparency and the depth to which light can penetrate.[1]

The next line of investigation concerns the character of the sea-water at different depths and the importance of such observations is twofold; first to give important information regarding the actual conditions under which marine animals and plants manage to exist and, secondly, to enable us by comparing the conditions present at different positions and at different levels to estimate the direction and strength of the movements of the deep-water masses.

For the investigation of the surface water, samples were taken by means of buckets of leather or wood that were lowered by hand, and as soon as they had been hauled up the temperature was taken by means of a thermometer. Simultaneously, readings were also taken of the air temperature with both wet and dry bulb thermometers, the height of the barometer was read and the strength and apparent direction of the wind, as registered by an anemometer, was noted; as this latter reading is not a simple record of the wind-force but is a combination of the actual wind-force and the movement of the ship, a record is also kept of the speed and course of the ship, so that from these factors the true force and direction of the wind can be calculated.

In connection with the oceanographic work it is essential that a record should be kept of the meteorological conditions, since these have a profound influence on the character and condition of the sea-water and, vice versa, the sea has a very important influence on the meteorological conditions.

The expedition was greatly indebted to the Air Ministry and its Meteorological Department for the loan of certain instruments. The first of these was a cup anemometer that enabled us to take an accurate record of the rate of movement of the wind in miles per hour, while the other was an Assman psychrometer for taking readings of the wet and dry bulb thermometers; from these readings one is able to deduce such things as the relative humidity of the atmosphere and the dew-point. Readings with these instruments were taken as part of the ship's routine every four hours while we were at sea, and at the same time a sample of the sea-water was collected and the temperature of the sea surface was taken by thermometer. A more

---

1. Gilson derived a relationship between the Secchi disc reading and the 'compensation point', the depth at which oxygen produced by photosynthesis just balances that consumed by phytoplankton respiration (see Part 5, page 318).

continuous record of the sea temperature was kept by means of a recording thermograph installed in connection with the intake of the engine-room; this gave us a continuous reading of the temperature of the sea-water at a depth a little below the surface, the depth varying from approximately 6 to 8 feet depending on whether the *Mabahiss* was fully loaded or was riding light towards the end of a cruise, when coal and water had been considerably reduced in quantity.

In order to take the temperature and obtain samples of the water in the deeper levels of the ocean, special apparatus has to be used and for this purpose the *Mabahiss* was provided with the following:

The Nansen-Pettersson insulating water-bottle

In this pattern the bottle, which consists of a central cavity, surrounded by a series of smaller chambers, is sent down open on the end of a thin wire rope having a diameter of 4 mm. This wire was coiled down on the small drum of the hydrographic winch and from there passed over a meter-sheave that recorded the length of wire out. In the end of the wire is a small eye-splice which is fastened to the top end of the bottle and when the bottle has been lowered down to the required depth and been left there for a few minutes, to enable it to take up the temperature of the water at that depth, for it must be borne in mind that the surface water in the tropics will be at a higher temperature than water a few fathoms down, a small brass messenger is sent down and this hits on a spring at the top end of the bottle and releases a catch that closes the bottle, which is then immediately hauled in and the temperature read before it can start to rise. With care, samples and temperatures can be taken with this apparatus down to a depth of 400 metres but we only used it, as a rule, to a depth of 200 metres and occasionally to 300 metres.

Ekman reversing water-bottles

In this pattern the bottle is held in a frame and before it is sent down the bottle is turned round through half a circle on a horizontal axis. This causes the bottle to open, the two ends being separated from the barrel of the bottle. On the side of the bottle are two, or sometimes three, metal containers for thermometers that also act by being reversed. When the bottle is sent down open the thermometers are placed with the mercury bulb at the bottom. In this ordinary pattern of reversing thermometer this mercury bulb is protected by an outer glass sheath that protects the bulb from the increased pressure that exists below the surface of the water; but sometimes an additional thermometer, of a different pattern, is added to the usual two, thus making three in all attached to the same bottle. This additional thermometer differs in that the mercury bulb is not enclosed in any protecting sheath, so that it is affected by both the temperature and the pressure.

When the bottle has been attached by means of clips on the side of the frame, it is lowered down and another bottle is attached to the wire at any required distance from the first and a third again is attached above this and so on. In this way a series of bottles at requisite intervals is attached to the same wire. The whole series is then lowered to the required depth and is left there for a short time to enable the thermometers to take up the correct temperatures; a small brass messenger is then sent down the wire and this strikes the spring at the top of the uppermost bottle and releases a catch that causes the whole bottle to turn over in the frame. As this happens a second messenger that was previously attached to the base of the first bottle is released and this slides on down the wire and strikes the spring of the second bottle and sends that off, and so on until the lowest bottle is reached. As the bottle turns over the two ends shut down tight to the barrel, thus enclosing a sample of the water from the depth to which the bottle has been lowered, and at the same time the thermometers are turned over and this breaks the column of mercury, the broken off column falling to the other end of the thermometer which is graduated so that the recorded temperature can then be read off directly; this temperature requires a small correction to be applied to it so as to give the actual temperature at the depth to which the thermometer was lowered because on hauling the thermometer up again it comes into water of a higher temperature than was present below and finally is hauled out of the water into air, which in the tropics has at times and seasons a very high temperature. In order to determine the necessary correction for this rise, which causes a slight expansion of the column of mercury, an auxiliary thermometer is attached beside the reversing thermometer in the same glass tube. The use of this second thermometer, in which the mercury bulb is not protected, and so is affected by both temperature and pressure, is to give an accurate indication of the actual depth to which the water bottle has been lowered. The wire rope to which the battery of Ekman bottles is attached passes over a meter-wheel that records the length of wire that has been let out, but this will only agree with the depth to which the bottle has actually been lowered if the wire is vertical all the way; in the event of there being a strong deep-water current, it is quite possible that although the upper length of wire may run down vertically the lower lengths may be swept out at an angle by the current so the bottle does not reach the fullest depth. Now by comparing the records of the two thermometers the one protected and the other unprotected and, therefore, recording a combination of both temperature and pressure, it is easy to determine the difference between the two and thus form an estimate of the pressure to which the thermometer has been subjected in its descent and, since the pressure increases regularly as one passes downwards though the water we can, from a knowledge of the pressure to which the thermometer has been subjected, calculate the actual depth to which the bottle has descended. In the majority of cases these two calculations agree very closely, but there are occasions on which they do not and we then accept the record of the unprotected thermometer as the true indication of the depth to which the bottle went and from which the water sample and the temperature reading were obtained.

As soon as possible after the samples had been obtained they were carefully examined by the chemists on board and an estimation made of the amount of oxygen dissolved in the water and pH concentration, while in a large number of cases an estimate was also made of the phosphates, nitrates and nitrites. Finally, every sample was analysed to determine the amount of the halogens, that is chlorine, bromine and iodine, present. The importance of this latter test lies in that from the result one can calculate the total salts dissolved in the water and thus arrive at a determination of the salinity of the water. Of the three salts, the chlorine is by far the most important, but small traces of the two other chemicals are present in combination and are estimated at the same time as the chlorine by the method employed.

The third main line of research is connected with the study of the bottom of the ocean and the character of the sea-floor. For the purpose of estimating the depth of the ocean the *Mabahiss* was fitted out, prior to her departure from Alexandria, with an echo-sounding machine of the Acadia type, manufactured by Messrs Hughes and Co. of London. The principle of the machine depends on the transmission of sound through water. Towards the after-end of the vessel, in the engine room, was installed the hammer that by striking a metal plate creates a sharp noise at regular intervals. This hammer is operated by a compressor that raises the air pressure and this in turn is suddenly released by an electrical contrivance, connected with the recording apparatus, that was installed in the lower chartroom on the bridge. As soon as the electrical current is broken, the hammer is released and a loud knock is made on the ship's bottom; the sound then travels down to the bottom of the ocean and from there is reflected back again and is picked up by a microphone situated in the ship's bottom in the forward

Fig. 7. Ekman water-bottles in their rack on deck; water-sample bottles in the lockers below. (*Photo:* H. C. Gilson.)

part. This creates an electric charge in the microphone and from there this is transmitted through an amplifier to the recording apparatus, so that the moment the echo is received, a current of electricity passes from a metal plate to a metal needle that is moving across a sheet of paper. The paper is specially prepared and is impregnated with starch and potassium iodide, so that the moment the electric current passes through the sheet the iodine is released and this combines with the starch to make a stain that shows up clearly on the white paper. The paper is fitted with a scale giving a range of 250 fathoms and as the depth becomes greater than this the record can still be kept on the paper by altering the timing of the hammer blows; this is accomplished by turning a wheel that is so adjusted that each notch alters the timing by 100 fathoms and by a complete turn of the wheel by 1,000 fathoms; the alteration of the position of this wheel is noted on the recording paper as plus 100, plus 200, etc., and in reading off the actual depth this amount must then be added to the depth as shown on the scale. A certain amount of correction has to be made in accordance with the salinity and temperature of the water through which the sound is passing, since this has a slight modifying influence on the rate of transmission of the sound; this is quickly and easily done by means of tables that have been prepared by the Admiralty. The particular apparatus that we were provided with was supposed to record down to 5,000 fathoms but as a matter of experience we found that it was very difficult to get any record below 2,500 fathoms. This was especially the case if there was any sea running and the reason appears to lie, at any rate to some extent, in the formation, owing to wave action, of a cushion of water mixed with small bubbles of air under the vessel. The whole apparatus is still somewhat in the experimental stage and requires a great deal of attention in order to keep it running, but doubtless this will be improved as the makers get more experience. The very great advantage of the apparatus is that it enables one to take soundings, while the ship is steaming, at a rate of about twenty-five to the minute and thus one can investigate the depths in detail, whereas formerly with wire soundings it took from one-and-a-half to two hours to take a single sounding, while the ship stopped and carefully manoeuvred all the time so as to keep the wire in a vertical, or 'up and down', position; and even then one might not be absolutely certain as to the exact depth at which the weight on the end of the wire struck bottom, since deep currents may deflect the wire out of the vertical.

The next observation was to obtain a sample of the sea-bottom and this was done by lowering some form of apparatus on the end of a long wire cord; the wire was passed over a meter-wheel that recorded the length of

FIG. 8. The central part of the chemical laboratory, with Mohamed titrating salinity samples. (*Photo:* H. C. Gilson.)

wire out and this served as a check to the result given by the echo-sounder. As a matter of practice we found that the depth as shown by the length of wire out was always some small percentage, about 2 per cent, more than the depth as given by the echo.

The *Mabahiss* was provided with a Lucas sounding machine for the purpose of taking soundings and bottom samples, but the position in which this was fixed in the ship, at the extreme stern end just over the propellor, was so unsuitable that it was found to be almost impossible to use the machine. In the first place the position of the apparatus rendered it impossible for the operator to communicate rapidly with the officer on the bridge who was controlling the vessel. Moreover, if the vessel drifted astern over the wire it was impossible to go ahead on the engines since the propeller would then cut the wire. Finally, the position was such that the maximum amount of strain was thrown on the wire as the vessel rose and fell in a seaway. As a result of these difficulties we lost in rapid succession a number of Baillie rods and Driver tubes, as well as hundreds of fathoms of sounding wire. Eventually we gave up the use of the machine altogether. In its place we used the hydrographic wire to the end of which we shackled either a Baillie rod, a Driver tube or else a Bigelow tube. The wire was passed over an accumulator and then over the meter-wheel slung on a davit on the port side of the ship on the well-deck and it was found that as a general rule the accumulator gave a very definite kick the moment the strain on the wire was released by the bottom-sampler striking the sea-floor. As a subsidiary check on the depth at which the sampler struck the bottom we also used the rate at which the wire was running out. Every ten metres was timed as it ran out by means of a stop watch and it was at once noticed, when the sampler struck the bottom, that the time was materially increased, the wire running out much more slowly when only under its own weight than when the extra weight of the bottom sampler was hanging on it. The accumulator consisted of a fixed wheel over which the wire passed; it then passed downwards under another wheel placed at the end of a metal rod working in a metal tube against a stout spring; from this wheel it passed up again and over the meter-wheel. As the strain comes on the wire the bottom wheel on the metal rod is forced up the tube against the spring. Thus this served two purposes; first, when the ship was rolling or pitching there was a considerable variation in the strain on the wire, the strain decreasing as the ship fell in the trough and increasing considerably as she rose on the crest of a wave, but by the give of the accumulator this strain was more or less equalized and no sudden strain was thrown on the wire; the other purpose has already been indicated and showed the moment when the weight of the bottom sampler struck the bottom, for the sudden

FIG. 9. The Priestman grab, open, is hoisted over the side. (*Photo:* H. C. Gilson.)

release of the strain enabled the spring to drive the lower wheel down with a sudden kick.

The principle underlying the construction of all the types of bottom sampler used on the hydrographic wire is much the same and consists in forcing a tube into the sea-floor by means of weights, which may or may not be detached in the process. Of the various types used by us the Baillie rod is fitted with a butterfly valve at the bottom, so that as it is driven into the bottom ooze the mud is forced up past the valve; on hauling the tube out of the mud and back on board through several hundreds or thousands of fathoms of water this valve prevents the bottom sample from being washed out. The great drawback to this particular apparatus is that the bottom deposit is churned up as it is forced past the valve and one cannot, therefore, obtain any conclusive evidence of stratification, if this character is present, as it often is, in the deposit on the sea-floor. The Driver tube is a larger and somewhat heavier form of apparatus and in this the tube is fitted with a glass inner tube into which the bottom deposit is forced; the sample can then be stored for subsequent examination in the original glass tubes. The metal tube which holds the glass tube is fitted with a spring valve that is supposed to be forced down by the detachable weight and should close below the bottom opening, thus also preventing the sample from washing out on the way up; in practice we found that in spite of all care in adjusting the weight and the valve before sending the tube down, in quite a number of cases the valve failed to operate properly and the tube came up empty.

By far the best type of bottom sampler for use with the hydrographic wire in deep water was undoubtedly the Bigelow tube. This apparatus has the added merit of simplicity, for it consists of a strong tube made in two sections that are screwed together. The bottom section that is forced into the mud is 5 feet in length and about 2 inches in diameter, while the top length of tube is provided with a heavy, 150 lb weight fixed in position. The tube was lowered down and the weight forced the bottom tube into the bottom ooze and it was found that in spite of there being no precautionary apparatus, such as valves, to prevent the washing out of the ooze, in nearly every instance the sample came up intact, the tenacity of the bottom deposit being quite sufficient to prevent its being washed out; it was only in the case of samples from comparatively shallow depths, where there was a large admixture of sand, that the enclosed sample was washed out on the way up. By means of this simple apparatus, cores ranging from 3 feet to over 5 feet in length were obtained and these show clearly the stratification, when such is present.

It will be clear to anyone that none of these forms of apparatus would be

FIG. 10. Hauling in the full grab. (*Photo:* H. C. Gilson.)

of any use on a hard bottom since the tube would not be forced into the ground; for such a bottom, use is made of the Snapper lead. In this apparatus the mechanism consists of two strong jaws operated by a powerful spring; immediately above these jaws is a weight and the jaws are held open by a short metal rod. The moment that the lead strikes the bottom the separating rod is dislodged and the two metal jaws are forced together by the spring. There seem to be two serious defects in this apparatus, the first of which is that the moment the Snapper strikes a hard bottom it tends to bounce back and thus the jaws do not close on the bottom itself but on the water just above the bottom, and the second is that the jaws are made of copper and are, therefore, too soft to bite off any rock fragment should it strike such a sea-floor; instead of the jaws biting off a fragment of the bottom they are themselves bent and distorted so that after one or two trials the jaws fail to meet properly and have to be hammered into shape again.

Fig. 11. The ship's complement: crew members and scientific staff.

In order to obtain large samples of the bottom in comparatively shallow depths so as to be able to make a differential count of the number of organisms present or obtain a sample of the occluded water for chemical analyses, we employed a grab of the type that is commonly in use by engineers in canal construction. The use of such a grab was first instituted by Petersen, of Denmark, who used a grab that brought up a sample having an area of one-fifth of a square metre; in shallow water a number of samples can be obtained quickly and thus an average can rapidly be estimated, but in deeper water and where time could not be spared for any very long survey of a given area, it was necessary to use a larger grab and one was manufactured for us by Priestman Bros, which brought up at one time a sample having an area of half a square metre. A slight modification of the apparatus was also introduced whereby the closing chain that in Petersen's model ran through the middle of the apparatus was replaced by two wire ropes that were outside the grab so that the sample of the bottom inside the grab was absolutely undisturbed. The apparatus was sent down open, but as soon as it hit the bottom the supporting chains were released and the weight was taken up on the two wire ropes thus pulling the jaws together. The contents of the grab were then examined and, after a sample had been kept, the rest was put through a series of graduated sieves so that all the animals and much of the coarser material of the bottom was preserved, only the finer mud being washed away.

The John Murray Expedition

Scientific staff

Leader	Lt-Col. R. B. Seymour Sewell, CIE, Sc.D., IMS
Deputy Leader	Dr E. F. Thompson
Biologists	Mr T. T. Macan
	Dr H. Faouzi
Chemists	Mr H. Cary Gilson
	Abdel Fatteh Mohamed
Surveyor	Lt-Com. W. I. Farquharson, RN

Ship's staff

Captain	K. N. MacKenzie
Mulazim Awal [Jr Lt]	Ahmed M. Badr
	Ahmad Sarwat
Chief Engineer	Mr W. J. Griggs, MIMarE
Mulazim Awal	Mahmoud Mukhtar
	Edward Morcos
Wireless Operator	Mr Lloyd Jones
Ries Bahari	Abd-Allah Diab
Rub Ries	Ahmed Ali Sorour
Bahari Maher	Ahmed Yousif El Said
	Ali Etaiwa Hussain
	Hussain Badr Abdel Aal
	Mohamed Ahmed El Hag
	Ahmed Ewaida Ewaida
	Moustafa Abdel Kerim Kendiel
	Ali Ali Moustafa
	Mohamed Mohamed El Salami

Engine-room staff

Ries Atashgi	Afifi Mohamed
	Mahmoud Ahmed
Rub Ries	Mohamed Hassan El Hindi
Atashgi	Soliman Said Ahmed El Manaili
	Ahmed Mohamed Haman
	Hassan Mohamed Ali
	Abdel Gawad Mohamed
	Mohamed Ahmed El Sanawi
	Ali Tantawi Saab
First Steward	Ibrahim Ahmed
Cook	Mohamed Mohamed Ali
Servants	Abdel Rahman Hamouda
	Ali Hamad Fadl
Carpenter	Abdel Ghani El Said
Stokers	Salim Ali Mahdi, taken on at Aden
	Ramazan Hassan, taken on at Zanzibar

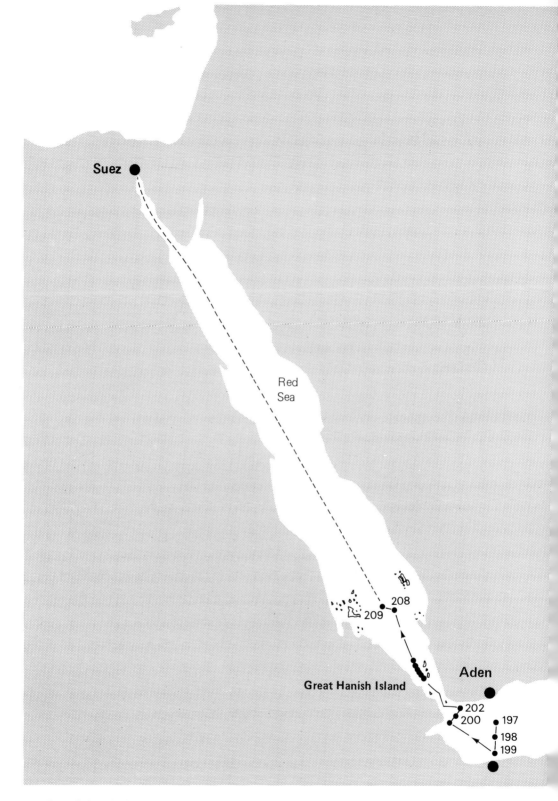

Fig. 12. Track chart, Cruise 1: Red Sea–Aden. Station numbers are indicated.

Chapter 2

Alexandria to Aden

3–5.IX.33 WE sailed from Alexandria on the morning of Sunday, 3 September, at about 7 o'clock. The wind was northerly, blowing with a force of about 20 miles an hour. As a result, as soon as we turned east towards Port Said we had the sea on our port beam and this caused the *Mabahiss* to roll a bit, but considering her size she is a remarkably steady little vessel. Apart from attacks of sea-sickness in certain members of the scientific staff, there were no incidents to record and we reached Port Said a little before 4 o'clock the following morning. Soon after we were anchored a lighter came off bringing several cases of scientific stores for us; among these were some that I had left at Port Said on my way through, while another contained the large grab, that had been made specially for the Expedition by Messrs Priestman Bros but hadn't been ready in time to come out with all the rest of our gear. Owing to a mistake, twenty-four cases of water-sample bottles, that had arrived in Port Said on the *Mashobra* on 1 August and were intended for various merchant ships that were going to take surface samples and temperatures for us, were also put on board, and these had to be returned to shore. The Port Officer himself came off a little later and the position was explained; but unfortunately two vessels had been allowed to pass through the port without the necessary cases being put on board. Having concluded our business we hoisted the signal for a pilot and just before ten o'clock we proceeded on our way through the canal. As we were being given a free passage through by the Canal Authorities, we were by the rules compelled from time to time to tie up to the bank to allow other vessels to pass us, and during one of these interruptions some of the scientific staff took the opportunity to land on the canal bank and stretch their legs for there was little or no room on board for taking exercise. In consequence of these delays it was not until sunset that we reached Ismailia and anchored for the night.

We left again at about 7 o'clock the next morning and on the way through we took the opportunity of overhauling and mending one of the otter-

trawl nets that had been damaged on the way out; a patch of the canvas   5–7.IX.33
covering had rubbed through and part of the net had been torn; as soon as
this repair had been effected, the net was lashed along the port side in
readiness for a trial haul. At the same time the chemists were busy getting
things ready in their department and, as the ship was quite steady, Abdel
Fatteh seized the opportunity to get quantities of silver nitrate weighed out
in preparation for the titration of the water samples, while Gilson was busy
constructing a rack to hold the water-sample bottles along the engine-room
bulkhead on the starboard side.

We reached Port Tewfiq (Suez) about four in the afternoon and anchored
for the night.

We steamed out of Suez at 7 o'clock on the morning of the 6th and ran
down the Gulf of Suez with the wind astern. During the forenoon all
hands were occupied in getting ready for a try-out of some of our gear, and
the large grab was hoisted out of its box and stowed away on the starboard
side of the well-deck. We reached a suitable ground about noon, and a
series of soundings were taken with the small Lucas sounding machine;
these ranged from 34.5 to 37 fathoms and were checked by the echo-
sounding apparatus, which recorded a depth of 35 fathoms, while a second
echo was recorded at a depth of 70 fathoms owing to the sound being
reflected back from the surface and passing down to the bottom and up
again a second time. According to Mr Tyler, our expert from Messrs
Hughes and Co. who was accompanying us on our first trip to see that the
apparatus worked satisfactorily, the character of the record indicated a
bottom of mud with a hard rock bottom about 5 fathoms below. We then
tried some of the water-sampling apparatus and after lunch we shot the
otter net and carried out a trawl for half an hour. There wasn't very much
in the net when it came up, but the catch included a varied assortment of
animals, several small fish, several echinoids and molluscs, among the latter
being two examples of a species of *Murex*, a sessile ascidian, black in colour,
with two other species of a different colour associated with it, two small
starfish and a tubicolous polychaete worm, red in colour and inhabiting a
tube constructed of mud particles. Taken all round, MacKenzie and I were
quite satisfied with the results; they had given us an opportunity of seeing
that the gear worked satisfactorily and of getting the crew acquainted with
the necessary procedure.[1]

1. MacKenzie's view of this first attempt to use the gear, recorded in his personal journal
   of the Expedition, does not tally with Sewell's! '6th Sept. At 6 a.m. proceeded to sea,
   where all scientific gear was put over the side and tested. The whole day spent in
   shooting [the] deep-sea trawl, a perfect exhibition of the uselessness of shore people on

7.IX.33   As soon as the trawl was back again on board we steamed to our anchorage off Abu Zanima and anchored for the night. It was nearly dark when we arrived and in spite of a nearly full moon one couldn't see very much of the place, but the next morning I had a good look at it. I little thought, when I left it in 1916, after being there for nearly six months with my regiment (the 23rd Sikh Pioneers) guarding the Manganese Company's works, that I should ever see the place again. In those days there had been a spidery pier of girders running out into the bay, but this appeared to have been replaced by a more solid construction. Doubtless it was necessary, for the old pier was a very gimcrack structure, and whenever our supply ship came alongside it the Captain had to be very careful not to bump into it or it would have given way. The bare rocks beyond the beach and the buildings on shore looked as hot as ever, and there was a lot of dust being blown off the desert by the wind.

    Although most of our scientific apparatus had been received on board, there were still three thermometers that had not arrived; these were of a special kind, graduated to record high temperatures, and were urgently necessary for work in the Red Sea, owing to the comparatively high temperatures that exist in the lower levels consequent on the shallowness of the entrance channel opposite Great Hanish Island, near Perim. Only two of the thermometers that we had on board were suitable and unless the other three arrived we should have been very much delayed in our work in this area. We had heard on the morning of the 2nd, the day before we left Alexandria, that they were expected and we had received all the necessary documents regarding them, so we had arranged that they should be collected for us by the Marine Biological Station (at Hurgada, see below) and be sent on at once to Suez. As we had not yet heard that they had arrived, we decided to stay where we were for the forenoon of the 7th and take the opportunity of trying the large bottom grab. Owing to its weight, a satisfactory method of getting this out and in again had to be devised; this was eventually accomplished and in due course I had the satisfaction of seeing it go over the side and be let down to the bottom. And that was about as far as my satisfaction went on this occasion, for when it was hauled on board again and opened, instead of the 6 or 7 cubic feet of mud that I had expected to get, there was only about one, and we were left wondering whether the meagreness of the sample was due to the presence of rock underlying the mud and so preventing the grab from sinking in properly,

---

board ship, most of them half sea-sick and flopping around decks like so many American tourists.' For permission to quote this and other extracts from MacKenzie's journal I am very grateful to his son, M. K. MacKenzie.

or to the sample being washed out on the way up. Neither explanation
seemed to be probable and a subsequent examination of the grab showed
us that we had omitted to remove the solid metal plates that had been
screwed on over the perforated gauze sheets that allow the water in the
grab to pass out when the grab sinks into the mud; and this of course
must have equally prevented the mud from entering the grab. During the
afternoon we received the expected wireless message saying that the
thermometers were at Suez, so we weighed anchor and proceeded back
to Port Tewfiq. There was now a strong head wind, blowing according
to the anemometer on the bridge at about 23 miles an hour, and this
raised quite a nasty head sea, so that the *Mabahiss* was shipping a good
deal of sea and spray, especially on the starboard side. As the companion
way down to our cabins opened on this side to the deck, we had to run
the gauntlet both going to and coming back from dinner in the saloon
that was aft. I managed to get to the saloon without mishap, but on
trying to get back after dinner I found that someone had turned out the
deck light so that the alleyway was in complete darkness and I over-shot
the door. While trying to find it the *Mabahiss* shipped a beauty and I was
soaked through.

We arrived back at Port Tewfiq at one o'clock in the morning of the 8th
and anchored outside the harbour for the rest of the night. Soon after
dawn we proceeded into the harbour basin and moored alongside HEMS
Monagym. It was like old times seeing this little vessel again. I hadn't seen
her for thirteen years, but during the war, when I was stationed with my
regiment at Tor and Abu Zanima on the Sinai coast, she used to come
down from Suez and bring us our provisions and mails, and she carried me
when I went up from Tor to Abu Zanima to inspect the second half of my
battalion and again when I went up from Abu Zanima to Suez to catch a
ship for Bombay when I got my first war-leave in 1916. We took in water
and received the parcel of thermometers that we had been waiting for, and
I also received from Allen and Hanbury's a parcel, that I hadn't been expecting, containing a supply of glucose for those who suffered from sea-
sickness! We left Port Tewfiq again at about 11.30 and steamed down the
Gulf with the wind now aft. Just at sunset a small school of porpoises
came alongside the accompanied us for a few minutes. We were to see
quite a lot of these animals during the next few months, but it is a very
different matter seeing them from the deck of a large vessel, such as a
P and O liner, to seeing them from the well-deck of a little trawler that is
only some 4 feet above the water level; the largest specimens were about 5
feet in length and their upper surface was a uniform dull brown colour,
and as they swam alongside it seemed as if they deliberately chose the

8–9.IX.33 foremost slope of a wave, so that they were helped along by the wave in much the same manner as one is when surf-riding.

Early the next morning we altered course to the west and steamed in towards Hurgada, where we were going to pay a call at the Egyptian Marine Biological Station that has recently been started there. There was a strong wind blowing about 25 miles an hour and this raised a short choppy sea that continually splashed up through the scuppers, so that the well-deck was awash and there was a considerable amount of spray coming inboard. We anchored off Hurgada at about 9 o'clock and soon afterwards two local fishermen brought off a message to say that Dr Crossland, the Director of the Biological Station, was waiting on the beach; so we sent off our motor boat and brought him and Dr Sambon, of Cairo University, off to the ship. After we had shown them round we all crowded into the motor boat and went ashore and they motored us out to the Biological Station that lies about 4 or 5 miles further up the coast. The road ran through the desert that is dotted over with the derricks of the oil borings, some of them in use, others discarded as they did not yield a sufficient supply to make it worth while to keep them going. All through this area the land has been formed by a raised coral reef and many of the masses of the harder corals are still intact *in situ*, though the more delicate branching forms, such as *Acropora*, have disintegrated and are now in fragments. There is no trace of any formation of limestone underneath the surface, such as one commonly finds under the sand in the raised coral reefs in other places, probably because there is so little rainfall in this area; in consequence, specimens of coral and mollusc shells can be picked out even by hand. We were shown over the station and some of us went out and had a look at the coral reefs, the fauna of which seemed to be a rich one. After lunch we motored back to the jetty and returned to the *Mabahiss*. About 4 o'clock we got under way and steamed down the Red Sea towards our first station.

We had now been at sea for a week and had more or less settled down to life on board a small trawler. Our first and greatest difficulty—and one which, in spite of all our efforts to reduce to a minimum, remained constantly present throughout the whole Expedition—was lack of room. There were seven of us on the scientific staff and with the exception of Lieutenant-Commander Farquharson, we were accommodated below deck amidships between the large forward hold and the engine-room and stoke hold. Farquharson, from the nature of his duties as Navigator and Surveyor, was constantly required on the bridge and so he was allotted a deck cabin on the port side, the only other cabin that opened on deck being that reserved for the Captain.

To reach our quarters and the laboratory we had to go down an accommoda-

tion ladder that descended at a steep angle to a narrow passage running   9.IX.33
across the width of the ship. Originally this lower deck had comprised a
small laboratory and the Scientists' Mess on the after side and four single
cabins on the forward side. In order to increase the laboratory space it had
been necessary to give up one of the cabins, that on the port side, and
throw this into the laboratory as the biological section, while the original
laboratory was reserved for the chemical work, the two being connected by
a narrow passage made by removing part of the dividing bulkhead, so that
we could all use the same sink. In this converted cabin a bench was erected
running along the ship's side below the porthole and a cupboard for the
storage of gear and a rack for our storage bottles against the inner bulk-
heads. Above the bench was fixed a rack for holding our large storage
bottles for alcohol and formalin, with which the bulk of our collections
were preserved. The two single cabins on the starboard side of the ship had
been thrown into one that was occupied by our two Egyptian colleagues.
This was fitted with a couple of bunks, the one above the other, below the
porthole that opened on the ship's side and the rest of the space held the
usual cabin wash-hand stand, a hanging cupboard, a writing table and a bookcase, in which was housed the greater part of the small reference library
that we had managed to get together, the rest of it being accommodated in
a small extra bookcase that the ship's carpenter had constructed in the
laboratory between the bench and the cupboard. In the double cabin there
was also room for a small settee, that would at a pinch hold three people.

    The inner cabin on the port side was the only one of the original series
that remained intact, and this I occupied; its dimensions were about 6 feet
square. Along one side ran the bunk, with a set of drawers underneath and
on the opposite side was a hanging cupboard, a small set of drawers and
the wash-hand stand, while in the corner was fitted a small extra cupboard
for taking stationery, note books, printed forms, etc. Between this cupboard
and the head of the bunk was a small seat below the porthole. There was
no writing table and if I wished to do any clerical work I had to fix a board
across the seat between the wash-hand stand and a slot on the side of the
bunk so that I was then penned in the corner. A single porthole opened
out from the cabin on to the well deck, and a similar porthole also opened
out of the two-berth cabin next door in addition to the porthole on the
ship's side. Unfortunately, these two portholes opened forward exactly
underneath the raised gangway that ran across the ship from side to side for
the winch-man, and immediately in front of this was the main trawling
winch itself, that very effectually cut off nearly all light, so that the porthole
was of very little use for illumination and when open permitted the entry
into the cabin of·a small amount of air that was thoroughly permeated with

9.IX.33 the smell of machine oil from the winch or of castor oil and tallow from the wire rope on the winch drum. It was thus impossible even on the brightest days to see to do anything in my cabin except by electric light, or, when the Chief shut down the dynamo for any reason, by an oil lamp which added its quota of heat and smell to the general atmosphere.[1] At the foot of the accommodation ladder a door opened on the after side of the alleyway into the old Mess room that had been converted into a three-berth cabin for the accommodation of my Cambridge colleagues. Nearly the whole of the available space in this cabin was occupied by the bunks and there was only just available space for a wash-hand stand and a small table, with a few drawers under the bunks. Beyond this at the end of the alleyway was the laboratory; there were three chemists on board and when they were all working at once there was, as can well be imagined, very little room to move about in; the biological side could only just accommodate two persons at the same time. Although there were three portholes opening on the ship's side, these were only about a foot above the water line, so that as soon as we put to sea these had to be closed and remained so until we got back to port again. A ventilating shaft came down from the deck above on each side to give us air, and each cabin and the laboratory was fitted with an electric fan, but these only served to keep the stale air circulating. With a temperature that at times ran as high as 93 °F, the state of the atmosphere down below can be better imagined than described; but even the imagination can hardly do justice to the state of affairs that existed when one of the biologists upset a bottle of formalin in the laboratory. Those that are accustomed to working with this preserving agent will not need to be told, but for the benefit of those who are unacquainted with the fluid I may state that it has a most penetrating and irritating odour that even in the weakest possible concentration causes the nose and eyes to smart and the eyes to weep copiously.

Below the well-deck there was a large fish-hold; but the forward part of this had been taken up by the refrigerator and the after quarter or third was now an additional coal-bunker, to enable us to carry some 30 tons extra coal and so increase the length of time that we could stay at sea. In the space that remained were stored the greater part of the dry stores, that had to be sufficient for forty men for a period of some twenty-eight days, and what remained over this was filled with as much of our scientific gear as

1. If things were bad below deck, they could be quite as unpleasant on the bridge. MacKenzie wrote that with a following wind 'smoke and ashes from the low funnel pour steadily into our little bridge and with such determined force that the nuisance has given all hands the appearance of coal heavers, and five minutes on the bridge is sufficient to ruin any suite [*sic*]'.

we could manage to stow away. As, however, there was not sufficient   10.IX.33
room for everything, a number of boxes of water-sample bottles and storage
bottles for specimens had to be stowed on deck round the base of the
funnel, while two large iron tanks, for the accommodation of extra large
specimens, were clamped to the deck aft, one on either side of the ship. On
the well-deck itself, in addition to the trawling winch and the necessary
fair-leads, gallows, etc., we had to find room for one or two barrels of
spirit and a case, containing two large carboys of formalin, the large grab
and any nets that were likely to be required, and still space had to be found
for those that were working the gear or were engaged in getting the
specimens out of the nets when they came up and roughly sorting them
out before they were sent down to the laboratory.

Another difficulty that we had to cope with was a complete ignorance of
the language spoken by the crew. We, of course, knew no Arabic and they
appeared to know no English, though as time went on and we became
better acquainted with each other, we managed to pick up a little of their
language and we gradually discovered that they, or some of them, also
knew a little of ours. All the world over, from time immemorial, the sailor
has carried out his various routine duties to the accompaniment of songs or
shanties, and these Egyptian lads were no exception. Hauling on a line or
holystoning the decks was carried out to the accompaniment of a series of
songs or choruses, but what these were about remained a sealed book to us
except for the refrain of the song that they sang when holystoning the
decks; during this work someone sang a number of verses at the end of
each of which the whole party would roar out a refrain that, so far
as we gathered, was an appeal that someone would 'marry me to a
negress'.

Farquharson and Tyler had now got the echo-sounder running smoothly
and we were taking soundings at a rate of about twenty-five to the minute
as we steamed along. As each sounding was taken, the hammer operated by
the air compressor in the engine-room came down on its metal plate with a
sharp thud that was audible all over the ship; during the night-watches the
noise was so loud that it seemed as if it was coming from just the other side
of the bulkhead of my cabin. During the first few days I found it very
difficult to get to sleep with this constant noise going on, and doubtless
others on board suffered in the same way. But after a few days we got so
used to it that it made no difference to us, so long as the apparatus was
working smoothly. On the other hand, we now found that if anything
went wrong with the apparatus or if, for any reason, it stopped, we suddenly
woke up.

We made our first official station on 10 September in Lat. 25°24′30″ N.;

10.IX.33   Long. 36°12′12″ E.; depth 2,240 metres. Farquharson, who had been studying the chart the previous evening, had informed me that about 11 o'clock we ought to be in the near vicinity of the deepest sounding that had ever been taken in the Red Sea, 1,200 fathoms, and I had decided to make our first station in this deep patch. By 11 o'clock, however, the depth, as given by the echo-sounder, was only 800 fathoms and I began to think that either we had missed the area or else that it was a myth; but a few minutes later the echo began to indicate a rapid fall in the sea bottom and before long it was showing a depth of 1,212 fathoms. The *Mabahiss* was then turned head to wind and we attempted to take a sounding with the Lucas machine. There was a strong wind blowing and a moderate sea running, and as the Lucas machine was right aft, immediately over the propellor, where the movement of the ship is at its maximum, conditions were not exactly favourable. We made our first attempt to get a sounding and a sample of the bottom with a Driver tube, but the wire parted after a few fathoms had run out, and we lost the sounding tube. After this we made two more attempts with a lighter Baillie rod but each time the wire parted and we lost the tube. At the fourth attempt we got a sounding of 1,230 fathoms, thus corroborating the result of the echo-sounder, but on attempting to haul in, the wire again parted and we lost a third Baillie rod and failed to get a sample of the bottom deposit. In the meantime we had started to take samples and temperatures of the water at different depths, but here again our bad luck still dogged us, for while attempting to get a temperature reading and a water sample from a depth of 30 metres the Nansen-Pettersson bottle failed to close properly; the bottle was readjusted and we were ready to try again, but this time the winch-man, instead of paying out the wire, suddenly hove in and before the winch could be stopped the bottle was pulled into the meter-wheel. Fortunately the wire did not snap, or else we should have lost the bottle; but one of the wire strands had parted and this necessitated making a new eye-splice at the end of the wire. While this was being done we started work with batteries of Ekman reversing water-bottles on the port-side wire, and even here our luck was out, for on one occasion the bottom bottle came up flattened out and the attached thermometer smashed to pieces. The only explanation that I can give of this accident is that, owing to an oversight, the bottle was sent down closed instead of open and the increasing pressure, as it was lowered down, had ultimately become too great for the metal sides of the bottle and these had suddenly been crushed inwards or imploded.[1] This

1. The gear losses at this first station did not augur well for the future. Indeed, any
    forebodings which Sewell might have had would have been well founded, for the
    Expedition lost a large amount of gear and some parts of the narrative read like a

proved to be the last of our mishaps at this station and from this point the   10–11.IX.33
rest of the work proceeded smoothly, the last battery of reversing bottles
being safely back on board just after dark. At times during the day the sea
had been so rough that we shipped quite a lot of water on the well-deck or
over the bulwarks amidships, and twice I had got caught by a wave and
was drenched. But salt water never did anyone any harm and with an air
temperature of 82 °F in the shade one soon got dry again or, at least, as dry
as one's own profuse perspiration would allow. While we drifted, as we
rapidly were discovering, we could see quite a number of animals floating
on the surface that we probably shouldn't have noticed when we were
steaming and at this station a large swarm of brown medusae (jelly-fish)
came floating by.

On the following morning at 11.30 the ship was stopped and brought
head to wind, and we made another attempt to get a sample of the bottom.
One of the large Bigelow sounding tubes was attached to the end of the
hydrographic wire by a length of rope and was put over the side. The
meter-wheel was set to zero and we commenced to pay out the wire; at first
the wire would not run out without the winch-engine working, but after
some hundreds of metres of wire had passed out, it ran off itself. The
sudden release of strain on the accumulator springs indicated that bottom
had been struck at 1,024 metres and at the same time the echo-sounder
gave a depth of 1,008 metres, which agreed very closely. We then commenced to haul in and we got the tube up until the shackle connecting the
wire with the rope was alongside. The wind was now on our starboard side
and the ship had drifted down over the rope, so that it was running
underneath her. We went slow ahead, turning the ship, and as soon as the
rope was free from the ship's side, started to heave in by hand. All was
going well and we were just getting the heavy bottom tube up, when the
rope suddenly parted and the Bigelow tube returned to the bottom! I had
intended carrying out a trawl as soon as the sounding was over, but we
now discovered that the eye-splice on the end of the trawl-warp was too
large to pass through the large meter-wheel and it was necessary to cut it
off and make a smaller one. This was an annoying defect in the meter-
wheel, and the one that we subsequently had made for us was modified in
the form of a snatch-block, to allow for the rope being adjusted and the
meter-wheel put on or taken off whenever required by merely opening the
hinged back of the block and passing the wire through.

As the making of a new eye-splice would take some time and as the

---

catalogue of disaster. Some of these losses were undoubtedly due to inexperience on the
part of both the scientists and the crew, but they do seem to have had a great deal of bad
luck too!

11–12.IX.33 weather was by no means favourable for scientific work, we abandoned our intention of trawling and steamed on towards the south so as to reach our next station about dawn the following morning. All day long the chemists were busy carrying out analyses of the water samples that we had obtained the day before and, as it was clear that they would not be in a position to deal with any more for another twenty-four hours and it was no use overloading them with work right at the commencement of the Expedition, I decided to confine our efforts to obtaining a sample of the bottom fauna. At the same time our experience of the last few days had shown that conditions for work were much more favourable in the early mornings than later in the day; in the early hours there was a good deal less wind and sea, the former getting up steadily towards mid-day or early afternoon, so from this point on we had to arrange that our stations were reached at dawn or soon afterwards. I was called at 6.00 the next morning and on coming up on deck I found that conditions were favourable, so the ship was stopped and work commenced at about 7 o'clock.

We first attempted to get a sounding and a sample of bottom with a heavy Bigelow tube; this was safely sent down and appeared to strike the bottom at 2,176 metres, the reading on the echo-sounding machine giving 1,145 fathoms. We at once started to heave in but the hydrographic winch began to give trouble; instead of running the tube up straight away, it stopped, when over 1,000 metres of wire were still out, for some twenty minutes, during which time the bottom tube swung free in mid-water. It was not surprising, therefore, that when we did get the tube back on board there was no sample of the bottom in it, though there were traces of soft yellow mud still adhering to the outside. We then attempted to carry out a trawl with the Agassiz net; this was lowered away and a sufficient length of wire paid out. We steamed ahead for half an hour during which the strain as shown on the dynamometer was just over one ton. Then, as there seemed, from the angle at which the wire was trailing out aft, to be some doubt whether the net was actually on the bottom, we reduced our speed to slow and the strain fell to 16–18 cwt. After an hour the ship was stopped and we commenced to heave in. At first the trawl-winch jibbed and refused to heave in but after a bit we got it to start and then, when there were still some 1,900 metres of wire out, there was a loud bang; the strong chain by which the meter-wheel was attached had parted and the heavy wheel shot away like a stone from a catapult, snapping the trawl warp as it went. It first hit the top of the hatch in the well deck, breaking off a segment of its rim, and then passed between Macan and myself and plunged into the sea about 25 yards out from the ship's side. Macan and I were only about 6 feet apart: I felt the wind of it as it went by and was spattered with oil and grease from it, so it was a pretty close thing. And it was Macan's birthday too!

So the only result of our attempt to trawl in the deep part of the Red Sea was the loss of our meter-wheel, the trawl and some 1,800 metres of our trawl wire. This put an end for the time being to our trawling, so we turned back to the deep patch and during the afternoon carried out a series of hydrographic observations. But our run of bad luck had not yet finished, for at 8 o'clock that evening, when Faouzi was taking the usual routine meteorological observations, the head of the Asman psychrometer came unscrewed and the whole instrument came clattering down from the lower bridge to the deck, smashing both thermometers. Never in my life could I remember having struck such a run of bad luck as we had experienced during the last three days;[1] the loss of about half our trawl wire and the meter-wheel was particularly trying, as this completely prevented us from trawling in really deep water until we could get some more wire, and without the meter-wheel we had no means of estimating the amount of wire out when we were using any of our nets. Just before we finished taking our hydrological observations the crew, who were fishing for shark from the forecastle as two or three had been swimming round the ship, managed to hook one. It was a species of *Carcharias*, about 5 feet in length, but on cutting it open we found absolutely nothing in either stomach or intestines.

Having concluded our observations we turned south again and at 8.30 the next morning we stopped to carry out the very necessary work of marking the trawl wire, so that we might know how much wire we were paying out when trawling. The ship was stopped and the heavy Bigelow bottom tube, which had been shackled on to the hydrographic wire, was put over the side and lowered away; bottom was struck at 938 metres but again on hauling in the tube we found it to be empty, though the outside was smeared with traces of the same bright yellow mud. We concluded that the mud was too soft to stick in the tube. We then proceeded with the work of marking the trawl wire. A 3-foot triangular dredge was shackled on to the wire and put over the side and as the wire slowly passed out over the gallows the length was measured and a series of marks, pieces of coloured cotton or cloth, were stoutly lashed on to the wire. Marking commenced at 9.15 and just before noon we had marked 1,000 fathoms; all this time the ship had been drifting to leeward at the rate of about a mile per hour. We then started to haul in and all went well until we came to the

1. MacKenzie was less charitable: '13th. Existing as if in a turkish bath, every day station work, every night steaming. The scientific results so far have not been good, and the loss of much valuable gear through inexperience and carelessness has been disappointing.'

13–14.IX.33   last 200 fathoms, but in this last length of the wire there were a number of kinks, caused by the wire having twisted round on itself; most of the kinks were straightened out without any damage having been done, but in the last 80 fathoms some of them were so bad that this length of wire had to be sacrificed and cut off. While a new eye-splice was being made in the end of the trawl wire, we took a sounding with a Driver tube on the hydrographic wire. On hauling in we found that the wire had over-run the depth and there was a tangle of wire round the bottom tube; this was freed and having taken the Driver tube off, the last length of the wire was again passed over the side, with a 20 lb weight attached, to take out the twists, and then the wire was coiled down on the drum without any damage having been done. As a result of our attempt we obtained a core, about 7 inches in length, of the bright yellow bottom mud.

As soon as the eye-splice was ready we shackled on the 2-metre diameter plankton net and in doing so we discovered that a further effect of the loss of half our trawl wire was that, owing to the tapering of the wire, the inboard part was now too large and its diameter too great to pass through the release mechanism of the self-closing apparatus, so this could not be used. The net was put over the side (Station 5) and lowered away and a length of wire, estimated to be sufficient to allow the net to fish at a depth of some 500 metres, was paid out. The net was back on board again about half-past six, just after sunset, with a moderate catch, the most important ingredient of which was a number of deep-sea prawns, bright red in colour, many of which were still alive.

On the morning of the 14th, we started work by carrying out a number of hydrographic observations and as soon as this was completed we sent a 4-foot Salpa dredge down to the bottom in a depth of 996 metres (Station 6). At first there was but little strain on the wire, the dynamometer showing only 15 cwt, but after we had been going slow ahead for about a quarter of an hour there was a sudden increase to nearly a ton and a half and it seemed clear that the net had caught fast in some obstruction on the bottom. At first, when we started hauling in, the strain was again considerable and the *Mabahiss* had to be manoeuvred up to the wire. Eventually the net broke away from the bottom and was hauled in and it was then seen that the lashing holding the net to the frame had in places carried away and the rods of the frame had been badly bent. The bag of the net contained nothing but bits of rock that appeared to consist largely of calcium carbonate, and a few dead lamellibranch shells; there was no sign of any living organisms.

As soon as the net was back on board we steamed on towards the south in order to get to an anchorage off Zukhair Island. The weather during the

last five days had been particularly trying, for we had had a continuous
following breeze with a very high degree of humidity. Accustomed to the
tropics as I was, I found it very trying, and the engine-room staff were
becoming badly upset by it; one of our engineers was down with fever and
several of the stokers were suffering from colic. As the next day was Friday,
the Mohammedan equivalent of our Sunday, MacKenzie and I decided to
give the men a day off. As we steamed south a large school of dolphins
came round and two or three of the larger ones stayed with us for quite a
long distance, keeping just a foot or two ahead of our bows. Occasionally
they sheered off for a few yards, but they soon came back to their position
just ahead of us and from the bow of the ship we could see them turning
over in the water, showing their lighter-coloured bellies.

As we steamed south next day the weather became more and more sultry
and oppressive. It was noticed that as we got nearer to the Straits of Bab-
el-Mandab the patches of Sargasso weed that could be seen floating on the
surface became more and more frequent. About 5 o'clock in the evening
we anchored off Zukhair Island and some of the men went ashore. On
their return, they reported that there was a coral reef growing out beyond
the beach and they brought back with them several good sized mullet,
numerous hermit crabs and several species of molluscs.

On the morning of the 16th we weighed anchor at 6.15, just as it was
light, and steamed out to a position at the extreme southern end of the
deep water of the Red Sea, where there was a depth of 260 metres and
where we carried out a series of observations. It was very noticeable that
the Secchi disc disappeared at much shallower depths than at stations more
to the north; here it could be seen down to a depth of only 23 metres,
whereas at previous stations it could be seen at 35 metres. This seemed
definitely to be correlated with the large amount of plankton in the upper
water levels. Thompson and Gilson, assisted by Abdel Fatteh, carried out a
complete series of hydrological observations and got clear evidence of
stratification in the water levels. On the surface there was a layer of water
flowing up into the Red Sea and immediately below this there seemed to be
an outflowing stratum. At a depth of 80 metres there was a zone of water
of lower temperature, approximately only 17 °C, that could only have come
from outside, and below this again lay the main mass of true Red Sea
water. A haul of half an hour's duration with the 2-metre plankton net at a
depth of 183 metres produced a very large catch of typical planktonic animal
life, sufficient to fill a 7 lb jar. The catch consisted for the most part of
siphonophores, pteropods and salps, these latter probably being examples
of *Salpa cylindrica*; associated with these were several eel-larvae (Leptocephali) of various sizes, a few small pleuronectid (flat fish) larvae with the

16–17.IX.33   two small eyes still on opposite sides of the head, numerous alima larvae and young stomatopods. After we had hauled in the plankton net I had intended sending down the Agassiz trawl, but as a precautionary measure I first sent down the conical dredge to ascertain the nature of the bottom. This had been on the bottom for only 5 minutes when it became fast on something. There was a very considerable strain on the wire and the ship was manoeuvred to bring her up to it. The dredge eventually came away and was hauled back on board. It was found that the metal part of the frame had been badly bent, for the opening was now triangular instead of circular, and the wire strop had parted so that the dredge was hanging by a single chain instead of by three. There could be little doubt that the dredge had been hung up on rock. The contents of the dredge were for the most part black sand, possibly of volcanic origin, since these islands at the south end of the Red Sea are all volcanic, and mixed with this were numerous empty pteropod shells, the dead shells of small sea-urchins and a few dead mollusc shells. Once again there was no sign of living animals. As the nature of the ground appeared to be so unsuitable, I abandoned the idea of trawling and we steamed south to a new position on the west side of Great Hanish Island, at which point there is a shallow ridge separating the Gulf of Aden from the Red Sea. Here we carried out another full series of hydrographic observations and again got clear evidence of the separation of the Red Sea water into two layers by an inflowing current of Gulf of Aden water, the temperature at 80 metres depth again showing a sharp fall to about 17 °C.

As soon as this work was completed we steamed to an anchorage on the west side of Great Hanish Island and a party went ashore in the motor boat, towing the dinghy. Before they had gone very far they had trouble with the motor, for the coupling gear connected with the shaft refused to function; so they all climbed into the dinghy and pulled in to the shore. We were somewhat surprised to find both this island and Zukhair Island occupied by armed Italian guards. I had always thought that these islands were British; somehow one always seems to take it for granted that islands that do not obviously belong to some other nation are part of the British Empire and I knew that during the war we had taken over several of these islands in the southern end of the Red Sea, for detachments of my own regiment had been detailed to attend to some of the lighthouses on the islands.[1] It was difficult to imagine why Italian soldiers should be posted

1. Sewell's somewhat imperialist tone would have seemed quite unremarkable to most British readers at the time. MacKenzie's journal is only marginally less patronizing: 'A visit from a canoe with two filthy natives and two smartly dressed native soldiers came as a surprise. The island, they said, was Italian, and the flag was kept flying ashore. They

here. However, they informed us that they were there to protect the Italian
fisheries vessels which presumably operate from some port in Italian
Somaliland or from Eritrea.

The following morning Farquharson, Macan and I pushed off in the
motor boat, towing the dinghy, to carry out some trawling and dredging in
the shallower water round the island, while the *Mabahiss* left the anchorage
to take hydrographic and other observations on the shelf that separates the
Red Sea proper from the Gulf of Aden. The island looks what it is, a
typical volcanic upheaval; for the most part it is absolutely bare of vegetation, though there is a patch at the top of the beach that is covered by a
low scattered scrub. All the rest, so far as we could see, is volcanic rock
and lava. In places round the shore there has been a marked degree of
erosion and this is especially evident in a small group of islands on the
south side of the bay, of which Double Peak Island is one. This island is
bordered by an absolutely flat rim that drops in a sheer cliff, the height of
which I estimated to be about 30 feet, and in places this is undercut or even
hollowed out into caves; but if this erosion was caused by wave action, it
must in places have been effected in times past, when the sea-level was
higher than it is today or the islands some feet lower, for its level is too
high for present-day conditions. The top of the cliff forms an almost straight
line across the face of the islands but in the more central parts are two
small peaks of varying hues, one of a sandy yellow colour and the other
madder-brown turning to black.

We landed on a sandy beach between outlying rocky promontories and
examined the foreshore. On the beach were numerous ocypodid crabs and
some sooty gulls were still breeding, for a few young birds and eggs were
seen. The beach consists of sand, shells and fragments of coral and beyond
the top is a low-lying area frosted over with a slight efflorescence of salt,
possibly caused by the sea breaking during storms over the top of the
beach, though during rain, which is rare in these parts, this area would be a
swamp. This flat area is dotted over with clumps of a grass- or reed-like
growth of a light green colour; round its periphery are outcrops of black
lava and these run out into the sea in ledges and promontories which
below the water level are fringed with masses of weed and in places are
encrusted with *Lithothamnion*. On the ledges are numerous *Chiton*, limpets
and whelks (*Buccinum*), while under loose boulders were numerous col-

---

were the guard. Who were we, and what did we want? Surprise indeed, as it was imagined
that this group belonged to Britain. It didn't, neither did or does it belong to Italy. Once
Turkish, and since the League of Nations had not yet decided to whom it should be
handed, Italy is getting in the thin end of the wedge.'

lections of *Dostia*; several species of *bêche-de-mer* (holothurians) were found lying in crevices and grooves in the rocks, and some of these were of a pale brick-red colour, that closely resembled the red of the *Lithothamnion* and some of the corals. A few yards out from the beach, coral begins to grow and forms a scattered, patchy reef with channels and areas of white sand. Judging from the fragments that were seen on the beach, the commoner species are *Acropora*, *Favia* and *Tubipora musica*, the red Organ-pipe coral.

Having completed our hurried examination of the beach we then re-embarked in the motor boat and carried out a successful trawl, obtaining a varied assortment of alcyonarians and sponges with a rich commensal fauna, the most striking animals being several pycnogonids and ophiuroids, the latter coloured to match the alcyonarians on which they were living. About noon we knocked off work and anchored the boat; we then pulled the dinghy into a sheltered little bay, with a clean sandy bottom between two of the rock ledges, inside the coral reef, and had a bathe. We had hardly got back into the dinghy when we saw two sharks, about 3 feet in length, quietly swimming up into the little bay where we had been bathing a few minutes previously! On returning to the motor boat after lunch we found that the motor had struck work and it was 3 o'clock before we could get it to start again; and even then it only worked fitfully. However, we managed to carry out another trawl before the motor finally refused to work, so we hoisted the mast and sail and started off towards the rendezvous where we were to meet the *Mabahiss* on her return.

While we had been working off the island the *Mabahiss* had made a couple of stations on the top of the ridge that separates the Red Sea and the Gulf of Aden. At the first station (Station 9) a complete series of hydrographic observations had been taken, but an attempt to trawl with a 4-foot triangular dredge in 250 metres had resulted in the net being badly torn on a rocky bottom and the sole catch was a small piece of dead coral. At the second station (Station 10) they had better luck and carried out a successful trawl with the otter net in a depth of 55 metres, obtaining a large collection of sponges and other forms of animal life, conspicuous among which was a large nudibranch mollusc of a bright red colour.

The next morning we left our anchorage at about 6 o'clock and steamed out into the deep channel that runs up from the Gulf of Aden to the ridge opposite Great Hanish Island. Here we stopped the ship and carried out a sounding with a Driver tube, getting a depth of water of 215 metres, while the echo-sounder gave a depth of 216 metres. On hauling in there was nothing in the tube, but as the outside of it was scratched it seemed probable that the bottom was hard, so we substituted a Snapper lead and let it go; this time we got some small fragments of rock.

As this ground appeared extremely unsuitable for trawling or dredging, we steamed on again until just after noon to a spot where the chart indicated a sandy bottom. This time we got bottom at 207 metres with the Snapper lead, which was bent but contained fragments of rock. We then attached a 3-foot triangular dredge to the trawl wire, with a light rope becket at one of the angles (Station 11). After towing for half an hour we hauled the dredge in and found that the becket had parted and the net had been badly torn. Entangled in the net were several masses of rock, on one of which was the stem of a growing hydroid and some empty serpulid worm tubes, but these were the only signs of animal life.

Having completed our work we steamed for Perim Island and entered the harbour about 4.15 in the afternoon. While we were still some 15 miles away, we experienced a sudden and most refreshing fall in the temperature; this was due, without doubt, to a fall in the temperature of the sea-water for the thermograph attached to the engine-room intake simultaneously recorded a drop of temperature from 32.5 °C to 22.5 °C, the fall occurring with amazing rapidity.

Soon after we had entered the harbour the manager of the Perim Coal Company, that appears to own the harbour, and the medical officer, came off to us. The Coal Company very kindly excused us from payment of the usual harbour dues and the manager issued a general invitation to all of us to visit the Club. He also informed us that the chaplain from Aden had flown over by aeroplane in order to hold a service that evening for the inhabitants of the port and said that any of us who cared to attend would be very welcome: it isn't every day that one has the chance of meeting a chaplain who will fly some 90 miles in order to hold a service for a handful of people, so eight of us, including our two Mohammedan colleagues, went ashore to the Club where the service was held. After the service the Club reverted to its original state and we were introduced to most of the residents. We stayed chatting with them and partaking of their hospitality until 8.30 and then the manager of the Coal Company sent us back on board in his launch and we passed a comfortable night in a temperature that was several degrees lower than we had been experiencing during the previous ten days.

We left the harbour at 6.15 the next morning in an atmosphere that was wonderfully fine and cool; it was almost the first cool morning that we had experienced since we started on our voyage. Our immediate programme was to make a series of stations across the head of the Gulf of Aden just to the east of the entrance to the Straits of Bab-el-Mandeb, and soon after half-past nine the ship was stopped and turned head to wind for the first of these. Ever since we had left Perim the colour of the water had been

19–20.IX.33 gradually changing until by the time we reached our station it was a brownish-green and was so turbid that the Secchi disc disappeared from view, as it was lowered down, almost at once; at a depth of 3½ metres it was invisible and I expected to find that there was a large quantity of microscopic life present in the water; but the result of centrifuging 100 cc yielded a surprisingly small amount, consisting mostly of the microscopic alga *Trichodesmium*, that has a red colour and is usually given the credit of being the cause of the Red Sea being so named, and a diatom, *Rhizosolenia*.

The depth of water at this station was just over 450 metres and it took the chemists a little over two hours to complete their observations. Work was over about noon and we steamed off to our second station, which we reached at half past two; here the depth was 415 metres, which agreed well with our earlier sounding, and a second complete series of observations were carried out. It was half past four when we finished, but the chemists decided that they would carry on with the third station, though this meant working after dark, so we proceeded still further to the south.

At this stage the weather began to get distinctly bad. There was a strong wind blowing from the north-west and this raised a nasty sea that repeatedly broke over the well-deck or splashed over the starboard side, while the little *Mabahiss* was rolling a good deal. These conditions proved to be too much for some of us; however our third station was reached at sunset and work started almost immediately. Cargo lights had been rigged in readiness over the well-deck, so that the chemists could see; the chief difficulty was in reading the temperatures on the thermometers, but this was got over by the use of hand torches, and, considering the general conditions, work proceeded remarkably well and was completed at 9 o'clock without a mishap, except for the loss of one messenger. The echo-sounder had indicated that we were in much deeper water than we had expected, so as soon as the chemists had finished, Farquharson took a sounding with a Driver tube on the wire and got bottom at 1,575 metres, the bottom deposit being a brown mud of which we obtained a 13-inch core. When this was over we steamed eastward and during the night ran out of this deep area into a depth of some 750 metres. I had arranged to carry out a trawl at 8.30 the next morning, but just before then we ran into a patch of very irregular bottom, the echo-sounder indicating a series of steep elevations and depressions. As conditions appeared to be unfavourable we ran on for another hour and then stopped and brought the ship's head to wind, the echo-sounder now showing a depth of about 1,100 metres and the weather being beautifully fine with an almost calm sea. A sounding with the Driver tube gave us a core of about 12 inches in length of greenish-brown mud,

similar to that obtained the previous night, so the Agassiz trawl was
shackled on to the trawl wire and after a little delay was put over the side
(Station 15). We left the trawl down for an hour and when we hauled it in
again we found that the wire had somehow got foul of one of the bridles,
so that the net had been dragged sideways and, of course, had captured
nothing at all except a few jelly-fish that had been taken on the way either
up or down. After this failure the ship's head was turned towards the
African coast, where I hoped to find shallower water and be able to get in
another trawl before nightfall, since in less depth it would not take so long
to send the trawl down to the bottom or get it back again. Instead of
getting shallower, however, the depth either remained the same or got
even deeper and at four in the afternoon the echo-sounder was still indicating a depth of about 1,100 metres and another sounding with the
Driver tube gave a depth of 1,155 metres with a core of the same brown
mud. The echo-sounder had now developed a fault, so we lay hove to
for an hour while Farquharson got the trouble corrected, and as meantime the repairs to the trawl had not yet been completed we postponed
our trawl until the next morning and steamed in towards the African coast,
going slow and turning off-shore again when we reached the 100 fathom
line.

The next morning at 8 o'clock we carried out a trawl (Station 16) with
some success, in spite of the fact that the Agassiz trawl was fishing rather
badly owing to the foot- and head-ropes being too long; the result of this
was that the head-rope, instead of being pulled taut by the drag on the
foot-rope, sagged in the middle and thus allowed the net to fish properly
only at the two ends. On emptying the net, which contained a mass of soft
mud, we found that we had captured a number of prawns, all of which
showed the characteristic pink colour of deep-water crustacea, while
sticking through the meshes of the net were numbers of flower-like colonial
alcyonarians of the genus *Virgularia* or some closely allied genus. On the
completion of work at this station we steamed northwards into deeper
water in order that the chemists might carry out observations at the first of
a line of stations that we proposed to take across the Gulf of Aden on the
longitude of Aden itself, 45° E. There was some delay in completing the
work as it was found necessary to readjust the position of certain blocks
through which the wire passed. To start with these were not quite in a
straight line with the hydrographic winch and the wire coming off the
winch at an angle pressed against the rollers and commenced to cut a deep
groove which would ultimately have cut right through them. After completing the hydrographic work we steamed on our northerly course again
in order to get into a position where from our previous work we expected

21–28.IX.33 to find a deep channel with water of some 800 fathoms depth and there carry out a mid-water trawl with the 2-metre diameter plankton net. We were rather later than we expected in reaching this deep area, and the net was not sent down until a quarter past five in the evening, so in order that the net should be back on board again before nightfall the trawl had to be a short one. The depth-recorder was attached between the trawl wire and the net and it was hoped that it would give us some indication of the exact depth at which the net fished, but on subsequent examination it was found that the recording apparatus had failed to function properly, for when the needle had started to rise as the pressure increased it had caused a large ink-blot on the paper that completely obscured the actual reading. We estimated that the net had been for the most part fishing at a depth of about 900 metres (Station 18) and although the catch was small it included a number of fine reddish-brown deep-sea medusae belonging to two genera, *Atolla* and *Periphylla*, as well as a few small black deep-sea fish of the genus *Cyclothone*. During the night of 22 September we experienced a strong set towards the west, which delayed our arrival at Aden somewhat, but we anchored in the harbour soon after 9.30 and later in the morning I went ashore and paid my respects to the Chief Commissioner. That evening four of us, at the invitation of the Chief Commissioner, visited the Union Club and later dined with him at the Residency. We got back to the landing jetty at about 11.15 p.m. and were waiting for our motor boat to come in and take us off to the *Mabahiss* when we saw a brilliant sheet of flame suddenly shoot up alongside the ship; the motor boat had caught fire! Apparently the fire was caused by a back-fire from the motor when starting her up, and this had ignited some petrol that had leaked out from the carburettor; fortunately no serious damage was done and the fire was soon put out.

During the next few days I spent much of my time in looking up old friends whom I had known in Aden during the war years. We were to have sailed again on the morning of the 27th; but, just before we were due to leave, the echo-sounding apparatus went wrong again, the ball-race, carrying the ball bearing of the motor, having seized up. Farquharson and Tyler hurriedly went ashore and scoured Aden to try and find another. They were fortunately able to get one, but it was too late to get this installed before nightfall, so we postponed our departure until the following morning; just before we sailed we said goodbye to Tyler, who was catching a ship home again. We were all sorry to part with him for he had been invaluable in getting the echo-sounder to run properly and in helping our Chief Engineer or anyone else who wanted a bit of machinery looked at.

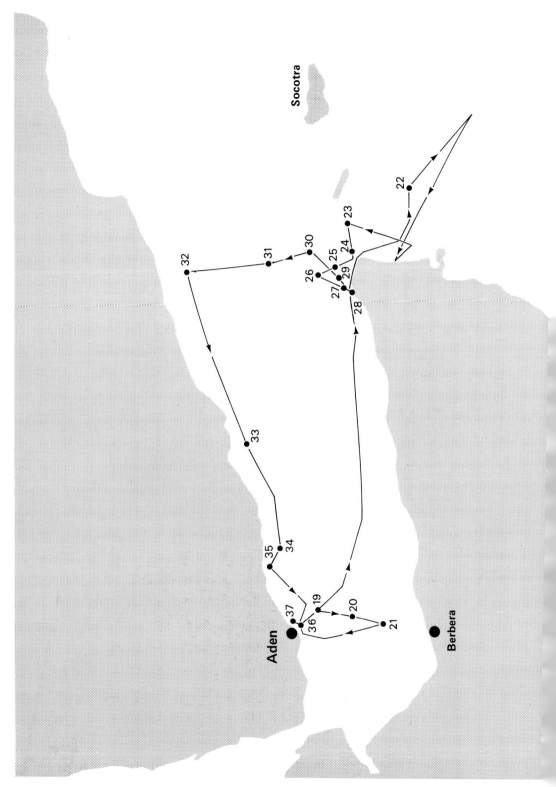

Fig. 13. Track chart, Cruise 2: Aden–Aden. Station numbers are indicated.

Chapter 3

The Gulf of Aden

WE left Aden at dawn on the morning of 28 September. All the previous day we had been taking in our sea-stores, among which was a quantity of freshly killed meat, which was put down in the refrigerator. While we had been in port we had had our fires drawn for a boiler-cleaning, and at first there was some difficulty in getting the refrigerator to work; this was eventually overcome, though precious time had been lost. On the night of the 27th the machine had again stopped work and later on in the morning of the 28th it was reported that our stock of meat was going bad. I inspected it and there was no doubt that the worst had occurred; after a consultation it was decided that the whole consignment would have to be dumped, so that at the very start of our cruise we were without any fresh meat.

For two days nearly all the spare time of the Chief Engineer had been taken up in trying to get the refrigerator to work but without success and the main result was that he had himself become badly gassed with the fumes of the machine. When I saw him at about 8 o'clock in the evening he was lying on the grating aft, feeling very sick, while his pulse was weak and soft; he was very drowsy and took a long time to reply to any question that was put to him. We had a camp cot rigged up for him on deck so that he could sleep in the open air; the following morning his condition did not appear to be any better and he was clearly unfit for duty, so after a consultation with Captain MacKenzie it was decided that we should put back into Aden and send him to hospital.[1] We got back to port at about 7.30

---

1. MacKenzie's journal entry about Griggs' hospitalization contains the first hint of a difference of priorities which is a common source of friction between captains and scientists on oceanographic cruises. 'In the Gulf of Aden, Chief Engineer having received a dose of gas while working at refrigeration plant has become seriously ill and neither of our medical men will express an opinion. 'Will he die?' I asked. 'Well we can't say, but we don't just know what to do,' and such is all the satisfaction one can get. The operating of marine stations being the primary point of view of all ocean scientists, I decided to immediately turn back and land Griggs into hospital in Aden.'

on the 29th. Colonel Phipson, the Port Health Officer, came off to us at once and after seeing Griggs took him straight off to the European General Hospital. This time we were anchored right up near the head of the harbour, as HMS *Penzance* was occupying our former berth, and on the morning of the 30th, HMS *Cornwall* came in and there was the usual coming and going of officers paying formal calls. The same morning the SS *Orontes*, one of the Orient Co.'s liners, dropped anchor in the harbour and through the P and O agents we were able to arrange that one of their engineers, who was an expert on cold storage, should come over and have a look at our machine. They had the same make of machine on their ship as we had and he overhauled ours, which he said was a beautiful little plant, and put it in a going condition.

Our Chief was well enough to be discharged from hospital on the morning of 2 October, and about 1.30 in the afternoon we again sailed, passing the fine Italian ship *Victoria* coming into harbour as we were going out. Just before we actually left a flight of fourteen pelicans flew over the harbour but unfortunately at too great a height for a photograph to be taken of them.

As soon as we got clear outside we began to experience a swell from the south-west that upset some of us. All the next day we steadily pursued our course down the Gulf towards Cape Guardafui; the weather was for the greater part of the day wonderfully fine and there was an almost flat calm. There were a number of porpoises about during the afternoon, but none of them came very near us. About tea-time we passed several large shoals of fish swimming near the surface, and hovering over these were a number of birds. At first I was inclined to take them for sea-gulls, but a closer scrutiny through field-glasses showed that they were a rather smaller bird. The whole of the back was a dusky brown colour and the underparts were white; the tail was rounded and the wings were slender and pointed; the bill was moderately long and more slender than a gull's. The flight was also quite different from that of a gull, with little or none of the usual soaring of the gull's flight. On the contrary, the wings were flapped frequently and the general character was more like that of the flight of a duck. It is possible that these birds were shearwaters and the position where they were seen was opposite the village of Ras Fartik on the African coast at a distance of about 7 miles from the shore.

Soon after we had left Aden the character of the sea-water had begun to change. During the 3rd and the morning of the 4th its colour had been a deep blue, but as we got nearer to the north African coast off Ras Fartik and Ras Alula this had gradually changed to a decided green, and about mid-day on the 4th we took a haul with the high-speed tow net. The catch

4–5.X.33 included a few copepods and *Sagitta*, but the bulk of it was made up of diatoms of several species and genera, and conspicuous among these were numerous examples of a *Ceratium*, probably *C. tripos*. It seems probable that this change in the character of the water is due to the influx of the Socotra current that carries a rich plankton from the East African coast into the Gulf. Associated with this change it was noticed that as we got further away from Cape Guardafui and the Gulf the temperature of the surface water got steadily lower and by 4.00 in the afternoon it was only 23.2 °C, instead of being about 29.0 °C. It seems probable that this reduced temperature is caused by an upwelling of deep water off the African coast.

At 9.15 p.m. on the 4th we were nearly opposite Cape Guardafui and as a result we were beginning to feel the lift of the swell coming in from the Arabian Sea. The weather was beautifully fine and clear and we passed Cape Guardafui at about 10 o'clock that night and by the following morning we were well out in the Arabian Sea. Our original intention had been to make for a spot off the African coast where a shoal area had been reported to the Admiralty. They had asked us to try and investigate the area and discover if there was any truth in the report, but the circumstances caused a change in our programme. We had been making much less mileage than we had expected and our speed over the ground was only about 4.5 to 5 knots, instead of the 7 that we had hoped for. Furthermore, just when it was likely to be wanted, the echo-sounder had begun to give trouble and, instead of giving a single clear knock, had developed a stutter. All night it was giving trouble and Farquharson and Lloyd Jones were working on it until early morning, but without any success, so at 8 o'clock we decided to alter our programme and instead of making for the shoal area we altered our course towards the spot that we had selected for a deep hydrographic station to the south-east of Socotra. One cause of our slow progress was in all probability the fact that we were steaming against the Socotra current, following through the gap between Cape Guardafui and Socotra where, according to the Dutch current charts, it may have a speed of some 50 miles a day.

During the morning we took another haul with the high-speed net and obtained quite a good catch, which for the most part again consisted largely of examples of *Ceratium*, this time of at least two species, one probably *C. tripos* and the other closely resembling *C. fusus*; associated with these were some colonies of *Trichodesmium erythraeum*, a small species of *Globigerina*, several species of copepods and a few *Sagitta*. The general colour of the water was a decided green and the resemblance between the two catches indicates a common origin, namely the East African Drift.

In order that the hydrographic work might be carried out in daylight, the ship was stopped at 3 o'clock in the afternoon of the 5th, although we were still some 20 miles from the spot that we had aimed at. As the echo-sounder was still out of action we had to trust to the chart to give us an indication of the depth, the nearest sounding showing 1,800 fathoms. We took observations down to 2,000 metres and then, as there was still time before dark, we took a sounding and obtained a good core of the bottom, consisting of a white clay, from a depth of 3,556 metres. During the process of heaving in the heavy Bigelow sounding tube the winch gave a lot of trouble and the drum appeared to be rubbing badly against the guiding rod that controlled the rollers.

Having completed work we steamed on towards the south-east to get to our next station and this time we made better progress than we had expected for we experienced a set towards the east from the branch of the African current that turns eastward along the south side of Socotra. We reached our proposed position at dawn on the 6th, but as there was time to spare we ran on for another four hours so as to put the station as far to the south-east of Cape Guardafui and Socotra as possible. At 10 o'clock the ship was stopped and work commenced, but in spite of the work that our engineers had done the hydrographic winch rapidly went from bad to worse and instead of going round in a circle the drum appeared to be describing an orbit shaped like an egg! It was impossible for us to continue, so work at this station had to be abandoned and we then steamed westward towards the African coast to try and locate the reported shoal. The echo-sounder was now functioning better and there was a distinct hope that we might be able to get our little bit of surveying done without any further trouble. As we approached the coast we ran into a belt of strong wind and moderate seas and as a result the *Mabahiss* shipped quite a lot of water over the weather side and somehow or other a good deal managed to find its way into the laboratory. Macan and I spent some time in mopping it up, but after an hour or two it was again as bad as ever. Right to the very end of the expedition, whenever there was any sea on the port side, water invariably managed to find its way down into the laboratory and we were never able to discover how it got there.

At about 3.45 a.m. we were in the vicinity of the shoal, but the echo-sounder had again struck work and, in addition, the weather had become cloudy and visibility was so poor that it was impossible to get a fix to give us our position. We decided to run in to an anchorage on the coast and stay there for the night, and then, if circumstances permitted, to carry out the survey the following morning. If this was not possible we would abandon the effort and return to the Gulf. We anchored at about 7.15 p.m. in a bay, Ghubbet Binna, on the north side of the promontory Ras Ali

8–9.X.33 Bash Kil, where we were sheltered from the southerly wind and so passed a quiet night.

We left our anchorage at about 5.15 on the morning of the 8th and as conditions were better we proceeded out towards the supposed shallow area. Farquharson had now got the echo-sounder to function once again and so for the greater part of the day we steamed backwards and forwards across the region but without finding the least trace of any shoaling, so that there could be little doubt that the reported shoal did not exist. Just before the survey was concluded, and while Farquharson was taking a sounding with the small Lucas machine by which he got a depth of 138 fathoms with a bottom of soft grey mud, a number of jelly-fish (medusae) drifted past the ship. By means of a hand-net we secured examples of two species; one was a small brown medusa with remarkably long tentacles (? *Pelagia perla*), and associated with this was a small crustacean megalopa larva that repeatedly darted for shelter into the sub-umbrella cavity; the other was a species of *Aurelia* that seemed to be thicker in the umbrella than the common European *Aurelia aurita* and was possibly *A. maldivensis* Browne. This latter species was the more predominant and just before we took the sounding we passed through quite a shoal of them. They were of a delicate mauve tint, the circular gonads being of a slightly darker colour.

On the completion of the survey we steamed northwards to make a station in the channel between Cape Guardafui and Socotra. As the following day was the anniversary of the Accession of King Fuad to the throne of Egypt, we attempted to send him a respectful message of greeting from the John Murray Expedition; unfortunately our good intentions failed to materialize for our Wireless Operator, owing to atmospherics, was unable to get our message through either that night or the following day.

We were in position for our next station at 6 o'clock on the 9th, being then exactly in the middle of the passage between Cape Guardafui and the nearest of the islands of the Socotra group, Abd al Kuri; so the ship was stopped and work commenced a few minutes later. Our observations were concluded soon after 8.30 and we then steamed in towards Cape Guardafui until we were in about 50 fathoms depth, when by way of preparation for a trawl we put over the conical dredge. The sample of the bottom thus obtained consisted of a coarse sand mixed with small stones and masses of encrusting barnacles, indicating a certain amount of rock on the bottom. However, we carried out a trawl (Station 24) in a depth that varied from 73 to 220 metres. When the trawl was hauled in again it was found to be badly torn, which was not altogether surprising, but the catch was fairly good and very varied, one splendid example of a crinoid (sea-lily) of brilliant colouring being entangled in the net. The major part of the catch consisted of sea-urchins with long stout spines, and there were a few fish. While we were trawling we experienced a strong and steady set towards the west, which was in conformity with the notice on the chart that also says that tide-rips occur in this area, doubtless caused by the swing of part of the Socotra current round Cape Guardafui. We also saw a fine specimen of a swordfish jumping out of the water; this particular species seems to be especially prone to this form of activity and usually carries out ten or twelve leaps out of the water before disappearing altogether.

After work was completed we ran in towards the coast and anchored off a village, composed of a number of mud huts, and off which several fishing boats were anchored. The following morning we got under way early and steamed out towards the north-west in order to get into water of some 450–550 metres depth for another station. Judging from the record of the echo-sounder the bottom here was very irregular and for a long time we couldn't get out of water of a depth of only about half this, for every time that the record showed a tendency to drop and we were expecting to get the depth that we desired, the bottom would rise again and we were disappointed. Eventually, at 10.30 we got the depth required and the ship stopped. The Driver tube was sent down and we got a depth of 630 metres. But unfortunately the tube did not close properly, a way that this particular piece of apparatus has, and as it came up to the surface the whole contents ran out of the tube; but they appeared to consist of a soft grey sand and mud. A snapper lead was then shackled on and sent down, but this failed to close as the bottom was too soft to give a sufficiently sudden impact. We then shackled on the Agassiz trawl and this was sent down, the net being towed on the bottom for an hour (Station 25); when it was hauled in again it was found that its contents were rather scanty, owing to the cod-end not having been tied sufficiently tightly. The catch, such as it was, consisted mostly of brown-coloured deep-sea medusae of the genera *Atolla* and *Periphylla*, but the examples of the latter genus were much smaller than the specimen that we had previously got on the 21st nearer the head of the Gulf of Aden. The chemists then got to work and while they were busy we collected some of the clumps of Sargasso weed that were floating near at hand; associated with the weed was a very interesting fauna. Some of the clumps were overgrown with colonies of stalked barnacles of the genus *Lepas*, and hiding among the fronds were three species of small fish, including a blenny and a small *Balistes*, several minute crabs and two examples of a sea-anemone. It was very interesting to note the way in which the coloration of all these various animals blended with that of the weed and thus served to conceal the animal.

Fɪɢ. 14. Getting the Agassiz trawl over the side, October 1933. (*Photo:* H. C. Gilson.)

When the chemists had finished, the Agassiz trawl was sent down again. 10–11.X.33
This time our luck was dead out, for the net had only been on the bottom
for about twenty minutes when it got caught on something. The strain on
the dynamometer suddenly rose to over 2½ tons, and then the rope strop
parted and the wire ran out freely. We then started to haul the net in and as
it came up we found several kinks in the wire, which looked very suspicious.
When the last length came aboard we found that the wire had parted about
30 fathoms above the trawl and we had lost the trawl and one of our swivel
shackles that had been specially made to stand a strain of 5 tons. Until late
that evening we were busy making a new eye-splice in the end of the wire
and in rigging another Agassiz trawl. When this was completed we went
slow ahead or drifted, so as to be in a depth of about 1,900 metres in the
morning.

The ship was stopped at 5.00 on the 11th and ten minutes later work
began at Station 26. The heavy Bigelow sounding tube was shackled on to
the hydrographic wire and sent down, and bottom was struck at 2,356
metres. When the tube was back again on deck we found that we had got a
fine core of greyish white bottom mud, about 2½ feet in length. In order
to get a record of the temperature and the character of the bottom-water,
we then sent down an Ekman reversing water bottle to 2,330 metres; but
when this came back again it was found that it had actually been on the
bottom, so it was clear that there was a certain amount of irregularity in
the sea floor. We then put the Agassiz trawl over the side and commenced
to lower that; but the process was a slow one as, owing to the loss of some
of our wire the day before, we had to put fresh marks on the wire as it was
played out. However, by 1.45 we had marked up to 1,400 fathoms and
were getting near the end of the wire on the drum. We then started to
trawl but as there seemed to be some doubt, owing to the irregularity of
the bottom, whether the net was actually down, we paid out another 210
fathoms a few minutes later and then went ahead trawling. On hauling in,
the catch was found to be moderately good and the rest of the afternoon
was spent in sorting it.

During the day, owing to the trouble we had been having with the
hydrographic winch, we got our Chief Engineer to have a thorough look
at it and he discovered that the drum had actually cracked right across. As
soon as work with the trawl was finished we therefore steamed in to the
coast and anchored for the night in a small bay just to the west of an
upstanding mass of rock known as the Elephant's Back from its resemblance
at a certain angle to that animal. Opposite our anchorage was a small fishing
village and a mile or two on the east side of the rock, just round the corner
from our anchorage, was a small town, with a Government House, flying

11–12.X.33

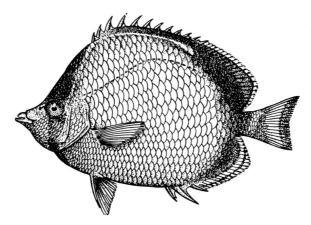

Fig. 15. *Chaetodon gardineri*, obtained at Station 27 and named in honour of Professor J. Stanley Gardiner (Reproduced from *Scient. Rep. John Murray Exped.*, Vol. VII, No. 1, Fig. 22.)

the Italian flag, and a wireless station. Until after midnight we were busy getting the hydrographic wire off the hydrographic winch on to the small drum of the trawling winch; this necessitated both winches working at the same time and the noise that we made was such that we might have been working cargo. One couldn't help wondering what the inhabitants of the village and town thought of us and whether they suspected us of landing contraband goods. We were astir early next morning and as soon as it was light enough to see we steamed out again and carried out a trawl with the otter trawl in shallow water (Station 27), in order, if we were lucky, to get some fresh fish for consumption. The nature of the ground appeared to be quite suitable and as large shoals of fish, mostly *Caranx* (horse mackerel), could be seen swimming near the surface, we were hopeful that our larder might be replenished. We left the trawl down for nearly two hours, during the latter part of which we ran over a deep gully, the bottom dropping to about 80 fathoms and then shoaling again. When the trawl was hauled, it was found to contain a fine collection from the biologists' point of view, but little or nothing from that of the fishmonger. There were a number of small fishes, mostly brightly coloured, the predominant colour being a bright pink with irridescent blue on the sides, and one small shark banded with dark brown on a lighter brown- or fawn-coloured surface. The most conspicuous part of the catch consisted of brightly coloured alcyonarians of various species and sea-fans, while a number of other fleshy forms had bright red tips to the polyps and these latter seemed to belong to the same species as that which we had previously obtained at Station 24. In addition, there were numerous small crabs and prawns, together with some sponges, squids, sea-urchins, starfish, etc.

On the completion of the trawl we steamed out to the 100 fathom line in
order to get a sample of the bottom with the grab. This was sent down and
brought up a good sample of the bottom, conspicuous on which was a fine
specimen of a sea-urchin with delicate, long, red spines.

While we were steaming in to our anchorage the previous night we had
carefully fixed the position of a depth of 800 fathoms where we wanted to
trawl. As soon as the grab was back on board we steamed out to this spot,
but we overshot the mark and when we took a sounding we found that we
were in 1,136 fathoms. As this depth was too near to that of Station 26, we
steamed inshore again and the echo-sounder showed a remarkably steep
rise of the bottom from about 1,100 fathoms up to 750, the bottom coming
up, as Farquharson expressed it, 'like the side of a house'. At 750 fathoms
the bottom became level and we steamed on to the flat for a short distance
before we stopped the ship and sent the Agassiz trawl down (Station 29).
We then went slow ahead for three-quarters of an hour, thinking that we
were trawling successfully all the time. Everything seemed to have gone off
quite well, but when we hauled the trawl in again and there were still about
200 fathoms of wire to come in, we found a true lover's knot in the wire,
so the strain on the wire was taken up on the nippers and the knot taken
out. We then went on hauling in slowly and when we got to the 115
fathom mark a dreadful tangle of wire and net came up together. There
were five or six great coils of wire looped round and round the trawl and
the trawl frame; the whole lot was hoisted in board and cleared and the
wire run on to the drum, but of course the trawl had not been fishing at
all. I have never before seen anything like the mess and can only suppose
that, as we were paying out the wire and letting the net down to the
bottom, it got caught in a strong upwelling current that was sweeping up
the steep bottom slope a little to seaward of where we were trying to trawl,
and that this had caught the light Agassiz net and had twirled it round and
round like a kite in a strong wind. Whatever the cause the result was a
complete failure to trawl, but fortunately no damage had been done to
either the trawl or the wire.

During the night of the 12th we steamed slowly towards the position of
the next station that was to continue our line of observations across the
mouth of the Gulf of Aden; by 5.30 we were in position and work started
(Station 30). Towards the end of our work two large sperm whales were
seen about a mile away on our port beam and as soon as work was completed we steamed slowly towards them until we were quite close. This
particular kind of whale has a habit as it swims of half turning over and
thrusting up one of its flippers above the water. It was interesting to note
how very easily two whales such as these, when swimming in line ahead,

13–15.X.33   might be taken for the great sea serpent when they came up to blow and showed the tops of their heads and the flippers simultaneously.

Having taken a photograph of these animals we steamed on to our next station (Station 31) and carried out a series of hydrographic observations. We then headed northwards towards the Arabian coast, making a dog-leg during the night in order to cross an area where the existing soundings indicated a ridge running out from the coast towards the south.[1] There certainly is a remarkable ridge in this area, for the evidence from the echo showed that on the east side of the ridge the bottom dropped, in the space of ten minutes or a distance of about a mile or less, from 800 to 1,600 fathoms, a slope at an angle of about 45 degrees.

Next morning we were in sight of the Arabian coast in a depth of some 600 fathoms. There was only a light wind blowing from the east and a slight sea, but as soon as we started work we found that we were either again in the clutches of the Socotra current setting us towards the north-west, or else in the Arabian coastal current setting up into the Gulf; in consequence it was extremely difficult, if not impossible, to keep our wires straight up and down. We finished our work at this station (Station 32) in the early part of the afternoon and all that night we steamed westward up the Gulf. Early the next morning we looked for a suitable trawling ground in a depth of some 700–800 fathoms, but it was not until about 10.30 that we got anywhere near what we were looking for. Then, just as we thought that we had reached a suitable spot, the echo-sounder suddenly indicated a rapidly rising bottom, the slope coming up at an angle of about 2 in 5, so we steamed on a little further and then found that we had been steaming over a ridge or plateau, for the depth increased again. At about 11.30 the bottom steadied down to a depth of some 700 fathoms and the ship was stopped and the heavy Bigelow tube was sent down, with an Ekman bottle about 20 metres above it. The bottom proved to consist of the usual green mud and we then put over the Agassiz trawl (Station 33) and towed it for one hour and three-quarters. The catch was small though interesting, and as soon as the net was back on board again we steamed still further west in the hope of getting some better catches before we put into Aden. Judging from our experience and that of the *Investigator*, which ran a series of stations along this coast in about 1907, the fauna gets much richer as one approaches the head of the Gulf.

1. This ridge, with its associated gully, is now known as the Alula-Fartak ridge. It was the most easterly of a series of similar NE.–SW. trending topographic features which were charted from the *Mabahiss* in the Gulf of Aden and which are now recognized as transform faults between the African and Arabian plates. See Part 5, p. 313, and R. W. Girdler, *Deep-Sea Research*, Vol. 31 (6–8A), 1984, pp. 747–62.

The following day, 16 October, was almost worthy of being called a red-letter day in the annals of the expedition. Early in the morning we were in a depth of about 550 fathoms. The day was wonderfully fine with only light airs blowing and the sea was almost glassy. A sample of the bottom showed the same green mud, and the Agassiz trawl was sent down about 9 o'clock (Station 34). As we were towing, the depth showed a tendency to increase, so we altered course in order to keep in the same depth or, if possible, get into water that was a little shallower. As the net was being hauled the trawl wire got caught in the door of the forward scupper and we had to stop hauling while it was cleared. This left the mouth of the net a little below the surface and, as there was no valve-flap in the net, a large number of fish immediately commenced to float up out of it. We immediately ordered the sea-boat away. The men, seeing what was happening, were remarkably prompt in getting away and they soon pulled round and recovered the floating fish by means of a hand net. When the net was finally back on board it was seen that we had made a splendid catch. There were quite a large number of big fish of the usual deep-sea type, as well as numerous prawns, crabs and other animals, and, as soon as we were able, we began to get these transferred to spirit in order to be ready for a second trawl a little later in the day.

We then steamed in towards the land to get into shallower water. I wanted to carry out a trawl in about 250–300 fathoms but owing to a mistake on the part of the officer on duty we went on until we were in only some 150 fathoms. As this was too shallow we turned round and steamed out again to the required depth. We first sent down the heavy Bigelow sounding tube (Station 35) to get a sample of the bottom and then the chemists carried out a series of observations on the temperature and collected samples of the water at the various standard depths; this was completed by about ten minutes to five and we then put the otter trawl over. As we had not had very much experience with this net we took rather longer time than perhaps was necessary in getting it to the bottom. When enough wire was out we steamed slow ahead and towed it for three-quarters of an hour, which was all that we could allow if the net was to be back on board before dark. The net was safely on board soon after 7 o'clock and again we had made a splendid catch. There were a large number of fish of various kinds, as well as numerous prawns and several magnificent spider-crabs; other ingredients of the catch were sea-urchins and a large number of deep-sea medusae of the usual red-brown colour. These latter must certainly have been caught on the way up and seemed to belong to the same species that we had obtained previously, though at considerably greater depths. This might possibly be explained by the upward migration of these

16–17.X.33 animals, for it is well known that many animals migrate towards the surface of the sea at night, sinking down again during the day when the sunlight penetrates down into the water. Such an upward migration from depths of some 400 metres might begin fairly early in the afternoon, as the effect of the sun's rays must at that depth begin to decrease at a very early hour.

All day long the weather had been nearly perfect and, as usual on days like this, there had been a lot of animal life on the surface, while masses of Sargasso weed were seen drifting by. I could see a fish, some 9 inches in length, hiding under one patch of weed, but I couldn't see enough of him to enable me to identify him. Later in the evening, while we were carrying out the second trawl, a large shoal of horse mackerel came by, many of them jumping out of the water, and following close behind came a school of dolphins, perhaps not actually treading on their tails, but in all probability feeding on the fish.

The next day, the 17th, we reached Aden and found a number of packages awaiting our arrival. Among these the most important were a new meter-wheel, that had been specially made by Munro Bros, London, to replace the one that we had lost in the Red Sea, and 1,000 fathoms of trawl wire from the RIMS *Investigator*, that had been sent over from Bombay by the Officer in Charge, Marine Survey of India, to take the place of the wire that had parted. These were just two examples of the great help and assistance that we received everywhere during the whole course of the Expedition and which helped so greatly towards the success of our work. So once again we were in a position to carry out deep-sea research work.

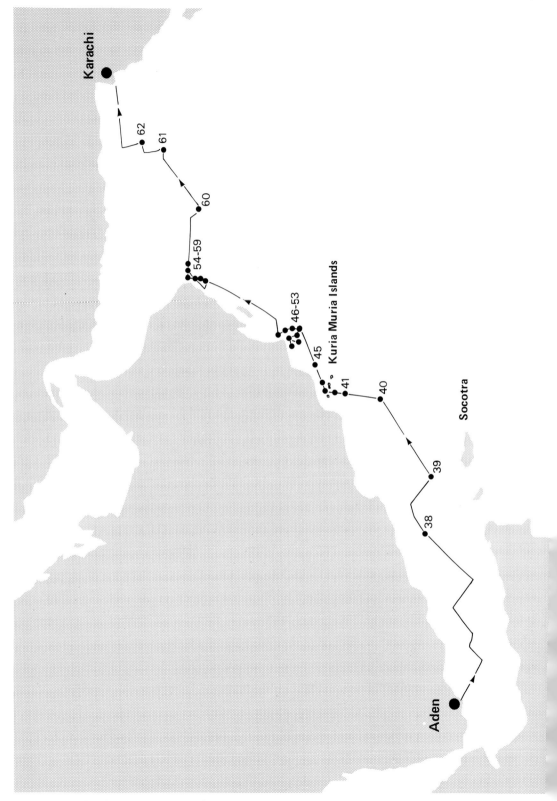

Fig. 16. Track chart, Cruise 3: Aden–Karachi. Station numbers are indicated.

Chapter 4

Aden to Karachi

WE left Aden on 22 October, soon after mid-day, and ran down the Gulf towards our first station that was to complete the series across the entrance.[1] The echo-sounder was running fairly satisfactorily and we steamed a zig-zag course so as to cross and recross the line where we expected to find a ridge, or possibly more than one, crossing the Gulf. While in Aden the P and O Co. had very kindly put their workshop on to the job of mending the drum of the hydrographic winch and they seemed to have made a good job of it, so during the first day out of port we occupied ourselves in transferring some 5,000 metres of wire off the small drum of the trawl-winch back to the hydrographic winch. That night the breeze freshened quite considerably and was blowing from east-north-east, while at the same time there was swell rolling into the Gulf from the east. In consequence a somewhat confused sea was running and although we were well down in the water, having just filled up with coal and water, the *Mabahiss* managed to roll and pitch a good deal and we were shipping a fair amount of water over the well-deck and the forward part of the main deck. As usual, some of it managed to find its way down to the laboratory.

About mid-day on the 23rd we ran over a marked ridge, the bottom coming up quite suddenly from about 1,100 fathoms to 300 or less, and we spent the next few hours steaming backwards and forwards across the ridge that is about 4 miles wide. At about 7.00 in the evening we stopped and attempted to get a sample of the bottom using the Snapper lead. We got no indication when the lead actually struck the bottom and so let the wire over-run and when we hauled it in again there was a true lover's knot in the wire about 30 fathoms above the lead. The lead, being comparatively light, was hauled in a few fathoms by hand and the wire was then made fast while the tangle was straightened out; finally, the wire was run back on to

1. Having been without fresh meat throughout the previous cruise, MacKenzie's journal records that they left Aden this time with 'no less than 20 live sheep closely packed on the limited space which our forecastle head offers'.

the drum without damage. Unfortunately, the Snapper had failed to close, so we did not get a sample of the bottom after all, and we steamed on again on our course towards the next station. One effect of this sudden uprising of the bottom is to cause a marked upwelling of water from below. On either side there were tide-rips, and a series of surface samples were taken at short intervals across the ridge in order to try and detect what changes were being brought about, but the only difference that we were able to detect was a slight fall in the temperature of the surface water from 28.2 °C to 28.0 °C.

We reached the position for Station 38 early on the 24th. Both wind and waves had moderated, though there was still a somewhat confused sea, with a few white horses and a swell from the north-east. We seemed to have passed out of the area of the Sargasso weed, but there was plenty of plankton in the water; the general colour was a greenish-blue and a few examples of *Porpita*, a colonial animal with a central buff-coloured flat disc and a surrounding ring of tentacles of a deep blue, were seen drifting by.

Work at first proceeded smoothly, but a little later Gilson, who had finished his series of observations with the Nansen-Pettersson bottle, decided to occupy his time by taking a few over-riding turns out of the wire on the small drum of the hydrographic winch. To do this he attached a weight to the end of the wire and passed some 120 metres of it over the side. Unfortunately, we were drifting steadily to starboard, the side over which he had passed the wire, and this resulted in Gilson's wire getting entangled with the wire on the port side, on which were the Ekman re-versing bottles, so that when Thompson started to heave in his string of bottles he brought up both wires together! The wires had to be separated and the starboard wire repassed under the ship before the Ekman bottles could be got inboard. This was successfully done and no damage to either wire was caused, but it was a good example to us of how easily two wires on opposite sides of the ship can get twisted round each other when the vessel is drifting.

When work was over we steamed eastward out into the Arabian Sea towards our next station, which we reached at 6.30 a.m. on the 25th. It was a bright, fine morning and there was but little wind, so that the sea was fairly smooth, with only a few white horses still persisting, though there was an appreciable swell from the south, presumably the aftermath of the south-west monsoon. While the chemists were busy with their observations at Station 39 and the collection of water samples and Macan was working the winch for them, Dr Faouzi and I busied ourselves in collecting some of the surface animals that drifted within reach of the hand net. Again there were a number of *Porpita* and a few were collected and preserved. However,

25–26.X.33   it proved to be extremely difficult to get a specimen in anything like a good condition, for at the first disturbance the animal sheds all its lovely blue tentacles and all that is left is the central brown disc. Among the animals that drifted by were several large *Beroe*, at least 6 inches in length, but all attempts to capture and preserve these completely failed, as the animal immediately dissolved into a mass of jelly and slime and the only parts that remained were the tougher bands of its ciliary plates. We managed to get some quite nice specimens of one sort or another, and among these was a pelagic actinian that I had never seen before. Thompson was at one time very tempted to jump overboard in order to try and secure a fine specimen that he saw drifting by just out of reach of the hand net.[1] Fortunately he didn't, for a moment or two later, when we went across to the other side of the ship, we saw a fine shark about 7 feet in length swimming a few yards away from us.

All the following morning we steamed eastward to get into position for making the first of a series of stations on a line running in towards the Arabian coast. The sea was wonderfully calm all day and there was an amazing profusion of animal life in the surface levels. Small flying fish were darting out of the water in large numbers. At the moment that they appear out of the water the pectoral fins can almost invariably be seen to be vibrating rapidly with a movement not unlike that of the wings of a dragon-fly in flight, but once the fish has steadied down there does not seem to be any further movement; nor could I detect any trace of the double line of ripple circles, caused by the tips of the pectoral fins touching the water at intervals, that Agassiz described and that I have myself seen in the case of larger species in Indian waters. Nevertheless, the track that was made by the rapid to-and-fro movement of the caudal fin as the fish again obtained a fresh impetus, after it had glided for some yards, was clearly visible. About noon there was such a profusion of life to be seen that I occupied myself for some time in trying to take a census of some of the larger species that could be recognized. I attempted to count the number of *Porpita* in a belt about 30 feet out from the ship's side; the numbers showed a great range and in consecutive intervals of four minutes each we passed 193, 23, 57,

1. From his slightly detached position, MacKenzie at this stage comments a little cynically on the antics of the scientists, though he is clearly rather happier about the state of his crew: 'Thompson and his staff have collected many deep-sea samples and the laboratory is daily a scene of intense activity, while Macan spends days repairing bottom nets or, with the Colonel, hanging half overboard trying to catch plankton with a butterfly net. . . . All hands are slowly settling down and the ship is slowly assuming the appearance she should, and not so much indicative of being run by a bunch of farmers, or I should say soldiers, which my crew really are.'

34, 14, 2 and then they completely disappeared, at any rate for a time.   26–27.X.33

When the ship was stopped for hydrographic work at Station 40 we again made a collection of interesting specimens by means of the hand net; among these were several examples of a rose-pink barrel-shaped ctenophore, as well as several other kinds including samples of *Bolinia*, but again we were unable to preserve any of them as they immediately disintegrated when placed in either formalin solution or any other preserving medium.

On the morning of the 27th the ship was stopped at about 5.30 and work commenced about half an hour later. Everything went smoothly at first but after a bit, when we were taking samples in the deeper depths, the drift of the ship caused the wire to stray out of the vertical. This necessitated a slight alteration in the position of the derrick holding the meter-wheel over which the wire was running, since the weight of the depth recorder, and several Ekman water-bottles, to say nothing of the weight of the wire itself, had pulled this out of the straight. As soon as the guy rope on the side against which the davit was pulling was unfastened, the davit swung inboard with a crash and the water bottle that had just been attached to the wire turned over and so released the messenger, which slid down the wire and set off all the water-bottles that had already been sent down but were not at the depths that we wished. The davit then had to be swung out again before we could continue our work and this, owing to the pull of the wire, was no easy matter. Eventually it was accomplished and we were then faced with the problem of getting the wire back on the pulley wheel of the accumulator, for when the davit swung in this had slipped off. This necessitated taking the strain off the wire and, owing to the thinness of the wire, it was no easy job. However, by fastening a stop on the wire and taking the strain on a stopper below this, we were able to release the strain on the wire above by paying out a little more and we then got the wire back in its proper position. All this caused a delay of about an hour, so that we didn't finish work at the station until about 10.45 a.m. We then steamed in towards the land. Ahead of us was the group of the Kuria Muria Islands with the Arabian coast in the distance; on the chart there was shown a depth of 800 fathoms with a bottom of mud, and this seemed a very suitable position for a bottom trawl, so we steamed towards it. For a long time the depth remained nearly constant at about 1,400 fathoms and then it started to shoal suddenly. As soon as we were in 800 fathoms, as shown by the echo-sounder, the ship was stopped and a sounding was made with the heavy Bigelow tube. Bottom was struck at 1,416 metres, but on hauling in we found that the end of the bottom tube was dented and there was no trace of any bottom sample in it. This seemed to point clearly to a rock bottom, and indeed with a rapid rise that we had just passed over this was

27.X.33 more than probable, so instead of the Agassiz trawl that I had intended to use we sent down one of the strong triangular dredges. During the short time that it had taken to make the change, we had drifted into about 500 fathoms. As soon as sufficient wire had been paid out, the dynamometer was applied and we started to steam slow ahead (Station 42). At first all went well; it was clear that the dredge was on the bottom and it seemed to be moving over it in a series of spasms, for the strain on the dynamometer varied rapidly from 15 cwt to 1.5 tons. We had been dredging for just over half an hour when the strain suddenly went up to over 2 tons and the rope strop on the nippers parted with a bang. The wire ran out freely and the ship went astern to ease the strain. We then started to haul in and at first there was a considerable strain on the wire, but when about 550 fathoms were still to come there was a sudden easing and from then on the wire came in quite easily. When we got the dredge back on board we found that the rope becket on one corner of the frame had also been carried away. The net was hoisted up on the derrick and swung inboard; there was a large hole in one side about half way down, but below this the rest of the net was filled with from $\frac{1}{2}$ to 1 ton of angular blocks of granite of all sizes from an inch or two to about a foot square. It seemed probable that the sudden easing of the strain, when we were hauling, was due to the tearing of the net and the escape of all the rock above the hole. There was only a little living material in the catch; for the most part this consisted of sponges, while there was also a little dead coral of the *Lophelia* type. Judging from the results, we had been dredging on a typical 'scree' slope, a continuation below water of the granite slopes of one of the islands.

While Stations 41 and 42 were being worked, a collection of surface-living organisms was made by means of the hand net. The richness of the plankton was amazing and it was most amusing to see how keen all the various members of the ship's staff, both officers and men, were to secure specimens; we ought to have had several hand nets instead of only two, for the competition was most keen. We secured a number of ctenophores, salps and a few patches of Sargasso weed, hiding in which were several small fishes, of a species of *Antennarius*, and a young balloon fish, *Diodon hystrix*, about 3 inches in length, that showed clearly a scheme of protective coloration, in addition to its protection of long pointed spines. While we were at work at Station 42 a number of long strings of salps, some of them at least 3 feet in length, drifted by and a few of these were secured. In one instance a fish, about 5–6 inches in length, was seen quietly swimming to and fro above the length of a long string; judging from its colour and general appearance this was also an example of *Diodon hystrix* but as we were unable to capture it, it is impossible to be certain on this point. Later

in the afternoon several shoals of small fish were seen, and as we approached
the land we were rapidly overtaken by a shoal of the lovely *Coryphaena*, the
dolphin of sailor folk, resplendent in a wonderful colouring of grey, light
blue and gold, while a little further off were some large horse mackerel
(*Caranx*), a school of true dolphins and a large shark.

About 5.30 that evening we anchored in a small bay on the south-west
side of Soda island, one of the smaller islands of the Kuria Muria group;
we soon had the motor boat in the water and a party went ashore. The
island is absolutely bare and its sides are composed of regular 'scree' slopes,
such as the one that we had just been dredging over. There seemed to be a
lot of seaweed about, much more than one is accustomed to seeing in
tropical waters, and on the beach there was a regular high-water mark
where the weed had been washed up. The beach itself consisted very largely
of dead coral that had been thrown up by the waves, so that it was clear
that some coral, at any rate, grew in the neighbourhood.

The next day we divided forces, Macan and I going off in the motor
boat to see if we could get any evidence regarding the presence or absence
of definite coral reefs, while Thompson and the other chemists with Dr
Faouzi remained in the *Mabahiss* to work stations in the deeper water at the
edge of the continental shelf. Macan and I set out in the motor boat about
8.15 and headed in towards the larger island, Jezirat Halaniya, but as usual
the motor began to give trouble and we had barely got away from the
ship's side when it struck work. I was in two minds whether to hail the
ship and get her to stand by until we could see whether the trouble could
be put right, or to let her go off and trust to providence and our motor
mechanic. Before I could make up my mind the motor did it for me by
starting again, but it was only a flash in the pan and the engine soon failed
again. By this time the *Mabahiss* was well away, so there was nothing to be
done but to hope for the best, and eventually all went well and we steamed
in for the shore against a current that was setting strongly to the west.
Swimming against the current between us and the island was a school of
dolphins, and we could clearly see them blowing as they came up to the
surface.

As we neared the island we found a small bay, in which were a small
dhow and two canoes, but as we approached the dhow put out to sea.
There were several of the inhabitants about and some of them came off in
the dug-out canoes and tried to sell us some fresh fish; they had some large
Caranx and a large bright pink 'rock salmon'. We explained as best we
could that the *Mabahiss* would be coming in to the island about 3 o'clock in
the afternoon and told them to go out to her then, but they failed to
understand us. For although they came off to the ship when she got in they

28.X.33   had already disposed of the fish, probably eaten them themselves, for they did not appear to have very much to live on. At the head of the bay there was a small village, the huts of which are composed of low stone walls, roofed over with fish skeletons and dried seaweed. At the south-west side of the bay is a reef of rock, thickly overgrown with seaweed of the same Sargasso type that we had been collecting out to sea. While we were talking to the villagers, our driver managed to stop the motor again and before he could get it to function we had drifted towards this reef until we were only a few yards from it. Having avoided the reef, we steamed out for a short distance and put down the small rectangular dredge on a sandy bottom in about 5 fathoms of water. We got a catch that consisted largely of weed and weed-haunting animals, and we then steamed further out into a depth of about 14 fathoms and made a series of observations on the water temperature and collected samples for analysis from various depths. We then ran eastwards up the coast and examined another rock reef, that turned out to be very similar to the one near the village, being also thickly overgrown with the Sargasso weed; it seemed not improbable that these and similar rock reefs around these islands or off the mainland are the principal source of the weed that we had been encountering in the Gulf, the weed being swept westward by the surface current, that at this time of the year sets strongly along the coast into the Gulf. Here we tried to carry out a dredge over a rather rocky bottom, but the dredge caught in the bottom and merely acted as an anchor, the engine refusing to move the boat, so we gave up the attempt and ran further up the coast towards the east where a magnificent promontory juts out into the sea. We ran close up to this to try and locate a shoal area that was shown on the chart but failed to find it, so we turned west again for a bit and then put the dredge down to act as an anchor and knocked off for lunch. After that was dealt with, we turned east again and had another look at the cliff, which is composed of a stratified sandstone, interspersed with bands of some harder material, possibly limestone. As a result of subaerial erosion by wind and rain, the softer strata have been weathered away leaving some of the harder bands projecting in overhanging ledges, that ultimately break off and crash down. There had been some quite recent falls of the rock and a number of large slabs were perched precariously on some of the lower slopes. We also carried out another haul of the dredge, this time on a bottom of clean sand, obtaining an interesting catch; it was then time for us to return to the small bay near the western end of the island where we were to meet the *Mabahiss* and be picked up again. The ship came in about 3.30 and anchored for the night off the village.

   While Macan and I had been away in the motor boat, the others in the

FIG. 17. A pause in paying out the trawl warp. Left to right: Thompson, Macan, Ali Etaiwa and Sewell. (*Photo:* H. C. Gilson.)

Mabahiss had made a couple of stations near the edge of the continental shelf. In the evening some of us went ashore and visited the village. There are about forty people living on the island and, according to Theodore Bent (*Southern Arabia*, p. 230), these people belong to 'the Jenefa tribe, who pursue sharks, swimming on inflated skins'. On this beach there was not a trace of true coral, though some of the lads brought back water-worn fragments of what seemed to be a hydrocoralline.

28–29.X.33

The next day, the 29th, we left our anchorage at dawn and steamed eastward towards the position of our next station. This was to be the first of a series running into the coast on the east side of the next headland, Ras Madraka. As we had several hours to spare, we filled in the time by seeing whether we could get a large surface seine net, that we had on board, to work. A pair of rather crude otter boards had been made by the ship's carpenter and these were shackled on to the two wings of the net, and the whole was then put over the side. The first attempt was a complete failure, for the boards simply lay on their backs and did not act at all. They were

29–30.X.33   hauled in again and some weights were attached to one side of them and then they were put out again; but even then they did not function properly and the two wire bridles persistently twisted round each other and so prevented the boards from separating. As the experiment was clearly not a success, we gave it up and steamed off to a spot on the chart where there is supposed to be a coral reef. On our way we passed close to the foot of the headland of Ras Sukhra; this is a bold cliff, about 600 feet in height, that drops almost sheer into some 20 fathoms of water. This cliff, like so many of the others that we saw along this stretch of the coast, is identical in structure with that on the Kuria Muria islands and is composed of alternating horizontal strata of sandstone and limestone that are weather-worn into ledges and ridges.

We reached the so-called reef at about 5.20 in the evening and after a sounding, to give us the depth and an indication of the bottom, we put a triangular dredge down (Station 45) and towed it for half an hour. It was dark long before we got the net in, and when we did so it came up with a hole torn in it; even so it contained such a splendid catch that we didn't get sorted out until after 11 o'clock that night. The bottom clearly was for the most part composed of *Lithothamnion* and hydrocorallines, with an occasional colony of true coral, but it is not a coral reef in the generally accepted meaning of the term.

The next morning we were at our station at about 5.30 and the chemists at once got busy taking water samples and reading temperatures. Having completed the work here, we steamed in towards the coast and made another hydrographic station about noon. Here again the bottom rose with a rapidity that was truly amazing; at one moment we were in water of 1,200 fathoms depth and the next it had risen up to 50 fathoms. In this depth we made a third station for the chemists and as they had finished by 1.30 I decided to try to trawl on the edge of the shelf, where the bottom drops so steeply. We steamed out to the 110 fathom line and then put the Agassiz trawl down (Station 48). We towed it for half an hour, during which time the strain on the dynamometer was jumping about violently—rather too violently as it turned out—and we got the net back on board again we found that it must have been on a rocky bottom and about half the net had been torn completely away. So badly was it damaged that it seemed doubtful whether we could repair it, and, as we looked like running short of nets, I sent off a wireless message to our Committee in England requesting that spare nets might be sent out at once to Bombay, so as to reach us before we left on our voyage across the Arabian Sea to Mombasa. The total catch from the trawl was almost biblical in its scarcity—only five crabs, a prawn and two small fishes!

We then steamed in to our anchorage on the west side of Ras Madraka:
this headland is again of the same type as Ras Sukhra and Halaniya Island,
though not quite so fine, and between this cape and Ras Sukhra there is a
long stretch of a sandy bay, on the beach of which quite a heavy surf was
breaking. The whole of this part of the coast seems to consist of the same
geological formation and the most probable explanation of the remarkably
steep drop in the sea-bottom along the edge of the continental shelf, that is
quite narrow here, seems to me to be a great scarp fault that has left this
series of sheer cliffs along the coast, and has submerged an area of land that
originally stretched southward.

After we had anchored, the Sheik of the neighbouring village came off
to see us, while a party from the ship went ashore. The Sheik told us that
there were about seventy inhabitants in his village; certainly all along the
coast there were little knots of men watching us as we came in, and he
wanted to know where the war was! This must have been a rather important
problem for him for he didn't appear to know which government he was
supposed to be under or whether he owed allegiance to the Sultan of Muscat
or to someone else. The shore-going party on its return again reported that
there was no sign of any coral on the beach.[1]

On 31 October we carried out our 50th Station, an event that was duly
celebrated at dinner that evening in a bottle of sherry. We left our anchorage

1. MacKenzie, who was with the shore party, made rather more of the visit to Ras
   Madraka. 'Late that evening, about an hour before sunset, we found anchorage under the
   black volcanic peaks of Ras Madraka. Landing in the pram was made with difficulty. A
   crowd of wild-looking natives, armed with rifles and the short curved silver ornamental
   Arab knife, rushed into the water to help us drag our boat ashore and clear of the heavy
   run. "Whom were we fighting?" was their first question. "Were we friends or enemies?"
   and from their looks I know that they did not believe us when we replied that we were
   merely peaceful fishermen. . . . A very quick bathe satisfied the most venturesome, and
   none of us felt too happy when with loud and threatening gestures the Arabs showed
   their annoyance and disbelief because we refused their invitation to join them in evening
   prayers. Up to the waists in water, we were thankful to have our boat afloat again, and
   just as we were scrambling aboard, our friends having finished salaaming in the direction
   of a sun which had now dipped, came running down the shore, and were positively
   offensive in their demands for food. "Rootie! Rootie!" they shouted in chorus, and so
   frantic became their cries that we thought it best to remain in contemptuous silence. In a
   twinkling, however, a canoe was swept down the beach, launched, and was quickly
   alongside us. Thus escorted, we made the ship where, on our own ground, they soon
   learned that their chances of obtaining food were nil. A careful watch was kept that
   night, for apart from our little experience, the Sailing Directions had duly warned us that
   the natives hereabouts were not to be trusted. Nothing of course happened, and before
   six the next morning the *Mabahiss* was hull down to seaward, and making way for
   trawling grounds anew.'

31.X–1.XI.33 off Ras Madraka early in the morning and steamed out from the land in order to carry out two series of observations in a line off-shore, in order to ascertain whether there was any evidence of upwelling deep water along this region of the coast. The chemists wanted to get observations in about 500 fathoms of water, and again in about 1,000 fathoms at the foot of the continental slope. We reached our first station according to plan and work was duly carried out; but when we tried to find the steep continental slope that we had hitherto been accustomed to, we signally failed. We steamed out from the coast over very uneven ground but the depth increased very slowly and we were eventually some 10 miles away from our first station before we got into, or nearly into, the required depth for the second series; it seems that the hill range of which Ras Madraka is the terminal land point is continued out under the sea for some distance. Our hydrographic work was completed by 12.15 and we then shackled the 4-foot triangular dredge on to the trawl wire and sent it down. As we were paying out the wire we found several over-riding turns in the wire on the drum, so we paid out the greater part of the wire and then hauled in the extra amount more than was actually required for the dredge. All this took time and it was 3.30 in the afternoon before we actually commenced to dredge. Everything appeared to go satisfactorily and there was a constant and steady strain on the dynamometer, with none of the jumping and jerking that we had previously experienced along this coast, so we left the dredge down for three-quarters of an hour and then hauled it in. The dredge came up just before sunset, and it was then seen that the rope becket on one of the chains had parted and the dredge was hanging by two only. There was remarkably little in the net; this was all the more disappointing as everything seemed to have gone satisfactorily and there was still in the net a little soft brown mud, which indicated that the bottom had been quite suitable for a trawl. By the time the dredge was up on deck it was too late to get to an anchorage before dark, so we stayed at sea for the night, drifting, and early the next morning we steamed in again towards the coast on the east side of Ras Madraka, making two more hydrographic stations on the way, and finally anchored for the night on the east side of the headland.

All through these last few days there was a most amazing profusion of animal life in the surface water. Perhaps the most common of the planktonic animals was a salp, *Pegea confoederata*, and at times there were as many as fifty examples in a cubic metre of water at or near the surface; these were all or very nearly all in the chain-forming stage and numerous bands of immature salps, as much as 3 feet in length, were quite common. In addition to the salps, there were numerous jelly-fish that seemed for the most part to

belong to the genus *Aurelia*, and quite a number of examples of the blue
pelagic mollusc *Ianthina*.

During the night a large dhow anchored near us and early next morning a canoe came off from her to try and sell us some fish; we availed ourselves of the opportunity and purchased a number of large *Caranx* (horse mackerel). On leaving our anchorage we steamed eastward for about an hour to a position where a coral reef is indicated on the chart; this is figured as having a lagoon with 7 fathoms of water in the centre and a rim of rock all round. As soon as we were over the spot we sent down the 4-foot triangular dredge (Station 53) and, while we were towing this, Farquharson, Thompson and Macan went away in the dinghy to sound round and see if they could locate the lagoon; they had no success and our echo-sounder indicated that there was a general depth of about 5 fathoms all over the patch. As soon as the dredge was down the jerking of the trawl wire clearly indicated that the net was on a rocky bottom and the strain on the dynamometer varied from 3 cwt to 1 ton 5 cwt. After the dredge had been on the bottom for about seventeen minutes there was a particularly violent jerk, the strain shot up to nearly 2 tons, and the rope becket on the nippers parted with such a jerk that the indicator needle of the dynamometer was carried away. The dredge rope ran out rapidly, but the ship was stopped and the brake on the winch drum gradually applied until the rope was checked. We then proceeded to haul the dredge in and as it came up it was seen to be full of such a mass of material that it would be impossible to get it in by hand. It was hooked on to the boom and was hoisted up and swung inboard, and we spent the rest of the morning and most of the afternoon sorting out the catch. Much of the contents of the net consisted of rock and rock fragments, mixed with a coarse sand and a number of dead mollusc shells; there was also a quantity of *Lithothamnion*, though not so much as on the reef that we had previously investigated to the east of Ras Sukhra. True reef-coral was again almost entirely absent though there were several examples of a small solitary coral. The most conspicuous part of the catch consisted of sponges and alcyonarians, and a queer twisted type of oyster. As one would expect on a sandy bottom, there were quite a number of molluscs of the *Cardium* and *Arca* type, while most of the bits of rock and the dead shells were inhabited by a number of small holothurians, of a species of *Cucumaria* that both attached themselves to the rock and covered themselves over with fragments of rock or shells, which they held in position by their tube feet.

All along this part of the coast the land was still bordered by steep sandstone cliffs, similar to those seen at Ras Sukhra and Ras Madraka; this sandstone is probably the main source of all the sand on the continental

2–3.XI.33   shelf, for there are conspicuous signs of weathering on the cliff face. Why there should be so little reef-forming coral on this coast is a problem at present unsolved. The water over the reef was of a pea-soup type, very similar to that seen at our anchorages on the two sides of Ras Madraka, and this is in all probability the general character of the water along most of this coast. The profusion of animal life in the surface waters suggests an upwelling of deeper water with an increased supply of mineral constituents, such as phosphates. Off both Ras Sukhra and Ras Madraka we certainly experienced a fall of temperature in the surface water, the thermograph in the engine-room indicating the occurrence of patches of water with a temperature some 2 or 3 °C below that of the general area; but our observations on the deeper water at the edge of the shelf and beyond do not appear to indicate any upwelling of water from any great depth and it seems likely that the fall of temperature round these headlands is due to local swirls, probably connected with changes in the currents round the points caused by changes in the tides. It was suggested that the absence of coral might be associated with the pea-soup character of the water, the thickness of the suspended matter interfering with the penetration of light through the water strata and thus inhibiting the life and growth of the coral polyps, but this seems hardly likely. On the other hand, smothering by the sand derived from the erosion of the cliffs also seems insufficient to prevent their growth, for, although mud may interfere with their life, many corals can clear themselves of sand with comparative ease.

On the conclusion of our work at Station 53 on 2 November we steamed eastward along the coast towards our next position, where we expected to find a depth of water of some 550 fathoms with a bottom of soft green mud and sand. We reached the indicated spot soon after noon on the 3rd, though we were rather longer in getting the required depth than we had anticipated; just as we were nearing the spot the bottom started to shoal rather rapidly, but after a minute or two the level steadied down and the ship was stopped for work to commence. The echo-sounder gave a depth of 520 fathoms and a Driver tube was shackled on to the hydrographic wire and sent down; we got no indication of when the tube struck the bottom and so paid out about 150 fathoms more wire than was actually necessary. On hauling in it was found that the bottom valve, as so often occurred with this type of tube, had failed to close and the sample of the bottom had been washed out on the way up, though some soft green mud was still adhering to the outside of the tube. We therefore sent down the Agassiz trawl (Station 54) hoping that on this occasion it would not be torn to pieces by rock as it so often had been further to the west on this coast. During the actual trawl the strain was steady and quite normal, so the net was left down for a full hour. On heaving in, just at the critical moment as the net was coming to the surface, the trawl wire again caught in one of the scupper doors and we had to stop heaving until it was cleared; the first indication that we had made a successful haul was the appearance of a number of deep-sea fish floating up to the surface through the mouth of the net. The sea boat was immediately ordered away and these were picked up, and I do not think that we lost any. The next indication of the richness of the catch was the fact that owing to the weight of its contents we were unable to haul the net inboard even when all the stewards and unattached individuals were roped in to give a hand. We managed to get the net about half way up and we could then see that the cod-end of the net was full of mud, so we left it hanging over the side and went slow ahead for a bit to wash some of it out; after a quarter of an hour or so much of the mud had gone back to the sea and we were then able to get the net on board. The most conspicuous thing about the catch was the enormous number of small brittle stars (ophiuroids); the side of the net that had been on the bottom was a tangled mess of them and the cod-end contained literally thousands. The whole catch was remarkably good though there was not a great number of different species present, but those that were represented were present in large numbers. In the net and mixed up with the soft green mud were a number of irregular blocks and lumps of a consolidated clay that had been bored through by some mud-boring animal; but the original maker of the borings was no longer at home—possibly he lay at a depth below that to which the trawl had dug and so the net had not succeeded in catching a specimen.

As soon as the net was on board we headed inshore to an anchorage, which we reached at about 6 o'clock and we anchored off Lashkarah village for the night. As we ran in towards the coast, the echo-sounder showed that the sea-floor rose steeply from the 300-fathom level to 50 fathoms in a distance of about ¾ mile, a slope of about 1 in 2½. Here the coast was by no means so rugged as further to the west; the hills lay further inland and the coast itself seemed to consist largely of sand and sand dunes, while in the middle distance were a few conical hills that had very much the appearance of pyramids rising up out of the desert.

The following morning, 4 November, we left our anchorage at about 7 o'clock and steamed off to another station, heading a little up the coast, to try and discover, if possible, whether there was any suitable ground for trawling with the otter net in a depth of water of about 250 fathoms. We reached the position of our first trawl at 8.40 and the ship was stopped in a depth of some 800 metres. Gilson had been working at the Driver tube during the last two days, trying to make the valve work properly, and so

4.XI.33 we shackled it on to the wire and sent it down to get a sample of the bottom; on this occasion it worked quite well and brought up a core of the bottom mud about 11 inches in length, that showed clear evidence of stratification; the upper 8 inches consisted of a brownish-green mud mixed with either sand or very small shells, while the lower 3 inches was of a grey-green colour and was composed of a finer material. The 4-foot Salpa dredge was then sent down (Station 55), but before it had been on the bottom very long it got caught in something, possibly the tough grey mud, and the strain on the wire increased to such an extent that the wire began to slip through the nippers. We stopped the ship and hauled the net in again and then found that the rope becket on the dredge frame had been carried away and the net had been torn away from the frame at one end. The net contained a large number of masses of a hard grey clay, and there was a mass of the same clay adhering to one side of the dredge; but there was absolutely no sign of any living organisms in the bag.

We then steamed inshore in order to get into a suitable depth for a second station. There was not a breath of wind stirring and at about 1 o'clock the surface of the sea, which was absolutely calm, was seen to be covered with a substance of a brick-red colour. Where this was banked up against the ship's side under the influence of the current it accumulated until the water was covered with a red scum, while in the distance several other similar dense patches could be seen. At first I thought that this scum was due to the presence of the small alga, *Trichodesmium erythraeum*, that is usually responsible for such a phenomenon and is sometimes the cause of the Red Sea earning its name; but when some was collected in the hand net it was found that the colour was due to a small protozoan belonging to the genus *Noctiluca* or a close ally.

The ship was stopped for another trawl in about 240 fathoms, but in view of what happened in the morning, instead of putting the otter trawl over, I sent down the 4-foot triangular dredge (Station 56). We started dredging at about 2.15 in the afternoon, but the net had only been on the bottom for a little over a quarter of an hour when we again got stuck fast in something and the strain on the wire shot up. We stopped the ship, but there was such a strong current running that it swept the vessel away from the wire and the strain continued to increase. At first the wire began to slip through the nippers, as it had done in the morning, and the jerking of this caused a slack loop of the wire to form; this immediately twisted round itself in a kink, but before we could do anything the strain had gone up still more, the rope strop on the nippers parted with a bang and the wire immediately ran out freely, at the same time taking the kink out. The wire was checked by the brake on the winch drum, but before we could haul in

we had to go ahead and steam up to the wire, taking the strain off it.   4.XI.33
Hauling in was very slow, and when we came to the length of wire that
would lift the dredge off the bottom, there was again such a strain on the
wire that everyone on deck was ordered to stand clear in case it parted.
Fortunately it didn't, and after a final burst of energy on the part of the
winch the dredge came off the bottom and everything was plain sailing,
though the strain on the wire still indicated that the net was full of something. We got the net to the surface and then hooked it on to the derrick
and heaved it in a bit more, when we found that the bag was full of green
mud, so we left it awash, while we went slow ahead, in order to wash out
some of the contents. After a short while we were able to get the whole net
up and inboard, fortunately intact, and it was then very obvious to everyone
that the mud was anything but clean, for it smelt strongly of rotten eggs
(sulphuretted hydrogen). We washed out all the mud that we could with
the hose and then put the rest through the sieves, but all that we got out of
it were about a dozen dead mollusc shells and the dead shells of two deep-

Fig. 18. Washing a dredge haul on deck, November 1933. Left to right: Thompson, Faouzi
and Sewell. (*Photo:* H. C. Gilson.)

4–5.XI.33   sea spider crabs, *Encephaloides armstrongi*. There wasn't a trace of any living organisms; nor would one expect there to be in a mud that was so strongly impregnated with this foul smelling gas.[1]

As soon as the dredge was safely on board we steamed inshore to a fresh anchorage for the night, this time off Ras al Hadd, the most easterly promontory of the Arabian continent. This part of the coast was again fronted by steep cliffs composed of stratified sandstone, though here they were by no means so high, nor was the stratification so well marked as further westward, but there could be but little doubt that the general structure was the same.

We left again soon after dawn the next morning and steamed out to a fresh station that we reached about 8 o'clock. We carried out our work and it was interesting to find that we were still in the zone of soft green mud smelling strongly of sulphuretted hydrogen; as at the last two stations, the bottom mud was quite soft, but even so the depth varied with amazing rapidity and as there was a strong current running it was practically impossible to keep in water of the same or anything like the same depth. When the ship was first stopped the depth as given by the echo was 330 fathoms, but by the time the Driver tube had reached the bottom, which was about half an hour later, we had drifted with the current and the recorded depth was 384 fathoms, and a little later, when we sent an Ekman water-bottle down, it had again increased to 437 fathoms. The exact opposite happened when we were trying to trawl (Station 57), for we started in a depth of 437 fathoms and within a quarter of an hour we had got into water of only 240 fathoms. A little later the depth increased again slightly, but the trawl was for the most part carried out in a depth of about 246 fathoms. At 10.30 the trawl got stuck fast on the bottom; we were by now getting quite used to this sort of behaviour in the region, so we hauled it in. The catch consisted of the same foul-smelling soft green mud and all the animal life that we secured consisted of a single dead gastropod mollusc, *Rostellaria delicatula*, and two examples of the same spider crab,

1. The discovery of anoxic conditions in the bottom sediments and of large areas with virtually no living benthic animals was one of the most important results of the Expedition but was not adequately explained at the time. As Sewell wrote, such conditions had been encountered in the relatively enclosed situation in the Black Sea (and in some fjords) but was quite unexpected in the open sea. The explanation of these conditions in the Arabian Sea is the combination of high surface productivity resulting in an abundant input of organic matter to the sediments coupled with relatively low oxygen content in the deep water masses (see Part 5, page 320), but Sewell was unaware of these factors until much later.

Encephaloides armstrongi, that on this occasion were just alive, though clearly   5.XI.33
moribund.

Having completed our work we steamed out into deeper water so as to carry out a series of observations in a depth of about 650 fathoms; here again we had the same difficulty, for the bottom altered so rapidly that it was impossible to keep in anything like a constant depth. We started work in a depth of about 650 fathoms but by the time the Driver tube had reached the bottom the depth had increased to 685 fathoms. On this occasion the Driver tube again refused to work, so we did not succeed in getting a core of the bottom, but a certain amount of mud was adhering to the outside when the tube came up and this again was green in colour and had a slight smell of sulphuretted hydrogen. We then let the dredge down (Station 58) and paid out an amount of wire that should have been sufficient, but the depth still continued to increase and about half way through the trawl it was 740 fathoms, so that it was a matter of some doubt whether the dredge had been on the bottom for very long. When it was hauled in all that it contained were a few polychaete worms, a single large red crab, *Paralomis* sp., and a little green mud mixed with some white stones. Although these results were not as satisfactory as we could have wished, they seem to show that a more or less lifeless area extends down to a depth of at least 655 fathoms and that throughout this belt the bottom consists of a soft green mud that is impregnated with sulphuretted hydrogen gas. What the ultimate cause of this condition may be in an area such as this is not easy to determine. Another region in which a similar state of affairs is known to exist is the Black Sea, and there the condition is generally attributed to the fact that it is an enclosed basin with a consequent stagnation of the deeper waters and bacterial decomposition of the organic matter on the sea-bed; but here on a steep continental slope, exposed to all the currents that are set in motion by the strong winds of both the north-east and south-west monsoons, no such explanation seems possible.

During the progress of the trawl we again ran through patches of water that were coloured a brick red by the same organism that had been so plentiful the previous day; this organism appeared to be very closely akin to *Noctiluca*, the protozoan that so often causes the phosphorescence of the sea, but in this case we got no evidence of phosphorescence and certainly there had been none in the sea during the previous night. Besides these protozoa, there were seen floating on the surface quite a number of dead squids that in life must have been over a foot in length, but none of those seen were complete, for in every case some part had been bitten off by a predaceous enemy. A number of brown rhizostomous medusae and numerous chains of the salp, *Pegea confoederata*, were also seen.

6–9.XI.33   All through the following night we steamed eastwards out to sea, and at 6 o'clock in the morning the ship was stopped in order that we might carry out a station (59), in some 1,000–1,100 fathoms. The heavy Bigelow tube was shackled on to the hydrographic wire and lowered away; bottom was struck at 1,071 fathoms and then hauling in commenced; but before we had got very far the small block over which the wire ran carried away, the friction of the wire having cut right through the wheel. Unfortunately the wire was damaged and one strand had parted, so we had to cut the wire and put in a long splice. It was lucky that the whole wire did not go, or we should have lost our only remaining Bigelow tube, one Ekman reversing water-bottle, complete with two thermometers, and some 1,750 metres of wire. When we got the Bigelow tube back again, we shackled on a 4-foot triangular dredge (Station 59) and carried out a haul; the net came up full of about a ton of soft green mud, but this time there was no smell of sulphuretted hydrogen. The actual catch was, however, very small and, after the labour of putting nearly a ton of the mud through the sieves, all the animals that we got out of it were two ophiuroids, a starfish, a holothurian, a mollusc or two and a few worm-tubes without the worms. It thus seemed probable that we were still in the zone of little or no life, though the general conditions appeared to be quite suitable.

On 8 and 9 November we were busy carrying out our first 24-hour station. The ship was stopped at 6 o'clock on the 8th and we sent down one of the small Bigelow tubes to get a sample of the bottom; this was quite successful and we got a core of *Globigerina* ooze, the first that we had seen. After that the chemists were busy with the usual collection of water samples and taking of temperatures at different depths until about 10 o'clock and then we carried out a horizontal haul with a series of five nets attached to the same wire at intervals (Station 61). At the extreme end we had the large 2-metre diameter plankton net and, at intervals that we calculated would correspond to about 400 metres of depth, we attached a string of 1-metre-diameter nets, finally putting on a fine silk net that we towed just below the surface. The whole string was lowered down and we started trawling, going slow ahead, but after a few minutes the ship drifted over the wire and the latter got caught on something. Before we could get it clear we had to stop the ship and as a result the 2-metre net actually came in contact with the bottom, but fortunately no damage was done and the trawl was continued at half speed. Just above the 2-metre net we had attached one of our depth-recorders; this seemed to work quite satisfactorily, so that from the record we were able to calculate fairly accurately the depth at which this large net had been fishing.

Later in the day the chemists carried out a second series of observations, and then at 11.30 at night we repeated our mid-water trawls. The nets were again sent down satisfactorily, but either the surface current had changed or else we steamed at a more rapid rate, for the wire trailed out aft at a much greater angle and so the nets were not fishing at depths that corresponded with those of the morning's haul. Incidentally, we learnt that our shackles for the 1-metre-diameter nets were not strong enough to stand the strain for one of them parted and the whole net was lost. The catches were interesting and we got several fine deep-sea prawns of the characteristic red colour, but I could not detect any trace of phosphorescence either in them or in any of the deep-sea fish that we got. One interesting fact came to light from a somewhat cursory examination of the catches and that was that whereas in the day catches we got a number of examples of a small scopelid fish, with numerous luminous organs(?) along its sides, not a single one appeared in the night catches. If, as one might suppose, this was due to migration, it would seem to be in the reverse direction to that which is usual, for most deep-sea animals appear to migrate up towards the surface at night, whereas these must have gone deeper.

We had now arrived at the end of our cruise and the ship was headed for Karachi. As we steamed across the open sea between Ras al Hadd and the coast of India we kept the echo-sounder going almost continuously in order to see to what extent I and others were right in our view that the few available soundings indicated the presence of a submarine mountain range running out from the Indian coast. The results of our echo-sounder proved eminently satisfactory, for we obtained clear evidence not only of one mountain range but of two running more or less parallel to one another with a deep gully between them. In places these ranges rose up from some 1,850 fathoms depth to as little as 480 fathoms, a height of about 8,200 feet; while the gully went down to some 2,000 fathoms, or about 900 feet deeper than the general line of the ocean bed. The contours of the ridges, as revealed by the echo-sounder, were extraordinarily like those of a land mountain chain, the tops of the hills alternating with valleys and ravines running down the sides, and it is difficult to explain the presence of such a deep gully except as an old and now submerged river-bed, that in the course of years cut its channel down to a level considerably greater than that of the then surrounding country. To the more northerly ridge we gave the name of the Murray Ridge, while the rising ground on the southeastern side of the gully, that seems to connect with a wide submerged plateau and on its eastern side appears to merge into the continental shelf of India, I have termed the Karachi Plateau.

Our work in the Gulf of Aden, which we had crossed and recrossed on several occasions, as well as traversing its length from east to west or vice

versa three times, had shown that the floor of this area is extremely irregular. No less than ten hill ranges run out from the Arabian coast in a north-
east to south-west direction, and between the ranges near the mouth of the
Gulf there are alternating deep gullies.[1] None of these ridges completely
cross the floor of the Gulf and the southern part is formed by a deep gully
that commences in the Gulf of Tajura at the western end and finally opens
into the Arabian Sea. All geologists are agreed that the Gulf of Aden is a
part of the Great Rift Valley system of Africa and that it has been formed
by subsidence, so that this deep gully might also be a now-submerged
river-bed. It was probably the presence of these deep and submerged gullies,
presumably old river-beds, that was the cause of one newspaper reporter
announcing to the world that we had discovered the Garden of Eden, the
fall of Adam presumably being accompanied by such a fall of the land level
that the Garden of Eden became submerged beneath the ocean.

The day before we reached Karachi the weather was swelteringly hot;
there wasn't a breath of wind and the surface of the sea was absolutely
smooth and oily in appearance. As we had an hour or two to spare, for we
didn't need to get to port before the late afternoon, Captain MacKenzie
stopped the ship and Lieutenant Badr, Dr Faouzi and I went away in the
sea boat in order to try and get a cinema photograph of the ship; conditions
were not too good for there was a heat haze over the sea, so that sea and
sky blended together at the horizon, but there was a wonderful reflection
of the ship in the water.

During the afternoon, as we steamed towards the port, we passed a
number of turtles swimming on the surface and there were innumerable sea
snakes.

We reached Karachi harbour at 4 o'clock in the afternoon. No sooner
were we in port and tied up to the jetty than our Chief Engineer drew fires
and shut down the steam, so that the dynamo stopped working and we
were without either lights or fans; under these conditions my cabin rapidly
became uninhabitable. However, we had barely arrived before several old
friends, whom I didn't even know were stationed in Karachi, began to roll
up. The first of these was Commander Jack Rattray of the RIM, whom I
had known years before in Aden and Port Blair in the Andamans; he was
now Marine Transport Officer and thanks to his kind offices the English
members of the Expedition were all made honorary members of the Sind
Club and I was thus able to secure a room in the Club for a few days.
Another old friend was Mr Campbell, who was in one of the banks, and
finally Mr Oddin Taylor, the Chief Engineer in charge of the great Sukkur

1. See also footnote, page 107.

Barrage whose acquaintance I had made on board the *Britannia* on my way home from India the previous April: he and his wife were down in Karachi for a few days. Between them all I had a great time and it was usually after, and on occasions long after, midnight before I got to bed; fortunately nobody gets up early in Karachi and few, if any, go off to business before 11 o'clock. Another old friend that I met in Karachi was Mr Howard, who used to be my Assistant Surgeon on the *Investigator* in 1910–11 and who was now Port Health Officer. Through his kind offices I was able to secure from the Municipal Laboratory some sterile agar tubes, so that, if the opportunity arose, I might be able to make an attempt at culturing any bacteria in the green mud that smelt so strongly of sulphuretted hydrogen.

The Karachi Port Authorities were particularly good to us, for not only did they not charge the Expedition any port dues but they went even further and their Chairman issued an order exempting us from any charges that we might otherwise have incurred, such as payment for water supplied to us, etc. We cannot thank them too heartily for the most generous manner in which they treated the Expedition.

The Chief had our boilers going again on the 16th, so I migrated back to my quarters on board and had a quiet night before we sailed on the 17th at about 12.30 p.m.

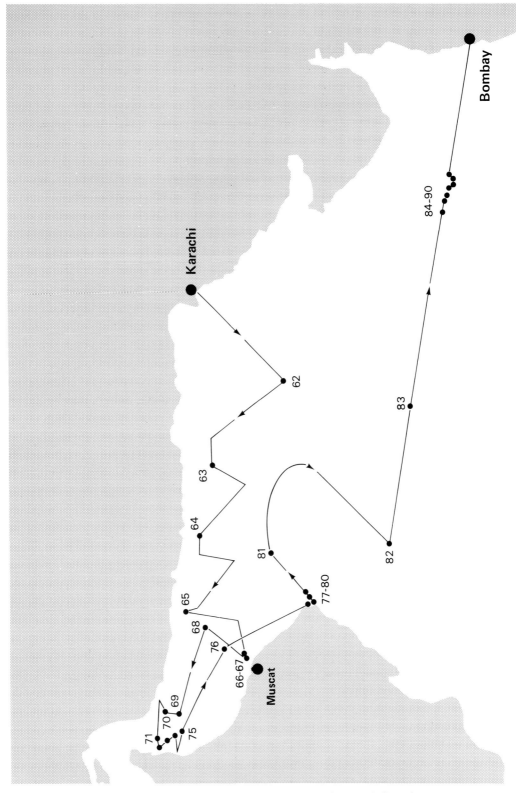

Fig. 19. Track chart, Cruise 4: Karachi–Bombay. Station numbers are indicated.

Chapter 5

Karachi to the Gulf of Oman, and Bombay

THE weather was very cloudy and misty when we left Karachi, and there was but little wind, so that we had a very quiet start. At first we ran towards the south-west, so as to make a dog-leg across the Murray Ridge and the Karachi Plateau before we turned north to reach the coast of Baluchistan. At about 5 o'clock that evening we ran into a light shower of rain, the first that we had seen since we left Alexandria. We were due to reach the end of our first lap on the following morning at about 8 o'clock, and at about 7.30 on the 19th the ship was stopped as we had reached the required position. The sky was cloudy and there was now a fresh breeze blowing from the north-east. The depth, as given by the echo-sounder, was 1,900 metres and when we sent the Bigelow tube down it struck bottom at 1,904 metres, a very close agreement. The bottom consisted of a tenacious grey clay, so we sent down the Agassiz trawl and carried out quite a successful haul (Station 65), the net arriving back on board a little after 1.00 p.m. There was a lot of clay in the cod-end of the net, so this was tipped out into a wooden box and we started to hunt through it for the specimens. As soon as the net was back on board we steamed off on our course to the north to get to our next station and this brought the wind round on to our starboard beam, so that the *Mabahiss* was rolling a bit and from time to time would ship a sea over the well-deck. Towards the end of the sorting process an extra large wave came over and capsized one of our bowls, in which were a number of small animals; these were at once swept away in the sea water, but we managed to recover most of them.

Towards evening the wind got up still more and we were now running across a choppy sea from the north-east complicated by a slow swell from the south-west, the result being a most uncomfortable motion. At dinner time Gilson was standing up to it well and was quite merry and bright, and Macan, as one would have expected from an experienced yachtsman, was completely unaffected; but Thompson and our Egyptian chemist Mohamed were both down and out and even Dr Faouzi had to discard his dinner before he had time to do anything with it, while the Chief Engineer was only saved from disgrace by retiring below to the engine-room. A curious thing that I have often noticed before is that engineers on board ship are much more comfortable down below in the atmosphere of the engine-room, with its reek of oil, than in any other part of the ship, whereas it would be hard to find anything more calculated to upset all other members of a ship's company.

By the morning of the 19th we were more or less under the lee of the land and conditions were more comfortable. Away to the north we could see the coast of Baluchistan in the distance and when I went up on the bridge to see how we were getting on and what indications the echo-sounder was giving of the character of the bottom, I found that we were apparently running exactly parallel to the line of a hill range, for the bottom was rising and falling in a most peculiar way. We seemed to be crossing a series of gullies and ridges, the depth varying continually between 110 and 800 fathoms, while, in addition, there were all sorts of curious cross-echoes coming from a slope some way to one side of us.

At 8.30 a.m. we were in exactly 1,000 fathoms by the echo-sounder and, as this was the depth that I was aiming at, the ship was stopped and we commenced work at another station (63). We first tried to take a sounding with a small Bigelow tube and 15 metres above it we attached to the wire a single Ekman reversing water-bottle to give us the temperature and a sample of the water. We got not the slightest indication of when the tube struck the bottom, so when we had paid out 100 metres more wire than the depth indicated by the echo, we stopped and hauled the tube in again and then found that it had penetrated the bottom, which was a soft grey mud, so deeply that the whole of the tube and about half of the extra weight that we had put above it had been buried. We then sent the Agassiz net down (Station 63) and carried out a haul; everything appeared to go off satisfactorily and the strain on the dynamometer was only just over 1 ton, which, as the haul progressed, increased to 1 ton 12 cwt. We left the net down for an hour, hoping to make a successful catch; but on hauling it in again we found that the rope-becket on the trawl frame had carried away and the whole of the net had been torn out of the frame and was still somewhere on the bottom. I can only suppose that the net had filled completely with the soft mud and that when it had been lifted off the bottom the weight had been too great for the net to stand and it had torn away from its head and foot ropes. The loss of this net was a most unfortunate occurrence, as it left us with only a single net for the Agassiz frame and that an old one that had already been patched more than once.

On the night of the 19th we ran towards the south-west in order to cross

19–20.XI.33   our submerged hill-range once again and try to get a more definite idea of
how it ran. We then turned north-west to get to a station where we could
carry out a trawl in about 250 fathoms. During the previous day the sea
had been of a definite green colour and at night, where the waves were
breaking and the water was disturbed, there was quite an amount of phosphorescence on the surface.

On the morning of the 20th there was still a fair breeze blowing but now
from the north-west, the force being about 4 on the Beaufort scale, and the
Mabahiss was rolling and pitching to an extent that was somewhat unpleasant. In the distance to the north we could just see the faint outlines of
the Persian coast. The ship was stopped at 8.30 a.m. and before long the
chemical section of the staff were busy taking a bottom sounding and a
water-sample in a depth of about 250 fathoms. Bottom was struck at 448
metres and the sample brought up consisted of a soft but tenacious grey
clay. Having lost our Agassiz net at the previous station, I had determined
to try the Monegasque trawl and Macan and Faouzi had been busy the
previous evening in getting it ready. By the time the chemists had completed
their job the net was shackled on to the trawl wire and it was then put over
and we towed it for about an hour (Station 64). I had expected that the
strain on the dynamometer would be somewhat more with this net than
with the Agassiz, but at the commencement of the trawl there was little or
no difference. As the trawl progressed, however, the strain rose steadily to
1 ton 5 cwt, or thereabouts, but at the end of the hour it suddenly rose to
over 2 tons and then, before we had time to stop the ship, fell again to less
than a ton. We cautiously went slow ahead again to see what would happen,
for the sudden release of the strain appeared to indicate that something had
carried away and I think we all felt that at the least the rope strop on the
frame must have parted. As we steamed slowly on, the strain again increased
to 2 and even to 2½ tons, finally settling down somewhere in the vicinity
of 2 tons. From this it appeared probable that we were fast on something,
so we stopped towing and started to try and heave in. At first the winch
made very heavy weather of it, so MacKenzie brought the *Mabahiss* round
and we steamed up to the wire. The winch then managed to drag in a foot
or two at a time as the ship dropped in the trough of a wave and gradually
we got the whole length of the wire inboard. During the process we got
broadside on to the sea and several waves quietly lopped over the side on
to the well-deck. I only just escaped being drenched by one, for I had gone
to sit down on a box on the weather side, but after a moment or two I
realized that I was exactly at the point where a wave would come over if it
could, so I moved away and a few seconds later a large one splashed over
exactly where I had been. When we finally succeeded in getting the trawl

up we found that the net was full of the same soft grey mud; there must have been about 2 tons of it in the net originally, but some and possibly a good deal had been washed out during he ascent. Even so, there was still nearly a ton of it in the cod-end, so we passed a rope round the net to take the strain off the frame and let the net hang in the water, while we went slow ahead and washed still more of the mud out. When we finally got the trawl on board we noticed that the mud had a rather queer, unpleasant smell about it, though this was not due to sulphuretted hydrogen gas, like the mud off Ras al Hadd. We carefully passed all the mud through the sieves but found not a trace of animal life in it with the single exception of the front half of a red deep-sea prawn that was almost certainly captured on the way up.

During the night of the 20th we again steamed first towards the south-west and then north-west so as again to cross, if it was still present, the submarine hill range that we had already noticed further to the east, running parallel to the coast line. At dawn we were steaming northwards so as to reach the position of the first of a series of stations that the chemists were going to make across the Gulf of Oman from north-east to south-west off Muscat. As we steamed towards the Persian coast the sea-bottom was remarkably flat, the depth for miles remaining almost constant at about 500 fathoms.

We were in the desired position about 9 o'clock and a sample of the bottom, taken with the small Bigelow tube, showed that it was composed of a soft green mud, without any appreciable smell. Judging from our past experience, this was the type of mud that we had already met with in the area where we had completely failed to find any animal life, and I therefore suspected that the trawl in this area too would prove to be absolutely barren. As, in that case, it wouldn't be worth while wasting a whole hour on it, I determined to send down the 4-foot triangular dredge, for at least one might hope to get some dead remains out of the mud, which we should in all probability not do if we used the trawl.

The dredge was duly carried out (Station 65) and my expectation that the area would prove a barren one was found to be correct, for we got absolutely nothing in the dredge except one valve of a lamellibranch and a few foraminifera.

We had now trawled or dredged in almost all depths between 250 and 1,000 fathoms in the Gulf or off Ras al Hadd and in every case there had been, for all practical purposes, a complete dearth of animal life. This raised a whole series of questions; firstly at what depth does animal life cease to exist in this region? The surface and shallow littoral zone appears to be extremely rich, but somewhere between the 50 and 250 fathom lines the

21–22.XI.33   bottom-living fauna disappears completely. Again, does the floating population (the plankton) peter out in the same way with an increase in depth or does that continue down to greater depths and only the bottom life disappear? Another question raised was whether the bottom-fauna, that in other regions we find at the depths occupied here by this azoic area, is absent altogether or does it occur in this region at depths either less or greater, depending on whether the local conditions have driven it upwards towards the surface or downwards into greater depths? It was clear that during our stay in the Gulf of Oman and the region of the Arabian coast we should have to try and find the answers to all these problems.

As soon as it was light on the 22nd, we started work at Station 66; this was to be a complete station, both hydrological and biological work being included in the programme. The chemists were soon busy and the small Bigelow tube was sent down to the bottom, the indicated depth being 610 metres, and brought up a bottom deposit of soft brownish-green mud without any offensive smell. It must be an amusing and rather unwonted sight to see a series of scientists solemnly smelling the contents of either a sounding tube or a trawl net as soon as it comes up, in order to see whether they can detect any trace of sulphuretted hydrogen; but after our experience in the region round Ras al Hadd we were very much on the look-out for any further samples from the bottom that showed a trace of this particular gas.

When the chemists had finished their work we shackled on the 4-foot triangular dredge and sent that down. As the general character of the mud appeared to indicate that we were in all probability still within the limits of the azoic area, I again decided to limit the dredge to half an hour, so the net was hauled in again at 10.30 (Station 66). Although it had been down for only a short time and the dynamometer had shown a strain of only some 14 cwt, the dredge was so full of the bottom mud that it was impossible to haul it on board without running the risk of the weight proving too much for the net, and we left it hanging over the side for a while and steamed slow ahead so as to wash some of the contents out. When enough had thus been got rid of, the net was hoisted up on the derrick and was swung in and emptied into a box on deck, from which it was carefully put through the graduated sieves. There were several bits of rock and some stones mixed with the mud, and on these were the tubes of serpulid worms, but the main ingredient of the catch were dead shells of the mollusc *Rostellaria delicatula* and there were actually three live examples and a few living worms inhabiting mud tubes.

It thus seemed that we had been working at or very near the lower limit of life in this area and it was to be expected that in still shallower water we should begin to find the real fauna of the region; we therefore steamed in towards the Arabian shore until we were in about 150 fathoms depth and prepared to send the dredge down again. Unfortunately, as the dredge was being put over the side the wire got caught between the roller and the frame of the gallows and was so firmly caught that we had to cut the wire out and a new eye-splice had to be made at the end. This delayed us for about an hour, but as soon as the wire was ready the dredge was sent down and we proceeded to carry out work at Station 67. At first there was but little strain on the dynamometer, but as the wire showed a continual series of slight jerks it seemed certain that it was actually on the bottom. After a few minutes, however, these jerks ceased and as the strain showed no increase we began to think that we must have drifted out into deeper water; this seemed all the more likely as our course was for the most part away from the shore. However, I determined to adopt a policy of masterly inactivity and a little later the recurrence of the oscillations in the strain indicated that the dredge was still on the bottom. As it seemed probable that we might hope for some living organisms at this comparatively shallow depth, I left the dredge down for a full hour. When we hauled it up, it came in quite easily; but as soon as we got it to the surface we found that the net was even more full of mud than ever, and we again had to leave it hanging over the side while we went ahead and washed some of it out. The mud was of the same brownish-green colour, but not quite so tenacious, as at the last station, and thus was more easily washed out. When we got the net inboard we put the rest of the contents through the sieves, but with the exception of several black stones and bits of rock, a few mollusc shells and serpulid tubes, which this time seemed to be empty, there were no indications of life; even at the shallow depth of 274 metres we were still below the level at which the fauna lives.

At the conclusion of this second trawl we were going into Muscat cove for the night in order to pay our respects to the authorities. While we were carrying out our second dredge we saw one of the Persian Gulf sloops, flying the White Ensign, enter the harbour, but before we had completed work she came out again. We should have liked to meet her, but at any rate we had the compensation of knowing that she wasn't occupying the best berth in the harbour.

It is the custom for every ship that enters the out-of-the-way little port of Muscat to send a party ashore on the southern horn of the cove and paint the name of the ship in large letters on the rock face. As we steamed in I was interested to see, among a number of others, the names of several RIM ships, including my own former ship *Investigator*. As soon as we were anchored, Captain MacKenzie and I went ashore to call on the Political

22.XI.33   Agent. The town lies at the head of the cove on a level piece of ground and is shut in on the land side by hills and ridges, composed of a black rock pitted with a number of holes that impart a pock-marked appearance to it. At each end of the sea front perched on the hill top is a fine old Portuguese fort, while a number of smaller outlying forts occupy the tops of small hills on the two spurs that run seaward on either side of the cove. We should never have been able to find our way through the narrow tortuous streets by ourselves, but an Arab who spoke English consented to act as our guide and show us the way. On our way we passed a number of houses, some of which had great carved wooden doorways, that were very fine and most picturesque. The road appeared to lead through several buildings that we later discovered to be the Customs House. Here another Arab came up and asked who we were and what we wanted so we attempted to explain that we wished to see the Political Agent and produced our visiting cards but we discovered that the Agent's house was still further on, through more doorways and up a narrow street. Eventually we reached our destination

Fig. 20. Muscat waterfront from the terrace below the British Consulate, November 1933. (*Photo:* H. C. Gilson.)

and were able to present ourselves. The Political Agent turned out to be Major Bremner, whose sister was married to Captain Vibart, RIM, a very old friend and shipmate of mine on the *Investigator*. In the course of conversation it transpired that our arrival was not unexpected, although, thinking that there was no wireless station at Muscat, we had not attempted to notify the port of our intended visit. However, the naval sloop that we had seen entering the harbour earlier in the day had reported to the Political Agent that they had seen an Egyptian Government vessel off the port 'in distress, steaming round and round in circles' but had been unable to get into communication with her, and had received no reply to a signal asking if assistance was required. As Bremner knew that we should be coming up the Gulf about this time he guessed what ship it was. Major Bremner very kindly took us for a motor drive along the coast road to Muttrah, the next town to the north, which commercially is really of more importance than Muscat itself, for it is here that all the camel caravans stop and their goods are loaded into dhows, of which there were about half a dozen anchored in the bay. The chief recreation of the younger section of the population of Muscat appeared to be hockey, and one of the first sights that we saw was a game between about half a dozen small boys that had been in progress in one of the streets that was only some 15 feet wide at the most. Unfortunately, a large black dog had appropriated the ball and the game was thus brought to a stop until the dog could be persuaded to give it up again, which he showed no intention of doing, though being quite friendly about it.

The next day a party went ashore to explore the town and four of us foregathered at the Residency to lunch with the Political Agent; in the evening he came on board to return our call and have a look at the ship. During the day we had sent a party ashore and duly added the name *Mabahiss*, in both English and Arabic, to those that already adorned the rock face. Late in the evening we steamed out again into the Gulf of Oman.

At about 7 o'clock on the morning of the 24th we reached the position for our next station (68) in a depth of 1,745 metres. The usual procedure was followed and the chemists had completed their hydrological work by about half past ten. The 4-foot triangular dredge was then shackled on to the trawl wire and was sent down and towed on the bottom for an hour, during which time the strain on the dynamometer varied between 1 ton and 25 cwts. When the net came up there was still a little green mud adhering to the frame, sufficient to show that the net had been on the bottom. Some more mud was clinging to the cod-end of the net, but its only contents were four examples of large salp, *Salpa hexagona*, that must

24–25.XI.33 have been captured on the way up, though unfortunately there were no means of telling at exactly what depth. So here again the bottom was completely sterile, though there is plenty of animal life in the shallow depths, while round Muscat harbour there is quite a fair quantity of growing coral and the fish are most prolific.

Our next station (70) was reached at about 8 o'clock on the 25th, the depth as given by the echo-sounder being 1,250 metres. After a little delay the chemists started work and carried out a series of observations at all the standard depths. While this was in progress the water at or near the surface was seen to be full of plankton, the most conspicuous objects being examples of large salp, *Pegea confoederata*, the same species that had been so abundant on the Arabian coast during our last cruise. As soon as the chemists had finished we steamed towards the north-east to reach the 100-fathom line off the Persian coast. We reached the required depth at about 1.30 p.m. and as soon as we had taken a sounding, a water sample and a temperature reading from the bottom, we put over the large otter trawl and towed it for an hour (Station 70). In spite of the bottom consisting of

FIG. 21. The sailors ashore in Muscat. (*Photo:* T. T. Macan.)

the same, or at least a very similar, soft green mud as that which we had so
frequently encountered before, the catch was quite good. It was a relief to
find some living material in the net after all the barren trawls that we had
been carrying out in this region. The most conspicuous ingredient of the
catch was the mollusc, *Rostellaria delicatula*, of which we obtained no less
than 213 examples, some of which had another species of small mollusc, a
Crepidula, riding on its shell. We also got a few examples of another species
of mollusc, a very fine *Pirula* that seemed to be more slender than the
common *P. investigatoris* and is probably the species that its author, Dr
Baini Prashad, one of my colleagues in the Zoological Survey of India,
named after me, *P. sewelli*. There were also at least five species of fish in the
net, as well as a number of other interesting animals, including starfish,
echiuroid worms with a fluffy zone round the middle of their length,
some crabs and prawns, and two locust shrimps. So altogether we got
quite a varied assortment of living animals and it was clear that we had
at last got above the azoic belt into a zone where there is quite a rich
fauna.

As soon as the net was up we steamed towards the Persian coast and
anchored for the night. In view of the reports that we had received regarding the general unfriendly attitude of the Persians, we were careful to
anchor well outside the 3-mile limit, so that they could have no excuse for
making trouble. In the distance we could see the town of Jask, that used to
be an important aerodrome for the Indian Air Mail, but which had to be
given up owing to the objections raised by the Persians.

The weather had been fine all day with, for the greater part of the time,
little or no wind, so that the sea surface had been quite smooth and in
consequence there had again been a lot of plankton about. During the
afternoon the predominant form was a small medusa, with long tentacles,
probably *Pelagia perla* or an allied species; we had captured some very similar, but somewhat larger, examples of this form a day or two before, so
that it seems to be widely distributed throughout the Gulf.

The following morning we got under way very early, at about 3.30, and
steamed off towards the west to get to a position right at the head of the
Gulf in a depth of about 50 fathoms. At this station (71) the bottom consisted of a coarse sand mixed with a little mud that refused to stay in the
sounding tube, though fortunately some still remained caught between the
two weights of the tube. As soon as the chemists had finished their
observations we again sent the otter trawl down and towed it for an hour.
This time the resulting catch was only a small one, though it seemed that
we were still within the zone of life and not in the dead area. We then
steamed towards our next station off the Arabian coast in much the same

depth of water; and this we reached at about 1.30 p.m. This time I decided to use the Agassiz trawl (Station 72). As soon as we started to tow, the dynamometer showed very great fluctuations in the strain and at one time it seemed clear that the net had actually got caught up in something on the bottom. However, it freed itself and at the end of an hour we hauled it in. When the net came up we saw that the frame had been badly bent and the net torn away from the frame at each end. Fortunately the net hadn't carried away altogether and in the cod-end was a large collection of sand and shells of numerous kinds, but mostly dead. Mixed with these was a large assortment of small animals and it took three of us working until sunset to get them sorted out. To add to the excitement, when the net came up it was seen that there was a sea snake in it, and when the cod-end was untied and the contents were shot into the box on deck, the snake came out early on and was buried under about half a ton of sand and shells. Since all sea snakes are poisonous, we had to be rather careful in digging for him before we could get on with the rest of the sorting. When we did eventually find him he was more dead than alive, and though he showed signs of recovery when dropped into a jar of spirit, it was too late from his point of view!

As soon as the net was back on board we steamed inshore to an anchorage off an Arabian village named Dubal Dibbah and anchored there for the night. Almost as soon as we were anchored a large boat put off from the beach and we were visited by some of the inhabitants, while a little later some of our people went ashore. The Arabs were at first very suspicious of us and mistook the Egyptian flag for that of Persia; it was very clear that they did not love the Persians. Our shore-going party saw something of the village and eventually had tea with the Sheikh, but all the time they were escorted by a band of some twenty men, all armed with rifles. Our little Egyptian colleague, Abdel Fatteh Mohamed, seemed to be a special object of their suspicion, and although he strenuously protested in Arabic that he was not a Persian but an Egyptian, nobody seemed to believe him and for long afterwards we used to tease him about what would have happened to him if he hadn't been under British protection. Had we been flying the British flag only, instead of both the Red Ensign and the Egyptian Government flag, there would have been none of the suspicion that we aroused, for the Sheikh informed Captain MacKenzie that he was under the protection of the British Government. However, he didn't appear to rely on this to too great an extent, for he seemed to maintain a small but quite efficient army and we were told that there were some 400 riflemen in the village.

We left our anchorage the next morning and steamed out into the Gulf so as to get to the 50-fathom level where I wanted to carry out a series of

observations with the grab; as this weighs something in the neighbourhood
of a ton and a half and has to be hoisted up on the derrick before it can be
swung out and lowered away, it is not the sort of thing that one would
choose to work with except in comparatively calm weather. The weather,
however, had been very good to us for some days past and this morning
was no exception for there was an almost flat calm. On this occasion, in
order to give us a good indication of when the grab reached the bottom
and thus enable us to avoid paying out too much wire and so run the risk
of the extra slack kinking, we rigged the dynamometer above the meter-
wheel, so that when the grab struck the bottom and the strain on the wire
eased up, the dynamometer needle would at once show the lessening of the
tension. The manoeuvre of lowering the grab proceeded smoothly and the
dynamometer gave a good indication, but a much better one was the sudden
release of the strain on the wire itself. We then hauled the grab in again and
proceeded to examine its contents, which consisted of dead mollusc shells
mixed with some sand and a little green mud. About a pound jar of the
deposit was preserved intact; the rest was passed through the graduated
sieves, but there was remarkably little in the way of animal life present.

We then steamed out further into the Gulf in order to get to the 80-
fathom level, but at the crucial moment the echo-sounder let us down by
refusing to function. As Thompson and Gilson wanted an hour in the
middle of the day in order to experiment with their light-recording apparatus, the ship was stopped while they carried out their trial and the
echo-sounder was being repaired. When this latter was got going again it
was found that we were in too deep water, so we turned round and steamed
in towards the Arabian coast until we were in the required depth. The grab
was then again put over the side and a sample of the bottom obtained
(Station 74). This time the dynamometer gave no indication whatever of
when the grab struck the bottom but the release of tension on the wire
showed that it was at 160 metres. Here the bottom consisted of a soft green
mud and sand, and after preserving a sample intact we took the opportunity
of aspirating off some of the occluded water so that our chemists might
analyse it and compare it with the supernatant water. All the rest of the
mud was passed through the sieves and this time we got many more
animals from it, including a number of small isopod crustaceans and a few
worms.

We then steamed in to the Arabian coast and again anchored for the
night off a small oasis, where there were quite a number of huts and
dwellings of sorts forming the village of Khor Fakkan. There was a good
sandy beach and all along it, between two outlying spurs from the chain of
hills that runs along the coast, was a dense mass of palm trees, while a little

27–28.XI.33   green scrub spread up the lower slopes of the spurs. Apart from this oasis the country appeared to be very bare and almost, if not entirely, destitute of vegetation. No sooner had we anchored than some of the local inhabitants came off to us and sold us some fresh fish, which provided a pleasant change in our menu.

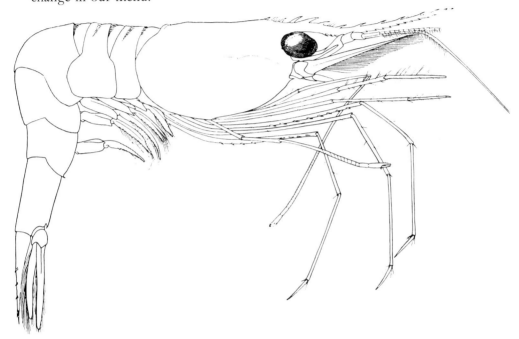

FIG. 22. *Plesionika minor*, a previously undescribed species of shrimp taken at Station 75 but not mentioned in Sewell's narrative.

We left our anchorage early next morning and according to the echo-sounder reached a depth of water of 110 fathoms at about 9.30. The grab was at once put over the side and lowered away and the moment of striking the bottom was at once indicated by the wire, though again the dynamometer gave little or no sign. It was at once hauled up again and as soon as it came to the surface it was obvious that it had sunk well into the bottom mud, for there was a lot of extra mud still clinging to the sides and the wire ropes. The contents were emptied out and examined but there was very little animal life, only a single mollusc and one locust shrimp. We then shackled on the otter trawl for Station 75. On the previous occasions we had been using bridles that were only 75 feet in length and it seemed probable that they were not long enough to allow the boards to separate sufficiently and fully extend the mouth of the net, especially as the two bridles showed a strong tendency to twist round each other. This time we

used bridles twice as long and inserted a light swivel-shackle between each   28–30.XI.33
bridle and the corresponding otter board. The trawl was down for an hour
and when it came up we found that we had obtained one of the largest
catches that we had seen up to that time. The main ingredient of the catch
was a large number (666) of sea-cucumbers, all apparently of the same
species; in addition, there were quite a number of fish, mostly small, as well
as several squids and some large chocolate-brown medusae. So large a catch,
even though it was not a very varied one, was something of a surprise after
the paucity of our previous ones.

While we were steaming out to our station we had passed a large school
of dolphins, but they were completely indifferent to our presence; they
passed quite close to the ship but took not the slightest notice of us and
proceeded quietly on their own course, up the Gulf towards the north-
west, which was in exactly the opposite direction to ours.

Having completed our work at Station 75 we proceeded out to the deep
area in the centre of the Gulf, which we reached on the morning of the
29th. Here we stopped to carry out hydrological observations, in a line
with some of our previous stations so as to complete a series right across
the Gulf, and hauls with the large plankton nets in order to discover, if
possible, whether the fauna was different in the different strata of water
that the chemists had shown to exist in the Gulf. Work commenced soon
after 8 o'clock and by 1.45 the chemists had finished and we shackled on
the 2-metre plankton net, together with a streamlined weight and the depth-
recorder, while at intervals, as the wire was paid out, we attached a series
of four other 1-metre diameter nets (Station 76). Sufficient wire, so far as
one could calculate, was then paid out so that the large net would be
fishing at about 1,600 metres depth, and the whole string was towed for an
hour. On hauling in, it was found that two of the nets, made of fine silk,
had split, but the catches in the nets that remained intact were quite satisfactory and a study of these should show whether there is any difference in
the fauna of the water strata, other than those usually associated with increasing depth. A casual examination of the contents did not appear to
indicate anything unusual regarding the inhabitants of the different levels,
but the fact that animals were captured at all depths seems to indicate that
the cause of the sterility of the bottom between the depths of 250 and 1,500
metres is not to be found in the water itself but must be sought in the mud
of which the bottom is composed.

Having completed our work, we set our course for Ras al Hadd so that
we might carry out a few more observations on the bottom mud of that
region before we left the area.

We steamed past Ras al Hadd about the middle of the morning of the

30.XI.33   30th and reached our destination at noon. As soon as we were in position we sent down the grab. The depth on this occasion was slightly less than at Station 56, being only 411 metres instead of 457, but as soon as we got the grab back there could be no doubt that we had hit on the correct spot, for the contents reeked of the same foul-smelling gas, and as the grab came up through the last few feet of water one could see bubbles of gas coming up with it. I at once proceeded to inoculate some culture tubes with the mud in order to try and culture any bacteria that might be living in it and might be the source of the gas. A large sample of the mud was treated with the aspirator and some of the occluded water drawn off for chemical analysis, while, since this treatment must of itself abstract some of the gas from the water, a further sample of the mud was allowed to settle and the water decanted off from it; the rest of the mud was then passed through the sieves, but there was no sign whatever of any living organisms.

I had proposed carrying out three dredges of about 150, 250 and 350 metres depth and thus try to determine the upper limit of the azoic zone. However, the bottom proved to be so irregular that before we had finished work at the first station we had already drifted into water of some 350 metres depth and so the Salpa dredge was shackled on and sent down at once (Station 77). We towed this for forty minutes and when we hauled it in again we found that it was full of the same foul-smelling mud, though the depth during the course of the haul had shoaled to 274 metres. On passing the contents of the bag through the sieves all that we obtained was a single crab.

We then steamed inshore for a short distance that brought us into a depth of 163 metres and Farquharson took a sounding with the small Lucas sounding machine; this brought up a sample of the sulphuretted hydrogen mud and as it was clear that we were still in the azoic zone, we steamed on a little further. The next sounding, in a depth of 102 metres, gave a bottom sample that was still green mud, but which did not appear to smell of sulphuretted hydrogen, so we again sent down the Salpa dredge (Station 79) for half an hour; when it came up it was again full of the same foul-smelling mud and the only sign of animal life was a fragment of a single locust-shrimp. We again started to steam inshore, but before we had gone more than a few ship's lengths the bottom 'came up like the side of a house' and we found ourselves in a depth of only 9–12 fathoms (Station 80). We then sent the dredge down again and this time after half an hour it came up full of coarse clean sand and shells including a varied assortment of animal life. This settled the question of the upper limit of the azoic zone for clearly it extends right up to the edge of the flat shallow-water area of the continental shelf.

Just to the north-east of this region the land runs out in a promontory, Ras al Khabba, and two of my scientists who landed there on our previous visit reported that the headland is for the most part composed of lava and basalt and is clearly volcanic in origin. It seemed just possible that the presence of the sulphuretted hydrogen gas might be due to this cause, but as all the volcanoes along this coast have long been extinct it did not appear probable that this was the solution to the problem and the fact that the dead zone extends far beyond the limits of the region where this foul gas is present indicates that there is some other factor at work, possibly bacteria, in which case I hoped that our cultures might give us an indication.

Having finished our work in this region we steamed north again into the deep area of the Gulf of Oman and carried out a complete station there, the chemists making a series of hydrological observations while the biologists carried out a trawl on the bottom with a Monegasque net (Station 81). Even in a depth of nearly 2,000 fathoms we were still in the region of grey clay with its usual paucity of animal life. After paying out nearly 3 miles of wire with the net at the end of it, and hauling it in again after an hour's tow on the bottom—a job that kept us fully occupied for the best part of six hours—all that we managed to get for our pains were two starfish and a single large deep-sea prawn, the latter having been caught, almost certainly, on the way up.

When we had finished this trawl we steamed again towards the southwest to reach another spot where the chemists wished to make further observations and in order to carry out a further survey of the region with our echo-sounder. This instrument had already enabled us to survey an area that a few years ago, with the old method of deep-sea sounding by wire, would have taken us some three survey-seasons to cover. Our results had been most interesting, for we had traced under the sea three great hill ranges running out from the coast in the neighbourhood of Karachi towards the west and south-west. The northernmost range runs nearly due west into the Gulf of Oman, parallel to the Baluchistan coast, while two others run, as I have already mentioned, in a south-west direction with a deep gully between them with a depth of about 2,000 fathoms, whereas the main area of the Gulf of Oman has a depth of only some 1,850 fathoms.

The weather continued fine, and for several days we had had an almost flat calm. During the afternoon of 2 December, we were steaming along at nearly 10 knots, considerably more than we had done hitherto. However, 'pride goeth before a fall' and at about 3 o'clock we gradually slowed down and finally came to a complete stop. On inquiring what had happened I heard that the whole of the floor of the engine-furnace had dropped out! The heat of the fires had melted the fire-bars and they were now lying in a

2–7.XII.33   semi-molten mass on the floor of the stoke-hold. It was impossible to do anything until this mass of iron had cooled sufficiently to allow the engineers to hoist it up and dump it overboard. New fire bars had to be put in, so it wasn't until about 8.00 in the evening that we really got going again and this delay cut our anticipated time short by about five hours.

During our run eastward across the northern end of the Arabian Sea to Bombay, where our cruise was to terminate, we carried out hydrological stations on the 3rd, 4th and 5th and on the next two days, the 6th and 7th, the biologists were thoroughly busy and were working at high pressure. On the first of these days we carried out one trawl (Station 85) in conjunction with the chemists and a second one (Station 86) independently, while on the 7th we made four stations, including two trawls (Station 87) and three hauls of the grab. Six stations in two days were rather too much, but as this was the only opportunity that we should get of investigating the continental slope off the west of India, we went all out to get as much done as was possible.

FIG. 23. The scientific staff in working dress, off Bombay, December 1933. Left to right, standing: Farquharson, Mohamed, Thompson, Macan, Gilson. Seated: Sewell, Faouzi.

This area appears to be a somewhat infertile one, for out of our four trawls we got very little, at any rate in the way of animal life, though we made one or two quite interesting discoveries. At the station in 286 metres (88) we got a good sample of the bottom in the grab and again a smell of sulphuretted hydrogen was noticeable, though not very marked. Here the bottom was composed of a grey clay-like material over the top of which was a layer of black or dark-brown mud or slime. This latter seemed to be of terrigenous origin for it was, at any rate in part, composed of vegetable debris and contained a dragon-fly's wing. It seems possible that it is derived from the outflow of the Narbadda and Tapti Rivers that pour their waters into the Gulf of Cambay, and that the debris is swept out of the Gulf by currents or tidal action and is deposited to the southward over the continental edge and the upper part of the continental slope. The presence of a bottom deposit impregnated with sulphuretted hydrogen could well account for the paucity of the fauna, but here again we have the problem of the source of this gas.

At our last station but one (89), we had a somewhat exciting time. We had sent the otter trawl down and this had been on the bottom for about three-quarters of an hour, during which time everything seemed to be going quite well, when suddenly the strain on the dynamometer, which had previously been in the neighbourhood of only 10–15 cwts, shot up to 3 tons, and before we could stop the ship the rope-becket on the nippers parted with a bang and shot over the side of the ship. The trawl wire ran out freely and the ship was stopped as soon as possible. We then commenced to haul in and at first there was a great deal of resistance, but this suddenly eased up and it seemed clear that the net, which must have been caught on the bottom, had at last come free. When we got it up we found that one of the otter boards was badly damaged; the iron shoe on the lower side was bent right round at a right angle and one of the wings of the net was badly torn. Entangled in the net was a large mass of calcareous rock and it seemed that we must have run over an unsuspected patch of this material, so that we were lucky to have got off as lightly as we did.

After another haul with the grab in about 50 fathoms we headed towards Bombay and reached there about 4 o'clock on the afternoon of 8 December. I think that we were all glad to get into port and have a rest, for during the last few days an epidemic of colds and what appeared to be a mild form of influenza had been going round the ship. Someone must have picked up the infection when we put into Muscat, for the first case started soon after that and since then several members of both the crew and the scientific staff had gone down with it.

As we steamed up the harbour past Colaba Point we saw that all the

8–9.XII.33 government ships were dressed and there were gay flags flying everywhere. We found that this display of bunting was in honour of the arrival of the new Governor of Bombay, Lord Brabourne, who had arrived from England by the P and O mail boat that morning. Our pilot took us to one of the government moorings near Middle Ground opposite the RIM Dockyard, where we were in the company of RIMS *Clive* and *Lawrence* in the next row of moorings and RIMS *Pathan* in the inner row, and as soon as we were safely tied up we proceeded to dress the *Mabahiss* with all the flags that we could muster.

The following morning Captain MacKenzie and I went ashore and introduced ourselves to our agents, Messrs MacKinnon, MacKenzie and Co. Ltd. They were extremely good to us and one of the partners, Mr Hogg, most kindly offered to put up for the night prior to our coaling as many of us as cared to come ashore. I arranged with him to take six of us, for I knew that every one of us would accept the invitation with much gratitude, for coaling, even at its best, is a dirty job and begins very early in the morning and goes on for most of the day. Having arranged to meet MacKenzie at lunch at the Taj Hotel, I left the office and went round to the Bombay Natural History Society's rooms, where I had a short chat with Sir Reginald Spence and Mr Prater. But after a minute or two they had to go off to take part in the functions connected with the departure of the Ex-Governor, who was due to leave by the P and O mail at noon. After they had gone I stayed on for a few minutes and then left to go to the Taj Hotel to get a haircut—and not before it was urgently necessary. I chartered a taxi and told the driver where to take me, but he explained that he couldn't get to the hotel until the Governor's procession had passed. He drove me round the back of the Prince of Wales Museum and there, at the corner of Hornby Road, we were held up, so he edged the car into a vacant space on the left of a row of other cars and carriages. Just at that moment the procession came along. First came a detachment of the mounted police and then a detachment of the Governor's bodyguard, very resplendent in full dress. This was followed by the Governor's state coach with the golden Umbrella of State and then came a second detachment of the bodyguard, while the tail of the procession was composed of a motor car in which were two police officers in full dress. Both sides of the street were lined with troops, but as soon as the procession had passed a gap was made opposite the end of our road and the policeman on point duty waved the line of cars on. All those on my right turned north in the direction from which the procession had just come; but my driver started up and then swerved down the road to the left. The next thing that I realized was that I was forming an involuntary part of the Ex-Governor's procession, coming immediately

behind the car with the two police officers in it—and so we went on for   9–13.XII.33
about 300 yards. I then thought that it was about time to get out of it, or I
might get more deeply involved in the farewell ceremonies, so I stopped
my taxi-man and, having attracted the attention of the officer commanding
the troops, got him to allow my taxi to turn down a side street and so get
to the hotel.

The next day I went off to the Haffkine Institute at Parel and introduced
myself and Dr Faouzi, who came with me, to Colonel Sokhay of my own
service, who was the Director. Through him I enlisted the services of his
department in the investigation of the foul-smelling mud from the Arabian
coast. He very kindly undertook to try and culture any bacteria that might
be present and in due course, when we got to Colombo about three months
later, I got the report. I also took Dr Faouzi round to the Imperial Institute
of Science and introduced him to some of the zoological staff there. Finally
I went round to the RIM Dockyard to see some of my old friends and
shipmates of former years.

On the morning of the 13th we were all busy getting the last of our
stores etc. on board and carrying out the usual port routine of health
inspection and preparation for sailing. Just before we left a large parcel of
books for the ship's library was brought off by the P and O launch, a
parting gift from Mr Hogg, to whom we were very much indebted for
many kindnesses during our stay in port.

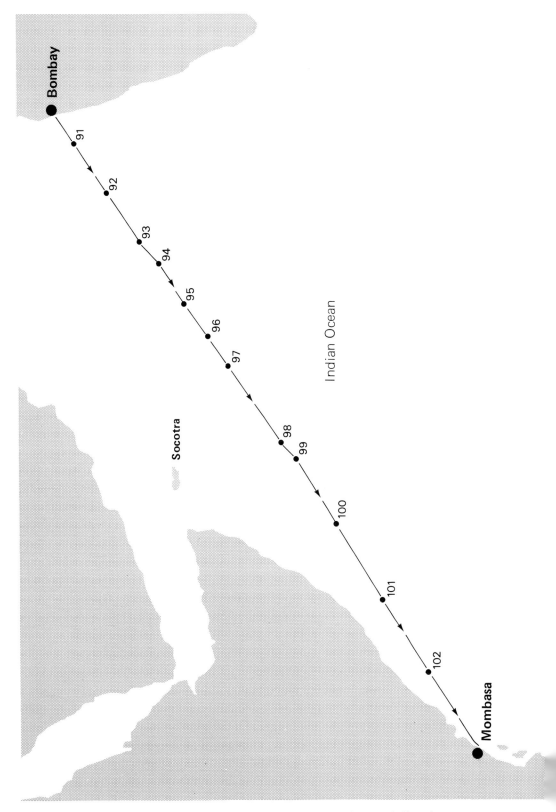

Fig. 24. Track chart, Cruise 5: Bombay–Mombasa. Station numbers are indicated.

Chapter 6

Bombay to Mombasa

WE left Bombay about 1.30 p.m. on 13 December and set our course towards the south-west for the long run across the Arabian Sea to Mombasa on the African coast, which we hoped to reach on the 31st and so be able to celebrate the New Year in port. The distance to be covered was approximately 2,400 miles and during nearly the whole of this we should be out in mid-ocean, away from sight of land and off the main steamship tracks, with nothing to occupy our attention except work; we were thus thrown back entirely on our own resources for any recreation and relaxation that we could look forward to. In anticipation of this state of affairs some of our Egyptian colleagues, who owned a gramophone, had invested in several new records which they had obtained in Bombay. Among these was one that they were particularly fond of and it usually happened that this record was put on during the dinner-hour. As their cabins were in the after part of the ship and were reached by the ladder that opened out of the saloon aft, we got the full benefit of the performance and its nightly repetition began, towards the end of the trip, to get monotonous. Since the return of the expedition I have discovered that this particular tune is almost as popular on the wireless as it was on the gramophone and very few weeks go by without it being broadcast by one or other of the jazz bands. I have thus learnt that it rejoices in the name 'Ali Baba', but as our gramophone record was in some foreign language, Spanish I think, I did not gather at the time what it was all about. Our other source of amusement and outside interest was the wireless news that our sparks managed to pick up. This was typed out and pinned up on the notice board in the saloon but here again our colleague Lloyd Jones showed a markedly limited, one might almost say parochial, interest and day after day almost the only news we got were items of information broadcast from Sydney in Australia; as Captain MacKenzie's and Lloyd Jones's wives were both in Australia the reasons for this bias were obvious, but I for one got rather tired of reading that the umpteenth suicide had occurred from Sydney Bridge.

As soon as we got clear of the land the north-east monsoon wind freshened and the sea got up, so that the *Mabahiss* started to roll somewhat.
Being loaded well down she began, as usual, to take seas over the well-
deck on the starboard side, though conditions were not too bad. At about
midnight on the first night out we ran into a belt of phosphorescence that
was as good as anything that I have seen. I had turned in about two hours
previously, but Thompson came down and woke me up and I went up to
the navigating bridge where MacKenzie and Thompson were. The whole
sea was a blaze of light on every hand. There was a brisk breeze blowing
from the north-east, raising a number of white horses and as each wave
broke it was a mass of greenish-blue light. As one looked further and
further away from the ship those patches appeared to lose their individuality
and blend into one another, so that the whole horizon was a soft uniform
glow. All along the ship's side, as we moved through the water, was a soft
glow, and stretching away aft a long streak of light marked our wake, with
a second narrow stream of light alongside it where the patent-log was
trailing through the water. At our forefoot, where the stem of the vessel
cut the water, there was a bright glow and each time that we dipped to a
wave this was accentuated as the water was thrust away on either side. It
was as fine a display of phosphorescence as I had ever seen, and I stayed on
the bridge quite a while watching it; it lasted altogether for about a couple
of hours and then gradually disappeared.[1]

The next morning at dawn we stopped for a hydrographic station on the

---

1. MacKenzie was also greatly impressed by this display of bioluminescence. 'The first
night at sea was one which will long be remembered by those of us called on deck before
midnight to witness the most weird luminous phenomena that I had ever seen on the
face of the ocean. Luminosity of the sea had frequently been observed in various parts of
the world's waters, but the continued brilliancy of that night exceeded anything we had
imagined possible. On approach it had the appearance of breakers on a low shore, and
had we been in the vicinity of land I certainly would have thought we were running
aground. On entering the luminous area one had the impression of meeting a very
choppy sea. In reality the sea was slight with light following wind; each wave seemed
greatly accentuated, breaking into a million flashes of white light which lit up the night
and gave the most extraordinary flood-lighting effect to the whole ship. For hours we
steamed through this apparently stormy sea, the imaginary waves and flashes of light at
times gave the idea of violent agitation, every minute one expected the ship to lurch and
roll and it was a most uncanny sensation to find her perfectly upright and steady. The
cause is said to be the presence of prolific organic matter in the water, and not one of
our scientists was able to give further explanation or reason.'

   Dr P. J. Herring of the Institute of Oceanographic Sciences suggests that the most
likely source of the bioluminescence on this occasion was dinoflagellates, since these
organisms emit their light only when agitated as, for instance, by the passage of a ship
through the water or the breaking of waves, as referred to in both accounts.

14–15.XII.33   edge of the continental shelf in about 100 fathoms. Work at this was over
by about 7.30 and we then steamed on again our course towards the African
coast. Macan and Faouzi were kept busy during the greater part of the day
in getting things ready for work in deep water; this entailed getting an
extra length of the *Mabahiss* trawl wire up from the hold, and first this and
then the thinner *Investigator* wire was shackled on to the main trawl wire
and was paid onto the winch drum. Eventually we had some 5,000 metres
of wire ready for work, for we intended next morning to carry out a trawl
and we anticipated that the depth of the water would be somewhere in the
neighbourhood of 2,200 fathoms, though this was merely a guess for there
was not a single sounding shown on the chart anywhere near the position
that we were making for.

The next morning the ship was stopped at 6 o'clock for work at Station
92, and the echo-sounder gave a depth of exactly 2,000 fathoms. The
chemists at once got to work and the small Bigelow sounding tube, with
an extra 25 lb weight, was sent down to the bottom but there was no
indication whatever of when it struck. On hauling in, it was clear that the
bottom had been reached and a core, about 15 inches long, was obtained of
a grey ooze full of rounded gritty particles, a typical *Globigerina* ooze. Water
samples and temperature readings were then taken at all standard depths
between 0 and 3,500 metres, and at the conclusion of this work the Agassiz
trawl was shackled on and sent down. There was a moderate breeze blowing
from the north-east and we rolled a bit, while from time to time a wave
lapped over on to the well-deck, but this did not interfere with us and
work proceeded smoothly.

During the process of paying out the 2,500 fathoms of wire we took the
clutch out of the winch-drum, so that the weight of the trawl and the wire
that was already out pulled the wire off the drum without our having to
use the steam. Towards the end of the paying-out process it became rather
difficult to regulate the pace with the brake alone, but as the wire was
trailing well aft, as we went slow ahead, there didn't seem to be any risk
involved. As soon as the necessary length of wire was out the nippers and
dyamometer were adjusted and we started trawling. Trawling was continued for two hours, and at 2.30 hauling in commenced; this proceeded
steadily until about 4.15 and then, when there were still some 690 metres of
wire still out, the wire came up in a tangle, having somehow got twisted
round itself. Unfortunately, this was not seen until it was too late and the
tangle came in over the gallows and jammed in the meter-wheel, parting
the wire with the loss of some 690 metres of wire and the trawl net. The
only causes to which I can attribute this fiasco are that the light Agassiz
frame, that had been fitted with a brand new net, did not sink as rapidly

during paying out as the trawl wire, so that the wire overran the trawl and
got twisted round it, or else that at this spot on the lower part of the
continental slope there is at this time of year, when the north-east monsoon
wind is blowing, an upwelling current of sufficient force to have twirled
the net round and so have caused a twist in the wire. As a result of this
accident I had to send off a wireless message to our Committee in England
asking that another 1,500 fathoms of wire should be sent out to us as soon
as possible, for we now had too little trawl wire to work in any depth
greater than some 1,800 fathoms.

All that night and the next morning we steamed on towards the south-
west and we reached the position for our next station at 3.30 on the
afternoon of the 16th. The depth was 2,193 fathoms by echo and as soon as
the way was off the ship we sent down the big Bigelow tube, getting a
splendid core of the bottom, 3 feet 6 inches in length. The whole length of
the core was full of *Globigerina* shells and there was a gradual transition in
the colour from cream at the top end to a dull grey in the deeper part, due
probably to a chemical change in the deposit with the formation of iron
sulphide in the deeper levels. After this the chemists took water samples
and temperature readings at depths down to 4,000 metres. As it was half
past ten at night before these observations were completed, the biological
work was postponed until next morning, so we steamed on during the
night and at 8 o'clock on the 17th the ship was stopped and we proceeded
to carry out a mid-water trawl with the 2-metre diameter plankton net at a
depth of about 500 fathoms using the self-closing mechanism (Station 94).
We were using a 1-inch rope for the throttling line and everything seemed
to go quite well until we sent down the messenger and released the closing
gear. We then started to haul in, but when we got the closing mechanism
up alongside it was found that the strain on the throttling line was very
much greater than we had expected and three strong Egyptian sailors were
unable to get the net in by hand; we had to hook the line on to the derrick
and haul the net in by stages, hauling in as much as we could and then
making fast again and hauling in another length of the rope. So great was
the strain on the rope that every moment I expected to see it part, but
fortunately it stood the strain, though I do not think that it would have
done so had it not been a brand new rope. When we came to examine the
catch there was very little in the net and it seemed probable that the throttle
line, that runs round the net about the middle of its length, had prevented
the net from opening to its full extent and thus from fishing properly.

Owing to the set of the current under the influence of the north-east
monsoon or wind we were making such good progress that I had intended
carrying out a 24-hour station on the 18th. Unfortunately, however, an

18.XII.33 epidemic of sickness began to go round the ship and it seemed to attack the scientists in preference to others. Macan had been rather seedy for some days and Thompson was suffering from a kind of heavy cold with severe headache—probably a mild form of influenza—and then Gilson went down with fever. As all three were living in one cabin it is not surprising that they managed to contract the disease from each other. I was thus compelled to cancel the 24-hour station and convert it into an ordinary station instead.

As we were somewhat ahead of our time in reaching the position of our station on the 18th, the ship was stopped and we drifted for an hour or so, so the chemists should not have to get up and start work in the dark. They actually commenced work at 5.30, but even so it was not until 1.30 in the afternoon that they had completed their observations. Unfortunately, we were not successful in getting a sample of the bottom; this, coming immediately after the long and interesting core that we had obtained the previous day, was very disappointing. There was a distinct, though not a very large, kick in the accumulator when 4,274 metres of the wire had run out; but on hauling the bottom-tube in it was found to be empty, so either the kick was a delusion, which is hardly likely in view of the close agreement between this depth and that given by the echo, or else the bottom was hard or the sample had washed out on the way up. At about 1.30 we put the large plankton net over the side (Station 95) and paid out 1,400 metres of wire—the same as in the haul the previous day—and at the same time the speed of the ship was regulated so as to keep the angle of the wire as close as possible to that of yesterday's haul. On this occasion we omitted the use of the self-closing mechanism and the resulting catch was distinctly better than on the day before when the mechanism was in use. This may have been due to the absence of the throttling line, the net thus being able to fish to its fullest extent, or to the fact that the net was fishing not only when it was being towed horizontally, but also during the whole of its ascent, when being hauled, through some 500 fathoms of water.

While the trawl was in progress there were a number of flying-fish darting out of the water, some of them quite close to the ship, and on several occasions one could see a larger fish chasing them; this latter usually seemed to be a *Caranx* (horse mackerel) and he frequently jumped right out of the water after the little fish in front. One or two *Coryphaena*, the sailor's dolphin, resplendent in the most wonderful iridescent colours, were also swimming round the ship.

The 18th saw the commencement of the Mohamedan feast of Ramadan and quite a number of our officers and crew strictly observed it, though, I understand, according to the law they need not have done so as they were on a journey.

After observing the fast all day long, sunset was greeted by a bugle call, and then a few minutes later came a second fanfare that I was given to understand corresponds to the British Army call commonly known as 'Come to the cookhouse door, boys' and the Mohamedan officers gathered in the saloon for a really hearty meal and I expect that they needed it after a day-long fast.

On the morning of the 19th the ship was stopped so that we might carry out another haul with the 2-metre plankton net at the end of the wire and several smaller 1-metre nets in series above it (Station 96). I hoped to so manage the trawl that the depth at which the bottom large net was fishing would be about 457 metres and when we got the net up and examined the depth recorder it showed that the net had actually fished at 420 metres, which was sufficiently close. All the nets made good catches and the cod-end of the large net was full of a mass of jelly-like material that turned out to be fragments of a giant *Pyrosoma*. An account of a similar specimen is given in the *Challenger* Reports and it is there stated that the specimen was markedly phosphorescent, so much so that the ship's officers amused themselves by writing their name on the surface of the animal with their fingers and seeing it come out in letters of fire. As soon as we got our specimen up, Faouzi and I took it down into my cabin that was dark enough even at the best of times, and we let down the dead-light and having turned off the electric light tried to induce the fragments of the *Pyrosoma* to exhibit its phosphorescent properties. There was absolutely no response and it seems either that this animal was not phosphorescent at all, perhaps owing to its broken state, or else that it only exhibits its phosphorescence at night time, which actually is the case with some of these animals. We also obtained a number of several species of fish, including two species of *Cyclothone*, the one colourless except for some rows of small black dots and the other a jet-black all over, the latter type occurring in those nets that had fished at a deeper level, as well as several hatchet-fish and prawns of various kinds.

On the night of the 19th at midnight we started to work our 24-hour station that had been postponed, and observations were taken at intervals of six hours throughout the period. In the first series the chemists took observations from the surface down to only 800 metres depth, but we had both winches working from midnight to about 1.30 a.m. so that during this period there could be no sleep for anyone on board. Just before dawn they started the second series, taking observations from the surface right down to the bottom at 4,230 metres; this took them until 11.30 and half an hour later they began the series that was again only a short one to 800 metres depth. When this was finished the biologists took over in order to get a bottom sample. The heavy Bigelow tube was shackled on to the end of the wire and was put over the side, but when some 2,000 metres of wire had run out we discovered a very bad kink in the wire and I was doubtful whether it would stand the strain; we decided that we had better give up the attempt and hauled the bottom sampler in again. There was no time to do anything to the wire before the chemists began their fourth and last series of observations at 6.00 p.m., but as they were only working from the surface down to 800 metres again, a kink at 2,000 metres did not seem to matter very much. By this time it was dark, or nearly so, and it is not possible to be quite certain as to what exactly happened, but when about 600 metres of the wire, with the required reversing-bottles attached at intervals, had been paid out, the ship gave a sudden lurch to a wave and this must have caused the strain on the wire to increase suddenly. The wire parted somewhere below the surface and we thus lost six reversing water-bottles and fourteen thermometers. The wire had probably begun to deteriorate as a result of constant use, for it had been in operation at about 80 stations out of the 97 that we had made, and at most of these it had been up and down several times.

All day long on the 21st we steamed on towards Africa, for although we had been at sea for eight days we were still not quite half-way across. The weather was moderately fine and what wind there was was astern. But we had now definitely got into the doldrums, though in this part of the ocean this area does not exhibit its typical character owing to the north-east monsoon, so that there is not a belt of continuously calm weather. We had, however, definitely got into a rain belt, for both early in the morning and again at night we got a heavy downpour. The only excitement during the day was the appearance of a large school of dolphins which came quite close alongside so that we could clearly see them swimming down the forward slope of the waves.

We were to have carried out another hydrological station on the morning of the 22nd, but the chemists had not yet completed there analyses of the water samples collected at the 24-hour station, so in order to fill in time and not get too far away from the position at which we wished to carry out our observations, I decided to carry out another mid-water trawl with the large plankton net. I had intended to try the self-closing apparatus again, but when we came to rig up the net we found that the end of the main wire was too thick to go through the guides of the self-closing gear, while the end-splice was too long and would not permit the messenger to slide down far enough to operate the release; we therefore had to be content with an oblique haul from approximately 2,000 metres to the surface. We completed the haul (Station 98) but the catch was disappointingly small. While the trawl was in progress a couple of sharks were continually swimming round the ship. Some of the ship's officers amused themselves by trying to shoot the animals, but none of them managed to score a hit. Right up to the end the sharks were sublimely indifferent to the attempts on their life and came nosing round the wire as the trawl was hauled in. During our various crossings of the Arabian Sea we were destined to see quite a number of sharks and they almost invariably exhibited the same coloration, a brown upper surface with a white belly and white tips to the pectoral fins. They belonged to the blunt-snouted kind and from their general appearance seemed to be examples of *Carcharias gangeticus*, the most voracious of all the Indian sharks. The wire also seemed to intrigue a shoal of *Caranx* (horse mackerel), for they kept swimming round and round it. They showed the most lovely colours, canary yellow tails and sides of an iridescent green, contrasting strongly with the dark grey of their backs.

As a result of an examination of the hydrographic wire it was clear that the outboard end was in a bad condition and in one or two places there were bad kinks. We cut off the part that had deteriorated and dumped it over the side and got up a spare coil of wire and spliced this on to the other end then reeled it off on to the hydrographic winch in preparation for our next station.

While this was going on we just drifted, and as the weather was fine, the wind having gone down considerably, there was quite a good assortment of planktonic organisms to be seen on the surface and floating round the ship. I occupied part of the time in collecting some of these with their attendant little fishes. The most frequent catch was a medusa of the genus *Aurelia* and nearly 50 per cent of those that I caught had a little fish with it. However, it is probable that the actual frequency of association of these two animals is not quite so high as this, for one could see the fish as a little shining speck in the umbrella cavity of the medusa and I naturally concentrated on capturing these rather than those in which no such speck could be seen. Even *Porpita* is sometimes accompanied by a small fish and I managed to capture one; this fish seemed to belong to a different species from those that inhabited the medusa. While we were at tea a whale came close by. As I went aft to the saloon I had noticed a couple of oily-looking patches on the surface of the water close astern of us and I was wondering what they could have been caused by when the whale appeared. Incidentally, when the whale passed to windward of us there was a most objectionable smell coming from it.

The repair of the hydrographic wire was completed by about 7 o'clock in the evening of the 23rd and then there was a short interval while the Chief was raising steam; at about 9 o'clock the chemists began work at Station 99 and this was completed at 1.30 on the morning of the 24th.

FIG. 25. Looking aft from the forecastle of the *Mabahiss*, Lieutenant Badr on the bridge, December 1933. (*Photo:* H. C. Gilson.)

Misfortunes never seem to come singly and unfortunately something now
seemed to have gone wrong with our wireless installation. Lloyd Jones,
our Wireless Operator, informed me that there was an earth somewhere in
the ship and that when he listened in he got nothing but a succession of
weird noises, like glorified atmospherics, and was quite unable to hear any
signals or messages, so that we were for the time being completely without
news and, what was worse, we were unable to send out any messages. I
had hoped to get two messages of Christmas greetings off, one to our
Committee and the other to my children in England, but neither of these
could be sent. It was lucky that the message asking for a further consignment of scientific gear to replace what we had lost at Station 97 had been
sent before this defect made its appearance.

I had hoped that during this voyage we might strike a depth of over
3,000 fathoms and so be able to record the existence of another deep. A
little to the south of our line there are two or three soundings on the
Admiralty chart of 2,900 fathoms and on the 23rd our echo-sounder showed
that we were in a depth of 2,910 fathoms, but then the bottom started
to come up again and on the 24th we were in water of less than 2,900
fathoms.

We celebrated Christmas Day by carrying out our 100th Station. At 9
o'clock the ship was stopped and we commenced work in a depth of 5,060
metres; it took us until late in the afternoon to complete the hydrological
work and then we sent the heavy Bigelow tube down and got a sample of
the bottom. In the intervals Gilson managed to carry out a few experiments
with the Harvey net and the results seemed to indicate beyond any doubt
that there is a much greater total quantity of plankton in these tropical
waters than is usually held to be the case, though I have never believed the
generally-accepted and oft-repeated statement that tropical waters are
markedly deficient in plankton. Furthermore, the results showed that the
greatest concentration of the plankton is to be found at a depth of some
35–45 metres and is not at the surface.

It was 6.30 in the evening before we got the sounding tube back again
and we then started to celebrate Christmas Day. The saloon had been decor-
ated with the Expedition flag and across the room were hung strings of
little coloured labels that the chemists used for distinguishing their water
samples, so that it looked quite gay. The Commisariat Department had
excelled itself and, though we had fared sumptuously all day, the climax
was reached at dinner, as the following menu sufficiently indicates:

25–26.XII.33

Hors d'Oeuvres

Mock Turtle Soup

Fish Mayonnaise

Asparagus au Beurre

Roast Duckling
Petit Pois   Cauliflower
Snowed Potatoes

English Plum Pudding
White Sauce

Fruit Salad

Assorted Nuts   Muscatels

Sherry   Port   Whisky

Cigarettes

The only unrehearsed effect was produced by our Head Steward, Ibrahim, who was unable to read English and was, in consequence, quite unable to distinguish one bottle from another and so gave us all port wine with the soup instead of the sherry.

All the next day we steamed south-westward towards our next station. The weather was gloriously fine and we seemed to have run out of the sphere of influence of the north-east monsoon, for the sea was, except for a slight swell, absolutely flat calm. There also seemed to have been a general change in the atmosphere, for it felt decidedly warmer and more sticky than before, and this suggested that we had run into an area of different water. There seemed to have been a slight change in the colour of the sea, for it was decidedly more green than before, but there was no change that we could detect in either the salinity or temperature of the water. There was apparently an increased amount of life in the water and at breakfast time there was an incredible number of flying-fish darting out of the water, disturbed and frightened by our passage. Hundreds of them together suddenly dashed out of the water and went planing away on either hand; I cannot remember ever to have seen so many at one time. As the day wore on their numbers got steadily fewer and fewer and one is tempted to correlate this with the depth at which the plankton occurs. In English waters it has been well established that the major amount of the floating population, and especially of the smaller crustaceans on which the fish feed, occurs at or near the surface at night, but that as the day wears on these little animals sink down to a deeper level. The same phenomenon has been shown to occur in the tropical part of the Atlantic Ocean, so that it is probable that in the early morning the plankton throughout the Indian tropics is also near the surface. Consequently the fish which are feeding on the plankton will be near the surface too and, if disturbed, the flying-fish will take to the air, whereas later in the day they may be feeding at a deeper level and so not be disturbed to the same extent by the passing of a ship.

As I came out of the saloon after lunch I noticed a big splash on our starboard beam about 100 yards out from the ship. While I was looking to see whether anything more was going to happen a great ray, that looked about the size of a billiard table and was probably larger, jumped clear out of the water and came down again with another great splash exactly like the first one. I only got a momentary view of the animal, but this was enough for me to see that on either side in front of the head there was a projecting horn and there is no doubt that the fish was a specimen of the giant ray, *Dicerobatis eregoodoo*. Just before we called at Karachi a specimen of this fish had been captured after a prolonged fight by one of the residents, Mr Tombasi, who very kindly gave me a photograph of it. His example measured 22 feet across from the tip of one fin to the tip of the other, and this one was probably much the same size.

The ship was stopped at 8.30 on the morning of the 27th and soon after we began work at our 101st Station in a depth of water of 4,285 metres. While work was in progress I occupied myself by collecting examples of the surface plankton. In the early morning, as on the previous day, there were a number of flying-fish darting out of the water on either hand; again the numbers showed a steady diminution as the day wore on, so that by noon there was not a single one to be seen, though at 7.30 there had been thousands. During the greater part of the day the plankton was quite scarce, but about 3.30 in the afternoon a number of organisms began to make their appearance. The most conspicuous of these was a small medusa that appeared to belong to the species *Pelagia perla*, or, at any rate, was remarkably like the pictures of this little animal. In the morning I had seen only a single example of this jelly-fish, but in the evening they were so common that in a space of half an hour I was able to collect thirty specimens that floated within reach and I could see many more that did not drift near enough to be caught. Associated with these jelly-fish were small black amphipod crustaceans; I rarely caught a jelly-fish without at the same time capturing at least one of these crustacea, whereas I could drag the hand net through the water for several minutes without capturing a single one unless a jelly-fish was also present.

28–29.XII.33   During the early morning of the 28th we again experienced a prevalence of the flying-fish but again they disappeared by about 10 o'clock. I was not up early enough to see these little fish at the height of their occurrence, but Farquharson and the officer of the watch both informed me that the best time to see them was just before dawn, when they occur in thousands and are so vigorous that they sometimes fly right over the ship as high up as the level of the bridge, whereas during the later part of the day they merely fly away from the ship.

About mid-day we ran into water of quite a different colour from that which we had previously been in. It was of a distinct purple-red and was somewhat patchy in its distribution, for we could clearly see darker patches with lighter blue-green water in between, so at 12.30 p.m. we put the high-speed plankton net over the stern and towed it for about an hour. The resulting catch contained quite a large assortment of microscopic organisms, for the most part diatoms of several kinds, with a few *Radiolaria* and *Globigerina* in all its glory with its protoplasmic processes all stretched out in a kind of halo round it.

That evening, at about 8 o'clock, we crossed the Equator and passed into the Southern Hemisphere. None of our Egyptian colleagues had ever been so far south, but there were no incidents commemorating this crossing of the line, such as one reads about in passenger and other steamers, for we were all far too busy to indulge in such matters. The weather was decidedly stuffy for the wind was dead aft and was moving at exactly the same rate as the ship herself, so that the anemometer on the upper bridge was completely stationary, the first time that this had occurred since we left Alexandria.

On the morning of the 29th the ship was stopped and we proceeded to carry out our 102nd Station. The weather was fine with only a light wind from the north-east, but there was now a strong current setting us towards the east or north-east and this made it very difficult to keep the two hydrographic wires on the opposite sides of the ship straight up and down. Indeed, it seemed to be almost impossible, and the first thing that happened was that the port-side wire ran under the ship as we drifted down over it, and then became fast in something on the ship's bottom. What the obstruction was could only be surmised; it might have been the projecting plate of the microphone that picks up the echo for the sounding machine, or it may merely have been barnacle growth, for we must by now have been pretty foul on the bottom, particularly if the bottom was anything like the ship's sides as far down as we could see. As we had been at sea continuously for some three and a half months, there had been ample time for a rich fauna and flora to have developed. However, whatever the obstruction was, we managed to get the wire free, but soon after that the two wires got

twisted round each other below the ship. This was eventually corrected and
work proceeded again. The hydrological work was completed at about
12.30 and we then sent the heavy Bigelow tube down to get a sample of the
bottom. We didn't get a very good indication of when the tube struck the
bottom, but it seemed to be at about 3,263 metres and this agreed well with the
depth as given by the echo-sounder which was 3,215 metres. On hauling it in
we found that we had got a good core of the bottom deposit that was a pale
yellow or cream on the surface but changed to a grey ooze at the deeper end.

I had intended to carry out a mid-water trawl as soon as the bottom tube
was up, but Captain MacKenzie pointed out that owing to the strong head
current and the foul condition of the ship's bottom, we were so far behind
our scheduled time that unless we got under way at once we should be
unable to get to Mombasa before nightfall on the 31st. Since a ship is not
allowed by harbour regulations to enter that port after nightfall, this would en-
tail our hanging about until the morning of the 1st, and I gave up the idea.

Throughout the 30th we steamed steadily on our course towards
Mombasa, but owing to our foul condition and the strong head-current we
were only able to make about 5 knots. Then, to delay us still further, our
boiler tubes got choked with soot from the Indian (Bengal) coal that, owing
to the coal restrictions in India, we had been compelled to take in at Bombay
instead of Welsh coal, and this finally necessitated our stopping while the
Chief cleaned his tubes. As we got nearer to the coast the character of the
water seemed to change again and its colour became quite blue. A surface
tow-net that we had out for an hour now yielded only a very small catch,
as was to be expected from the colour of the water, for a blue colour
always means an absence of living organisms. The delay caused by having
to clean boiler tubes was the cause of our not arriving off Mombasa until
nearly midnight on the 31st, and so after all we had to anchor for the night
off the port and only got in early on the morning of the New Year's Day.

After nineteen days at sea we were all very glad to get into port, and it
was especially pleasant to see a really green country again after the barren
coasts that we had been working along during our three previous cruises. I
wasn't up early enough to see Mombasa from the sea, for by the time I
came on deck we were already in the entrance to the harbour which extends
up between the mainland and the island on which Mombasa and the port
of Kilindini are situated. Most of the buildings are situated on the island
and there are only a few across the harbour on the mainland, much of
which appeared to be virgin jungle, though there are large areas of what
seemed to be open grassland. We eventually tied up to the jetty just astern
of an Italian ship, and shortly afterwards our fires were drawn and we were
once again without lights or fans on board.

1–8.1.34   Later in the morning Farquharson, Faouzi and I went ashore to visit the General Post Office at Mombasa and try to get some parcels and letters that were said to be there waiting for us. As it was New Year's Day there were only one or two clerks present and they informed us that all the things that we wanted were in the Kilindini Post Office on the jetty alongside where we were lying! Nothing further could be done that day, but the next morning I went to the Kilindini Post Office only to be told that all our mail was in the GPO at Mombasa where we had been the previous morning. Our Chief had had the same experience, so I told the clerk what I thought about his department and he then undertook to get the parcels and mail sent down to the Harbour Post Office for us, which he did, and eventually we got them about mid-day on the 2nd.

After visiting the post office on the 1st we went off to pay our respects to the Political Resident. None of us knew where he lived or where his office was or even his name, but the driver of the taxi that we hired said that he knew, so off we drove. He took us straight to his private residence and we found that the Political Resident was out, but Mrs Fazan, his wife, very kindly invited us in and provided us with a drink, which we very gratefully accepted. After chatting for some time we said goodbye and drove to the Mombasa Club to pay our call there. We duly wrote our names in the visitors' book and left cards for the President and Secretary; the Club was absolutely deserted though it was very evident that there had been New Year's Eve celebrations there the night before and this was possibly one predisposing factor for the marked absence of anyone there the following morning.

The next day the Political Resident, Mr Fazan, came on board and returned our call. He very kindly invited the three of us to stay with them for a few days—an invitation that we all gladly accepted. On our last morning Mrs Fazan very kindly arranged that the junior officer in charge, Mr Dove, should show us round the fort that is partly Arab and part Portuguese and is now used as a jail. Another day five of us hired a couple of cars and drove out into the country for a picnic. We first went towards the south to the top of some hills from which we got a magnificent view of the country round, and from such a bird's-eye view one could quite well understand what a magnificent country for game it must have been in the past before ruthless slaughter decimated the herds. In the afternoon we went down to the sea-coast for a bathe at a place called Tiwi that lies within the coral reef. The reef was interesting, for spreading out from the present sandy beach is a wide shelf of reef-rock that is still covered at high tide but at low water is left high and dry with numerous small shallow pools of water on the surface. Beyond this old reef is a wide belt in which

the water is of considerable depth—some 5 fathoms—and then outside this
again is the recent reef that is only just uncovered at low tide. It would
seem probable that the inner raised reef is an older formation and was in
existence before the occurrence of the universal fall of sea-level that took
place some 4,000 years ago, and that the outer present reef has been formed
since that time. Behind the raised coral reef the beach consists of sand and
masses of coral rock, while dotted about were a number of rounded
fragments of pumice that occurred all over the Indian Ocean in the two or
three years following the explosion of Krakatoa in 1883. Mombasa itself is
built on a raised coral formation and much of the stone used for building is
quarried out of the island and is called by the inhabitants 'coral', though it
would probably be more correct to call it coral-rock; judging from the part
that I examined and that is exposed in the moat and round the foundations
of the fort, the rock is a coral-conglomerate and contains a number of
fragments of coral that still retain much of their original structure, but the
mass of the rock is not coral in the strict meaning of the term.

Some of the members of the Expedition had hoped to get up country to
Nairobi for a day or two and see something of the wild game. At the
commencement of our stay in port these hopes ran high, for it was
rumoured that the captains and chief engineers of all ships visiting the port
were granted free passes on the railway. Captain MacKenzie and Dr Faouzi
each interviewed the local railway authorities and they were led to believe
that free passes would be issued to all members of the Expedition if they
wished to go, and several of us made plans for going up to Nairobi for at
least one day there. However, when the final decision of the authorities in
Nairobi was received it was learned that all that the railway was prepared
to allow us was a return ticket for one-and-a-quarter fare; this was, perhaps,
as much as one was entitled to expect from the railway, but the officials in
Mombasa had raised our hopes rather high so that the concession came as a
great disappointment and no one went after all.

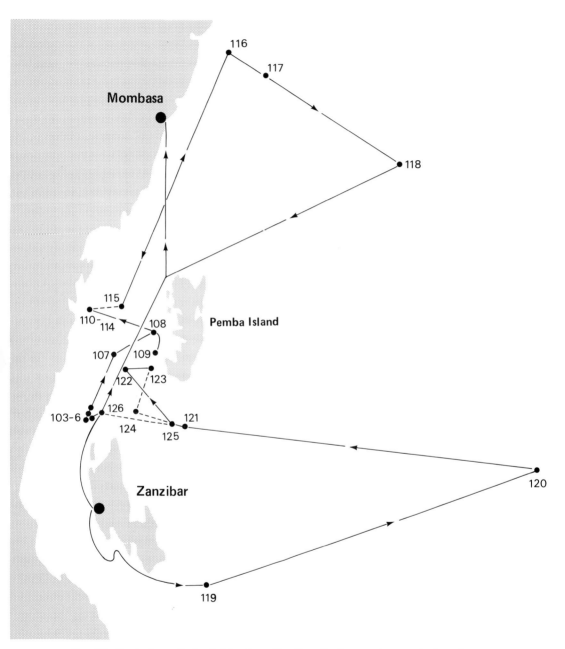

FIG. 26. Track chart, Cruise 6: Mombasa–Zanzibar. Station numbers are indicated.

Chapter 7

Mombasa to Zanzibar

9.I.34 WE left Mombasa on 9 January at 11 o'clock. There was a quite a stiff breeze blowing from the north-east when we left the shelter of the port and it wasn't long before the *Mabahiss* was pitching and rolling in a lively sea. The port authorities had asked us to try and locate a shoal patch that is shown on the Admiralty chart just off the entrance to the harbour. The general level of the sea-bottom in this area is about 20–22 fathoms, but on the chart are two small areas in which the depth is given as 6 and 4.5 fathoms respectively; what the port authorities really hoped was that we should be able to prove that there were no such shallow patches, for they were very doubtful regarding their actual existence. This, of course, we couldn't do for it would have necessitated a regular survey of the whole area and we couldn't spare the time for it. Instead, we ran several lines of soundings with our echo-sounder and we found that, in the region where these shallow patches are shown on the chart, the sea-floor is very irregular and, as there are extensive coral reefs in the vicinity, there is no reason why there shouldn't be coral-heads and patches in the area which might well have grown up from the bottom.

While we were steaming backwards and forwards across this area it was interesting to note the differences in the sea-water. The inshore water, that was presumably coming off the reefs and out of the harbour on the ebb tide, was a bright green colour and contained quite a lot of a grass-like weed floating on the surface, while a little further out to sea the water was a deep and clear blue. Between these two masses of water was a definite line of drift weed, partly of a grass-like type (?*Cymodocea*) and partly of a Sargasso type, this latter being in all probability derived from the reef itself.

As soon as we had made sufficient soundings to indicate that the occurrence of the shoal-patches was at least probable, we steered to the south on our course for Zanzibar in order to report ourselves to the Political Resident there and obtain official sanction to work off the coast, for the whole coastline along this part of Africa belongs to the Sultan of Zanzibar and is not British in the strict sense; we were, incidentally, carrying mails for Zanzibar.

During the early part of the night, as we steamed southward, our Navigator took the opportunity of swinging the compass; this occupied us for about an hour, but in spite of this and the northerly current that was running against us we covered the distance from Mombasa to Zanzibar, about 126 miles, in some twenty hours, so the *Mabahiss* was making good progress.

At about 8.30 on the morning of the 10th we stopped off the anchorage on the west side of Zanzibar and took the pilot on board and proceeded to an anchorage off the south side of the town near the British Residency. A couple of hours later Captain MacKenzie, Dr Faouzi and I went ashore and paid a formal call on the Sultan and the British Resident. The Resident, Sir Richard Rankine, was away somewhere in the island but the Chief Secretary, Mr MacElderry, very kindly asked four of us to lunch and we accepted for ourselves and the Chief Engineer. Having paid our calls we were taken round to the Zanzibar Museum and were introduced to the Curator, Dr Spurrier, who is a real enthusiast and who insisted, in spite of his age, in taking us round and showing us all his treasures, or as many of them as time would allow. Among the interesting exhibits in the museum are a number of letters, reports, etc., from Dr Livingstone and Mr Stanley. Dr Spurrier told us that a few weeks previous to our visit a school of whales had come ashore near the town; altogether there were about forty of them and they measured about 17–18 feet in length. Some they managed to tow out to sea again before they died and these swam away, but a number of the others died and the stench from their rotting carcasses was so bad that they had to tow them out to sea and let them drift away. The species of whale appears to have been the false killer, for by all accounts they were of a uniform black colour both dorsally and ventrally, whereas the closely allied Caa'ing Whale has a white belly. After lunching with the Chief Secretary, we returned on board and in the evening several of us were taken for a drive round the neighbouring part of the island.

We left Zanzibar early on 11 January and steamed northwards towards Pemba Island. As soon as we were in 50 fathoms of water, we commenced our biological work. We first carried out two hauls of the grab in depths of approximately 50 and 100 fathoms; in the first of these the sea-bottom consisted of a coarse sand mixed with shells, and the sample contained little or no animal life, but at the second haul the bottom was mixed with a certain amount of mud and here we got several small holothurians and a few solitary corals. It is usually at about this depth that one gets the greatest number of animals in the grab, probably because at about this depth the

11–12.I.34 fine organic detritus, that is drifting about in inshore waters, is deposited on the bottom; in other words, this is Murray's 'mud line', where fine mud and debris are deposited and sand- and mud-feeding organisms, such as holothurians and other echinoderms, can find sufficient nourishment.

Having finished our two hauls, we were on to the 150-fathom line and carried out a third haul with the grab, getting a good sample of a green mud with a superficial coating of a brownish-yellow colour; there was, however, little or no animal life in it. When it was over we shackled on the Agassiz trawl and sent it down for an hour (Station 105). The result was a very good catch and quite a number of the animals obtained seemed to be different from anything that we had hitherto seen, but until the experts have submitted their reports on the various species it is impossible to be absolutely certain on this point.

As soon as the trawl was up on deck we got under way and steamed southwards again towards Zanzibar island in order to get to an anchorage for the night. We dropped anchor at about 4.45 in the afternoon in Mkokotoni Bay, opposite a small village or township near the north end of the island where there were two or three quite nice-looking houses just at the top of the beach among the trees. A little later several of us went ashore for a bath.

Early the next morning we left the shelter of our anchorage and steamed out into the open to get into water of a depth of 100 fathoms for a trawl. There was a strong wind blowing from the north, force 5 on the Beaufort Scale, and we steamed out straight into the teeth of it, so that the little *Mabahiss* was soon pitching more than was pleasant. About 8 o'clock we were in the required depth and we sent down the big Bigelow bottom-tube and one reversing water-bottle, to give us the data necessary for the trawl, and as soon as these were up again the Agassiz trawl was put over (Station 106). As the trawl progressed our course altered somewhat and before long we were steaming across the set of the seas. Macan in the meantime had got busy with the bottom sample and had just got it out of the tube when we shipped a sea over the well-deck and the core went sailing away into the scuppers. We managed to rescue most of it, if not all, but it was now in fragments, so that we didn't know which bit should join on to any other. All the time that we were trawling we were constantly shipping water on board, but apart from this everything went off satisfactorily and when we hauled the net in we found that we had got a very good catch.

As soon as the trawl was back on board we steamed off towards the north to get into deeper water for a second haul and at the same time to get nearer to our proposed anchorage for the night. This time we were not so successful; the trawl was sent down in 240 fathoms (Station 107) and everything went satisfactorily to start with. When the trawl had been down for about three-quarters of an hour, however, the strain on the dynamometer suddenly shot up from about 8 cwts to over 2 tons. I immediately yelled to the bridge to stop the ship and this was done before any serious damage had resulted; but when we got the net up we found that it must have caught in a rock or some similar obstruction, for the loop in the bridle had pulled out from the thimble and the bars of the frame were somewhat bent. Fortunately, the net was intact, so that we had not lost any of the catch. This was only moderate in amount, though it contained several interesting animals.

When this second trawl was over we steamed eastwards toward Pemba Island and anchored in calm water for the night in Chaki Chaki Creek. From our anchorage, before it became too dark, we could see some red-roofed houses on shore. Later several lights could be seen, but we had got in too late for anyone to go ashore and for most of the evening the biologists were busy sorting, labelling and preserving the catches. Among the animals obtained in the second trawl were a number of deep-sea prawns of a beautiful pink colour and a water-colour sketch was made of one of these before it was put in spirit, for a short period of immersion in any preserving fluid rapidly destroys the colours of these animals.

We left the shelter of our anchorage early the next morning and steamed out into the deep channel that runs towards the north-west between Zanzibar and Pemba islands and then turns northwards between the latter island and the mainland of Africa. Owing to the existence of this deep channel we were able to carry out quite a number of deep trawls in water that was comparatively calm, for although there was throughout our stay in the region a strong north-east wind this channel was on the lee side of Pemba. The sea was not quite so troublesome as on the previous day, but even so it was sufficiently rough for an occasional wave to come over the windward bulwark on to the well-deck. We steamed out into water of a depth of about 425 fathoms and then stopped and carried out our 108th Station. Everything went well until we were hauling the Agassiz net in again and then, owing to the wind being on our starboard beam, the ship drifted down over the wire and it became necessary for the officer of the day, Lieutenant Sarwat, to alter course so as to get the wire clear; shortly after we had done so, we shipped a green sea over the curve of the bulwark and a mass of water flopped down on deck and into the Captain's cabin, the door of which was open. Sarwat got blamed for not keeping the course that Captain MacKenzie had given him, but it was not his fault for he clearly couldn't keep on the same course when the trawl wire was hard under the ship. However, he carried out the true naval tradition by passing it on to us on the well-deck. When the trawl was up we found that the

13–14.I.34 endless chain that carries the foot- and head-ropes of the net had snapped. Included in the catch were two earthenware bowls of a light biscuit-coloured pottery, both of which were slightly broken round the rim, but otherwise were in a remarkably good state of preservation; the pottery appeared to me to be recent, but the bowls had clearly been on the sea-bottom for some time as they were overgrown with serpulid-worm tubes. Later, when we got back to Zanzibar, I took them to the museum and asked Dr Spurrier to look at them and tell me whether pottery of that type was manufactured in the neighbourhood; the bowls had been made on a potter's wheel but the general type was one with which Dr Spurrier was not acquainted and he suggested that they might have been made in Muscat and have been thrown overboard from a passing dhow.

As soon as we had completed our first trawl we steamed in towards Pemba Island into ground of about 325 fathoms for another cast of the trawl, which in the meantime had been repaired (Station 109). Everything went off well, though at the commencement the jerking of the dynamometer indicated that we were trawling over rough ground. Towards the end of the trawl the echo-sounder showed that we were approaching a bank; we could clearly see the record of the echo coming back from the bank, which was some little distance away from us, and we tried to manoeuvre the ship so as to avoid it, but our efforts were not crowned with success and eventually we passed right over it. The strain on the dynamometer rose from 10 to 17 cwts but that was the only appreciable effect.

When we had got the trawl safely back on board we steamed towards Pemba Island to a new anchorage for the night in Port George. Our course to the anchorage lay up a narrow inlet with coral reefs on either side and it was very interesting to see, dotted over the reef and especially near the extreme edge of it, several small islets covered with thick vegetation but with the sides so eroded by wind and wave action that the general shape of each islet was like a mushroom with a markedly overhanging top and narrow pedicle. On the inshore side of the reef the islands or the mainland were all fringed with small vertical cliffs, or in places by overhanging ledges, and it is clear that there is a great deal of erosion going on here in spite of the protection of the reef; in one island the base of the pedicle was hollowed out in a series of small caves and in another there was an actual perforation right through the base. After steaming up the creek past the reefs we anchored off the village and some of us went ashore for a visit, and were all much struck by the general cleanliness both of the village and of the inhabitants.

Early the next morning we left the shelter of our anchorage and steamed out into the channel, and as soon as we were outside set our course for the position where we had carried out our last trawl the day before. As we had been rather pressed for time we had carried out this trawl without taking a 14.I.34 sample of the bottom or getting a sample and temperature reading of the deep water and we hoped to fill this gap in our knowledge. As things turned out we did not get a sample of the bottom for the deposit consisted of sand that refused to stay in the tube, but we successfully obtained the water sample and temperature reading.

As soon as this was accomplished we steamed off towards the African coast to our next station (Station 110) in a depth of about 200 fathoms. There was very considerably less wind than we had been experiencing during the last five or six days, so that the sea was almost calm, and we successfully carried out our trawl, though the resulting catch was not very large. As soon as the trawl was back on board we made all preparations for a second trawl with the Agassiz net in about 50 fathoms. During the course of the morning the wind had got up again and the ship was now rolling a good deal and was taking an occasional wave over the bulwark, but we managed to carry on without much inconvenience. The Agassiz net was put over the side about 3 o'clock in 50 fathoms, but almost as soon as it was on the bottom the depth began to shoal and before long we were running into a depth of only 25 fathoms (Station 111). Our course was altered and the depth increased to nearly 90 fathoms, but at this point the trawl caught in some obstruction. The strain on the dynamometer suddenly shot up to a ton and a half and then the net came away from the obstruction with a jerk. It was impossible to say exactly what had happened, but it seemed probably that the rope strop on the bridle had carried away. The strain had fallen almost to nothing and we went on with the trawl, but in a few minutes the strain shot up again and, after varying about 1½ tons for a moment or two, increased to over 2 tons and the strop on the nippers parted and the line ran out. The ship was stopped and we started to haul in the net; when it arrived alongside it was seen that the rope-becket on the trawl frame had parted and the frame itself was considerably bent, while the net itself was badly torn and contained very little.

We then steamed in towards the African coast and made our way between some islands into a sheltered anchorage for the night in Manza Bay, a few miles to the north of Tanga, the roofs of the houses of this town having been clearly visible from the ship as we were carrying out our trawls earlier in the day. As we steamed up to our anchorage we could clearly see that here too most, if not all, of the islands on either side of the channel showed signs of erosion; their edges were all undercut and the islands were in consequence mushroom-shaped, so that, as in the island of Pemba on the opposite side of the channel, there can be little doubt that the sea is slowly but steadily eroding the land away. A little further up the creek in which

14–15.I.34 we were lying was the wreck of a steamer and one wondered how she came to be there, for it seemed hardly likely that a vessel would accidentally run aground in such a sheltered anchorage. One suggestion put forward was that she was a relic of the attack on Tanga during the Great War, but she looked hardly dilapidated enough for an eighteen-year-old wreck.

The next morning, as soon as it was light enough to see, we left our anchorage and steamed out again through the entrance channel to get into water of a depth of 50 fathoms for a haul with the grab. The depth was reached soon after 7 o'clock, and as the grab was already shackled on to the wire on deck it did not take long to put it over the side and send it down. Even so, in these few minutes we had drifted into deeper water and bottom was actually struck at 62 fathoms. The grab brought up an interesing collection of reef-haunting forms, including sponges, corals and alcyonaria, but it was barely down on deck again before we were in 100 fathoms, so it was hurriedly hoisted out and sent down again, this time striking the bottom at a depth of 120 fathoms. Here the bottom consisted of a coarse sand and contained little or no animal life. A third haul with the grab was made in 193 fathoms and this time we got a sample of a grey-green mud, but again with little or no animal life. These three stations were so close to each other that it was clear that the bottom dropped very steeply from the edge of the reef.

On the completion of these hauls the grab was stowed away in its box and preparations were made to carry out a haul with the otter-trawl in about 350 fathoms. There was a little delay in shooting the trawl as the otter boards fouled each other, but they were soon cleared and the trawl was sent down (Station 115). As there was plenty of time and everything appeared to go satisfactorily, the trawl was left down for an hour and a half and we secured a splendid catch; there were at least twenty species of deep-sea fish present and among these were some thirty-eight examples of a species, *Setarches guntheri*, of a lovely red colour. There were also numerous large deep-red prawns and several octopi, as well as thousands of small delicately-coloured ophiuroids (brittle stars) and several large red ones that seemed to be the same species that we had previously obtained in a haul in the Gulf of Aden near Cape Guardafui.

This completed the work that we could do in the sheltered area of Pemba channel, and on the completion of the trawl we steamed northwards to get to our next station off the African coast to the north of Mombasa, where Farquharson wanted to do some survey work, since the 100-fathom line appeared to lie much further off the coast than was shown in the chart, and where the chemists were to commence a hydrological section extending out from the mainland. As soon as we got away from the lee of Pemba Island

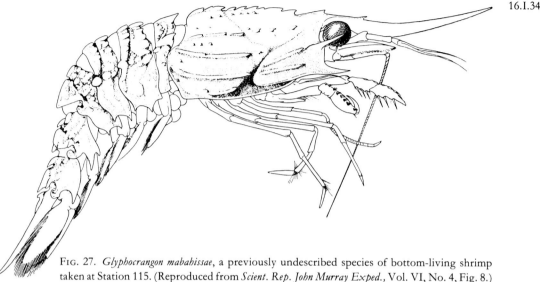

FIG. 27. *Glyphocrangon mabahissae*, a previously undescribed species of bottom-living shrimp taken at Station 115. (Reproduced from *Scient. Rep. John Murray Exped.*, Vol. VI, No. 4, Fig. 8.)

we began to take seas over our bows and the well-deck was awash. During the early part of the night the wind and sea continued to get up and we had a somewhat uncomfortable time, but by the following morning the sea had gone down quite considerably. Unfortunately the sky was overcast, so that though the echo-sounder was working satisfactorily, Farquharson was unable to fix our position with any very great degree of certainty and so we did not succeed in adding very much to the chart.

At 8.30 the ship was stopped for our hydrological station. Work did not proceed very satisfactorily because the drum of the hydrographic winch again started to give trouble, this time jamming so that the forward and reverse gears could not be interchanged. However, after working on it for some time the 2nd Engineer managed to get it going again.

Work in the biological section had been severely handicapped during the last day or two owing to Macan going sick. This was the first sign that our stay in Mombasa had had a serious effect on the health of the ship's company; from now on we had a number of cases of illness owing to several members having picked up malaria there, and at the same time the weather became most trying, so that conditions were by no means conducive towards rapid recovery. We at once instituted a regular course of quinine for everyone on board and thus Dr Faouzi, who acted as Medical Officer to the Expedition throughout the whole voyage, had yet another duty thrown on his shoulders; for unless someone in authority sees that the dose is duly swallowed there are always a number of individuals who quietly and sur-

16–17.I.34 reptitiously discard the dose, for the taste is anything but pleasant and one result is often an attack of indigestion.

On completing the work at Station 116 we steamed eastward to our next position that was to be in 500 fathoms depth. The wind and sea were getting up again and, as we were now steaming about east-south-east and so almost at right-angles to the wind and seas, the *Mabahiss* was rolling heavily. We carried out work at Station 117 and then proceeded still further out in order to get into water of 1,000 fathoms depth. Towards evening of the 16th we were taking quite a lot of water over the rail on both sides and the ship was rolling to such an extent that a number of us were affected. Even Captain MacKenzie was none too happy and about 10 o'clock that night he altered course more to the east, partly to make up for our drift to leeward and partly to bring the seas more on our bow and less on the beam; but at 1 o'clock we were pounding heavily into a head sea and MacKenzie ordered half-speed. We all had a somewhat disturbed night; twice the ship rolled so heavily that there was a crash in the laboratory and something had gone by the board. On the second occasion I found that quite a number of things had cascaded off the laboratory bench, in spite of having been carefully wedged in so that they shouldn't move. Several tubes of specimens were on the deck and the tops of two glass kilner jars had been stove in. I started to clear up the mess and a few minutes later Faouzi came along and gave a helping hand and between us we got things straight again.

We reached our position at 7.30 on the morning of the 17th, so the ship was stopped and we proceeded to carry out our work at Station 118. The chemists did their job first and then we sent down the Agassiz trawl and carried out a haul at a depth of 1,792 metres. In spite of the weather, everything went off satisfactorily and we secured quite a good catch. Macan, unfortunately, was showing no signs of improvement, indeed if anything he was worse. Two of the crew had also gone sick, one with high fever and the second with inflammation of one of his arms. After consulting with Dr Faouzi, it was decided that we should turn round and proceed back to Zanzibar and put our invalids into hospital.[1] My original intention had

---

1. The Expedition had by this time been proceeding for rather more than four months and relations were understandably becoming a little strained, particularly those between MacKenzie and Sewell. During this cruise between Mombasa and Zanzibar things were exacerbated by a combination of bad weather and sickness. Sewell makes relatively light of both factors, but for MacKenzie, with rather little concern for the scientific results they were much more significant: 'The monsoon was exceptionally severe [and] our ship was continually under much water. Pitch and toss, roll and lurch. Station work was

been to steam still further eastward so as to get into water of 2,000 fathoms   17–18.I.34
and there carry out a complete station, both hydrological and biological,
but this would have entailed steaming eastward for fully another day and
would have delayed us getting our sick into hospital for two days. So at 5
o'clock on the evening of the 17th we turned our bows towards the west
and having now both wind and sea with us we made such good progress
during the night that on the morning of the 18th we were already to the
west of Pemba Island and reached Zanzibar at about 2.30 in the afternoon.
The Port Health Officer's Assistant came off to us at once and about half
an hour later took all our sick cases ashore to hospital. In the meantime
Faouzi and I settled down to work in the laboratory, for owing to Macan's
illness there had been an accumulation of bottles and specimens to be dealt
with and stowed away. The results of the last two trawls proved to be most
interesting; most of the crustacea seemed to be identical with species that
the *Investigator* had taken in Indian waters, but among the fish were two
examples of *Ipnops murrayi*, a fish that carries a large luminous organ on the
top of its head. This species was taken by the *Challenger* in both the Pacific
and Atlantic oceans, though at considerably greater depths, but no specimens had ever been obtained in Indian waters by the *Investigator*.

We left Zanzibar again about 4.00 in the evening and steamed round the
south side of the island, passing Chumbi Island on the way. I went up on
the bridge and had a good look at it; my interest in the island was due to

---

attempted with great difficulty, all hands soaking wet, all muscles strained and tired, for
the constant hanging on and attempts at steadying oneself had become laborious.
Steaming at night right into a big sea, and stopping at daylight for another shot at
hauling up the mud and life 6,000 feet below the surface. So severe was the strain on the
little ship that more than once we had to ease her down, and I became worried as to just
how long everyone would stand the extreme discomfort. My cabin, with ports and door
tightly closed, became a steaming hot-house, and even so sealed each wave striking the
door sent gallons of water running through my room, drawers, desk, everywhere. To
get out was often not only difficult but dangerous. . . . The health of the ship rapidly
decreased. In two days, sickness and fever broke out and then it was that malaria took its
grip. Three members were struck down and lay in a serious condition. Macan and the
carpenter ran high temperatures, 105 during the day and only the good Lord knew what
they were at night.'

According to MacKenzie's journal, the decision to put the sick ashore in Zanzibar was
taken by him, with the implication that Sewell would not have done so. He certainly felt
that Sewell's judgement was being adversely affected by the urge to complete the scientific
programme—an urge that was not shared by all the ship's company: 'The call or urge of
science must indeed be strong. Our scientists worked hard and long and to them the
discomfort must have been far greater than it was for us. The ship's crew cared nothing
for science. What was it all for anyway? A natural enough question, and one not even
Sewell could answer with satisfaction.'

18–19.I.34   the fact that the giant robber crab (*Birgus latro*) had been reported to occur in this island and the authorities at the British Museum had asked me to try and visit the island during the course of the Expedition and see whether I could get any evidence of the actual occurrence of the animal. After passing Chumbi Island we steamed in towards the coast and eventually, just after sunset, came to anchor in Menai Bay, about a mile from the shore; here we stayed for the greater part of the night as the Chief wanted to clean out his boiler tubes, and we were all glad to get a quiet night.

At about 6 o'clock the next morning we steamed out into the open sea again towards our next station. At first we were under the shelter of land, so that there was not much wind or sea, and for the first time for several days the stewards did not trouble to put the fiddles on the table in the saloon; but about two hours later we ran out from under the lee of the island and then we got the full force of the wind from the north-east. It was not blowing quite so heavily as it had been, but as the day wore on the strength increased and we experienced a nasty steep and confused sea from the north or north-east.

At a quarter past ten we were in a depth of about 550 fathoms, the bottom according to the echo-sounder going down rather steeply. The ship was stopped and we began work at Station 119. Our first attempt was to get a sample of the bottom and we sent the heavy Bigelow tube down on the hydrographic wire. It appeared to strike the bottom at 1,050 metres and all of us who were watching carefully for the kick on the accumulator were completely deceived, for when we had hauled the tube in again it seemed clear that it could not have been on the bottom at all and this was corroborated by the echo-sounder that by now was giving a deeper reading. So we sent the tube down again and this time from a depth of 1,228 metres we obtained a core of grey-green mud. We then sent the Agassiz trawl down for an hour and got a small though interesting catch (Station 119).

As soon as the trawl was back on deck we steamed eastward towards our next position. During the day the wind had been steadily rising and the sea getting higher until there was quite a steep sea running: as soon as we were well under way, the movement of the ship got much more marked, as one might have expected, and by 9 o'clock at night the *Mabahiss* was decidedly uncomfortable, pitching up and down and every now and then smacking into an extra big sea with a jar that could be felt through the whole ship. All through the night we steadily pounded into the head seas, making our way to the north-east to our next station. Eventually Captain MacKenzie had to slow down, as he was afraid of straining the ship, for as she slammed into each on-coming wave there was a thud and one could feel the ship quiver from stem to stern.

At about 9 o'clock the following morning we were in a depth of about 1,600 fathoms and as there was no likelihood of our getting into much deeper water unless we steamed on for at least another twenty-four hours, when we might be in water of 2,000 fathoms depth, I decided to make the station where we were, though I had hoped for a greater depth. As soon as we stopped, the movement of the ship became much easier, though even so the conditions were difficult and unpleasant for work. The heavy Bigelow tube was shackled on and was put over the side and lowered away; bottom appeared to be struck at a depth of 2,900 metres, which was considerably less than we expected. We stopped and then let the wire run out again and this time we appeared to strike bottom at 3,010 metres. Unfortunately the ship drifted away from the wire and the sideways pull on the davit resulted in this suddenly swinging round inboard and the wire slipped off the wheel of the accumulator and was caught on the sharp edge. It was impossible to swing the davit out again as long as the strain was on the wire, so we had to fix a stop on the wire and take the strain off. The davit was swung out again, but it was then found that the wire was badly damaged, so it had to be cut and a short splice put in before we could haul the Bigelow tube in again. When eventually we got the tube up we found it had struck bottom and had brought up a core of grey *Globigerina* ooze. We then carried on with the hydrological work and Gilson also took a number of hauls with the vertical Harvey net. Finally a reading of the transparency of the water was taken by means of the Secchi disc. When all this was completed the Agassiz trawl was shackled on and sent down (Station 120). We trawled for an hour and then hauled the net in again, but it was a slow process and it was nearly 5.30 in the evening before the trawl was back on board again and the catch was quite a small one. No sooner was the net on board and the wire coiled down on the drum than Captain MacKenzie turned the ship round to head back towards Zanzibar. While we were turning, the seas came broadside on to us and we rolled our weather bulwark under and took a green sea on to the well-deck. Before we knew what was happening we were struggling in about a foot of water to save the catch; fortunately, as I have already mentioned, it was only a small one for otherwise we couldn't have saved it.

We then steamed in towards the coast with the sea on our beam and in consequence we were rolling so much that work in the laboratory was impossible; such things as sorting bowls were promptly rolled off the table and one had to hang on to anything handy to prevent oneself from following suit. On deck, the well-deck was a flood of water for a sea came over the weather bulwark every few minutes.

That night we all had a thoroughly uncomfortable time for the *Mabahiss* was rolling very considerably and on the weather side the seas were fre-

21–22.I.34   quently breaking over the ship. The general wear and tear was now beginning to tell on the ship's company; Thompson was sea-sick, the Chief was feeling none too well (and when the Chief admitted that it means that he was really seedy), and Gilson had an attack of fever.

Early on the morning of the 21st we altered course towards the northwest and got into water of about 600 fathoms or less, and we then stopped the ship and proceeded to carry out work at Station 121 at the eastern end of the channel that runs up between Pemba and Zanzibar islands. When we started work the echo-sounder gave a depth of only 510 fathoms, which was less than we expected, but a sounding with the heavy Bigelow tube showed that this was correct. We then put the Agassiz trawl over the side and lowered it away. As I hoped to get into rather deeper water as the trawl progressed, I let out an extra length of wire, but even so, when we hauled the net in again it was obvious that it had never been on the bottom. It seemed clear that there must be a strong deep current flowing in between the two islands and that this had prevented the light Agassiz net from reaching the bottom.

As soon as the trawl was back on board we steamed towards the northwest, passing round the south end of Pemba Island and eventually reached a quiet anchorage in Kingaje Bay. We were glad to be back in calm waters, for the last three or four days had proved a very trying time for us all; the strong wind and steep seas had made the little *Mabahiss* pitch and roll to an extent that had to be experienced to be believed. Work in the laboratory was almost impossible, and work on deck, when we were trawling, meant that one was perpetually having a shower-bath from spray thrown up over the vessel or even an occasional complete sousing as she shipped a heavier sea.

We left our anchorage just after dawn the following morning and steamed out to the west of Pemba Island into a depth of water of about 400 fathoms; the weather was quite pleasant and either the wind had moderated considerably or else, owing to the shelter of the island, we felt it much less than previously. All preparations were made for a haul with the otter net (Station 122). This was put over the side but, unfortunately, there was some delay in tricing up the trawl wire aft and during the process the two otter boards collapsed on the sea-bottom and somehow or other became twisted round each other, so that when we hauled the net in again after an hour and a half we found the two bridles twisted round each other for about half their length, while one of the wings was also twisted round and round itself. This had prevented the net from opening properly, so that our catch was only a moderate one. As the cod-end came up it looked as if we had taken part of a haystack, for sticking out through the meshes of the net were

hundreds of delicate stalk-like objects, examples of an alcyonarian, *Vir-*
gularia or an allied species, and mixed with these were several examples of a
flower-like form in which the polyps, of a dark-blue colour, were arranged
at intervals up the stem in groups of three.

As soon as the trawl was over we steamed towards Pemba Island, so as
to get into rather shallower water for another trawl. I wanted to get one in
about 250 fathoms and so when we were in a depth of 280 fathoms the ship
was stopped. Here the character of the sea-bottom, as recorded by the
echo-sounder, did not look any too promising, so I decided to use the
4-foot triangular dredge instead of the otter trawl, and it was as well that I
did so (Station 123). As the dredge proceeded, the depth of water got less
and less until eventually we were in only 125 fathoms, and on hauling in it
was found that one of the lugs at a corner of the net to which a chain was
attached had completely broken off, so that the net was hanging by only
two, out of the three, chains; the net itself was badly torn and the greater
part of the contents consisted of stones and concretions that appeared to
have formed on the bottom.

After we had anchored for the night in Mkoani Channel, the District
Officer and the doctor came off to visit us and stayed to dinner.

The next morning, owing to a couple of quiet nights and a more peaceful
day, our invalids were all feeling better. We left our anchorage and once
again steamed out into the open sea through the channel between Pemba
and Zanzibar islands in order to get as near as possible to the spot where
two days previously we had tried to carry out a bottom-trawl but had
failed to get the net to the bottom owing to the strong deep current. This
time we took additional precautions; we used the much heavier Monegasque
trawl, instead of the Agassiz, and tied an additional 50 lb weight to its cod-
end (Station 124). As the net was being sent down we found that there was
a very strong subsurface current setting in a north-westerly direction towards the gap between Pemba and Zanzibar and this swept the net away to
such an extent that the wire ran out from the ship's side at an angle of
about 45 degrees. As more and more wire was paid out the weight of this,
combined with the weight of the net, gradually dragged it down until
eventually it appeared to have reached the bottom and we then began to
trawl. When we hauled in it was clear that the net had actually been on the
bottom for part, at least, of the time, though it was doubtful whether it
was there for the full period of the trawl and the catch was only moderate
in amount.

After completing our work at this station we steamed back again into
the Pemba channel and carried out a haul with the grab, getting a good
sample of a stiff grey clay, with a superficial covering of reddish mud, from

23–28.I.34   a depth of some 400 fathoms. As soon as this was over we returned to our anchorage of the previous night and a little later Captain MacKenzie and I went ashore to dine with Mr Rolleston, the District Officer. During the course of conversation at dinner it transpired that he and I had already met the previous summer in Cambridge. He asked me whether I knew the Director of the Zoological Survey of India in Calcutta, who had the same name. I explained that I actually was the individual that he referred to, whereupon he remarked: 'Oh! then it was you who told me the story of the man who ordered a gin and bitters before dinner in the Athenaeum Club.'

The next morning we left our anchorage and steamed southwards to Zanzibar, carrying out a haul with the grab in 100 fathoms on our way, and thus completing our work in this area. We reached port that afternoon and I was glad to learn that our invalids were progressing satisfactorily and would in all probability be able to rejoin us before we sailed for the Seychelles. We stayed in Zanzibar for a week, during which we were able to see something of the town; from our anchorage on the south side of the town we got a view of bungalows with red roofs standing back among the trees, from the top of one of which the Union Jack was flying to denote that it was the official residence of the Resident. A little to the west were square blocks of buildings rising from the top of the beach and a stone landing jetty, that was, however, only serviceable at high tide; at low tide even a small boat could not get in to it and one had either to be carried out to the boat or else walk along a wooden plank that was propped against the bow of the boat and that thus provided a steep and singularly insecure footing down to the sandy beach.

The town itself struck one as being clean and well-kept; the streets are very narrow and are only just wide enough for a motor to pass along, but many of the houses are provided with magnificent carved wooden doors, some of them studded with brass spikes that are kept highly polished and gleam like gold in the bright sunlight. The north and east part of the town is occupied by a perfect rabbit-warren of a native bazaar, in which the streets are only just wide enough for a rickshaw, while on either side are innumerable small shops, the chief contents of which appeared to be cheap Japanese goods.

As I have already mentioned, I was anxious to get to Chumbi Island to try and get evidence of the existence there of the giant robber crab and the Assistant Port Officer, Captain Somers, very kindly arranged to take me there, so on the morning of the 28th at 7.30 he called for me and took Lieutenant Badr and myself off in his motor boat. Somers was going down that way for a morning's fishing and on the way down he told me that the crab was quite well-known from some of the neighbouring islands, speci-

28.1.34

mens having been taken at Koshani Island on the west side of Pemba and two had been taken at Muona-Muona lighthouse, one example having actually climbed up to the light itself during the night. When Badr and I first landed on the island the tide was low, so we took the opportunity of walking right round it and of examining the coastline. Everywhere the island consists of raised coral-rock and on all sides, but especially on the south-east and east, this is being eroded away to such an extent that in places the rock overhangs the beach by as much as 5 to 15 feet, while the face of the cliff provides a home for numerous *Chiton*. At the foot of this cliff there is a smooth glacis of eroded rock, covered in places with a thin stratum of sand and worn into numerous potholes and small pools. Below low-water level the reef is largely composed of sand or eroded coral-rock and is much overgrown by sea-weed. I could see but little live coral on the reef itself, though in places on the east or open-sea side there were a few small isolated colonies of a species of *Coeloria*. The pools on the reef contained a certain amount of weed and showed the usual fauna, with numerous small hermit crabs on the smooth glacis and small blennies in the pools, while the common locust shrimp, *Gonodactylus chiragra*, and the red-eyed reef crab were conspicuous.

The surface of the island is composed of very rough coral-rock that has weathered into jagged points and holes and is overgrown with thick jungle, a common ingredient being a species of *Euphorbia*, the branches of which are set with long, stout and extremely sharp spines. Searching for any signs of the robber crab in such surroundings was not easy and though we did our best the only result was a rapid destruction of both skin and clothing. The lighthouse keepers on the island, however, seemed to know the animal quite well and said that it often came to the lighthouse at night, presumably attracted by the light. They promised to bring a specimen to the ship the following morning but, alas, never did so.

During our stay in the harbour the weather improved considerably and the surface of the sea, especially in the anchorage, was quite smooth. On 25 and 26 January there were thousands of examples of a jelly-fish, *Aurelia* sp., floating on or near the surface and, where the wind drifted against the ship's side, there were hundreds of them packed together so closely that they were touching. The prevalence of this jelly-fish at this time of the year appears to have been widespread, for Mr Latter, whom I later met in Colombo, told me that on his way out, when in the neighbourhood of Cape Guardafui on 5 February, he had passed 'through shoals of pink jelly-fish off the Somali coast (both before and after passing Cape Guardafui) and a few were seen on the following day, though then only at considerable intervals'. It seems probable that these were the same species that were so

28–30.I.34   abundant in Zanzibar harbour and it would be interesting to know whether the appearance of enormous shoals of this species is an annual occurrence.

The day before we were due to sail we received an intimation from the Sultan of Zanzibar that he would be pleased to receive the members of the Expedition, and especially the Egyptian members, at a private audience at 10 o'clock the following morning. That morning Captain MacKenzie and the Chief Engineer, our four Egyptian Coast-guard Service Officers, and myself, all in full uniform, together with our two Egyptian scientists, left the ship and were driven to the palace where we were received by His Highness.

As soon as we got back to the ship preparations were made for our departure and we sailed for the Seychelles at noon. Unfortunately, Macan had had a relapse of his malaria and so, after all, we were unable to take him with us and he had to be left behind in hospital for further treatment; but we arranged for him to be sent over to Colombo as soon as he was fit enough to travel, so as to rejoin us there before we left after our refit for our cruise through the Maldive Archipelago.

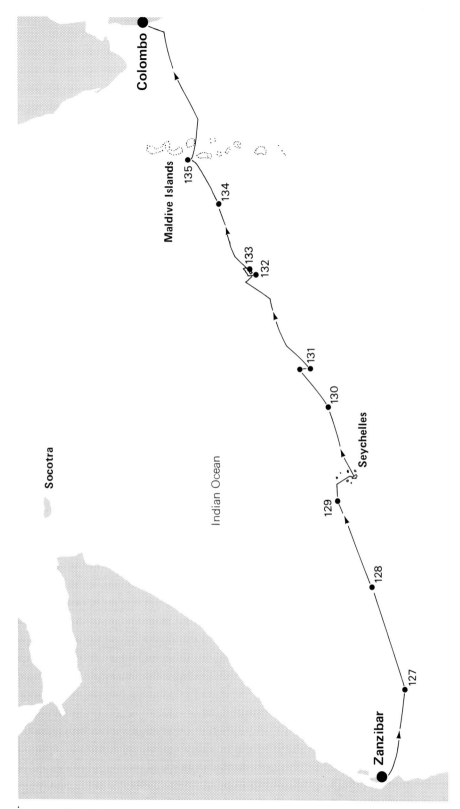

F<small>IG</small>. 28. Track chart, Cruise 7: Zanzibar–Colombo. Station numbers are indicated.

Chapter 8

Zanzibar to Colombo via the Seychelles

30.I–1.II.34 WE steamed out of Zanzibar harbour at noon on 30 January and at first, as we ran south under the lee of the island, things were quite comfortable; but about half past three in the afternoon we got out from the shelter of the land into the open sea and the *Mabahiss* began to roll a good deal with the sea on her port beam. As soon as we got under way Faouzi and Mohamed got busy in the laboratory and soon had everything stowed away, so that there were no loose bottles or other glass gear to go rolling about the bench or the deck. We seemed to be making very good progress, though it was too soon to form any opinion of what the *Mabahiss* would do when we encountered the strong current of the north-east monsoon. While bathing in Zanzibar harbour some of us had dived down in order to have a look at the ship's bottom below the waterline, and we were surprised to find very much less growth than we had expected. It seemed probable that our stay in Mombasa had killed off a certain amount of the weed, for a fairly large stream flows out into the upper end of the harbour and this must bring down a considerable quantity of fresh water, especially when it rains, and thus reduce the salinity of the water to an extent that might well be harmful to marine life.

We had a very disturbed night on the 30th, for the *Mabahiss* was rolling considerably and there were several crashes in the laboratory, in spite of our care in stowing things away. To add to the general discomfort a lot of water accumulated on the floor of the laboratory and three times during the night I was awakened by the sound of water swishing to and fro and had to turn out and swab it up.

The next morning the sea was considerably less and the movement of the ship was consequently easier. All that day we steamed on towards the south-east and after another somewhat disturbed night we reached the position that we had fixed on for our next station (127) at 7.15 on the morning of 1 February, so the ship was stopped and we started work. The echo-sounder had not been working very satisfactorily, partly owing to the disturbed state of the sea, but it indicated that we were in a depth of about 2,231 fathoms, so we shackled on the heavy Bigelow tube and sent it down. In the meantime Thompson had started work on the other side of the ship taking water samples and temperatures, and everything seemed to be going satisfactorily. However, as we were heaving in the bottom tube the hydrographic winch suddenly stopped with a jerk and examination showed that the drum had cracked right across, thus putting a complete stop to any further deep work. All through the course of the Expedition we had been having trouble with this drum, especially when we were trying to work a deep station. It had started to spread when we were trying to work a station to the south-east of Socotra and we had had it strengthened while we were in Karachi, and now it had cracked across and so couldn't be used at all. As we still had some 700 metres of wire out with an Ekman reversing-bottle and the heavy Bigelow tube at the end, we had to get a stop put on the wire and take the strain off by hauling in a length of the wire by means of a block and tackle. When this had been done we cut through the wire and, having made a loop on the end, we attached this to the spare drum of the winch and hauled the rest of the wire and the instruments on board again. In the meantime we ran the extra length of trawling wire, that was on the small drum of the trawling winch, on to the main drum so that this drum should be ready to take the hydrographic wire as soon as we could get the drum of the hydrographic winch to turn. But this was by no means an easy job, for when the drum cracked right across the two parts opened up and jammed hard against the brake so that it couldn't be moved. As we were quite unable to get on with any further work until we had completed all these arrangements, we got under way again, abandoning further work at this station, and proceeded towards the Seychelles. The change in our course now brought the sea on to our port bow and the movement of the ship was much easier. Most of the 2nd was spent in getting the length of hydrographic wire off the broken drum on to the trawling winch; this was completed by 4 o'clock in the afternoon and all that had then to be done was to splice the two lengths of wire together where we had had to cut them the day before. This was done as soon as it was light enough to see on the morning of the 3rd and at 11 o'clock the ship was stopped for work at Station 128. We took a sounding with the heavy Bigelow tube and got a good core of the bottom, which consisted of a cream-coloured ooze, from a depth of 2,250 fathoms and then carried out a complte hydrographic ex-amination of the water at all intermediate depths. As the somewhat cum-brous trawl winch could not be run at the same speed as the lighter hydro-graphic winch, we were rather longer than usual in completing our work, but this did not matter very much as during the previous day we had

3–6.II.34   struck a favouring current and so had made rather better progress than we had anticipated. The weather had also improved very considerably; the wind had dropped and there was now very little movement in the ship. Indeed, if it had not been for a swell from the north-east we should have been running on an even keel.

While work was in progress I kept a look-out for any planktonic organisms that might be floating on the surface, but on this occasion I saw nothing at all. The colour of the sea was a deep blue and the transparency of the water was greater than it had been previously, which in itself indicated that there was little or nothing in the way of animal or vegetable life present in it. From time to time we could see a few flying-fish of a small variety darting out of the water, but their numbers were very small.

Later in the afternoon there were several birds flying round the ship and this seemed to indicate that we were once more getting near land, and just before sunset we could see Bird Island in the Seychelles group silhouetted against the sky on the horizon, though it was still about 50 miles away.

We commenced work at our next station (129) at 7 o'clock on the morning of the 5th, and as soon as that was completed we crossed the edge of the Seychelle Bank and steamed in towards Port Victoria in Mahé Island. We were off the port by midnight and anchored there to wait for the dawn. Early on the morning of the 6th the pilot came off and took us in to the anchorage. Mahé, the chief port and town of the Seychelles group, is a very picturesque little place; little red-roofed houses are dotted about the lower slopes of the hillside and the mass of the island rises up behind until it meets the clouds, most of the slopes being covered with a dark green foliage, interrupted in places by grey masses and walls of granite rock. Low down near the harbour two larger buildings, the hospital and Government House, are conspicuous. The entrance channel is narrowed and tortuous and at one point runs near to one of the smaller outlying islands; coral reefs jut out from the shores and one steers a winding course between marks that indicate their limits. We finally anchored close in to the jetty, with a large dhow not far off, while several trading schooners and brigs were tied up to the jetty or were lying in the inner harbour. A number of inhabitants were already out fishing off the edge of the reef for mackerel (*Caranx*) in their canoes (*pirogues*), and as soon as we had been given pratique by the Port Health Officer, who is also the Medical Officer in charge of the hospital, several boat-loads of enterprising individuals came off and tried to sell us curios; among these were such things as the double coconut, walking sticks made of the vertebral column of sharks and a small specimen of

the giant robber crab that the owner informed me had been captured on
Aldabra Atoll.

Later in the morning several of us went ashore and paid our official call
on the Administrator, Dr Walsh, whose real appointment was that of Chief
Justice but who was acting as Governor while his junior officer carried out
the judicial functions. Having paid our respects we were taken to the
Club and there met Captain Lanier, who commands one of the coasting
brigs that ply between the Seychelles and Mauritius and who was acting as
Port Officer and Pilot during the absence from duty, owing to ill-health, of
the real incumbent. He very kindly arranged to take some of us for a drive
in the evening to show us something of the island and we drove towards
the south end of the island for some 17 miles. The road was by no means
good in places and at times the gradient was so steep that the car, which
was a 6-horse-power Fiat, had considerable difficulty in getting to the top
even in low gear. At one point, where we had to stop to allow another car
to pass us, it looked as if we should go backwards down the hill, but
MacKenzie hung on to the handbrake and at the crucial moment, when the
engine got going again, let go and we managed to climb the rest safely.
The scenery was very fine; for most of the way the road ran close to the
shore and all along there were great grey boulders of granite sticking up
among the trees or dotted along the foreshore, where they alternated with
stretches of white sand or occasional clumps of mangrove trees, with their
queer basket-like roots, while a little offshore ran a coral reef that was
covered with a quantity of weed of various kinds. Nearly every available
square yard of the land is cultivated and is covered with coconut palms,
which furnish most of the commerce of the island. Scattered all along the
road were houses and occasional villages, each with its Roman Catholic
church and its police station. The great majority of the inhabitants are
of very dark complexion and appear to have a strong admixture of the
African element in their make-up; they all speak a French patois that
those of us who could talk French found very difficult to understand
when they were talking among themselves, but when they spoke to us
they were much clearer and more distinct, though they pronounce the
J or G like a Z.

The next morning four of us went for a drive in a car that our agent had
very kindly put at our disposal. This time we went over to the north side
of the island and visited the wireless station that was erected during the
war and was bought in 1929 by a private individaul who had a scheme for
picking up the broadcast news and re-broadcasting it locally; apparently the
scheme had not been a success. We stayed and chatted for a time with
Captain Fane, who was managing the plant for the owner who was away

7–9.II.34   somewhere in Africa, and then we returned to the ship and later lunched at Government House.[1]

All day since breakfast we had been taking in coal, a supply of 50 tons having been sent down especially for us to ensure that we didn't run short during our long trip from Zanzibar to Colombo. This was completed about half past three and in the evening we were visited by the head of the Eastern Telegraph Company and one of his assistants, who were anxious to have a look round the ship. Farquharson demonstrated the working of the echo-sounder, which interested them very much for they had very kindly given us their assistance in carrying out certain repairs.

The Seychelles are generally regarded as a beachcomber's paradise for living is dirt cheap. Fish appear to swarm on the reefs and in the water just off them, and I heard that there was a scheme afoot to establish a fish-curing and canning industry in the island so as to provide some other means of livelihood beyond the usual coconut plantations, but the chief difficulty would be in finding a market for the produce, and I doubt whether it could be made to succeed.

At about 9.30 on the morning of the 8th we picked up our anchor and steamed out of the harbour. The weather was wonderful with hardly any wind and the only movement in the ship was a slight dip to the swell that was rolling in from the north-east. There was no sign of the north-east monsoon and we all hoped that the high winds that we had been experiencing off the African coast and that they had also had in the Seychelles, where the velocity had attained as much as 60 miles an hour, were its concluding effort. For the time being we also had a surface current with us so that we got along quite well.

The morning of the 9th was cloudy with a little rain and at 9 o'clock the ship was stopped and we commenced work at our station in a depth of

1. MacKenzie's account of the visit to the Seychelles is much more typical of the sailor than is that of Sewell, for it was clearly one of the best runs ashore of the whole Expedition: 'It has been said that once one of HM ships called at the Seychelles to spend a day but stayed a week. We called to spend four hours taking on coal but stayed forty-four'. The Seychelloises were particularly impressive: 'The Seychelles girls, what sailor has not heard of them? Tall and dark with the vivacity of their race, the latest Paris and London models displayed on slim and graceful figures, a life-long mannequin parade, each one prettier than the other. . . . Such a charming accent, but Lord what hairy legs.'

But the hospitality of the local officials was even more overwhelming and MacKenzie's journal gives the impression that, for those whose religion allowed them to participate, the Seychelles stay was one long series of receptions with no shortage of drink which they were reluctant to leave. ' "Must we go? Can't another night be spent ashore?" was the cry all round. "No," I said, "We cannot stay, we've got to go. Colombo lies ahead." "The skipper's married and doesn't care, but we'll come back to Mahé." '

2,368 fathoms. This was completed by about 4.30 in the afternoon and we then proceeded on our course towards our next station (131) that was to occupy us for some twenty-six hours. We reached the position at about 5.30 in the evening of the 10th and before we commenced our scientific work we carried out sea-boat practice. Work began at about 5.45 and for the whole of the next day we drifted quietly, taking observations at intervals of six hours. During the night, in addition to the chemical work, we carried out a haul with the mid-water nets and secured a number of interesting fish, some of them with luminous organs, but the most interesting part of the catch were several colonies of *Pyrosoma*, that, as their name indicates, were on this occasion highly luminous. As soon as we had got the catch on board, Faouzi and I took these specimens down to the laboratory and tested them for luminescence; the moment we touched one of the specimens it broke out in a pale greenish light that at first was quite bright, but which decreased in intensity at each application of the stimulus, made by stroking the colony with the fingers, until at last there was no response at all. After a few minutes' rest the power to produce light returned again and there was but little diminution in the intensity of light produced.

During the following day we again carried out a haul with the mid-water nets. The sea was calm and of a deep-blue colour, indicating that there was very little life in the upper levels, and this was corroborated by the Secchi disc that could be seen down to a depth of 34 metres. A few jelly-fish (*Aurelia*), were seen drifting by, as well as a specimen of a pelagic actinian, but otherwise there was little or nothing to be seen. When the nets were sent down there was a light breeze blowing from the north-west, while the surface drift carried the ship towards the south-west, the total result being a drift to the south. As soon as the large 2-metre-diameter net had got down to about 200 metres it began to draw away from the ship in a direction towards the west-north-west, and this lateral movement reached its maximum when the net was down at about 350 metres. As more wire was paid out the wire gradually came back to the vertical up and down position, and the same process was repeated when we were hauling the net in. It seems probable that there was a strong deep current at a depth of about 350 metres setting towards the north-west or west, since the ship was herself drifting towards the south.

The day haul yielded a number of interesting animals from various depths. We again secured a colony of the luminous *Pyrosoma*, as well as several of the same small fishes, but in the large 2-metre-diameter net were two fishes that we had not previously captured. One of these was of moderate size, and its general shape resembled a *Macrurus*, a genus of fish with a prominent snout and large eyes that in past days had earned for it among a succession of Surgeon-Naturalists on the *Investigator* the name of Joe Chamberlain fish, from a supposed resemblance (in profile view) to that eminent statesman. In this instance the gape of jaw was far in excess of anything that I had seen in any species of *Macrurus* and the jaws were armed with a few large fangs. The second fish was a specimen of *Malacosteus indicus* Gunther, that was originally captured by the *Challenger* and was described by Sir John Murray in the narrative of the Expedition, and our specimen agreed exactly with this description, especially in the character of the two luminous organs on the side of the head, the anterior of which is leaf-like in shape and has a very clear red irridescence, while the lower and more posterior organ is slightly angular and of an opaque greenish-yellow colour.

Having completed work at this 26-hour station by about 7 o'clock in the morning of the 13th, we steamed on towards the north-east and during the following night we crossed a slight elevation of the bottom, the depth of water decreasing to about 2,150 fathoms and then dropping again to 2,230 fathoms; this was the depth of water when we started work on our 132nd Station at dawn on the 14th. On this occasion everything went satisfactorily and we took water samples and temperature readings down to a depth of 3,500 metres. As soon as this was completed we shackled on the heavy Bigelow tube and sent it down, getting a good core of the bottom, about 4 feet in length and of a biscuit-colour in the upper half and grey below, from a depth of 4,080 metres. While the sounding was being taken a school of dolphins appeared in the offing; there were quite a number of them and some of them were jumping clear out the water. The majority of specimens were about 6 to 10 feet in length but with the school were two animals of a much larger size; one of these came quite close to the ship and I was about to take a shot of it with the cine-camera when it sheered off and I got nothing. This example was at least 20 feet in length, though in other respects it appeared to resemble the dolphin in general shape and had a dorsal fin of the usual type; it was brown in colour and had a rather pointed snout, like that of a porpoise, so that it was in all probability a specimen of the bottle-nose whale.

We completed work at the station at about 3 o'clock and immediately after got under way again and steamed off in the direction of Kardiva Channel, that runs across the centre of the Maldive Archipelago. At first the depth was more or less constant, but at about 6 o'clock we suddenly ran over a high ridge, the depth shoaling to as little as 858 fathoms. We then altered course and steamed northwards for a spell, crossing the ridge again. It was clear that this was the Carlsberg Ridge that had been crossed, a little to the south of our present position, by the *Dana* during her voyage

round the world.[1] Unfortunately, at this stage in our voyage we couldn't   15–16.II.34
spend very much time in mapping the ridge, but we decided to steam first
east, then south and then west again for periods of three hours so as to
cover as much of the ground as was possible in the time that we could
spare. However, during this period we did not again get into such shallow
water and for the greater part the depth remained about 1,500 fathoms. As
we steamed east again on the 16th the depth gradually increased until we
were in a depth of about 1,700 fathoms and the ship was stopped so that
we might carry out a trawl on what we supposed was the eastern slope of
the ridge. The chemists first carried out observations on the water conditions down to a depth of 3,000 metres and we then tried to get a sample of
the bottom with the heavy Bigelow tube. This was sent down in a depth,
as given by the echo, of some 3,500 metres, but the tube came up empty.
We then sent down the Monegasque trawl (Station 133), paying out nearly
all the available wire, namely 4,250 metres; this was if anything rather on
the short side, but I hoped that by carefully regulating the pace of the trawl
we might with luck get a bottom haul. Unfortunately there was a strong
surface current running from the north-east and a breeze from the north-
west, so that it was very difficult to regulate the pace. However, when we
got the trawl back again it was clear that it had been on the bottom for at
least a part of the time, for the chief ingredient of the catch consisted of a
number of irregularly shaped blocks of a black stone, that looked like coal,
but which a subsequent examination by a geologist in Colombo showed to
be dolerite, one of the basalt series of rocks and of volcanic origin.[2]
There was no trace of any mud or ooze in the trawl net and it seemed
probable that our failure to get a bottom sample with the Bigelow tube
was due to the bottom being mostly, if not entirely, composed of this rock.
With the stones were a few deep-sea animals, such as several colonies of
white hydroid, pieces of a sponge and three deep-sea sea-urchins of the
genus *Phormosoma*, all of which must have come from the bottom, while

1. In retrospect the Carlsberg Ridge was the most important topographic feature surveyed
during the Expedition, because of its significance in the theories of plate tectonics and
sea-floor spreading developed during the 1950s and 1960s (see R. W. Girdler, *Deep-Sea
Research*, Vol. 31 (6–8A), 1984, pp. 747–62). This passage in Sewell's journal was clearly
written some time later, for at the time they were unaware that the ridge had already
been named and initially they called it the 'Murray Ridge' (see Part 5, p. 313).
2. J. D. H. Wiseman's analysis of these basalt fragments, published in the Scientific
Reports of the Expedition, was the first comprehensive account of such rocks from a
mid-ocean situation and demonstrated that they were quite different from the continental
basalts from India which Sewell had expected them to resemble. Moreover, the gully
from which the samples was obtained was later recognized as the axial valley of the ridge,
typical of divergent plate boundaries (see Part 5, page 313).

other specimens, such as fish and prawns, might have been captured on the way up.

As soon as the trawl was back on deck we steamed on our course again, expecting the depth of water to increase steadily, but during the following night we again ran across a high ridge, the depth of water decreasing this time to 950 fathoms, before it dropped very irregularly to about 2,000 fathoms. It thus seemed clear that we had not carried out our series of observations on the eastern slopes of the Carlsberg Ridge, as we had thought, but in a deep gully on the top of the ridge.

During the night we developed trouble with our electric light. While we were still taking the catch out of the net all the lights in the ship suddenly went out and we had to carry on as best we could by the light of hand torches. For quite a while the fuses blew out as fast as the electrician put them in and the engineers were kept busy trying to locate the cause of the trouble. At first all the blame was put upon the chemists, who had an electric heater making distilled water in the laboratory, but after this had been completely disconnected the lights still went out, so the engineers had to find some other cause. The next one that they settled on was the echo-sounding machine, but this was also shown not to be the cause, and what they ultimately decided to be the *fons et origo* of the trouble I do not know, but eventually they got the lights to work again.

We reached the position of our next station (134) at about 6 o'clock on the 17th; but as the Chief wanted to clean his boiler tubes we just drifted until this work was completed. At about 9.30 we started work taking water samples and temperature readings, working with various instruments on either side of the ship and everything going satisfactorily until about the middle of the morning, when the two wires managed to get twisted round each other somewhere beneath the ship, but we managed to get them clear again after a little while. As soon as the hydrological work was over we sent down the heavy Bigelow tube and took a sounding. We struck bottom at 4,305 metres and obtained a splendid core, 62 inches in length, of a reddish-yellow soft ooze, the type of deposit that is termed red clay; Sir John Murray, in his account of the bottom deposits of the Indian Ocean, has shown that there is a patch of this in the north-eastern part of the Arabian Sea. It seems probable that its presence in this locality is correlated with the existence of the Carlsberg Ridge that separates the Arabian Sea basin into two regions to the north-east and south-west respectively; it is the former that is floored with the red-clay deposit.

The weather was still very good and there was hardly any sea running at all, just an easy swell from the north; as a result the plankton seemed to have come up nearer to the surface and was concentrated at a higher level than in rough weather. Another sign of the fine weather was the presence round the ship, while we were working at the station, of a large shark which had a blunt snout and was of a general brown colour with lighter patches on the belly and the tops of the pectoral fins; its length I estimated to be about 10 to 11 feet.

Late in the evening of the 18th we reached the position of our 135th Station; the last one that we were to do before we put into Colombo for our refit. It was essential that we should get our work over by 7 o'clock the following morning, for as there are no lights on any of the Maldive Atolls we had to get through Kardiva Channel by daylight, and we had to allow a good margin since we were certain to find a strong current running through the channel towards the west and so against us. We started work at about 8.45 and continued all night. The chemists carried out their part of the programme first and then Faouzi and I took over and carried out a deep trawl with the Monegasque net. As time was then getting short, things had to be hurried somewhat, but we managed to trawl for an hour and get the net back on board again by three minutes past seven. The catch was such a poor one that there was some doubt whether the net had been on the bottom during the whole time. On the other hand, our catches off Bombay had also been comparatively poor and it seems probable that the western slopes of the continent of India to the north and the Maldive Archipelago to the south are a naturally barren area.

As soon as the trawl was completed we headed for Kardiva Channel, but as we had drifted some 17 miles towards the south-west during the time that we were working at the station, we were rather later in reaching the western end of the channel than we had expected. On our way through we passed quite close to several of the atolls and islands; these are a very pretty sight with their white beaches of coral sand and a belt of almost emerald-green water over the outer reef, while the islands themselves are covered with dark-green vegetation. Between tea and sunset we passed close to Malé, the island residence of the Sultan of the Maldives and the centre of trade for the whole archipelago; there were a couple of Maldive brigs and several dhows lying off the island in the lagoon. The island itself appeared to be almost wholly occupied by buildings and houses, and the town is enclosed within an almost continuous city wall. On an open piece of ground, outside the city wall and between it and the sea-beach, a football match was in progress, while somewhere in the island someone was flying a kite. Like all these coral islands, the land is thickly covered with trees and bushes, conspicuous among which are the tall palm trees. Just as we ran out of the channel into the open water of the Laccadive Sea that lies between the Maldives and India we passed close to another big school of porpoises

19–22.II.34   that were jumping out of the water. During our next cruise through the Maldive Archipelago we were to see quite a number of such schools and it seems possible that these animals congregate in the sheltered waters in and around the atolls in the early spring months for the purposes of breeding.

For the next two days we steamed across the Laccadive Sea towards Ceylon and reached Colombo harbour about 5 o'clock on the afternoon of 22 February and, soon after, fires were drawn in preparation for our refit. The Port Medical Authorities at once came off and inspected the ship and, as we had been away from our home port for over six months, they insisted that before we could be dry docked for inspection the ship had to be fumigated to get rid of the rats. At first they said that they would do this with sulphur dioxide gas, but I protested strenuously as this would corrode all our scientific apparatus that was made of metal and would contaminate all our chemicals in the laboratory. After considerable discussion and argument, they eventually agreed to fumigate us with hydrocyanic acid gas, though they had never before done this with a ship but had on several occasions used this gas for fumigating 'go-downs' that were used for the storage of grain. Arrangements were made to evacuate the ship and the fumigation was then carried through without any mishap. As soon as the fumigation was over the ship was put in the hands of our agents for a complete overhaul and refit, and the crew were turned on to repaint the cabins, while a firm of engineers undertook the job of casting a new drum for the hydrographic winch. While all this work was in progress we had to live on shore and I had arranged with our Committee at home that I could send my scientific staff up to the hills for a week's rest and holiday. Thompson, Gilson and Mohamed went off to Kandy for a week, while Dr Faouzi took the opportunity of going for a visit to Madras, in order to see something of the work of the Government Fishery Department there.

Captain MacKenzie, the Chief and I all went to the Grand Oriental Hotel, while Lloyd Jones and our four Egyptian Officers went to the Bristol Hotel. Captain MacKenzie was joined by his wife, who had arrived in Colombo the day before we did on her way to England from Australia. MacKenzie's health had been none too good during our last cruise, but with his wife to look after him and with freedom from anxiety and responsibility, he rapidly improved.[1] After six months of cramped confinement on board we all found life on shore extremely pleasant and the

1. MacKenzie's journal for the passage from the Seychelles to Colombo is disjointed, rambling and highly critical of the scientists, and particularly of Sewell. MacKenzie was clearly quite ill and was feeling the strain of his responsibilities and of being confined in

swimming baths at the Galle Face Hotel were a great attraction; too great, as it turned out, for later both the Chief and I suffered as a result of bathing either too frequently or too long, he with inflammation of the ears and I with a most dreadful cold of the regular influenza type with infection of the nasal sinuses.

A few days after we got in and while our party was up in Kandy, Farquharson, the Chief and I hired a car for the day and motored up to see them and something of the country. We left Colombo at about 7 o'clock in the cool of the morning and at first we drove through the coconut planta-tions on the low-level ground, but after about an hour we began to climb up and were soon among the tea and rubber plantations. We stopped for half an hour or so at Peredenya to have a look at the Botanical Gardens and reached Kandy at about 11 o'clock. After lunch the Chief and I went off to see some of the sights of the place; we first drove round Lady Houghton's Drive and then along several other hillside roads, all of which seem to have been named after the wives of former Governors—Lady Gordon's Drive, Lady Macallum's Drive, etc.—and from each of these we got a splendid view of the country round. After that, we went down to the river to see the elephants attached to the Temple of the Sacred Tooth having their daily bath. As they lay motionless on their sides, they looked for all the world like great rock boulders in the stream; later on they were put through their paces and tricks by their mahouts and were duly rewarded with pieces of sugar cane, whilst the mahouts were rewarded with the usual baksheesh. When this performance was over we went on and visited the Sacred Temple itself; unfortunately the Sacred Tooth in its special shrine was not open for inspection, so we did not see it, and the rest of the Temple had little or nothing to recommend it—the shrines seemed very tawdry and the frescoes of souls in torment for various earthly offences were dreadfully crude; one came away with the firm conviction that the place wasn't worth seeing. Even the guide who took us round was woefully ignorant; we saw several statues of Buddha in different attitudes, some

---

cramped and uncomfortable conditions. Even after he was feeling better, in Colombo and in the company of his wife, his feelings were still fairly strong. 'Forty men in a bird cage, hop, hop, hop—a blasted iron bird cage. There wasn't room to move. Our wings were clipped and sore, our legs were losing power, and all the exercise for some of us was the wiping of a perspiring body with a filthy towel. . . . Faouzi was alarmed. Something must be done. Nineteen men walked to hospital the first day in. He made a report, a strong one. The Expedition would make or break, it looked like break. . . . "Right," I said, "I'll take the responsibility," the Leader wouldn't. A spell ashore for everyone. All hands off the bird cage. Clean paint and fumigate, smoke her out, blow her through, get her clean. They stayed in Colombo for almost four weeks and sailed greatly invigorated.

reclining, others in the attitude of blessing, the earth-touching attitude and so on, and I asked him in how many different ways the Buddha was portrayed, but he didn't know.

We left Kandy again soon after tea and had a most interesting drive down again to Colombo. The views that one gets as one drives down seem to be much finer than those that one sees on the way up, and it was interesting to watch the gradual change in the vegetation as we got lower and lower until we came out again in the coconut plantations. The last part of the drive was done in the dark and our driver seemed to be very anxious to get us back to our hotel as rapidly as possible so he trod on the juice and took all sorts of risks, until he was roundly sworn at by Farquharson in the best Navy style. The latter part of my stay in port was somewhat marred by my having to pay a visit to the dentist. One of my few remaining molar teeth suddenly started to give trouble, and as I did not relish the idea of going off to sea for a month or so with a doubtful tooth in my head, I went off to have it attended to. The dentist decided that it had better come out, but this was easier said than done and it was over an hour before he had completed the job, by which time the last state of my jaw was worse than the first—and that night I was due to dine at Government House with the Governor, Sir Edward Stubbs. Fortunately, the dinner was such that I could manage to eat a little and his wines were excellent. While we were in Colombo I celebrated my birthday and by a happy coincidence that very morning I received a cable from England congratulating me on being elected a Fellow of the Royal Society, so the double event was duly celebrated that night by a little dinner.

During our stay I was, thanks to Mr Wait, the Acting Chief Secretary to the Government, introduced to the representative of the Government of the Maldives. He not only very kindly gave me a letter of introduction to all the headmen of the various atolls, but on behalf of his government he most kindly undertook to provide the Expedition with a boat during our stay in the Archipelago, so that I could detach a party for magnetic and geodetic work; this latter branch of investigation was to be carried out by Major Glennie, RE, of the Survey of India, who was lent to the Expedition for this purpose and who joined us during our stay in port.[1]

---

1. Glennie made conditions on the *Mabahiss* even more cramped, according to MacKenzie. 'This trip we had three additional members to the crew—Major Glennie, RE, and his two servants. Glennie, who is an expert at swinging pendulums . . . came down to Colombo with a retinue of servants, waggon loads of instruments and gear, and heaven knows how many bearers. The *Mabahiss* wasn't half big enough for him. He'd require at least ten servants and the whole foredeck for gear. The Indian Army officer? Do they, I wonder, brush their own teeth?'

We were due to leave Colombo on the 16th, so on the 14th the *Mabahiss* was hauled up on to the slipway and her bottom was examined, scraped and treated with a coat of anti-fouling composition. On the 15th the Chief took in our supply of coal and got his furnaces going again. As soon as the dynamo was started, Farquharson started the echo-sounder to see that it was running properly and he then found that something had gone very wrong either in the amplifier or in the receiving part of the apparatus. As this couldn't be put right until the following day, we had to postpone our sailing until the 17th, but at any rate this ensured that we didn't go to sea on a Friday!

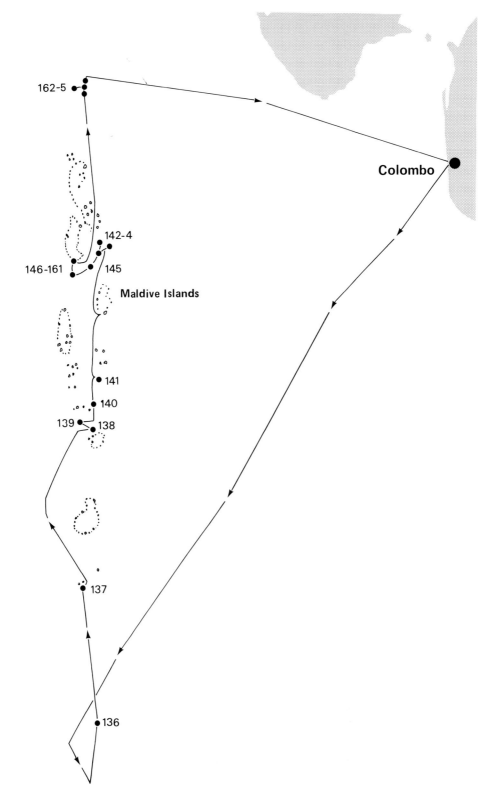

Fig. 29. Track chart, Cruise 8: Colombo–Colombo. Station numbers are indicated.

Chapter 9

The Maldive Archipelago

WE left Colombo late on the morning of 17 March and just as we were getting our anchor in a shore boat came up alongside and I heard myself hailed from it. On looking to see who was calling me I discovered that the man was an old friend of mine from Calcutta, Lieutenant-Commander Dick Collins of the RIM, who was on his way to England on leave and was sailing in the BI Steamer *Modasa* that was anchored just alongside us. But the next minute we were off, so I didn't have time to talk to him for long.

The weather was extremely good and during the next two days we made excellent progress, covering 240 miles in the first day and 235 in the next. What current there was, was with us in our course to the south-west, but most of our increased speed was due to the ship being once again clean below the waterline and to our having taken on Welsh coal in Colombo. We were heading for a point in the deep channel that lies between the southern end of the Maldive Archipelago and the Chagos group, so that we might run a line of soundings through this channel and carry out a hydrological station there. On the run down we crossed a deep gully of about 2,000 fathoms near the south-west corner of Ceylon and then the depth shoaled again, but as we proceeded still further to the south-west the depth gradually increased until it was about 2,400 fathoms. As we neared the southern end of the Maldive ridge the depth again got less until we were in some 1,500–1,600 fathoms and it stayed about this depth for some time. Just when it was wanted, as we were passing between the Maldive and Chagos archipelagos, the echo-sounder gave out, so that we could not tell what the depth was. On examining the apparatus, Farquharson found that the transmitter had cracked and it was necessary to replace this before the apparatus would again function. There did not seem to be any obvious reason why this piece of metal should suddenly have burst; but it seemed probable that it was a result of that curious phenomenon known as fatigue in the metal, for the machine had been running almost continuously for some six months. As changing this would be a long job, he suggested that we should occupy the time by putting in our 136th Station; we were not very far off the position which had been selected for this, so at 7 o'clock on the 21st the ship was stopped and work commenced. While we were in Colombo we had received both the new coil of hydrographic wire and the trawl wire for which I had cabled; during our run down we had been busy getting the hydrographic wire coiled down on the new drum that we had made for the hydrographic winch. We shackled on the heavy Bigelow tube and sent this down and it appeared to strike bottom at a depth of 3,555 metres. This agreed closely with what we expected, judging from the soundings given on the chart, but on hauling in there was not the slightest trace of any bottom deposit on or in the tube. We then carried on with the hydrological work and completed the taking of water samples and temperature readings and then set the bottom tube down again. This time we struck bottom at 3,630 metres which agreed so closely with the first sounding that there could be little doubt that we had struck bottom on that occasion also, but again there was not the least trace of any bottom mud on the sounding tube and I can only conclude that in this channel the bottom is composed of hard rock that is swept clean of all deposit by a strong deep current.

We finished our work at this station by 3 o'clock in the afternoon and almost at the same time Farquharson got the echo-sounder going again, so we then steamed almost due north towards Addu Atoll, the most southerly of the Maldive group, which we were due to reach at about 8 o'clock the next morning.

We approached the atoll in the early hours of the morning of 22 March. All that could be seen at first was a thin dark line stretching across the horizon ahead of us, but as we got nearer this resolved itself into a series of islands, covered with thick vegetation. To the west lay Gan Island, then came a gap and ahead of us was another island, Wiringilli, followed by another wide gap, beyond which lay a small island, followed by a long narrow belt of land that stretched away to the northward. The westerly islands were thickly covered with trees, but on the east side these were replaced by the graceful palm trees, springing up either in clumps or singly from a low bush scrub. Each island was fringed by a shelving beach of white sand, outside which the shallow water over the reef showed a lovely emerald-green, bordered in its turn by a belt of white where the rollers, even on a calm day, break in a mass of foam. All the islands are low-lying and flat, their topmost level being only a few feet above high-water mark.

At about 7 o'clock we steamed into the gap on the south side of the atoll

22.III.34   between Gan and Wiringilli islands, where the chart shows a channel with a depth of water of about 10 fathoms. We got well into the channel, the leadsman giving 10 fathoms of water, but one could clearly see patches of coral growing on the bottom and MacKenzie didn't like the look of it, so we turned and ran out to sea again. We then steamed eastward past Wiringilli Island and finally entered the lagoon through the channel between Wiringilli and Mulakadu islands, where there is a greater depth of water. During our run into the western of the two channels I could clearly see the little isolated island on the outer reef off Gan Island that is shown on the chart originally drawn by Moresby one hundred years ago, so that in spite of the constant erosion that is going on in most of these coral islands of the Indian Ocean, this little islet has not yet been destroyed.

Ahead of us, as we passed through the entrance channel, lay the quiet waters of the lagoon, while stretching away on either hand in a semi-circle towards the north was a chain of islands of very varying sizes. As we approached the northern part of the lagoon a series of small islands, stretching westward ahead of us, marked the northern limit of the reef, that in this atoll is for the most part free from land, only one small islet—Bushey Island—marking the patch of reef that intervenes between the two northern entrances. In the north-east corner of the lagoon beyond the lagoon reef we could see several boat sheds and a few houses dotted along the top of the beach and sheltered by the trees.

We anchored in the north-east corner of the lagoon and soon after both the dinghy and the motor boat were in the water. Farquharson and Sparks went off in the dinghy to try and locate a channel through the lagoon reef by which the motor boat could get in to the island, and having found one they put down a buoy to mark the passage. In the meantime all Major Glennie's gear for his pendulum observations was stowed, in readiness to be sent ashore, in the motor boat, and about 11.30 he, Captain MacKenzie, Thompson and I went off and met the dinghy as she was returning. We then took her in tow and steamed in through the reef, which in this corner of the lagoon is decidedly patchy in character. There was a line of dead coral showing well above the water and running about north and south along the edge of the reef, and having steamed in past this we turned our nose in towards some boat sheds on the northern end of Heratera (or Putali) Island. As we approached the shore a native boat put off from the beach to meet us; in this was the headman of the village and I duly presented my letter of introduction from the Maldivian Representative in Colombo. As it was low tide there wasn't sufficient water to allow the motor boat to get close in to the beach, so all Glennie's gear had to be transferred to either the Maldive boat or the dinghy and be ferried across the interval.[1]

It was nearly noon by the time that I got ashore with the last lot of Glennie's gear, and by that time his tent was up and he was ready to commence his observations, so I wandered off to investigate as much of the island as was possible in the time at my disposal. Glennie had established himself at the north end of the island of Putali and between this and the next island to the north, Midu-Huludu, there is a channel connecting the outer reef with the lagoon. The seaward end of this channel forms a wide bay, the floor of which is composed of coral fragments thickly overgrown with a grass-like weed and across which there is a line of 'coral horses', marking the old position of the island face before erosion had broken up the land and created the wide bay, which is now a home for all sorts of animals; small crabs were scuttling about among the coral debris, while lying half concealed among the weed were long mottled holothurians, *Synapta*, and a few shorter and stouter black ones, (?)*Holothuria atra*; numerous small fish were swimming about in the weed and two or three fine eels of a mottled grey colour were also seen. Having had lunch with Glennie and Thompson at the former's camp, I wandered southward along the island Putali. The northern end of the island is under coconut plantation and then comes a series of lakes, some of which contain water that is nearly or quite fresh, while others are somewhat brackish. The water in these lakes is shallow and gets so heated up by the sun that its temperature was high enough to be unpleasant to the feet, but even so there is a large fauna, especially numerous being a species of mollusc, *Pyrazus palustris*, the shells of which form a fringe around the margin. Further southward some of these lakes seem to have dried up and all that was left to mark their original sites were some wide expanses of dried mud covered with dead mollusc shells. Along the seaward side of the island there is a raised rim of coral fragments, the hurricane beach, that in places appears to have been recently added to, for several white masses of coral were scattered over the top of the older black fragments, while in others the sea seems to be gradually breaking through into one of the lakes. All this southern end of the island

1. MacKenzie was greatly taken by the Maldives and the Maldivians and devoted the final eight pages of his journal to his shore visits here. He was impressed by the friendliness of the people and was surprised by their relatively high technology. Wandering around alone on Addu Atoll, he was taken to the house of the headman and given soda water from a machine, he was cooled by a petrol-engined punkah and shown navigational instruments lovingly cared for. Finally: 'Books on navigation were produced. Nories tables, so well known to all sailors, but the surprise of all was Brown's *Nautical Almanac* for 1934. The very almanac we had tried so hard to get in Bombay, and here they had it in the Maldives.'

22–23.III.34   is covered with a scrub jungle that is so dense that unless one keeps to certain used paths it is difficult, if not impossible, to force one's way through. The lagoon beach of the island is in places undergoing erosion, for a line of sandstone was exposed along a stretch of the beach and the bushes at the top were being undermined and their roots exposed.

Having explored as much as the time would allow, I returned to Glennie's camp and at 5 o'clock the motor boat came in to take Thompson and myself back to the *Mabahiss*; Glennie was going to remain on shore all night carrying out his experiments. By this time the tide had risen considerably and the buoy that we had put down in the morning was no longer visible; owing to the shortness of its anchoring rope it had become submerged, but the increased depth of water made it easy to cross the reef and the clearness of the water gave us a good view of the upper surface, which is covered with numerous growing colonies.

The next morning we got out the grab and took a sample of the bottom from a depth of 40 metres in the anchorage and when the grab was opened on deck and the contents emptied out, we found that the deposit, which consists of a white chalky mud, smelled of sulphuretted hydrogen. But the degree of concentration of the gas was not sufficient to kill off all the fauna, for in the mud we found quite a number of animals, echinoderms, lamellibranch molluscs, crabs, a single locust shrimp and some polychaete worms. The presence of the gas came as a surprise and it seems probable that in this instance the source of it must be the decomposition of organic matter, derived either from the nearby reef or from decaying vegetable matter washed off the island and swept across the reef into the lagoon by every rising tide.

Having completed his experiments, Glennie came off about 1.30, and as soon as his gear had been hoisted on board and the motor boat and dinghy hoisted up we got under way and steamed out of the lagoon through the south-east channel. As soon as we were clear of the entrance we turned up the east coast of the atoll until we were opposite the position where Glennie had taken his observations. We then turned in towards the reef until we were as close as MacKenzie considered safe and then turned and ran a line of soundings in a due easterly direction, so as to get a section of the bottom contour and enable Glennie to make certain calculations that he needed in connection with his gravity tests. After running out as far as the 1,000-fathom line we turned north and set our course for Kolumadulu Atoll, which we sighted about 3 o'clock in the afternoon. As we steamed along the atoll rim we passed a number of islands between which the reef appeared to be continuous. Large numbers of flying-fish kept jumping out of the water and planing away on either hand. The sea surface was par-

ticularly calm and one could clearly see the manner in which the fish uses
its tail-fin as a propellor even after its body has risen clear of the water;
furthermore, it was very clear that the fish can alter its course in the air and
in several instances I could see the fish balancing from side to side, as it
went, with a sideways roll. There were a number of boats out fishing and
in this atoll the boats are of a different type from those that we saw either
in Addu Atoll to the south or further north. In other parts of the Maldives
the boats end at the bows in a fine upcurved prow, but in Kolumadulu the
boats that we saw all ended bluntly without the high curved point.

We entered the lagoon through a fine channel on the south-eastern part
of the reef and anchored in about 31 fathoms of water not far from one of
the fishing villages, but exactly opposite a small uninhabited islet, Timarafuri, which Glennie had selected as the site for his next series of observations. While we were anchoring, the leadsman who was taking soundings
managed to get the lead-line round the propellor and just at that moment
one of the Maldive boats came off from the village with the headman on
board. At first they wouldn't come near the *Mabahiss* because they said they
hadn't got permission, but we informed them that we had permission for
them to do so and when they came near I presented our letter of introduction, which they duly read and returned with smiles, saying that it was
quite all right. One of their men then dived down and freed the line from
the propellor, after which all Glennie's gear was piled into the motor-boat
and he was sent ashore.

In this atoll some of the smaller islands on the southern and south-
eastern face appear, so far as one can see from the ship, to be gradually
extending in a north-easterly direction, for this end of the islands was often
only covered with a low bush scrub instead of with large trees, such as
were present on the other parts of the islands. Timarafuri seems to be
undergoing erosion on its lagoon face for a strip of beach-sandstone runs
along the shore and many of the bushes on the island overhang the top of
the sandy beach and are having their roots gradually exposed. The general
vegetation of the islands on this part of the atoll seemed to be rather more
dense than on the islands on the corresponding part of the reef in Addu
Atoll and here there were many more large trees of the *Baringtonia* type.

We left the lagoon early next morning and steamed out again through
the south-eastern entrance, leaving Glennie behind to carry on with his
observations. We then turned north along the outer rim of the atoll until
we were opposite Glennie's camp and then turned and ran a line of
soundings at right-angles to the atoll rim as far as the 1,000-fathom contour.

At about 8.30 we stopped the ship and proceeded to carry out work at

24–25.III.34   Station 138. The chemists began operations by shackling on the heavy
Bigelow tube and above this was attached an Ekman reversing water-bottle,
to take a water sample and temperature reading of the bottom water. The
tube appeared to strike the bottom at 1,970 metres, but the wire was by no
means up and down owing to the ship drifting under the influence of a
strong surface current towards the south-west. The depth by the echo was
1,830 metres and on hauling the Bigelow tube in again it was seen that the
Ekman water-bottle had been on the bottom and a loop of the hydrographic
wire had got foul of it, so the bottle had failed to work and we got neither
a water sample nor a temperature reading; and the Bigelow tube was empty.
There was a little coarse coral sand in the water bottle that must have come
from the bottom, but that was all the indication that we got of its nature.
We then sent down the Agassiz trawl. We had received our new length of
wire when we were at Colombo and while we were at anchor in Addu
Atoll we had run this on to the trawling winch, so that now we once again
had plenty of wire for trawling purposes. As the wire had not been put on
the drum under any strain, we had to be careful to see that we got no loose
turns on the drum as we were paying out, so we went slow ahead and
allowed the wire to be pulled off the drum by the strain of the net in the
water, the speed being carefully controlled by the brake. When we had paid
out nearly 3,000 metres of the wire the dynamometer was applied and we
commenced to trawl. The net was down for an hour and we then commenced to haul in. When there were still some 2,000 metres of wire to
come in, the Agassiz trawl and the last part of the wire came up in a
tangled mass, the wire being twisted round the trawl frame in a series of
great loops, exactly as it had been at Station 29 off Cape Guardafui. The
winch was at once stopped and after passing a line round the tangled mass
it was hoisted in and we spent the next hour or more in getting the wire
untangled and coiled down again on the drum. So all our work at this
station had proved a complete wash-out. It seems probable that here too
there is a strong deep current that had caught the comparatively light net
and had twirled it round and round, thus getting the wire twisted round it;
such a current would prevent any but the larger and heavier particles from
settling on the sea bed and this would thus also account for the fact that
the Bigelow tube came up empty and that the only trace of the bottom was
a little coarse sand caught by the reversing water-bottle. The results of
our analyses of the water samples from Station 136 in the gap between
the Maldive and Chagos archipelagos indicated that there is a deep
bottom current flowing westward into the Arabian Sea basin, and
probably this holds good for the more northerly region in which we were
working, the current sweeping through the gap between Haddummati

and Kolumadulu atolls, in which the depth of water is some 1,100 fathoms.

In the evening we returned to our anchorage inside Kolumadulu Atoll and sent the motor boat in to bring off Glennie as soon as he had completed his observations. While waiting for him to come off, we swung out the grab and took a sample of the lagoon bottom. Here we got a clean sand mixed with a large number of small shells; there was only a little animal life in it, but we obtained a few pieces of a sponge with a commensal brittle star (ophiuroid) living in its cavities, two prawns and a few polychaete worms. We aspirated off some of the water from the bottom sample and tested this for sulphuretted hydrogen gas, but there was no trace of any, so that it was clear that conditions here were quite different from those in the north-east part of the lagoon in Addu Atoll.

At dawn on the 26th we left our anchorage in the lagoon and steamed up the east side of the atoll towards a position where a depth of water of about 500 fathoms was shown on the chart between Kolumadulu and the next atoll to the north, Mulaku; but, as we got near, the bottom started to rise and eventually we stopped the ship and carried out work at Station 140 in only 515 metres of water. At first we tried to get a sample of the bottom with the Driver sounding tube, but, as usual, this failed to function properly (it is a most unreliable piece of apparatus), so we then sent down a Snapper lead with an additional 50-lb weight above it and got a small sample of a coarse sand. The 4-foot triangular dredge was then shackled on and sent down and we towed it for an hour. On hauling it in again we found that we had got a very meagre catch, though the animals obtained clearly indicated that the dredge had been on the bottom, so it seems probable that there is a very poor fauna here. Mixed with the catch were a few small fragments of conglomerate rock and dead coral, so that this channel too seems to be swept clean by the bottom current.

As soon as the dredge was back on board we steamed off to the north in order to get to an anchorage in Mulaku Atoll before nightfall, for it would be extremely dangerous to be steaming about among these atolls at night as there are no lights or marks of any kind. It is very difficult to locate a particular opening into these lagoons where there are few or no islands on the reef, but eventually we found one, though on this reef there is hardly any land left and the reef runs on for miles with only an occasional sand-clay or rock above the general water-level. We anchored near the entrance channel, with a small island a little to the north of us, and a little later we sent the grab down to get a sample of the bottom. At the first attempt the grab came up with a piece of shell-conglomerate caught between the jaws; growing on this was a fine collection of sponges and hydroids. We then sent it down again and this time got a good sample of a coarse sand, mixed

26–27.III.34   with a certain amount of *Lithothamnion* and a few solitary corals and polychaete worms. Mohamed collected a sample of the occluded water and tested this for sulphuretted hydrogen, but could detect none.

We left our anchorage early on the morning of the 27th and steamed northward up the deep channel between the atolls that throughout the greater part of the Archipelago are arranged in a double series. The weather was fine and we made good progress. On our way north we ran through a narrow belt of water stretching in a direction from north-east to south-west, which was the direction of the wind, that was discoloured with a surface scum of a brick-red tinge; this was almost certainly caused by the presence of a microscopic alga known as *Trichodesmium erythraeum*, for on the following day the water in the lagoon of South Malé Atoll was then seen to be similarly discoloured and a microscopic examination showed the presence of large numbers of this organism.

We reached South Malé Atoll soon after 4 o'clock in the afternoon and, steaming in through the entrance channel, came to anchor off Sultan's Island. Almost immediately a boat put off from the shore and we were visited by no less than three of the Ministers of State—the Minister of Foreign Affairs, the Minister of Fisheries and the Minister of Health, who also acts as Port Officer, as well as by the Private Secretary to His Highness the Sultan. They all appeared to be very young to be holding such high positions of state, but a few months prior to our visit there had been a bloodless revolution in the Archipelago and all the previous high officials had been arrested and put on board a motor boat, the only casualty being in the case of the Minister of Finance who, reports stated, had been ducked in the harbour. The captives had then been sent away to Colombo and their places filled by the younger men of the revolutionary party. They were all highly educated and spoke English and Arabic perfectly, most if not all of them having been educated in Cairo. They told us that they had received information regarding the visit of the John Murray Expedition from several sources, the most recent being from their representative in Colombo, and they were willing and anxious to do all that they could to assist us; they had already arranged that we should be provided with a boat for our detached party and were sending an official with it to see that everything was done to help.

About 5 o'clock in the evening many of us went ashore and we were met at the jetty by the Private Secretary and one of the Ministers, who showed us round the island. The town was larger than I had expected and I was informed that it houses no less than 7,000 inhabitants. All round the town there is a city wall, with gateways at intervals; along the seaward side the wall is loopholed for guns, though the only guns that I saw were some old

Portuguese ones, relics of the time when Portugal owned the island. In the middle of the town is the minaret, from the top of which the Mohammedan priest summons the faithful to prayer. Several wide streets run through the island, from north to south and east to west, and at one part there is a street of houses just outside the city wall where all the Hindu traders are located, the true inhabitants of the island being, of course, all Musulmans. Along the main street are numerous little houses, each set in its own little garden in which were a number of fruit trees, such as the mango, lime or the breadfruit tree, while, in addition, there were plantations and a number of flowering shrubs and trees such as the frangipani and the gold mohur tree. The streets are kept wonderfully clean and even in the bazaar there was an absence of smells that was particularly noticeable after India.

After we had peregrinated the town we were taken back to the Customs House on the jetty and were given a repast of small cakes and a drink of a fizzy sweet nature, either bright pink or yellow in colour; I got a bright pink one but I was unable to decide what it was supposed to be. While we were at tea we were introduced to the Prime Minister, another young lad, and he very kindly presented me with three small Maldive copper coins, of which 120 go to the rupee. Finally, we said goodbye and, as our own boat had not come in for us, we were sent back to the ship in the royal barge, a beautiful long slim craft with a pointed bow and stern, that was built in the island and is propelled by eight oars a side.

The following morning two of the Maldive Ministers came off to look round the ship and we showed them our equipment and explained the workings of the various types of apparatus. His Highness the Sultan had intimated that he would be pleased to receive us in audience at 2 o'clock in the afternoon, so, after lunch on board, five of us, Captain MacKenzie, Lieutenants Badr and Sarwat, Dr Faouzi and myself, set off from the ship and were met on the jetty by the Private Secretary. As we were a little ahead of our time, we had to wait in the Customs House for a few minutes while an admiring throng crowded round. During our short walk to the palace every resident that possessed a camera took the opportunity of getting a snapshot of us, and it was surprising the number of cameras there were on the island. On reaching the palace we passed through several doors and round a number of corners and it would be extremely difficult for any one not acquainted with the building to find his way to the Sultan's apartments; but whether this was an integral part of the measures taken for His Highness' safety or merely a result of haphazard building I cannot say. Eventually we were shown up a short flight of stairs into the audience chamber and after a few moments we were joined by His Highness, who looked a really patriarchal figure. He was elderly, with a white beard and

28–29.III.34   moustache and long grey hair falling over his shoulders, and he was clad in a robe of purple-blue with a train carried by an attendant, and on his head a purple and white pugaree in the top of which was an upright gold ornament. He seemed very shy and retiring and spoke in a quiet voice; as he could speak neither English nor Arabic but only Maldavian, that seems to be a compound of Arabic, Urdu and Singalese, all conversation had to be carried on through his Private Secretary, who acted as interpreter. He expressed himself as being very pleased to see us and to be able to help the Expedition in any way, and hoped that we had received and would receive every attention and assistance in the various atolls. I attempted to reply suitably and conveyed to His Highness the thanks both of the John Murray Committee in England and of the members of the Expedition for all that he was doing to assist us. After that the conversation became a little less formal and the Sultan, who is very interested in music, asked whether any of us could play an instrument. Dr Faouzi admitted that he could play the violin and immediately an instrument of sorts, that resembled a cross between a violin and a cornet, was produced. In this instrument the sound-box of the violin had been replaced by a metal trumpet. Dr Faouzi did his best to play on it but he found the balance of the instrument something of a handicap and, as he himself admitted, the result was hardly a success. Then, after a few more formalities, the Sultan said goodbye to us and departed; he and his train-bearer having a slight difference of opinion as to which side of his chair he was to go and they got rather tied up in consequence; but eventually this was adjusted and he left us with the Private Secretary, who showed us out and back to the jetty, and we were seen off by him and several of the Ministers of State.

We left our anchorage off Sultan's Island at dawn on 29 March and steamed northwards towards Fadiffolu Atoll, where we were to pick up the Maldive boat and detach our magnetic and geodetic party. The sea was flat calm for there was no wind, except what we made ourselves, but this was sufficient to keep things fairly cool. From time to time flying-fish darted out of the water and sped away over the surface, leaving a train of circular ripples where their tails had touched the water. We made good progress and soon after 3 o'clock in the afternoon we entered the lagoon of Fadiffolu Atoll through a wide entrance, on each side of which is a wooded island. On the eastern side beyond the island was a long uninterrupted stretch of reef, with a line of rock or boulders—owing to the distance it was impossible to decide which—along its edge and beyond that another small wooded island with a sandy beach. The island near the entrance appeared to have been driven back from the edge of the reef towards the lagoon. It may seem strange to speak of an island having been driven across a reef,

but this is exactly what happens in these coral atolls, for as the island is   29.III.34
eroded away on its seaward face by wind and waves, the sand is swept
round by currents on to the lagoon side and is there deposited on the lee
side of the island, so that the washing away on one side and the piling up
on the other causes these islands to migrate across the surface of the reef
from the seaward edge towards the lagoon. Near the edge of the reef in
this instance was a line of raised rock, that in all probability marked the
original position of the island, and then between the rock line and the
island itself came a wide area of shoal water. The island is covered with a
low bush scrub, with only a few scattered palm trees, while all around it, as
far as one could see, is a sandy beach. In some of the islands to the north
there seemed to be clumps of low bushes or trees standing in the water,
like mangroves, but whether this was actually the case or whether it was
merely a mirage-effect is was impossible to say.

As we steamed across the lagoon, the general level of the lagoon floor
appeared to be uniformly flat, but from time to time we passed a submerged
sandbank that did not appear to be indicated on the chart. Fortunately,
these sandy shoals show up so clearly as green patches in the blue of the
deeper water that it is an easy matter to steer clear of them. Soon after 4
o'clock we anchored off the island of Difuri on the eastern side of the
lagoon; the dinghy and the motor boat were lowered and were loaded up
with the gear for the detached party and Glennie, Farquharson and Gilson,
who was detailed to act as driver for the motor boat in order to save the
Chief from detailing one of the engine-room staff, went off to establish
their first camp. In the meantime we got the grab out of its box and
hoisted it up on the derrick, in preparation for sending it down as soon as
men were available, in order to take a sample of the lagoon bottom. It was
lowered away but unfortunately did not close properly and so the sample
brought up was only a small one. This sample consisted of a mixed mud
and sand in which there were a number of small masses of a black material,
which appeared to be heavy. Mohamed took a sample of the occluded
water and this was found on examination to contain sulphuretted hydrogen
gas to the extent of 3.9 mg/litre, rather less than we had found in the mud
from Addu Atoll but still sufficient to be quite appreciable to one's sense
of smell. It seemed probable that here too the presence of the gas is associated with the profuse vegetation on the neighbouring islands, Difuri island
being covered thickly with scrub in which several palm trees and other
large trees are growing. We were preparing to send the grab down again
when Captain MacKenzie, having had a report from Farquharson that there
was a submerged rock near the ship, shifted our anchorage into deeper
water further off from the reef. By this time it was getting dark, so we

29–30.III.34 postponed our attempt to get a second sample of the bottom until the following morning.

Soon after we had anchored, a large shark, about 8 feet in length, was seen swimming round the ship; its presence very materially altered the views of some of the lads, who had been under the impression that sharks did not enter these lagoons and that, therefore, it was perfectly safe to bathe from the ship.

Early the next morning we put the grab over and obtained a good sample of the bottom, which on this occasion consisted of a cream-coloured ooze in which the strength of sulphuretted hydrogen was somewhat less than nearer to the reef, being only 2.26 mg/litre of occluded water.

At about 8 o'clock we got under way and steamed across the lagoon and out through the southern entrance into Kardiva Channel, and at about half past nine, when we were well outside, we stopped the ship and sent down the Agassiz trawl in just over 400 fathoms (Station 143). In view of the strong deep current that we suspected must run through the channel, and in order to avoid a repetition of the net getting caught up and twisted round the wire, we weighted the trawl frame by the addition of two Driver weights, each about 50 lbs. The net went down and the trawl was carried out without a hitch, the result being satisfactory and yielding a good catch. As soon as the net was back on board we steamed back again into the lagoon, this time by a different channel, and headed for the main village that lies on one of the islands on the west side of the atoll where we were to pick up the Maldive boat for our detached party.

Almost as soon as we were anchored several boats came off to us and we learned that they had been warned about a fortnight before that we should be coming; so the system of communication between the various atolls, in view of the fact that they do not possess any wireless apparatus, appears to be very efficient. The headman of this atoll had been educated in the University of Cairo, or rather in the big Muslim College there, and spoke both Arabic and Hindustani in addition to his own Maldivian language. He informed us that we could take the pick of all the boats in the atoll. I asked him whether we could give the crew of the boat any baksheesh, but he emphasized that this was state business, that they were only too pleased to be able to help the Expedition in any way possible and that if I attempted to give the crew money they would resent it; but they would be glad to accept such things as biscuits or tea, which to them were luxuries. As we were still busy sorting out the catch that we had made in the trawl, we took him along and showed him some of the things that we had caught; he admitted that he had never before seen fish like them, but he maintained

that they got better fish than those in their nets—and from his point of   30–31.III.34
view, no doubt they do.

Later in the evening Captain MacKenzie went ashore with the headman
and selected a suitable boat, and after he returned to the ship, as soon as it
was dark, partly with a view to testing our stock and partly to give the
inhabitants a firework display, he sent up several rockets and burnt some of
our flares. Unfortunately, the rockets were seen by our detached party,
some 17 miles away on the other side of the lagoon and, as they hadn't
been warned, they were doubtful whether they were distress signals or not,
so they came across in the motor boat to see whether we were all right or
had run on a reef. They appeared alongside about midnight, but finding
that everything was all right they went back again having made a 34-mile
trip for nothing.

The next morning at dawn we carried out a haul with the grab. On this
occasion it took us about half an hour instead of the usual ten minutes, for
when we had got the grab on the bottom we discovered that the rope of
the derrick had got badly worn and that one strand had parted; so we

Fig. 30. In the Maldives: visitors alongside, March 1934. (*Photo:* H. C. Gilson.)

hauled the grab up until it was alongside and then made it fast while a new rope was rove through the blocks, and when this was done we hoisted it inboard. Here the bottom consisted of a coarse sand mixed with coral fragments and shells; as we were in the near vicinity of one of the major openings of the reef there must usually be a good strong current setting into the lagoon and, doubtless, this prevented the finer particles from settling.

About 8 o'clock the Maldivian boat came off from the village and, having made fast to a hawser that we passed aft, we got under way and towed her down to where we were to meet our motor boat. All Farquharson's and Glennie's gear was then transferred to the Maldive boat and we hoisted our motor boat aboard and steamed back, towing the Maldive boat, until we were off the island where they were going to carry out their second series of observations. Having arranged a rendezvous off an island in South Malosmadulu Atoll where we were to meet and pick them up again nine days later, we said goodbye to them and steamed out into Kardiva Channel to a position which we had selected for a 24-hour station. We reached the spot about 4 o'clock in the afternoon and having attached a kedge anchor to the end of the trawl wire this was passed over the side and lowered away, the depth of water being 270 fathoms. When sufficient wire had been paid out, the wire was triced up and the nippers and dynamometer put on the wire and we swung to the wind and tide. We commenced work with the Ekman current-meter about 5.45 p.m. and observations showed that there was a surface current setting towards the south-east down to a depth of about 100 metres, whereas below that depth a deeper current was running westwards. As we were taking current observations every two hours, and it took us very nearly that length of time to make a single series of observations, we had a very strenuous time all the next day.

I had expected to get away from this station and carry out a deep trawl before putting into Horsburgh Atoll, which was to be our headquarters for the next week, on 1 April, but unfortunately Captain MacKenzie developed high fever and was quite unfit to navigate the ship and couldn't trust his Egyptian deck officers to take us safely into the atoll, so all that we could do was to stay where we were and carry on our observations. We continued the series with the Ekman current-meter, but took observations at four-hour intervals instead of every two hours, as we had been doing previously, and in the afternoon we attempted simultaneously to make some hauls with the plankton nets. The surface current running past the ship rendered it impossible to send the nets down vertically, and at our first attempt the net got caught on some obstruction on the ship's bottom. After a little delay we managed to free it, but when we got it in and sent it down the second time a shift in the wind caused the *Mabahiss* to swing and the net got foul

of the wire of the current-meter on the opposite side of the ship and it was
some time before we could disentangle the two wires. This was eventually
done, but by this time we were all convinced that the game wasn't worth
the trouble and we postponed our vertical or, rather, oblique hauls with
the nets until the current observations were concluded. We carried out the
first of our hauls in the afternoon, and early on the 2nd I was called and we
carried out a second series of hauls between 3.30 and 5.15 in the morning,
so as to be able to compare the conditions present in the dark and in
daylight.

Fortunately, Captain MacKenzie was now better and at 6 o'clock we
commenced to haul in the trawl wire and get up the kedge anchor. As soon
as possible the kedge anchor was detached and the Agassiz trawl shackled
on to the wire; at half past seven we put it over the side (Station 145) and,
having triced the wire up aft, commenced to trawl. The net was down for
an hour during which time the strain, as shown by the dynamometer, was
only 5 cwt. The catch was good and varied and we got a number of fish
and a large quantity of small prawns and some very fine sponges and
pennatulids.

As soon as the trawl was over we steamed westward and passed through
the entrance channel into Horsburgh Atoll about 1 o'clock in the afternoon.
Soon after we were through the entrance we shackled on the otter trawl
and towed it, as we steamed across the lagoon, for about an hour (Station
146). I wasn't at all hopeful regarding the probability of our catching very
much, but MacKenzie was very anxious that we should, if possible, catch
some fresh fish for consumption and as a matter of fact we made quite a
good haul. The catch consisted of a number of fish of various sizes, most
of them comparatively small but some of large size; mixed with these were
a number of small crabs, starfish and squids. As the trawl was being hoisted
in, several sharks came around and started to feed on the smaller fish that
were getting through the meshes of the net; the sailors promptly put a line
and shark hook overboard and managed to catch one of them.

Having finished the trawl we steamed to our anchorage in the north-
eastern part of the lagoon and soon afterwards put the grab down in about
15 fathoms of water; here the bottom consisted of a soft cream-coloured
mud that on this occasion showed not the faintest trace of sulphuretted
hydrogen gas.

A little later in the afternoon a party of us went ashore and landed on
Fehendu Island on the north side of the lagoon. When we got ashore we
were met by several of the local inhabitants from the village on the island,
and I produced my letter of introduction, which was duly read and returned.
As there was only one man in the whole crowd who appeared to be able to

2–3.IV.34   talk Hindustani, and not very much of that, and to understand even less, though that may have been my fault, we didn't manage to get very far in our attempts at conversation, though I gathered that they had been warned that we might be visiting the atoll.

I then walked round the island and studied the conditions that exist at the present day, paying particular attention to such changes as appeared to have taken place since the island was visited by Professor Stanley Gardiner, of Cambridge University, in 1899. A considerable degree of erosion has taken place during the interval, especially on the north side about the middle of the island, and at the present day the two sides are separated by only a few feet of land, so that in a few more years the island will have become divided into two. To a less degree erosion is going on along the whole of the north side and the greater part of this face of the island is fringed with a belt of the old reef-rock, eroded on its seaward face into a small vertical cliff and weathered on the upper surface into numerous pits and holes.

After discussion with Captain MacKenzie it was decided that on the following day we should leave the motor boat, with Thompson and Gilson on board, to carry out hydrological investigations in the lagoon, while the *Mabahiss* carried out biological work at the western end of Kardiva Channel. We left our anchorage about 6 o'clock and as soon as we were under way the otter trawl was again put over the side, for the success of our haul the evening before encouraged us to hope that we might still further replenish our larder. The net was towed across the lagoon and when we got near the entrance the ship was stopped and we commenced to haul in; at this stage things began to go wrong. The strain had gradually risen to nearly 1½ tons, and though we got the wire in until the swivel shackle was past the gallows, we then found that the net was hard on something on the bottom. The ship now drifted down over the wire bridles until these were hard along her side, so the trawl wire was slacked away. Lieutenant Badr, who was aft, reported that the bridles were clear of the propellor and Captain MacKenzie ordered slow ahead in order to turn the ship. Then came a sudden strain on the bridles and the next moment both of them parted at exactly the same level; it seems clear they had been caught and cut by the propellor as we went ahead. As the depth was only some 20 fathoms we hoped that we might be able to hook a grapnel into the net and recover it from the bottom, so for the next two hours we steamed backwards and forwards over the spot dragging hooks, but without success.

The ship was then anchored while MacKenzie went away in a dinghy and put down a mark-buoy at the edge of the reef on the eastern side of the entrance channel to facilitate our entering and leaving the lagoon; when this was down we steamed out into Kardiva Channel. Just outside the

3–4.IV.34

entrance the bottom drops down very steeply. We first put the grab over in a depth of 225 metres, but all that we got for our pains were a few small lumps of coral rock; we then sent down the 4-foot triangular dredge (Station 149) and towed that for an hour, at the end of which time we hauled it in with about 2 tons of coral detritus, sand and shells in the net. The strain on the net was such that we had to leave it hanging over the side while we went slow ahead and washed a good deal of the finer sand out. Eventually we were able to get it inboard, but there was very little animal life in the catch.

As the day was now getting on and it was imperative that we should pass through the entrance channel into the lagoon by daylight, we turned back towards the atoll and on our way put the grab over twice more, but on each occasion we got little or nothing, and it seemed clear that the bottom on the south side of the atoll is, for the most part, composed of either coral rock or a coarse detritus into which the grab could not bite. We then steamed into the lagoon and returned to our original anchorage, where we were soon after rejoined by the motor-boat party. We had now completed work at 150 stations and the event was duly celebrated at dinner that night in a bottle of wine.

At 6 o'clock the next morning, 4 April, the two chemists, Thompson and Gilson, again pushed off in the motor boat to continue their investigations into the hydrological condition of the lagoon, and the *Mabahiss* steamed out through the entrance and turned to the south-west in order to get into deep water off the western end of the channel. The depth of water increased rapidly as we got away from the atoll and before long we were in 250 fathoms of water, and then equally suddenly and to our great surprise, the sea-floor commenced to rise again until we were in a depth of only 30 fathoms, which was very much less than anything shown on the chart in this area. The depth continued at this level, with an occasional small peak rising up towards the surface, for some distance and so we altered course more to the west to try and get into deeper water. Before long we reached the edge of the bank and the bottom then dropped down very steeply. We tried to make our first station in a depth of about 350 fathoms but all the time there was a very strong surface current setting us towards the west and into deeper water. By the time we had got our sounding and bottom sample we had drifted into a depth of 471 fathoms, and before the dredge was over the side and down to the bottom this had still further increased, according to the echo, to 500 fathoms. The trawl (Station 152) was carried out quite successfully, though the depth of water ranged between 600 and 285 fathoms. When we started to haul in, the strain on the wire increased to an extraordinary extent, so much so that the winch could hardly cope

4–5.IV.34   with it, but we persevered slowly and gradually the wire came in. Although we were then in a depth of only 285 fathoms and there were still 1,000 metres of wire out, the line was straight up and down so that it seemed clear that it was caught on something on the bottom. Eventually it came clear and we got the dredge safely back on board, with the single exception of the 50-lb weight that had been fastened to the cod-end, for the rope attaching this had parted and the weight was lost. The catch was small, but included several bits of dead coral rock, much of which was stained black by manganese dioxide, together with some greenish-brown mud and sand.

Having completed the dredge we ran back on to the bank and put the 4-foot triangular dredge over again (Station 153) in a depth of 130 fathoms and this time we got a small, though varied catch, again mixed with fragments of coral rock.

At our last station for the day we steamed into the western end of Kardiva Channel until we were in a depth of 250 fathoms and, as we had previously trawled with the Agassiz net at this depth in the eastern part of the channel with complete success, we put this net over and towed it for some thirty-five minutes (Station 154). The strain on the wire during the latter part of the trawl showed a great range of variation, rising to 5 cwt or more and then suddenly falling to zero; we stopped the trawl and hauled the net in again and when it came up we found that it had been torn to shreds. Fortunately it was a very old net, and in any case wouldn't have stood much more work; but owing to the tears the catch was practically nil, though a few small fish were entangled in the meshes.

We then returned to the lagoon, passing the motor boat as we went in, and on this occasion we anchored in a new place off Inafuri Island in the western part of the lagoon.

The next morning we again left our anchorage at 6 o'clock and steamed out through the entrance, towing the motor boat. We cast off the motor boat, with Thompson and Gilson on board, as we passed through the entrance, for they were going to carry out a series of observations there on the changes in the sea-water and the currents in and out of the lagoon at different states of the tide, and we then turned westward towards our trawling ground on the slopes of the Maldive ridge. As we steamed out towards the open sea we again ran over the ridge that we had crossed the previous day and, being now on a different course, it was beginning to be clear that there was here a large submerged bank, the existence of which had not been suspected. In order to get some idea of its extent we ran southwards in the direction of Toddu Island until we reached its southern extremity and then turned eastward; here the depth gradually increased until it was 150 fathoms and we then turned north again so as to cross the

bank at a different angle. Having picked up the edge, where it rose steeply
from the floor of the channel, we headed westward and steamed right
across the bank until we reached its western end and then turned slightly to
the south of west to get into deep water.

I had originally intended to carry out a trawl in a depth of about 1,250
fathoms, and at the same time to get some idea of the general contour of
the western slopes during our run out and back again, and thus be in a
position to pick up depths of 800 and 1,000 fathoms for trawling during
the next two days. However, as our survey of the shallow bank had taken
up most of the morning, I changed our programme and decided to put the
trawl down when we had reached a depth of 800 fathoms. The west side of
the Maldive ridge drops down so steeply that we soon found ourselves in
water of 1,000 fathoms depth; the ship was immediately stopped and the
Monegasque trawl was sent down (Station 155), but before it had reached
the bottom we had drifted into water of 1,230 fathoms depth and so the
process of paying out the wire took longer than I had anticipated. As we
had to get away by 3.30 in order to get back to our anchorage before dark,
or else stay out and drift for the night which would have used up a considerable amount of our reserve of coal, I had to cut the trawl short and the
net was down for only half an hour, so that the resulting catch was small.
We eventually got to the entrance of the atoll just at sunset and found our
hydrographic party in the motor boat still hard at work; as we passed them
they informed us that they would not be finished until about half past nine
and would we please keep some supper for them.

The next morning we again left the lagoon at 6 o'clock and steamed out
across the bank until we were in a depth of 800 fathoms. Here we tried to
take a sounding and get a water sample and a core of the bottom deposit
before we put the Agassiz trawl down. While we were paying out the
sounding wire we ran into deeper water, as usual, and although we paid
out over 1,500 metres of wire we got no indication of when the tube struck
the bottom. We then hauled the tube in again and as the last length of wire
came in it was clear that we had overrun the depth, for the last 50 metres of
wire were tangled round the water bottle and the stray-line of the sounding-
tube; so we did not, after all, get a water sample, but we had collected a
good sample of the bottom, which consisted of a grey mud in which were
numerous Foraminifera, mostly *Globigerina*. We then sent the Agassiz trawl
down (Station 156) and although we paid out more wire than should have
been necessary for the depth, when we hauled it in again it was clear that it
had not been on the bottom at all. The catch consisted of several red
deep-sea prawns and some fish, mostly small, but one was a splendid
big fellow of a dark-black colour with comparatively small eyes and

6–7.IV.34 an enormous head with a small protrusible mouth on the ventral aspect.

We then ran eastward again in order to put down some more soundings on the submerged bank but, unfortunately, at the crucial moment the echo-sounder went wrong and before we could get it going again we were right on the bank and so missed its edge. At about 3.45 in the afternoon we stopped the ship and put the 4-foot triangular dredge down for half an hour on the bank (Station 157); this time the result was a magnificent catch consisting largely of a species of sea-urchin, *Centrostephanus*, of which we got 550 examples, while in addition there were in the net 50 specimens of a large brachiopod, several bright yellow crinoids and large quantities of a solitary or branching coral. As a result of this haul the biologists were kept busy until midnight, sorting and preserving the various specimens.

On the morning of the 7th we again steamed out into the channel to continue our work in the deep water to the west, while the chemists carried on with their observations in the lagoon. On our way to the trawling ground we again crossed the unknown bank and on this occasion we got very clear evidence of a marginal ridge, the depth shoaling to 125 fathoms at the margin and then dropping to 130 fathoms over the general level of the bank. We then ran out into deep water and at 8 o'clock the Agassiz trawl (Station 158) was put down in about 500 fathoms of water. As it was probable that we should drift into considerably deeper water, due allowance was made in the amount of wire paid out, and during the trawl the echo-sounder gave a range of depth from 786 to 1,170 metres. When the net had been down for about three-quarters of an hour, there was a sudden jump in the strain, as indicated by the dynamometer, and as, judging from our previous experience, this probably meant that the net was foul of some rock on the bottom and would, if we persisted, get badly torn, we stopped the trawl and heaved in. The resulting catch was small but varied and there could be no doubt that the net had been fishing on the bottom.

We then ran towards the north again, so as to be able to trawl on our way back with the current on our port side and thus keep the ship clear of the trawl wire, and about mid-day we sent down the Monagesque trawl in a depth of about 700 fathoms (Station 159). Unfortunately, before we could carry out the trawl the echo-sounder gave out completely, so that we were unable to determine the actual depth at which the net was fishing. During at least part of the trawl the sea-bottom, judging by what came up in the net, consisted of a soft grey *Globigerina* ooze, very similar to that which had been obtained by the sounding rod from a depth of 1,450 metres as Station 156, so that it is probable that we were working at a depth of approximately 950 to 1,450 metres. On hauling in there was considerable strain on the wire, but the net came in without any mishap and on this occasion the

catch was fairly good and included a specimen of the largest deep-sea fish   7–8.IV.34
that I have seen.

As soon as the trawl was back on deck we steamed direct to Horsburgh
Atoll, for as the echo-sounder had failed we could not carry out any more
observations on the topography of the submerged bank. On our way across
the lagoon to our anchorage in the north-west corner we passed the motor
boat, the engine of which had ceased to function, so we passed them a line
and towed them home.

When we anchored, I had the grab put down to get a sample of the
bottom, which turned out to consist of a soft cream-coloured mud that
again smelled of sulphuretted hydrogen gas and here analysis showed that
the gas was present in a concentration of 7.7 mg/litre. This concluded the
work that we could carry out in this area, for the next morning we were due
at our rendezvous to pick up our detached party.

One of the most interesting of our discoveries is the submerged bank at
the western end of Kardiva Channel. The area of the bank appears to cover
about $16\frac{1}{2}$ in a west-north-west/east-south-east direction and to be some 13
miles across from south-west to north-east. However, at the north-east part
of the bank the 135-fathom contour shows a tongue-like extension towards
the north and it is possible that this may be due not to an actual extension
of the bank in this direction, but to the presence of a detached submerged
islet, having a relationship to the main bank similar to that shown by
Toddu Island to Ari Atoll to the south; a more detailed survey than we
could afford the time for would be necessary to decide this point. Around
at least part of the rim there is a clearly-marked raised margin over which
the depth of water is only 125 fathoms, whereas over the main area of the
bank the depth is from 130–135 fathoms. The top of the bank is extraordinarily flat and, judging from the results of our dredging, consists of coral
rock. It would seem probable that we have here another atoll that was
originally one of the western series and must, of course, have been formed
at the surface of the sea, but that since its formation it has undergone
subsidence to a depth of 125 fathoms, possibly as a result of seismic changes.
To this bank we have, with His Egyptian Majesty's consent, given the
name King Fuad Bank, in order to perpetuate the recognition of the great
interest that His Majesty has taken in the John Murray Expedition and the
fact that the expedition was carried out in one of His Egyptian Majesty's
ships.

On the morning of the 8th we left our anchorage in Horsburgh Atoll for
the last time and, having picked up our buoy at the entrance channel, we
steamed round the western side of the atoll, and then turned north to
South Malosmadulu Atoll to reach our rendezvous and pick up our

8–10.IV.34   detached party. As we steamed into the atoll we sighted their boat in the offing and ran up alongside. Only Farquharson was on board as Glennie was on one of the islands carrying out a series of pendulum observations, and it transpired that they were not expecting us until the following day. The arrangement had been made that we should pick them up on the 11th day and MacKenzie had calculated this from the date on which we had put the party ashore on Difuri Island, whereas Farquharson and Glennie had apparently been calculating the time from the date on which we had actually left them at the western end of Faddiffolu Atoll. As they hadn't finished their work, we lay quietly at anchor in the lagoon and the crew were able to have a day off work, which they had thoroughly earned. During the morning we put the grab over and got a sample of the bottom, which turned out to consist of a rather coarse sand. A little later the Maldive boat came off with a message from Glennie to say that he would be ready to come on board at dawn the next morning. As there was not a breath of wind stirring we told the headman of the boat that we would give them a tow back to their own island on the other side of the archipelago if they were off at sunrise, but if later than that we should not be able to as we had to get up to Minikoi by dawn the following day.

During the day Sparks was very busy overhauling the echo-sounder and trying to get it to function again. But the fault seemed to lie in the valves of the amplifier and if these were burnt out, as seemed likely, there was not much hope of our being able to get the apparatus to work again until we could get to Colombo and get some new ones.

At dawn on the 9th the Maldive boat with our party was sighted about a mile away and MacKenzie made the welkin ring with a series of hoots on the siren to hurry them up, but the Maldive crew were all singing lustily as they pulled at their oars—there being not even a breath of wind—so our hoots were not heard and even the wisp of steam from the siren wasn't noticed; however, they effactually woke up all the ship's company so that we were all on deck to greet the party when they came alongside. Farquharson's and Glennie's kit was quickly transferred to the *Mabahiss* and a tow rope was passed to the boat, and we then steamed out through the entrance channel into Kardiva Channel and headed east for Faddiffolu Atoll, where we gave the Maldive crew some biscuits, tea and sugar as baksheesh and said goodbye to them. We then steamed northwards across the lagoon and out through one of the entrance channels at the north-east corner of the atoll and then ran northwards for Minikoi. Throughout the whole day the weather was a flat calm and the sea like glass. We reached Minikoi soon after dawn on the 10th and as we steamed up the east side of the atoll we had a good view of the SS *Horst* that had run aground on the reef at the

northern end of the atoll a few years before; she was carrying ingots of tin   10–11.IV.34
and the metal was still being salvaged out of her. When the *Horst* ran
aground another steamer stood by and attempted to get her off the reef,
but she too went aground and one of the harbour tugs from Colombo and
the salvage ship from Perim had to go to their assistance. They succeeded
in getting the second vessel off the reef, but the *Horst* was too hard aground
and so had to be abandoned to her fate.

During the night the engineers were hard at work on the motor boat;
this had been giving a lot of trouble during the past few days and the
motor had finally refused to function. They managed to get it to work
about 9 o'clock in the morning and then Glennie's gear was loaded into the
boat and we prepared to push off. Our programme was that Glennie should
be put ashore for his last series of pendulum observations and that I should
accompany him and, after that, Gilson and Mohamed were to take the
motor boat on and carry out a series of hydrological observations in the
lagoon. Meanwhile, the *Mabahiss* steamed out to the west and carried out a
trawl in about 1,000 fathoms of water on the western side of the atoll in
order to fill a gap in our series that had been caused by the two previous
trawls at about this depth turning out failures, the one owing to the trawl
getting tangled up with the wire and the other owing to the net not having
got to the bottom.

As the motor boat was heading in towards the narrow entrance channel
the motor again refused to function and we began to drift towards the reef
where, in spite of the complete absence of wind, quite a heavy surf was
breaking; so the oars were got out and it looked as if we should have to
pull the heavy boat in to the shore, a distance of about a mile. Fortunately,
one of the big racing canoes had come off from the village with the lighthouse keeper and the headman of the atoll, and we were able to pass a rope
to them and they gave us a tow into the lagoon. We anchored in the
lagoon off the northern end of the island and Glennie's gear was put ashore;
I landed with him and after a short interval the motor was persuaded to
work again, so Gilson and Mohamed went off to carry out their series of
observations.

As soon as Glennie had settled down to work and the tide was low
enough, I wandered on to the reef at the northern end of the island and
when I had seen all that there was to be seen here I worked down the
eastern side and back again along the lagoon side. It was very interesting to
see the different character of the land face on the two sides and to compare
the condition of the island and reef at the present day with the account
given by Professor Stanley Gardiner of his visit thirty-five years earlier.
During the interval a certain amount of erosion has taken place and the sea

11–12.IV.34   has broken across the northern end of the island, forming a complete break in the vegetation, while at the same point a number of large fragments of rock have been torn off the outer face of the reef and have been thrown up on the surface. It was dreadfully hot on the reef during the middle of the day and my notebook and camera were plentifully bedewed with drops of perspiration; unfortunately, early on in the day something went wrong with the shutter of the camera and instead of opening and closing when I pressed the button, it got into a reverse action and closed and opened instead, so that most of the photographs that I took were complete failures. It was not until I got back to Colombo and had the films developed that I knew that anything had gone wrong and so much of my labour was of no avail. The motor boat was to have come to take me off at 5 o'clock in the evening, but when the time came Gilson and Mohamed were still busy at the south end of the lagoon taking observations. We could see them in the distance running a line of stations across the lagoon, so that I knew that the motor hadn't again broken down. Eventually they finished their work and having picked me up we got back to the *Mabahiss* about 6 o'clock.

In the meantime the *Mabahiss* had carried out a trawl (Station 162) in about 1,000 fathoms on the western side, but the resulting catch had turned out to be very small and disappointing and in this respect closely resembled the trawls that we had done further to the north of Bombay in December, so that it seems probable that all down this western side of India and the Laccadive-Maldive ridge the fauna is poor. As there was not sufficient depth of water in the entrance channel for the *Mabahiss* to enter the lagoon and anchor there, we had to steam off towards the north until we were clear of the atoll and drift for the night.

Early the next morning we steamed round to the south-east side of the atoll and proceeded to carry out a series of hauls with the grab. The *Mabahiss* was first brought into a depth of water of 150 fathoms and the grab was sent down; we got a good sample of the bottom that consisted of a green sand but had very little animal life in it. Then we slowly steamed in towards the reef until we were in 100 fathoms and took another bottom sample, again getting a specimen of green sand. As the bottom outside these atolls goes down very steeply, we were by this time close to the edge of the reef on which the swell was breaking, and with the example of the *Horst* before our eyes it was clearly inadvisable to attempt to get any nearer, so we backed out into deeper water and sent the grab down for a third time in a depth of 200 fathoms. Up until now the grab had been working perfectly, but it now started to give trouble; at the first attempt it failed to close, so we sent it down again and this time, having struck bottom at 400 metres,

when we hauled it up again we found the jaws had jammed and refused to
open. At last, when we had succeeded in forcing the jaws apart, we found
that there was very little in the grab, what there was being again a green
sand.

After this we steamed back again to the north-east corner of the atoll
and sent the motor boat in for Glennie, who came off at 2.30. The lighthouse keeper and the headman came off in one of the racing boats to say
goodbye to us, this particular boat being the champion boat of the atoll.
Every year, they told us, they hold a regatta and on one occasion the
Commander in Chief of the East India Squadron, who had visited the atoll
in HMS *Effingham*, had presented a small admiral's pennant to the winning
crew of the canoe race, and now each year this pennant is raced for and is
flown for the year by the champion boat.

During the greater part of 12 April we steamed steadily on our course
for Colombo. In our original programme we had arranged to proceed to
Cochin harbour at the conclusion of our work in the Maldives, but owing
to the restriction by the government of India of the imports of foreign coal
we had been compelled, when we called in at Bombay, to take Indian coal
instead of Welsh, and the result had proved so unsatisfactory that we
decided to change our programme and return to Colombo and thus avoid
being compelled to take Indian coal again.

About 6 o'clock in the evening of the 12th we altered our course so as to
run a line of soundings across Wadge Bank off Cape Comorin. While we
were in Colombo for our refit the RMIS *Investigator*, the survey ship of the
Marine Survey of India, had put into port after carrying out a survey of
this area. As she had failed to find any trace of a shoal patch of some 5
fathoms that is shown on the Admiralty chart, Commander Sanderson,
who was an old shipmate of mine, had asked us to run across the bank, if it
didn't take up too much of our time and take us too far out of our course,
in order to corroborate their results. We too failed to find any trace of the
shoal, and we then set our course once more for Colombo, where we duly
arrived at about 4 o'clock on the 13th and tied up to our old moorings at
the head of the harbour. A little later Major Glennie and his party and gear
were put ashore. We were all very sorry to say goodbye to him, and everyone sincerely hoped that he had enjoyed his trip with us as much as we had
enjoyed having him on board.

Unfortunately, owing to our having changed our programme and returning to Colombo, instead of going to Cochin as was our original intention, a number of parcels that had been sent out to us from England
did not arrive before we left again, and these had to be sent on after us
to catch us at our next port of call, which was to be Aden. While in

13.IV.34   port we were glad to welcome on board a number of visitors who came to have a look round the ship; among these were two officers from one of the ships of the Bibby Line, which was engaged in taking water samples and temperature readings for us on their passage between Colombo and Aden.

Another unfortunate result of our change of plans was that a cylinder of methyl chloride gas for our refrigerator engine had not arrived in Colombo; as the weather was now beginning to get hot, this was all the more urgently necessary. By a stroke of good luck HMS *Hawkins* happened to be in port and we were able to get a small quantity from her, and our Contractor, Mr Fred Taylor, was at the last moment able to secure a further supply for us, so that we had sufficient to see us through until we got to Aden; but this delayed our departure for twenty-four hours, so that we were not able to leave for Aden until a day later than we had expected.

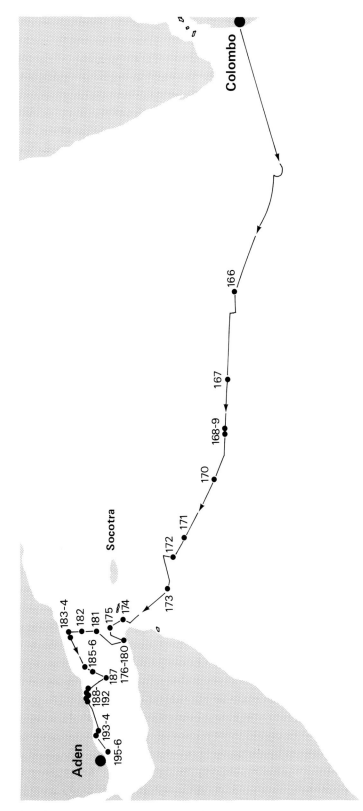

FIG. 31. Track chart, Cruise 9: Colombo–Aden. Station numbers are indicated.

Chapter 10

Colombo to Aden

Wᴇ left Colombo on 19 April at about 11 o'clock in the morning, and I think that we were all glad to get away and be able to feel that at last we had our noses turned towards home. The moment we got outside the breakwater we bumped into a bit of a head sea with a cross swell owing to the waves being thrown back by the breakwater. For a bit we shipped quite a lot of water over the well-deck and one extra large wave came right over the forecastle in a green flood. As a result of the tossing of our little craft it wasn't long before the usual crowd were down with sea-sickness; Thompson was the first to feel the effects, for throughout the whole expedition he never seemed to get accustomed to the movement, though he never gave in and, *mal de mer* or no, he always carried on with his work. Certainly our last cruise had not been calculated to acclimatize anyone to a seafaring life, for there had been little or no wind during the whole twenty-eight days, and in the shelter of the atolls and lagoons the sea had been a flat calm. but the wind had since freshened and it was blowing with a force of about 4 in the Beaufort Scale from the south-west, but by the following day it had veered to the north-west, so that the sea was on our starboard bow. We made good progress, and on the 21st we reached the eastern end of Kardiva Channel about 10.30 in the morning, which was somewhat earlier than we had expected. As we approached the Maldive Islands we came under their lee and the sea abated somewhat, so that we were not rolling and pitching quite so much as before, a change that was much appreciated by some of us. We steamed through the channel and, when we got to the western end, we ran a further line of soundings across King Fuad Bank. Having reached the western edge, where it drops steeply into deep water, we turned northwards to try and run along its edge for a bit, but there was such a strong current setting us to the west that when we once got off the bank we never seemed really to get on to it again, though the level of the sea bottom showed a considerable range of variation, rising and falling where, presumably, promontories ran out from the main mass of the bank towards the west. At about 6.30 in the evening, just as it was

getting dark, we approached the western side of South Malosmadulu Atoll
and having got into about 150 fathoms of water we turned and steamed
due west in order to get the correct slope of the bottom, as this was
required by Major Glennie in connection with his pendulum work. The
wind was now blowing from the west-south-west and there were several
rain storms in our vicinity, but the majority of them passed by some distance
away from us.

The next morning the weather had improved somewhat and it was
beautifully fine; we had run out of the cloudy area about 10.30 the previous
night and the wind went round to the north-west raising a slight sea from
that direction, while a swell was coming up from the south-west. We again
came across large schools of dolphins, some of which kept with us for some
distance before they turned away, and during the early hours of the morning
there were a number of flying-fish about, but with these exceptions and a few
birds that appeared to be shearwaters there was but little life to be seen.

After completing our section off South Malosmadulu Atoll, we had
turned towards the north to reach the first of a series of stations that we
were going to put down across the Arabian Sea along the line of Lat. 7°
N. We reached our position about 10 o'clock on the morning of the
23rd; all the previous night we had been getting considerably greater
depths by the echo-sounder than we had anticipated, and instead of about
2,400 fathoms, as indicated by the chart, we had got about 2,700 fathoms. In
order to make quite certain that we had sufficient wire for a bottom trawl in
such depths, I had got up an extra length of wire of 440 metres and this was
shackled on to the end of the wire on the drum of the trawl-winch.

As soon as the ship was stopped we shackled on the Monegasque trawl
and put this over (Station 166); the depth was now given as 2,580 fathoms
and, having paid out sufficient wire, we trawled for two hours. On starting
to haul in, the winch worked very badly and it looked as if the overhaul
that it had had in Colombo had not done it any good; one of the bearings
ran very hot and had to be constantly cooled by buckets of water. When
we got the net up it was seen that, strong though it was, it had been badly
torn or rubbed through, and the cod-end was full of rounded or angular
manganese nodules, concretionary masses coloured and impregnated with
manganese that had formed on the sea-floor.[1] We had collected 125 kilo-

1. Manganese nodules basically consist of manganese and iron oxides and hydroxides
   arranged in concentric layers around a nucleus. They were first discovered during the
   Challenger Expedition when large quantities were dredged from the deep Pacific.
   Individual nodules range in shape from spheroidal to flat and vary from a few microns
   in diameter to vast masses weighing several tons. Ever since their discovery the nodules
   have been of considerable scientific interest, originally because there was uncertainty as

23–24.IV.34   grams of these and mixed with them was a small quantity of mud; but there was not a sign of any living organisms, so it seems safe to conclude that this area of the bottom is a completely azoic one and in this respect is similar to the area further to the north around the southern coast of Arabia and the Gulf of Oman. As soon as the trawl was up the chemists took over and commenced to make temperature observations and collect water samples at all standard depths between the surface and the bottom, and then about midnight we shackled on the heavy Bigelow sounding tube and sent this down. Bottom was struck at 4,850 metres, which agreed very well with the depth as given by the echo-sounder, and on hauling in we found that we had secured a very fine core of a soft reddish-coloured ooze that seemed singularly free from *Globigerina* or other foraminifera. There could be little doubt that this was the red clay recorded from this part of the Arabian Sea basin by Sir John Murray.

During the time that we were working at the station, several sharks had been swimming round the ship accompanied by their little pilot fish (*Naucrates ductor*) and by several sucker fish (*Echeneis* sp.). The sailors amused themselves by putting a line with a shark hook over and succeeded in catching three of them. There didn't appear to be very much planktonic life in the surface waters, but I saw a few examples of the usual pink-tinged medusa, *Aurelia*, some of which were accompanied by a small fish, and one or two small medusae with long tentacles, probably *Pelagia perla*. While we were carrying out the hydrological work the new drum of the hydrographic winch that we had had specially made for us in Colombo to replace the one that had cracked, commenced to give trouble, for, although it had been made extra strong, it at once began to spread when the strain of taking samples in deep water was thrown on it. Owing to this spread the drum started to rub against the rod that operated the guide-rollers and the resulting noise was perfectly dreadful; a later examination of the drum showed that it had actually cracked. This again necessitated the transfer of the hydrographic wire to the small drum of the trawling winch, which already

---

to whether they were of terrestrial or extra-terrestrial origin. It is now known that they are produced in the deep sea, but the precise manner of their formation is still uncertain.

During the John Murray Expedition, manganese nodules were obtained only at Station 166 and did not apparently produce much excitement on the part of the Expedition members. This sample is referred to in Wiseman's account of the basalts from the Carlsberg Ridge in the Expedition Reports, but is not dealt with in any detail.

Commercial interest in deep sea manganese nodules has developed since the 1950s, not so much for the high concentrations of manganese and iron which they contain, but for the much smaller amounts of more valuable metals including copper, nickel and cobalt. Nodule recovery systems are already being actively developed and this resource may in the future supply a significant proportion of requirements of their contained metals.

had coiled on it a length of hydrographic wire and the wire that we had been using for the Ekman current-meter; as these had to be transferred elsewhere before we could coil the hydrographic wire on the drum, we were busy all the afternoon of the 24th making these changes.

The ship was stopped for our next station (167) at dawn on the 25th, but we were not able to begin work immediately for it was found that the eye-splice on the end of the hydrographic wire was too small to admit the passage of the pin of the shackle of the depth-recorder and so a new eye-splice had to be made. As soon as this was done the heavy Bigelow tube was shackled on and sent down. The depth when we stopped the ship, as given by the echo-sounder, had been 4,460 metres, but the bottom-tube struck the sea-floor when only 4,060 metres of wire had run out, so that it was clear that the sea-bottom was somewhat irregular in this area. On hauling in we got a good core of reddish-cream ooze that was rather more gritty than the last and seemed to have many more foraminifera in it, so that it more nearly approached a *Globigerina* ooze in its general character instead of being a red clay. The chemists then carried on with the hydrological work and this was completed about 1.15 in the afternoon.

During the afternoon the wind went round to the north-east and the *Mabahiss* made good progress on her westward course. There were a number of flying-fish about, but otherwise there was little or no animal life to be seen. As we steamed westward that afternoon and the following night the bottom showed a considerable range of variation in the depth, which continued to be great; at first the depth was about 2,700 fathoms and then had risen to 2,200 fathoms, but at about 9 o'clock in the evening it dropped again to about 2,500 fathoms.

According to our calculations we should by now have been getting into the neighbourhood of the Carlsberg Ridge if, as seemed probable, this extended from Socotra to the Chagos Archipelago, but when I turned in the depth was still over 2,200 fathoms. I therefore arranged that if and when the depth shallowed up to 1,750 fathoms, I was to be called and we would put the trawl down so as to get a haul on the eastern side of the ridge. At about 11 o'clock I was wakened up and told that we were in 1,800 fathoms and I repeated my request that the officer of the watch should call me when we got into 1,750 fathoms. At 3 o'clock on the 26th I was called and was told that we were then in water of a depth of 1,500 fathoms; it was clear that we were once again over the Carlsberg Ridge, so I routed out the other biologists and we prepared for a trawl with the Monegasque net. This was ready by 3.30, but by this time the depth had increased again to 1,620 fathoms and I then learnt that before I was

26–27.IV.34   called we had passed over a ridge on which the depth was only 1,350 fathoms.

The trawl was hoisted over the side and was sent down (Station 168). I had selected the Monegasque trawl because the indications given by the echo-sounder seemed to point to the bottom being rather rough. While we were still paying out the trawl wire, the depth increased still further to 1,740 fathoms, but at last we had a sufficient length of wire out and the nippers and dynamometer were put on and trawling commenced; we left the net down for an hour, during which time the strain on the dynamometer never varied from 1 ton 18 cwt. It took us until 9.15 to get the net up again, and when we got it on board we found that the rope becket on the frame had carried away, the frame had been badly bent and one of the stirrups had been broken across; it looked as if the net had caught in some obstruction on the bottom and that this had caused the rope becket to part and the stirrup on that side had then caught in the obstruction and had been bent backwards until it snapped across. The catch was very small, but caught in the net were some small fragments of a rock that seemed to be a foraminiferal limestone and it seems probable that this part of the ridge is composed of this material and that it was in this rock that the net had caught.

In order that the chemists might, if possible, put down a hydrological station on the top of the ridge or near the crest, we then steamed back on our course for an hour, but we failed to get any less depth, most of the bottom being at about 1,800 fathoms; so we then turned west again and at about mid-day we got to the top of a second ridge, or perhaps a continuation of the one that we had crossed, for the depth again shoaled to about 1,500 fathoms. The ship was again stopped and the chemists carried out a series of observations on the character of the water and when that was completed Gilson took a series of observations with the Harvey net.

The next morning at 6.30 the ship was stopped again for another station and on this occasion the chemists started first by sending down the heavy Bigelow tube to get the depth and a sample of the bottom. There was a marked kick when the tube struck the bottom at a depth of 3,705 metres, but when we got the tube back again we found that there was not only no bottom sample in it, but not even a trace of mud on the outside; this, taken in conjunction with the marked kick, made us think that the bottom here must be a hard one. We then proceeded with the hydrographic work and this went badly, for when we had sent down a string of Ekman water-bottles we found on hauling them in again that the messenger had failed to release the trigger and so the top bottle had not turned over, and in consequence none of the string had worked, so we had to send the whole string down again a second time. This time we put two messengers on the line together to make quite sure that they worked, and the result was successful. Having completed work with the Ekman bottles we again sent down the Bigelow tube to make sure, if possible, that the bottom was hard, and to make assurance doubly sure we lashed on to the side of the Bigelow tube a Baillie rod that would retain the contents if the bottom was soft. This time bottom was struck at a depth of 3,685 metres, but so great was the kick that the wire jumped off the wheel of the accumulator and kinked, and one kink caught in the ball-bearing block through which the wire was running. A moment later as the ship rose to a swell this kink suddenly straightened out with a jerk and some of the strands parted. This necessitated taking off the strain of the bottom tube by means of a stop and cutting the wire and putting in a splice before we could haul the tube in again. This was eventually done and the Bigelow tube was hoisted in soon after 2 o'clock in the afternoon; it was again empty, but the Baillie rod was full of a soft *Globigerina* ooze that must, on both occasions, have been washed out of the Bigelow tube on the way up. We then decided to put down the Agassiz trawl and in order to make sure that it reached the bottom we attached to the frame 150 lbs of additional weights, while a 50-lb weight was attached to the cod-end. I also paid out much more wire than should have been necessary and we towed the net for an hour (Station 170), but on hauling in there was practically nothing in the net and one was left wondering whether, in spite of our precautions and the additional weights, the net had ever been on the bottom. During the trawl the wire had streamed out towards the west and observations showed that there was a surface current setting us to the eastward at a rate of about a mile a hour; even so, the net should have reached the bottom and it is possible that here too the fauna is scarce or absent altogether.

While we were working this station a large number of sharks, more than we had seen at one time throughout the whole voyage, were continuously swimming round the ship and most of them were accompanied by pilot fish and sucker fish. They all seemed to belong to the same species; their colour was a brown fading to white underneath and with white tips to the dorsal and pectoral fins. The only shark that I know in Indian waters that shows this coloration is *Carcharias gangeticus*. In all there must have been at least twenty of these brutes, some of them of considerable size. The crew got out a shark hook and put it over the side with a lump of meat on it and two of the ship's officers had a rifle, and between them they did quite considerable execution. Throughout the greater part of the day the flying-fish kept coming out of the water on our port side in batches. Later in the

27–28.IV.34 day we could see a number of medium-sized fish that seemed to belong to the tunny family and were in all probability the kind known as the bonito, jumping out of the water, and where this was going on a number of gulls were flying round, obviously attracted to the spot. It was interesting to note that as soon as the dolphins came near the ship the sharks immediately sheered off.

We finished work at this station about 6 o'clock in the evening of the 27th and, having got under way, we steamed in a west-north-west direction towards the channel that runs between Cape Guardafui and the westernmost island of the Socotra group; this course took us along the line of the Carlsberg Ridge and the depth of water continued to be in the region of 2,000 fathoms.

At 6 o'clock in the evening of the 28th we stopped for our next station (171). The weather was wonderfully fine all day and in the morning there had been hardly any breeze. In the early morning there were numerous flying-fish darting out of the water but, as usual, their numbers showed a marked falling off as the day wore on. We had now quite definitely got into a strong surface-drift that was setting towards the east at a rate of about 1 knot; as this was against us we were rather later than I had expected in getting to our position and this compelled us to work at night. The biologists started operations by putting over the Agassiz trawl (Station 171) and, as on the last occasion, it seemed possible that the net had not reached the bottom at all; to make sure that it got there this time we put still more additional weights on the frame and I paid out considerably more wire than was, theoretically, necessary. The depth, as given by the echo-sounder when we commenced operations, was 2,200 fathoms, but when the net had been down a little time this decreased to 2,100 fathoms. We first paid out 5,500 metres of wire, but when this was out we found that there was a bad over-riding coil a little further on the drum of the winch, and as this was the last station at which we should be working in such deep water and so have so much wire out, we decided to pay out more wire and take this over-riding coil out. We therefore paid out another 300 metres of the wire and then recoiled about 150 metres of it again; so we thus had between 5,600 and 5,700 metres of wire out. The net was left down for two hours and we started to haul in at 10 o'clock. The net came up shortly after midnight and in it was a moderate catch, the predominant part being a number of echinoderms and a single fine blind deep-sea fish, *Benthosaurus* sp. The chemists then took over and started taking a bottom sample and carrying out the usual hydrological work. The heavy Bigelow tube was shackled on to the hydrographic wire and was sent down. Bottom was struck at 3,800 metres and we started to haul

in again, but when only some 200 metres of the wire had been got in, a
splice in the wire came in over the meter-wheel and, the strain being too
great, the splice pulled out and the Bigelow tube and 3,600 metres of
wire went to the bottom! This left only sufficient wire on the drum to
carry out temperature and hydrological observations on the water down
to 2,000 metres depth, and on the completion of this work Gilson made
a series of observations with the Harvey net. Work was over soon after
5 o'clock on the 29th and we then steamed off on our course towards
Cape Guardafui, but about 3 o'clock in the afternoon we stopped again in
order to carry out a mid-water trawl with a series of nets (Station 172). The
depth, as given by the echo, had now increased to about 2,500 fathoms. We
shackled on the 2-metre diameter net at the end of the wire and 50
metres above this we attached a 1-metre diameter net; three other 1-metre
nets were attached at intervals to the wire and the lengths paid out were
such as we calculated would be sufficient to get the lowest net down to
2,000 metres depth, while the other nets would be fishing at depths of
1,000, 500 and 250 metres respectively. We towed the whole string for two
hours and then started to heave in. The first three nets came up all right,
but we found that the lowest 1-metre diameter net had completely carried
away. The extraordinary thing about this was that the shackle by which the
net had been attached to the wire was intact but all four of the wire bridles
had parted. Then when we got up the large 2-metre diameter net we found
that there was a huge hole in one side of it. The only possible explanation
seems to be that for some unknown reason the 1-metre net had carried
away and then had been captured by the 2-metre diameter net and had
burst its way through that, snapping one of the strong longitudinal bands
of canvas that run down the length of the net as a support. It seems hardly
probable that the strain of towing the smaller net through the water could
have snapped four strong wire bridles or that the weight of the small net
could have burst a strong canvas band in the big net; one was left wondering whether some large marine animal had blundered into the small net
carrying this away and then, in its struggles to rid itself of this encumbrance,
had blundered through the large 2-metre net that was fishing some 50
metres lower down. While the trawl was in progress we could again see the
dolphins chasing smaller fish, which from time to time jumped right out of
the water, while a number of birds, of a uniform dark-brown colour,
hovered overhead and occasionally swooped down to pick up something
off the surface; they were probably shearwaters but they were too far away
for one to be able to recognize their species.

During the following night we encountered a very strong current that
was setting us back towards the east or south-east, so that we were three

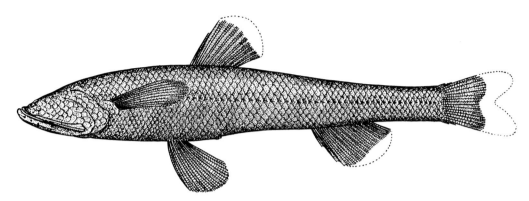

FIG. 32. *Bathymicrops sewelli*, a blind deep-sea fish named in honour of Sewell and presumably the specimen referred to in the narrative as *Benthosaurus* sp. (Reproduced from *Scient. Rep. John Murray Exped.*, Vol. VII, No. 1, Fig. 7.)

30.IV.34   hours late in getting to our next station (173). The depth was now about 4,440 metres, but during the previous day the chemists had got up an extra length of hydrographic wire and, after splicing this on to the wire on the winch, had run it on to the drum, so that they were able to work right down to the bottom. At first we tried to work with two wires, one on each side of the ship, the Nansen-Pettersson bottle on the starboard wire and the Ekman reversing-bottle on the port side. This had been our usual custom, but on this occasion we found that it could not be done. The surface current was setting us to the east at a rate of about 2 knots and this necessitated so much manoeuvring of the ship to keep the port wire up and down that the starboard wire trailed so far aft that there was a distinct danger that it might be caught round the propellor. We thus had to confine our work to one wire at a time and this caused the work to proceed so slowly that it was 6.30 in the evening before we had finished. There was little or no wind all day, occasional light airs from the south west, and the sea had been a flat calm, but in spite of these favourable conditions there had been little or no plankton to be seen on the surface, and curiously enough there wasn't a single shark swimming round. This was such a contrast to the station over the Carlsberg Ridge three days previously that one could not help wondering what could be the cause; both stations were on or near the line of steamer traffic between Aden and Colombo, which might possibly be a suitable haunt for these scavengers, and one wondered whether there was anything in the character of the water over the Carlsberg Ridge that might give rise to conditions that were more suitable or more attractive to them.

    During the night of 30 April we still had a strong head current against us and it was now clear that this was setting out of the Gulf of Aden through the channel between Cape Guardafui and the Socotra group of islands. According to the Admiralty current charts such a current might have been expected in the month of June, but this year conditions seemed to be a month or so early; this corroborated what Captain Brodie of the BISS *Karanja*, one of the ships that were engaged in taking water samples for us, had told me when I met him in Mombasa, namely that from his experience he had reached the conclusion that on many occasions in the Arabian Sea one finds the conditions in any given month correspond best to those that are shown on the Admiralty charts for the month following.

By breakfast time on 1 May we were once again in sight of Cape Guardafui, but owing to the strong head current it was past mid-day before we were in the middle of the channel between the Cape and the island of Abd al Kuri, where we were going to carry out a repetition of the station that we had made on our outward cruise the previous October. As we steamed up towards our position we continually put up a few flying-fish; these were big fellows and as we watched them come out of the water there could be no doubt that their large pectoral fins vibrated rapidly, rather more rapidly than the beat of the wings in a bird's flight and more nearly resembling the movement of the wings of an insect. This same movement could again be seen whenever the fish accelerated its flight by the to-and-fro movements of the tail fin as it dropped near the water. A number of the fish were also seen to alter the direction of their flight and many of them swung away downwind before plunging back into the water.

Soon after noon we stopped to carry out work at Station 174 and, as at this point the depth of water is only some 900 metres, we were finished in under three hours. I had hoped that we should find a certain amount of Sargasso weed floating about in this region, for when we were on our way out there had been a lot of it in the Gulf of Aden and with this strong surface current setting out of the Gulf it was only reasonable to suppose that some might be swept out with it; but there wasn't a sign of any.

We then steamed on towards the north to get to our next station. We were now back again in the Gulf and wished to repeat the series of five stations that we had run across the entrance to the Gulf of Aden during our outward voyage, in order that we might be able to determine the seasonal changes that take place in this area. It was after 7 o'clock in the evening before we were able to commence work, but whereas this had taken five hours on the first occasion, this time we had finished in a little

FIG. 33. The Agassiz trawl bent on a rocky bottom, 2 May 1934.
(*Photo:* H. C. Gilson.)

2.V.34   over two-and-a-half, which shows clearly how increased experience enables
one to save time.

   When our work was completed we drifted for some four hours while the
Chief cleaned his boiler tubes, and we then headed south-west towards the
Elephant Back Rock on the northern coast of Italian Somaliland in order to
put in some more biological work in that region. We were still a long way
off the African coast when I came on deck at about 7 o'clock, but by 9.30
we were in a position in a depth of 400 fathoms and I sent the Agassiz
trawl down (Station 176). At first it looked as if the trawl had got hung up
in something for the wire, after it had been triced up aft, ran out towards
the port beam at almost right angles to the ship; after a bit, however, it
gradually came aft and it seemed clear that there was a strong current
setting the ship off the coast. As the trawl progressed there was comparatively little strain on the wire, the dynamometer varying between 17 cwt
and 1 ton, and the echo-sounder indicated that the bottom was dead flat.

We got quite an interesting catch which included about thirty specimens of   2–3.V.34
a small transparent holothurian. We then steamed on until we were in a
depth of only 200 fathoms, when we sent the Agassiz trawl down again
(Station 177). This time, as the wire was being paid out, we drifted into
somewhat shallower water and the echo-sounder indicated a depth of
only 140 fathoms by the time sufficient wire had been paid out. As soon
as the wire was triced up aft we started to trawl, but on this occasion
our luck was again bad, for before very long the strain began to go up
and down in an ominous manner, jumping from 15 cwt to over a ton
and a half and then suddenly falling again to 9 cwt; after about twenty
minutes we got stuck fast in something and the strain went up to nearly
2 tons, so we stopped the ship and started to haul in. When we got the
trawl up we found that the rope becket on the frame had parted and the
frame itself had been bent into the shape of a U, while three of the extra
weights on the frame and the weight at the cod-end of the net had completely disappeared. Even so, there was a small catch in the cod-end,
consisting mostly of sea-urchins, so our labours were not altogether in
vain.

After we had got the remains of the trawl on board we shackled on the
grab and carried out a series of hauls, taking samples of the bottom at
depths of 50, 150 and 200 fathoms. At our first attempt at the 150-fathom
depth the grab came up with a large mass of rock caught between its teeth,
so we sent it down a second time. At all three positions the bottom consisted
for the most part of a mixture of green sand and mud and there was quite a
rich fauna, consisting mostly of polychaete worms and lamellibranch
molluscs.

It was interesting to see how familiarity with the working of the heavy
grab had also resulted in a curtailment of the time occupied in taking a
haul; when we put the grab over in a depth of 100 fathoms in this part of
the African coast on 12 October it had taken us forty minutes to make a
haul, but on this occasion the time taken in sending the grab down to the
bottom in 150 fathoms and getting it back on board was exactly nine
minutes.

On completing our work here we steamed off towards the north to get
to the third of our series of stations across the mouth of the Gulf. We
reached our position about 7 o'clock on the morning of the 3rd. There was
now quite a fresh south-easterly breeze blowing and on our way northward
the *Mabahiss* had been giving an occasional lurch as she struck a wave on
her starboard bow, but as soon as we stopped the wind was only sufficient
to keep the temperature cool and not strong enough to make conditions
unpleasant for work. Work proceeded smoothly and we had completed our

3–4.V.34   hydrological observations in about three hours, and we then steamed on to the fourth of our stations which we reached about 3.30 in the afternoon. Unfortunately the echo-sounder had again gone wrong, and this time it seemed as if the damage was really serious, for the combined efforts of Farquharson and Lloyd Jones failed to get it going again.

Before we actually reached our station and while work was in progress we saw several animals that attracted our attention. While we were steaming northwards we were followed from one station to the next by a whale that, from time to time, could be seen to come to the surface to blow; when first seen it was quite close to the ship's side and I dashed down to my cabin to get my camera in order to photograph it, but before I got back on deck it had dropped too far astern. Then, just as we were finishing our work at Station 182 at about half past five in the evening, we again saw a large animal quite close to the ship; it swam rapidly past us close on our starboard side where Gilson was taking water samples with the Nansen-Pettersson water bottle, and he was quite certain that he saw a pair of horizontal tail flukes behind a long slender fin rising from the middle of the back. He estimated the length at about 15 to 20 feet, and the colour certainly seemed to be brown. If this description is correct, then this animal was certainly a whale and might be the same species that we had seen at Station 132 in the neighbourhood of the Seychelles. The character of the dorsal fin—long and slender—agrees with the description of the killer whale (*Orca gladiator*); on one occasion many years ago on the *Investigator* I saw four of what I took to be this species in the Bay of Bengal. I happened to be below at the time but I immediately dashed up on deck with the camera and there, off the port bow about 150 yards away was a large animal, swimming just below the surface, but with *two* fins showing, a low and somewhat square-shaped one in front and a long slender one that rose for some distance above the water behind. Clearly this was not a whale and in length it appeared, so far as I could judge, to be considerably more than 20 feet; I should put it at about 30 feet or even more and though it was too far off and the light too bad for me to be able to distinguish its colour, I am inclined to think that this may have been an example of the large whale-shark (*Rhineodon typicus*).

We finished work at this station about 6.30 in the evening and then steamed northwards to the last of our stations across the entrance to the Gulf. Our previous work in this area had shown that there is a submarine ridge, one of the series of such that traverse the Gulf of Aden, running from north-east to south-west across this part of the Gulf and I hoped to run a dog-leg across it and so increase our knowledge of its contours. However, the failure of the echo-sounder rendered this out of the question, so we steamed straight to our next position and began work there at 7

o'clock on the 4th. This was a repetition of Station 32 and, as we had taken
a sample of the bottom on the previous occasion, we didn't trouble to take
another so that our work was completed in just over an hour and a half,
whereas on the earlier occasion it took us five hours.

We were now once again in the region of a rich surface fauna. While
work was in progress a large scarlet-coloured *Pyrosoma* colony, looking
exactly like a deflated inner tube of a motor tyre, drifted close by on the
surface. The sea boat was immediately lowered and one of us went off in
her to try and secure the specimen but unfortunately it couldn't be found.
The day before, while we were steaming northwards, MacKenzie had seen
what must have been another specimen of the same animal, for he described
it as looking like a motor tyre of a red colour.

As soon as work at Station 183 was over we steamed off to get into
water of about 800 fathoms depth in order to carry out a trawl. On this
occasion, as an experiment, we fastened a strip of netting between the two
cross bars of the frame of the Agassiz net to act as a head net and prevent
any animals, and especially quick-swimming animals such as fish from
escaping the net in an upward direction. Unfortunately we were unable to
get any exact indication of the depth from the echo-sounder, but as soon as
we were in the approximate depth, as indicated by the soundings given on
the Admiralty chart, we sent down a Driver tube that we had modified on
board, by removing the valve apparatus at the bottom end, so that it would
act like a Bigelow tube. We ran out some 2,560 metres of wire without
getting any indication of when the bottom was struck and, as this was
clearly excessive, we quite expected to find that the last part of the wire had
been on the bottom and was, in all probability, tangled round the bottom
tube. We, therefore, hauled it in carefully and noticed that when about
1,300 metres of the wire were still out there were distinct traces of mud on
the wire, so that the remainder must have been coiled on the sea-floor; but
the wire continued to come in steadily and eventually the bottom tube
came up with a short core of green mud in the tube. It thus seemed probable
that the depth was about 1,270 metres and, assuming this to be correct, we
sent down the Agassiz trawl and towed it for a couple of hours (Station
184). Everything went well, but when we hauled the net in again at the
conclusion of the trawl we found that we had got only a small catch, in
spite of the net having been fishing all the time. This paucity of the fauna is
all in keeping with the general indications obtained from our previous
work in this area that as one proceeds eastward along the Arabian coast the
fauna gets less and less until this condition culminates in the completely
lifeless area in the vicinity of Cape Ras al Hadd. One feature of the catch
was the presence of a number of fragments of dead coral, such as *Caryo-*

4–5.V.34   *phyllia*, *Lophohelia*, or similar branching forms; in addition there were a few solitary corals, but every specimen was dead and eroded. The major part of the catch, so far as living forms are concerned, was composed of about thirty examples of a thick-skinned holothurian. As soon as the trawl was up on deck we again sent down the bottom tube, and this time we got a clear indication that the depth was 1,270 metres, so that we had been working in water of about 100 fathoms less than I had hoped for, but without the assistance of the echo-sounder it is impossible to select any given depth for a trawl.

As soon as work was concluded we steamed westwards and early on the following morning the ship was stopped for another trawl. As soon as it was light Farquharson had worked out our position and from the chart gave us a probable depth of water of 1,972 metres; the sounding that we took a few minutes later gave a depth of exactly 2,000 metres with a bottom of green mud. We then put down the Agassiz trawl (Station 185) and towed it for an hour and a half; on this occasion the resulting catch was distinctly good, but there was a very significant absence of any free-moving animals, such as fish and prawns, and this gave rise to a suspicion that the netting between the two cross bars of the frame was not acting, as we had hoped that it would, as a means of preventing such animals from escaping the net, but, on the contrary, it was serving as a warning and was giving the fish and prawns sufficient time to make their escape before they were actually trapped by the net itself. The net came up so full of mud that we had once again to leave it hanging over the side for a time while some of the mud was washed out before we could get it in-board. The catch was certainly much more prolific than the haul that we had made the previous day, and this again seemed to bear out the view that there is a gradual increase in the fauna as one proceeds westward up the Gulf.

After completing work at this station we steamed for about an hour out into deeper water and put down a series of mid-water nets, the bottom one being at a depth of about 1,000 metres (Station 186). Here again the result was a good haul at all depths, and it was interesting to find that we had again got a number of examples of the deep-sea medusae of the genera *Periphylla* and *Atolla*, which we hadn't seen for quite a long time; indeed the previous occasions on which we had got these medusae in any quantity had also been in the Gulf of Aden during the month of October.

There were again several of the large crimson *Pyrosoma* colonies to be seen, and while we were carrying out the trawl a large example, that both I and the officer on the bridge estimated to be about 5 feet in length and with a width of some 9 inches, drifted by; another one was seen about 4 o'clock that same evening and yet a third early the next day, so there seemed to be a fair number of them about. Dr Faouzi suggested that it might have been colonies of *Pyrosoma* of about this size that he had seen one night when we were working off the Arabian coast in October or early November; these were long luminous objects, about 3 feet in length, that had drifted past the ship, at some depth below the surface when we were at anchor or were drifting; on the other hand they may have been long chains of salps that were very common at that time.

As the chemists wished to get a series of observations on the temperature and chemical characters of the water in a position mid-way between our two series of stations across the Gulf, we steamed well out into mid-channel and at about 10 o'clock that night they carried out work at a hydrological station (187) in a depth of water of some 1,650 metres and over a bottom of green mud. We then steamed in again towards the Arabian coast and at half past ten on the 6th were in position for another cast of the Agassiz net. The depth of water as given by a sounding was some 300 fathoms and the bottom was again green mud, a good core being obtained. The Agassiz trawl was then shackled on and sent down (Station 188). At the commencement of the trawl the pace at which we were steaming appeared to me to be too fast, so I asked the bridge for a reduction of five revolutions, but apparently my request was misinterpreted and translated into a request for five *additional* revolutions. When we hauled the net in after an hour it was clear that it had never been on the bottom at all, so we put it over again and this time, to make sure that it did get down, I let out an excessive amount of wire and the pace was carefully regulated. On starting to haul in there was a considerable strain on the wire and this, combined with a certain amount of carelessness on the part of some of the crew, resulted in one of our best men getting his fingers badly pinched as the tricing rope was let go aft; fortunately no bones were broken. When the net came up there was a large hole in it and this I attributed to the net having filled with such a quantity of the bottom mud that the strain on the net, which was getting old, was too great for it to stand and so some of the meshes had given way. The cod-end was still full of mud and this was carefully put through the sieves, but there was little or no animal life in it—a very different result from our two previous hauls.

We then ran inshore into water of a depth of only 50 fathoms and sent the grab down (Station 189); this came up with a good sample of a green sand mixed with a little mud, and to our surprise there was a slight, though distinct, smell of sulphuretted hydrogen gas. We hadn't expected to find this gas present so far to the west. We later put the grab down again in depths of 100, 150 and 200 fathoms and in each case got a good sample of the bottom, but none of these showed any trace of gas. It is possible that

5–7.V.34   the concentration of the gas in this area may be stronger at one season of
the year than at another and, if so, this might account for the very im-
poverished fauna that we had obtained at the previous haul of the Agassiz
net in 300 fathoms.

From the 100 fathom depth we obtained in the grab no less than fourteen
examples of a species of locust shrimp, *Squilla investigatoris*. This particular
species had been obtained in this vicinity several years before by the *Investigator*; the story told was that there had been about 500 examples caught
in one haul of the trawl, so, thinking that the animal must be quite common,
the Surgeon-Naturalist on board sent some 480 to the cookhouse where
they had been turned into prawn curry which had been much appreciated
by the Officers Mess. The remaining twenty examples he had kept, but
when he got back to the Indian Museum in Calcutta at the end of the
survey season he had discovered that these examples represented a new
species that had never been seen before. It was roughly estimated that the
value of each of the specimens, being from the scientific point of view co-
types, was about one pound sterling, so that the total value of the prawn
curry was about £480!

Having completed our hauls with the grab we steamed further westward
in order to repeat a trawl that we had made on this coast in October at
Station 34 and that had given very good results. In the meantime the net
had to be repaired and, as the seaman who usually did this work was the
one who had had his fingers pinched and was therefore *hors de combat*, this
work fell on Macan, so that he had a busy time; but everything was ready
to time and on the morning of the 7th at half past seven we stopped for
another station (193).

There was a slight breeze blowing from the south-east, but this was
barely sufficient to turn the anemometer and the sea was like the proverbial
mill-pond. As this was a repeat station, we attempted to reproduce as far as
possible the conditions of the earlier trawl and so see whether we could get
any evidence of seasonal changes in the fauna. The resulting catch was not
so good as on the earlier occasion and many of the ingredients appeared to
be different. This might, however, be quite well accounted for by a slight
difference in our actual position; Alcock has recorded how in his day the
Investigator tried to repeat a trawl which had yielded immense numbers of
bird's-nest sponges (*Hyalonema*) on the first occasion, but at the second
attempt they did not get a single specimen. I had a very similar experience on
the Burma coast, when I attempted to repeat a trawl at a position that was
in sight of land and where we had every facility for enabling us to fix our position with certainty. My object was to try and get another example of a lovely
ophiuroid (brittle star) with branching arms, *Trichaster flagellifer* v. Mattens

(*T. elegans* Ludwig) a single example of which had been obtained during the
previous survey season and which, apart from this specimen, had never
been recorded outside the Pacific Ocean; not a single specimen of *Trichaster
flagellifer* did we get, but we captured some twenty-two examples of another
species of the same genus *T. acanthifer* Doderlein, which at that time had
never been described. With these results in mind I was not, therefore, very
surprised to find that the two hauls did not appear to correspond very well.

As soon as the trawl was on board the biologists were busy getting the
decks cleared for another haul that we were going to make in a depth of
about 100–150 fathoms. While we were steaming in towards the land one
of the largest schools of dolphins that I have ever seen came bounding
over the water towards us and I dashed down to my cabin and got the
cine-camera in time to get a good shot of them; these examples appeared to
be about 5 to 6 feet in length and were a brown colour.

Having reached our station in 120 fathoms we put the Agassiz trawl
down for the last time (Station 194), for as soon as we left Aden on our
final cruise we should be working in and around the southern end of the
Red Sea again and our previous experience had shown that the only form
of apparatus that was of any use in that area was the 4-foot triangular
dredge.

As we approached the station we ran into quite a different mass of
water. Hitherto along this coast the water had been of a green colour and
had been extremely rich in plankton, the current, setting westward, carrying
a number of organisms from the Arabian coast region into the Gulf of
Aden. Now the surface was setting eastwards in the Gulf and the general
trend of these currents conformed to the scheme shown in the Admiralty
charts for the month of June, although we were only at the beginning of
May. The water was clear blue in colour and though I devoted quite a lot
of time, while we were trawling, to searching the surface, I failed to detect
a single animal. The same paucity or complete absence was noticeable in
the Sargasso weed, of which at this time of the year there was none to be
seen, though in the months of September and October masses of it had
been quite common.

On this occasion, as there was no hurry, I left the trawl down for a
couple of hours in the hope of getting a good catch; and we most certainly
did, for when the net came up it was about one-third full of animals and
was quite free from the usual mass of mud. The chief ingredient of the
catch was an enormous collection, between 4,500 and 5,000 examples, of a
sand-dollar *Laganum depressum* or some similar species; these were all of a
dirty green colour and as we picked them out of the catch the colour came
off on our fingers until they were deeply stained. The next most prolific

7.V.34 ingredient was a species of lobster, *Puerulus angulatus* (Spence Bate); there were 150 of these and, as the species is a well-known one, I for once broke my usual rule and seventy of them were sent to the cookhouse. There were

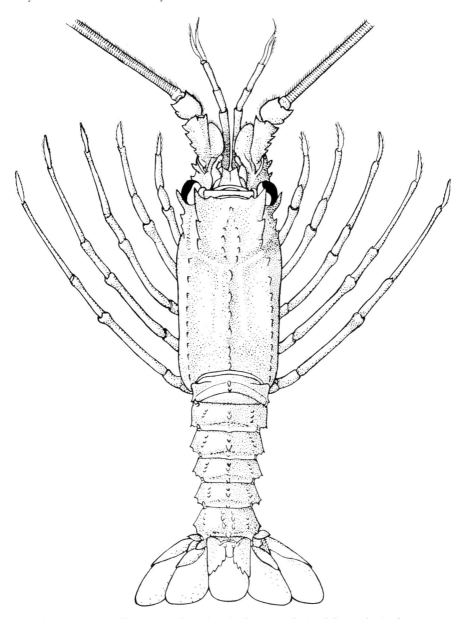

FIG. 34. *Puerulus sewelli*, a previously undescribed species of spiny lobster obtained at Stations 24 and 194 in the Gulf of Aden. (Reproduced from *Scient. Rep. John Murray Exped.*, Vol. V, No. 5, Fig. 4.)

also numbers of fish of a large variety of species and numerous starfish and
other invertebrates. Without any question this was the catch of the season
and a fitting close to our trawling with the Agassiz net.

Having completed the trawl, we steamed on towards Aden so as to be in
position the next morning for a repetition of the work that we had done at
Station 36 the previous October. The chemists were soon busy, Thompson
and Gilson working the batteries of Ekman water-bottles on the port-side
wire and Mohamed carrying out observations with the Nansen-Pettersson
water bottle on the starboard side. As we were due to reach port later in
the day, the deck staff were all very busy getting the ship cleaned up and
repainted and some of the men were working alongside in the dinghy,
scraping and cleaning the waterline.

To reach out from the ship's side and clip a messenger on to the hydrographic wire was easy enough for the other two, who stood well over 6
feet in their socks, but for Mohamed, who was only about 5 feet 4 inches in
height, it was a different matter and he had to stretch himself out to the
utmost over the bulwark to reach the wire. He had sent the bottle down
and was reaching out to send down the messenger and close the water
bottle, when his feet slipped from underneath him and he took a neat
header over the ship's side into some 200 fathoms or water; unfortunately,
he was, I think, the only member of the ship's company who could not
swim. As, however, he hit the water within a foot or so of the dinghy in
which two men were at work, he was promptly hauled out and safely
returned to the ship without having suffered, except from the shock; but it
was fortunate that he didn't actually fall over the side 2 feet further on for
then he would have fallen into the dinghy and might have hurt himself.

Having completed work at the station, we steamed on and entered Aden
Harbour about half-past three in the afternoon.

For some time past Captain MacKenzie's health had been gradually
giving way and the day before we were due to reach port he developed
high fever, so, as soon as the usual port formalities were concluded, Dr
Faouzi took him ashore and got him admitted to the European General
Hospital under the care of Colonel Phipson of the Indian Medical Service.
Colonel Phipson very kindly asked me to go and stay with him and, as the
Chief was going to draw fires and examine the boiler for a suspected leak,
and that means no lights or fans on board, I was very glad to accept and
spend a couple of nights in the same bungalow that I had occupied when I
was Port Health Officer during some months of 1915.

The evening before we were due to sail we had the first serious accident
of the whole voyage; we were busy transferring a number of boxes, containing part of our collection for shipment to England, and certain articles

8.V.34   of apparatus that had been lent to the Expedition for return to their respective owners in India when the ship's carpenter, Abdul Ghani, who was helping to lift a heavy crate, slipped and the crate crashed down on his foot. He was taken off to hospital and put under the X-rays and it was found that he had broken three of the bones of his foot. He was put into splints and bandages and we were able to take him on with us and I am glad to say that the bones completely united and he eventually fully recovered.

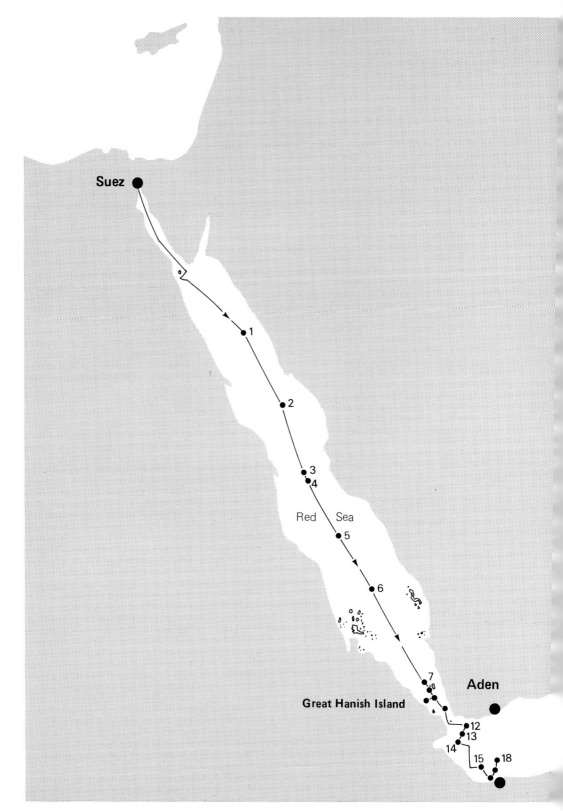

F<small>IG</small>. 35. Track chart, Cruise 10: Aden–Red Sea. Station numbers are indicated.

Chapter 11

Aden to Alexandria

WE were due to leave port on the 14th and an hour or two before we sailed MacKenzie rejoined the ship; he was better and had completely lost his fever so we were hopeful that there would be no recurrence of his illness. On leaving port we steamed due south in order to put in a series of hydrological stations across the head of the Gulf of Aden and thus repeat our observations of last October so as to detect the seasonal changes that occur in this area. There were three stations in all on this line and the first was carried out about 4.15 in the afternoon, while the next two were worked late that night and early the following morning, thus completing our section between Aden and Berbera on the African coast. Work at this last station (199) was over at about 7 o'clock on the morning of the 14th and we then steamed westward to get into the position of our next station, which was the most southerly of the series that we had previously run across the southern entrance to the Straits of Bab-el-Mandab.

We reached out position about 6.30 in the evening and work was at once commenced, but before we had had time to do more than collect a few samples and take temperature readings in the upper levels we were compelled to abandon work for the time being. Captain MacKenzie again developed high fever, with a very rapid pulse, and was in a state of delirium; the vibration and noise from the two winches, the one on the well-deck just outside the Captain's cabin and the other on the forward part of the lower bridge just overhead, was too much for him to stand in his state of ill-health. Throughout the night of the 14th we drifted idly, hoping that by the morning MacKenzie would be sufficiently recovered to enable us to continue our work. As we lay drifting, a passing vessel came across to us to see if we wanted any assistance and on receiving our assurance that we were all right, steamed off again on her course.

During the 14th a fresh breeze was blowing from the east, with a force 3/4 on the Beaufort Scale, but this died down and on the following day the sea was quite calm. Fortunately, MacKenzie was better and so we were able

to continue our work. At our first station at the southern end of the section   15–17.V.34
across the Gulf the sea-water had a most peculiar and unpleasant colour, a
sort of dirty green-brown; a sample was collected and examined, the contents being separated by means of the centrifuge, to see what plants or
animals might be causing this unusual colour; but the examination gave
very little result and it seemed that the water, which was probably coming
out of the Gulf of Tajura, might owe its character to some purely local
peculiarity. The transparency of the water was very low; unfortunately, no
observation was taken by means of the Secchi disc but as the Ekman bottles
were sent down they were visible to a depth of only about 5 metres below
the surface, while a shark swimming about only a few feet below the surface
was only just visible. Later in the day, when we steamed out into the
middle of the Gulf to carry out work at the middle of three stations, we
passed out of this dirty water into water of a clear blue-green colour; here
the transparency was markedly greater than it had been on the occasion of
our outward journey, for on that occasion the transparency of the water
had been only 8.5 metres in mid-channel and 3.5 metres on the Perim side,
whereas now it was 35.5 in mid-channel and 26.0 off Perim. The Sargasso
weed was still conspicuous by its absence, though one of my chemists
reported that he had seen a small mass of it the previous day, and on the
evening of the 15th we succeeded in securing a small floating colony on
which was a small swimming crab, while associated with it were several
small fish which, however, we were unable to secure.

Owing to MacKenzie's health it was impossible for us to do any work at
night, as the working winches kept him awake. We were thus unable to
carry out quite as many stations as I had hoped, but we managed to cram
an extra number into the day-time; we carried out three hydrographic
stations on the 15th and no less than three hydrographic stations and four
hauls with the grab on the 16th, while on the 17th we made one hydrographic station and carried out two hauls with the 4-foot triangular dredge.
The work at these stations confirmed our previous observations on the
marked paucity of the fauna in the deeper water of the south end of the
Red Sea. At one station we again got exactly the same type of fauna that
we had previously found, namely a small hydroid colony and a number of
serpulid worm tubes; but, after treating these latter with an anaesthetic for
over an hour, there was no sign of any living inhabitant. In the shallower
depths we got the same concretionary calcareous rock, some samples of
which clearly showed that they were being formed *in situ*, for embedded in
the rock were fragments of dead coral.

At our last station (209) on the 17th we had a somewhat exciting time.
The ship was stopped a few minutes after 12 noon and the 4-foot dredge

17–18.V.34   was sent down to the bottom, the depth, as given by the echo-sounder, being 200 fathoms. By 12.30 we had paid out sufficient wire and the meter-wheel was then taken off and the nippers and dynamometer applied; we then tried to trice the wire up aft, but a strong current swept the ship away from the wire until the tricing line was out to its fullest extent. We then tried to manoeuvre the ship up to the wire, but the strain on the trawl wire rose steadily to over 2 tons and our further attempts to manoeuvre the ship seemed to indicate that we were completely anchored by the dredge on the end of the wire. The wire was then running out almost at right angles to the ship on our port beam and there was a considerable strain on it; we started to heave in and slowly the wire came in over the gallows until there were about another 400 metres to come. At this point the strain suddenly eased up and the net came in. When we got it up to the surface we found that the net was about two-thirds full of greenish-brown mud and must have weighed about 2 tons; we got it in-board and the contents were passed through the sieves. There was very little animal life in it apart from a very few small live corals and a few polychaete worms. Mixed with the mud were numerous animal remains, such as the shells of pteropod molluscs or of lamellibranchs and some small dead corals and the spines of sea-urchins. With these were numbers of masses of calcareous rock, that seemed to fall into two main types; firstly flattened masses, the surface of which was honeycombed and pitted and on which were empty serpulid worm tubes so that these must have come from the surface of the mud, and secondly rounded or angular masses of rock that appeared to be lighter in colour and softer in texture and that showed no sign of having been on the surface so that they were probably formed beneath the surface of the mud.

There can, I think, be little doubt that there is some chemical change going on in these deeper waters of the south end of the Red Sea that is inimical to animal life.

Midnight on 17 May saw the last of our observations; the work of the John Murray Expedition came to an end and I, at any rate, was sorry, for there are all sorts of problems that have arisen during the course of our several cruises that need further investigation before we shall be in a position to give the final answer.

For the next three days we steamed steadily northwards towards Port Tewfiq and all hands were kept thoroughly busy; the scientific staff were fully occupied in packing up our collections of animals and water samples, and getting these ready to be handed over to our Agents in Port Said for transmission to England; our Egyptian Officers were very busy getting the ship cleaned and repainted, so that by the time we reached Alexandria the little *Mabahiss* should again be in her accustomed Coast-guard dress and

bear as little resemblance as possible to the rather untidy research trawler
that she had been during the last nine months. The final effort was made
on the afternoon of the 19th when the two davits, with their accumulators
and the meter-wheels over which the hydrographic wires had run, were
taken down and were stowed away in the hold. The weather continued to
be fine and, thanks to a cool breeze that blew steadily from the north-west
or thereabouts, the temperature was far cooler than it had been when we
steamed down the Red Sea the previous September. A number of gulls
were now accompanying us, flying round and round the ship, and on the
18th I saw in the distance a fine swordfish jumping out of the water and
falling back again with a splash and for the last time I was able to note the
extraordinary way in which this large fish keeps on repeating this
manoeuvre for some ten to twelve times in succession before he finally
stops and fails to reappear; presumably this action is for the purpose of
getting rid of any external parasites that may be present, but, if so, they
seem to take a good deal of dislodging.

We reached Suez about 11.30 on the evening of 21 May and anchored
for the night. Almost at once one of the Coast-guard motor launches came
off to us bringing a few letters and the next morning a number of Coast-
guard officials and officers came off to welcome us back again and brought
several bouquets of flowers for us. They were unfeignedly glad to see us
back again, for I think that some of them were rather doubtful, when we
set out on our Expedition, whether they would ever see their little ship
again.

We left Suez a little before noon on the 22nd and steamed into the canal,
just ahead of a couple of tankers, and at intervals we were hailed by passing
boatmen or Coast-guards and Customs men, who waved to us and cheered
us as we went by. One man, who was on duty at one of the signal stations,
began by carrying out his usual routine and stood strictly to attention as
the Government Coast-guard ship steamed by, but a moment later his
feelings got the better of him and he danced and waved to us—but, alas,
this breach of the regulations was observed by his superior officer and as
we steamed away up the canal we could see him being ticked off for this
breach of proper decorum.

As we carried no searchlight and so could only go through the canal by
daylight, we had to anchor for the night at Ismailia and here again we were
boarded by more of the Coast-guard officials, among whom was Hamdi Bey,
the head official of this particular province, who very kindly invited us all
to a reception that he was giving in our honour at Port Said on the evening
of the 24th.

Later in the evening all hands were mustered on deck and Captain

24–26.V.34 MacKenzie congratulated the officers and crew on the splendid manner in which they had carried out their duties throughout the course of the Expedition and informed them that the Government of Egypt, acting through the Director of the Coast-guard Administration, had in recognition of their fine work promoted all non-commissioned officers and ratings in the service to a higher grade, the sole exception being one of the Rub Ries, Ali Eraiwa Hussain, who had already been promoted when we were in Colombo.

We left Ismailia at dawn the next morning and, steaming steadily through the northern section of the canal, reached Port Said about noon and almost at once we were again boarded by the officials of the Coast-guard Service and the Captain of the Port.

I discovered that the Port Captain, who was supervising the supply of water-sample bottles and the necessary labels to those merchant service ships that were taking observations for us, had run out of labels, so Mohamed and I set off post haste to find a printer who would put the matter in hand for us at once. We were at last fortunate enough to find one and he guaranteed that the work would be carried out immediately and a supply of labels be ready in time to be put on board the next outward-bound vessel that was due to pass through the port a few days later. In the evening I went ashore again to see our agent and then went on to the Casino Palace Hotel, where I met several officers of HMS *Enterprise*, which was lying in the harbour a little to the north of us; and a little later I was joined by Mohamed and we stayed on shore for dinner, returning to the *Mabahiss* about 10 o'clock.

The next morning was Empire Day and all the British ships in the harbour were dressed; but there was no holiday for us for during the course of the morning our agents sent a lighter alongside us and took off all our boxes of gear, specimens and so on. There were in all about seventy of these, of various sizes, but the prize one was a huge case that Farquharson had had made to take all the surveying instruments that had been lent to the Expedition by the Admiralty and this was so heavy that it had to be hoisted up on the derrick and swung over on to the lighter.

In the afternoon we all went ashore to the reception given by Hamdi Bey, the Director of the Eastern Province Section of the Coast Guards, and to which a number of British and Egyptian officials had been invited in order to meet us. After tea several speeches were made, congratulating us on the work that we had done and on our safe return, and then we all trooped down to the courtyard and were photographed. When this was over we had to say goodbye for we were due to leave port at 7 o'clock. We actually left about half an hour earlier and before long we were out in the Mediterranean on our way to Alexandria, where we were due to arrive at

Fɪɢ. 36. Sewell in IMS uniform, about to pay an official call ashore, May 1934.
(*Photo:* H. C. Gilson.)

26–29.V.34   about 4 o'clock the following afternoon. The weather continued good and though there was a stiff breeze from the north-east, this was on our starboard quarter and we made good progress.

We were off Alexandria early in the afternoon of the day following and one of the Coast-guard motor boats came out to us with Mr Albani and another officer of the engineering branch of the Coast-guard Service on board. We hove to and these two officers were transferred from the motor boat to the *Mabahiss* in our little dinghy; there was quite a sea running and they had a somewhat rough passage, but at last this was safely accomplished and we then carried out a series of steam trials, so that they could satisfy themselves regarding the conditions of our engines before we went into port. As soon as this was over, which was a few minutes before 4 o'clock, we headed for the entrance to the port and steamed into the outer harbour.

As soon as we were in, a couple of motor boats put out to us bringing out Mr and Mrs J. C. Murray, who had come all the way out from England specially to greet us on our return, together with El Miralai Ahmed Fuad Bey, the Director of the Egyptian Marine, Salama Bey, the Director of the Egyptian Coast-guard Service, as well as several other officials and newspaper reporters. We then steamed into the inner harbour, with the two motor boats keeping station in our port and starboard quarters, and before long we were once again tied up to the jetty from which we had sailed nearly nine months previously. There was a large crowd of friends and relatives of our Egyptian colleagues on the jetty and the members of the Egyptian Fisheries Department, and as soon as we were safely tied up we were overwhelmed and our decks were packed with a crowd such as the *Mabahiss* had rarely, if ever, accommodated previously. Rear-Admiral Wells Pasha, RN, the Head of the Ports and Lights Service, came on board and congratulated us on our safe return and a little later some of us went across to HEMS *Sollum* that was tied up on the other side of the jetty and met several more of our friends, whom we hadn't seen since we left.

On the 27th we had another pleasant little ceremony on board, for Mr and Mrs Murray came down to the ship and all hands were mustered; Mr Murray then made us a little speech in which he thanked us for the way in which we had carried out our work and presented each of us with a medal to commemorate the Expedition; and on the following day we all attended a reception that was given in our honour on board HEMS *Sollum*.

The University of Cairo had very kindly invited the members of the Expedition to come up to Cairo to a reception that they and the Minister of Public Instruction were giving in our honour; so on the 29th we travelled up to Cairo and during the next few days had a busy time there. On the

30th King Fuad received Mr Murray, Captain MacKenzie, Lieutenant-Commander Farquharson, Mr Griggs and myself in audience at the Koubbeh Palace and I was thus able to thank His Majesty for allowing us to call the submerged atoll in the Maldive Archipelago that we had discovered, King Fuad Bank, and for the interest that he had throughout taken in the work of the Expedition, and also to inform him of the splendid way in which both officers and men had carried out their duties on board the *Mabahiss*. That afternoon we attended the reception given by the Minister of Public Instruction and in the evening I lectured to the University on the work of the Expedition and at the close Mr Murray presented the medals, commemorating the Expedition, to Dr Faouzi and Mr Mohamed who had been unable to attend the muster on board in Alexandria when the rest of us were given ours.

Fig. 37. The John Murray Expedition Medal presented to the participants at the end of the cruise. This example is the one presented to Captain MacKenzie, which is now in the possession of his son, K. M. MacKenzie.

The greater part of the next three days was occupied in sightseeing and our party in Cairo was joined by Mr T. H. Murray, another son of Sir John, who had flown all the way from Rhodesia in order to meet us; he had, unfortunately, been held up on his way so that he didn't arrive in time to greet us on our arrival in port, but joined us a few days later in Cairo.

So far as the scientists were concerned, our work was now over and all that remained was to hand the *Mabahiss* back to the Egyptian Government; this entailed a certain number of formalities, for the vessel had to be put into dry-dock for inspection and all the ship's gear had to be gone over and checked, so Mr Murray, Captain MacKenzie and Chief Engineer Griggs returned to Alexandria and the rest of us said goodbye to our Egyptian colleagues and left Cairo on the afternoon of 3 June for Port Said in order to join the P and O SS *Ranpura*. At Port Said we were met by several of the Coast-guard officials who very kindly gave us all assistance possible in getting our gear on board, and late that night we sailed for England, arriving at Plymouth on the 16th.

In conclusion I am very glad to be able to take this opportunity of expressing my thanks and my great appreciation of the splendid manner in which all those who were associated with me in the Expedition carried out their duties. Many of my scientific colleagues had had no experience of work of this kind or the nature of life on board a small ship on the high seas; but in spite of all discomforts, and only those who have suffered from sea-sickness can realize what these discomforts were like, they carried out their work in a manner that was beyond all praise. Of the ship's staff I cannot speak too highly; they one and all did their utmost to ensure the success of the Expedition and to help us in every possible way. To many of our Egyptian colleagues such a voyage was something entirely foreign to their ordinary experience; it took them to strange lands and unknown waters and entailed what to them was before unknown, a prolonged absence from home and their fellow countrymen; but in spite of all hardships they were invariably cheerful and hardworking and I know that I am speaking for us all when I say that we, as a result of the experience, have formed a very high opinion of the personnel of the Egyptian Coast-guard Service.

PART 3

Biographical notes on the principal participants

Lt.-Col. R. B. Seymour Sewell

Scientific Leader

Robert Beresford Seymour Sewell was born at Leamington, Warwickshire, in 1880, the second son of the Reverend Arthur Sewell and Mary Lee Waring. During his childhood the family moved to Weymouth where Sewell attended Weymouth College and obtained an Exhibition to Christ's College, Cambridge, in 1898. Before going up, however, he studied zoology for six months under the biometrician Weldon at University College London.

He obtained a 'Double First' in 1903 and, after two years as a junior demonstrator at Cambridge, he entered St Bartholomew's Hospital in 1905 and became qualified MRCS and LRCP in October 1907.

In 1908 he entered the Indian Medical Service to begin an association which was to last for more than twenty-five years. His first appointment was as Medical Officer attached to the 67th and 84th Punjabi Regiments, but in 1910 he became Surgeon-Naturalist to the Marine Survey of India and Hon. Assistant Superintendent in the Zoological Section of the Indian Museum at Calcutta. He thus made the same move to zoology as so many of his predecessors, including T. H. Huxley and, indeed, John Murray.

Sewell's job as Surgeon-Naturalist on the RIMS *Investigator* was technically to look after the health of those on board and to pursue his scientific interests on the side. Since, however, the medical workload was by no means heavy, most of his time was devoted to marine biology and oceanography, his major interest for the remainder of his life, and from 1911 to 1913 he was seconded as Professor of Biology to the Calcutta Medical College.

Having married the day after the declaration of the First World War, Sewell served from 1914 to 1916 in Aden, where he became Port Health Officer, a period to which he refers several times in his narrative. From 1916 he served first in Sinai and then with Allenby in Palestine.

After the war Sewell returned to India as Superintendent of the Zoological Survey. Subsequently, he once again became Surgeon-Naturalist to the Marine Survey until his appointment as Director of the Zoological Survey and Head of the Indian Museum in Calcutta in 1925. In 1933 he retired from the Indian Medical Service, finally leaving India to return to the United Kingdom via Egypt only four months before the *Mabahiss* sailed from Alexandria.

Following the John Murray Expedition, Sewell retired to Cambridge where, however, he continued to work in the Department of Zoology. During the late 1930s he was busy not only with the Expedition Reports and his current taxonomic research, but also with the editorship of the *Fauna of British India* which he continued until the year before his death in 1964, at the age of 83. In 1946 he was able to spend four months in his beloved India at the invitation of the newly independent government as an Adviser on the reconstruction of the Zoological Survey and on the formation of the Anthropological Survey and of the Central Fisheries Research Institute. The offer and acceptance of such an appointment clearly reflected both the respect which he commanded with the Indian authorities and his own commitment towards a country with which he felt a great affinity.

Fig. 38. John Murray/Mabahiss Expedition (1933–34) scientific staff, Back row, left to right: Abdel Fatteh Mohamed (Chemist); Lt.-Com. W. I. Farquharson, RN (Surveyor and Navigator); H. C. Gilson (Chemist); and T. T. Macan (Zoologist). Front row, left to right: E. F. Thompson (Chief Chemist); R. B. Seymour Sewell (Leader and Zoologist); Hussein Faouzi (Zoologist and Ship's Doctor).

His seventy or so scientific contributions, published over a period of more than half a century from 1903 to 1958, cover a wide range of topics, including physical oceanography and geography of the Indian Ocean region, taxonomic and ecological studies of a wide variety of animal groups from the coelenterates to the fishes, and even anthropology. But from about 1912 onwards his main interest was in the taxonomy and distribution of the Copepoda on which he published several major works, including those based on the collections made from the *Mabahiss*, which are still highly respected.

On a personal level he was, according to C. F. A. Pantin, a well-loved figure at Cambridge, but was at the same time a somewhat private man who was rather difficult to get to know well.[1] Pantin attributed this to the absence of old friends who could have shared the memories of his Indian days rather than to a lack of social qualities. But the tone of Sewell's John Murray Expedition narrative suggests that his background and experiences as a member of the Raj in British India had made him a rather formal man, acutely aware of protocol and status, and this formality may have made him seem somewhat distant, particularly to the younger generation.

Nevertheless, he appears to have been a very successful scientific leader on the *Mabahiss*, welding together an Anglo-Egyptian team without any hint of the acrimony or rivalry between the two nationalities which could so easily have developed. Indeed, the only indication of a personality clash during the voyage is that between Sewell, the formal Englishman, and MacKenzie, a rather forthright Scot. Tensions resulting from the sometimes irreconcilable claims of science, championed by the Principal Scientist, and of the ship, represented by the Master, are not unusual even on modern oceanographic cruises which are generally much shorter than that of the *Mabahiss*. During the John Murray Expedition, however, the differences appear to have been aggravated by a genuine clash of temperaments, and it is to the credit of both men that they did not allow them to get out of hand nor to affect their respective subordinates among whom relations seem to have been excellent.

A. L. Rice

1. C. F. A. Pantin, London, Royal Society, 1965. *Biographical Memoirs of Fellows of the Royal Society,* Vol. 11, p. 147–55, Most of the above biographical notes are taken direct from Pantin's obituary.

K. N. MacKenzie
Captain

Kenneth MacKenzie, Master of the *Mabahiss* for the John Murray Expedition, was born at Oban in western Scotland in 1897. However, he was brought up in the home of his grandfather, the minister of Baugh on the Hebridean island of Tiree. As a lad, he was familiar with Gaelic and he played the bagpipes from an early age. Although he attended the island elementary school, he was sent to the mainland for his secondary education—to the Highland village of Kingussie in Inverness-shire where he lived throughout each school term with his uncle, the minister. Thus he was truly a 'son of the manse', although any thoughts of entering the church were dispelled by the onset of the First World War. He was the first recruit from Tiree, joining the colours before his seventeenth birthday by entering the 8th Argyll and Sutherland Highlanders. Shortly afterwards he was designated a piper whilst enduring a hard and thorough training in Scotland. He joined the British Expeditionary Force in France in 1915. While in the Somme trenches he was promoted to Lance Corporal, but after a few months his health broke. He had a year in an English hospital before being honourably discharged in April 1917 as 'permanently unfit'. Throughout his later life he was an easy prey for diseases and illness culminating in serious heart trouble from which he died in 1951.

Having left the Army, he took first a course in the new science of radio telegraphy and obtained his first-class certificate on the day after the Armistice. Thereupon he went to sea as a telegraphist, sailing mostly on the trans-Atlantic liner *Pretorian* and the Blue Funnel Line's *Titan*. On *Pretorian* his radio station was in a wooden hut built on the boat deck. Twice these huts were swept overboard in Atlantic gales and his diaries record his relief at having been off watch on each occasion. After nine months of this service, by which time he was rated as a First Wireless Operator, he resigned from the radio company and, forsaking the life of an officer, joined the Union Castle cargo ship *Dromore Castle* as an ordinary sailor. He took this step in the hope that he would eventually secure higher promotion. The *Dromore Castle* served him well, for he sailed on her for almost four years, being steadily promoted through the grades of sailor, able-bodied seaman, lamp trimmer and bosun. On presenting himself for examination for the Second Mate's certificate he was rejected because his time as a lamp trimmer, a petty officer, was not counted due to an anomaly in the Board of Trade's regulations. So to make up this time he returned to sea for a voyage as a quartermaster on the *Duendes*. His qualifying sea-time completed, he studied for, and in September 1924 passed, his Second Mate's certificate. After a brief spell on a North Sea Coaster, he sailed for eighteen months as Third Mate and later as Second Mate of the new Glasgow tramp *Golden Cape*—a ship which disappeared with all hands shortly after he left her—to sit for and to pass his First Mate's certificate. So qualified, in September 1926 he joined the famous old City Line of Glasgow. In 1929 he passed his Master's certificate and sailed as Second Mate of their *City of Valencia* on the South African passenger and mail service. Whilst docking in London's West India Dock after such a voyage, he saw a small wooden auxiliary sailing barque fitting out. The after pilot, sharing his poop docking bridge, confirmed that this was indeed Captain Scott's old ship *Discovery* being fitted out for another voyage of exploration for a British Commonwealth Antarctic expedition. Immediately Kenneth MacKenzie's mind was made up, and no sooner had the *Valencia* tied up than he was round to the *Discovery* for a job—any job. He was referred to Captain John K. Davis, her Master and an Antarctic navigator of fame and long experience. Almost immediately, Captain Davis accepted MacKenzie as Chief Officer, being impressed by his enthusiasm rather than his knowledge of sailing ships, the Antarctic and scientific research which were beyond his experience.

The City Line granted him leave of absence with continued promotion, and so he embarked on this great adventure. He sailed with *Discovery* on the two BANZARE Expeditions under Sir Douglas Mawson—as Chief Officer in 1929/30 and then, on Captain Davis's retirement, as Master in 1930/31. On these expeditions *Discovery* mapped the Antarctic coastline between 61° and 180° E. with the necessary accuracy and conviction to form the basis of the Australian Antarctic Territory Act of 1936—the founding of Australian Antarctica. These expeditions were conducted with a sense of urgency owing to Norwegian whaling and territorial ambitions and with a sense of importance owing to the thirst for scientific knowledge, especially of marine biology, meteorology and magnetism. These expeditions discovered and named MacRobertson, King George V, Princess Elizabeth and Banzare Lands, and a large, newly discovered bay at 70° E. was named MacKenzie Bay. On the completion of these expeditions MacKenzie commanded *Discovery* for her return voyage to London around Cape Horn—one of the last British ships to round the Horn under sail. She returned to the River Thames in August 1931, having been away for two years, and was returned to her owners in excellent condition, her Antarctic work having been accomplished without damage or injury to the ship or any of her complement despite the dangers she had encountered—certainly a reflection on the abilities of her Masters and crew.

MacKenzie returned to the City Line in 1932 as Chief Officer of their

City of Dieppe. This service included a voyage to Australia where he met his wife-to-be. He married at the end of that year with the resolve to leave the sea—a wife needing, in his view, constant care. However, his name as a ship-master in scientific circles stood highly and the John Murray Expedition offered him command of their expedition ship *Mabahiss*—an invitation he initially declined, but later accepted as it was such a special undertaking. Again the City Line granted him leave with promotion, and so he joined *Mabahiss* in July 1933 for her voyages of research in the Red Sea and the Indian Ocean.

In July 1934, Mackenzie returned to London and once more rejoined the City Line, but this time as Assistant Marine Superintendent in their London office. However, later that year he left the Company and joined the London Midland and Scottish Railway Company in a similar position, based at Euston Station, to work in the management of their large fleet of cross-channel and ferry steamers. In 1936 he was appointed Marine Super-intendent and Harbour Master of the LMS harbour of Holyhead, with responsibility for the Irish Mail services and the port. Shortly after, in 1938, his health started to deteriorate and life became a struggle against a failing heart, although he continued to work. He died in 1951 at the age of 53, leaving a widow, two daughters and a son.

K. M. MacKenzie

Lt.-Com. W. I. Farquharson
Second-in-command of the ship and Navigator

Ian Farquharson was born in Cumberland in 1900, the eldest son of a doctor. Educated at Osborne and the Royal Naval College, Dartmouth, he caught the last few months of the First World War as a midshipman in 1918 and served for a short time on a minesweeper before transferring to the Hydrographic Service.

In 1921 he joined the *Fantome* as an Acting Lieutenant and surveyed the Torres Strait and part of the Great Barrier Reef. When this Australian commission ended in 1924 Farquharson transferred to the *Kellett*, working mainly in the Thames Estuary. From 1925 to 1928 he served in the *Iroquois*, surveying the approaches to Hong Kong and Singapore, returning to the United Kingdom for a further season in the *Kellett* in 1928.

Another period abroad, from 1929 to 1931 was spent in the *Ormonde* surveying in the Arabian Gulf and off the coasts of Cyprus and was followed by a further spell in British waters, this time surveying off the western coasts of England and Scotland in the *Beaufort*.

Farquharson's secondment to the John Murray Expedition was an enjoyable experience of which he often spoke in later years. He had an affinity with 'boffins' (as he liked to refer to scientists) and enjoyed long-standing friendships with many whom he met over the years, including those on the *Mabahiss*. Perhaps because of the formality necessary in his secondment from the Navy, Farquharson's duties during the Expedition were established in greater detail by the organizing committee than were those of any of the other participants. In addition to the normal duties of the second-in-command of a small vessel, he was responsible for all navigation and surveying, including the sounding work, and produced the volume on the topographic results which appeared in the Expedition Reports.

But Farquharson's main contribution to the Expedition lay in a quite different direction. He seems to have got on well with everyone in the ship, an important fact in view of the rather uneasy relationship between Sewell and MacKenzie. In the opinion of at least one of his shipmates, Farquharson was an 'outstanding personality who should take most of the credit for welding into a team the varied mixture of race, profession and upbringing that went to sea in *Mabahiss*'.

In late 1934, shortly after his return from Egypt, Farquharson was given command of the *Beaufort* for surveys of the sea lochs and islands off the west coast of Scotland. When the ship was immobilized due to the Abyssinian crisis in 1936/37 he continued with the survey with a shore-based party but was detached to sail the *Stork* to the East Indies, with the rank of Acting Commander. During 1937 he was seconded for a period to survey Lake Windermere and was able to renew his friendship with Macan.

Leaving the west coast of Scotland survey in 1938, he was appointed Superintendent of the Tidal Branch, a post he held for eighteen years. During the war years he was at the Admiralty in Bath, 'sailing' a desk in a job which, although shore-bound, held considerable interest for him. One of his assignments was to calculate the tidal drift which would carry ashore on the coast of Spain the body of the 'The Man Who Never Was'—a dead man, dressed in naval uniform, with a briefcase manacled to his wrist, containing bogus documents about a planned invasion which was intended to mislead the Germans.

In 1945 he retired from the Navy with the rank of Commander, but continued his work in the Tidal Branch, being transferred to Cricklewood in North London where, following the disastrous east coast floods in 1953, he worked out a flood-warning system. For this work he was awarded the

OBE in 1954 and received an Honorary M.Sc. from the University of Liverpool.

On leaving the Hydrographic Department in 1956 he was offered a post with the Canadian Hydrographic Service, subsequently embraced in the Marine Sciences Department, to work on the St Lawrence Seaway project. He emigrated to Ottawa where he thoroughly enjoyed the Canadian open-air way of life, and took to curling and snow-shoeing for relaxation.

In Ottawa he introduced rigorous methods of tidal observation and analysis and continued these from 1963 at the newly opened Bedford Institute of Oceanography at Halifax, Nova Scotia, where he was in charge of a tide and tidal-current programme covering several thousands of miles of the continental shelf from the Bay of Fundy to the Gulf of St Lawrence. During his three years in Halifax, Farquharson not only employed moored, recording current-meters for the first time in Canada, but, in the words of one of his colleagues from those days, 'used his great gift of cheerful, friendly, sociability to help bring together the technicians, surveyors and scientists working together for the first time at the new institute'.

After retiring from the Bedford Institute in 1966 he took part in the NIO (now IOS) Expedition to the Indian Ocean early in 1967 but continued to live in Nova Scotia where, he said, he could study tidal ebb and flow in Mahore Bay and Crow Cove from his front and back windows respectively!

In 1973, never having had a day's illness in his life, he was struck down with a severe aneurism of the aorta. Returning to Britain, he underwent a major operation from which he recovered physically, but suffered brain damage.

He now lives quietly in a nursing home in Devon, alas unable to communicate properly with his old friends. I know he would wish me to convey his fondest regards to them all.

J. Farquharson

E. F. Thompson
Senior Chemist and Deputy Leader

Ernest Freeman (Bill) Thompson was born at Palmerston, New Zealand, on 5 January 1906. He attended the University of New Zealand, graduating with a B.Sc. in 1927 and an M.Sc. in 1930. From 1927 to 1930 he was an

Assistant Curator at Canterbury Museum in New Zealand, after which he moved to the University of Cambridge, where he held a demonstratorship in the Department of Zoology from 1930 to 1937. On Stanley Gardiner's recommendation, Thompson was appointed Deputy Leader and Senior Chemist on the John Murray Expedition, having been sent to Plymouth and to Scandinavia early in 1933 to learn the latest analytical techniques. On his return to Cambridge he prepared a Ph.D. thesis on 'Physical and Chemical Factors of the Environment of Animals in the Red Sea, Gulf of Aden, Gulf of Oman and North-western Indian Ocean', clearly based on data obtained during the Expedition. The thesis was approved in December 1936 and the following year Thompson was appointed as a hydrologist at the Bermuda Biological Station in a programme overseen jointly by the Woods Hole Laboratory and the Royal Society.

In 1940 Thompson moved to Canada to teach ichthyology and zoology in the School of Agriculture and Fisheries at the University of Laval and in 1943/44 he worked as a Fisheries Investigator in the British West Indies.

The year 1944 brought him to the Bingham Oceanographic Laboratory, Yale University, where he served successively as Research Assistant, Curator and Research Associate until 1966. During this period Thompson's research was mainly concerned with the life history of the winter flounder, *Pseudopleuronectes americanus*, especially as revealed by the structure of its otoliths. It is unfortunate that owing to other duties at Yale, coupled with a general disinclination to set pencil to paper in writing up his results, this work, like so many of the John Murray results, was never published.

Aside from teaching at the graduate level in oceanography, where he became noted for his lucid discussions of Coriolis force, he held official appointments as lecturer in zoology, oceanography, meterology, and biology from 1945 to 1966. During this time he 'gently navigated a generation of Yale undergraduates through the science distributional requirements and acquired the affectionate title of "Tides" Thompson from his grateful students' (*Yale Alumni Magazine and Journal*, October, 1982). He also served on the staff of the Summer Institute for High School Teachers of Mathematics and Science for several years.

In 1959 Thompson was appointed Associate Dean of Freshman Year and, five years later, Dean of Ezra Stiles College, Yale. He served in this latter post with exceptional distinction until his retirement in 1973, by which time he was known as the 'Dean of College Deans' who claimed never to have been shocked by an undergraduate!

Thompson was a Fellow of Davenport College from 1945 to 1964 and of

Ezra Stiles after he assumed the Deanship. He died at New Haven, Connecticut, on 28 August 1982 and is survived by his wife and a son, Patrick Andrew, a physicist.

D. Merriman

Hussein Faouzi
Biologist and Ship's Doctor

Hussein Faouzi was born in Cairo in 1900 and initially pursued a medical career, obtaining his M.B. and B.Ch. degrees from the Egyptian School of Medicine at Kasr-el-Aini in 1923. For two years he worked as an ophthalmic surgeon in the Egyptian Department of Health, but in 1925 he abandoned medicine for the study of natural history, a decision which completely changed the direction of his life.

Faouzi travelled to France where he studied zoology, botany, geology and general physiology in Paris, and took specialist courses in applied zoology and hydrobiology and fish culture in Toulouse, obtaining his *Licence-es-science* in 1928. During the summer of that year he visited the marine laboratory at Roscoff and received his first real introduction to marine biology for, on the suggestion of the head of the laboratory, Professor Prenant, he undertook a short research project on the formation of the calcareous tubes of serpulid worms.

Back in Paris, Faouzi registered as a research student in the Department of Comparative Anatomy at the Sorbonne where, for two years, he worked under Professor Wintrebert on the female gonad of the sole. He was now firmly set on an oceanographic career; during his time in Paris he attended lectures at the Institut Océanographique on biological and physical oceanography and, before returning home, he made an extensive tour of European marine institutes, visiting laboratories in Britain, France, Germany, Norway, Denmark, Italy and Monaco, and making many valuable contacts with established oceanographers.

These efforts were rewarded when he returned to Egypt in 1931, for on the departure of R. S. Wimpenny he was appointed Director of Fisheries Research within the Coast-guard and Fisheries Administration and was based in Alexandria. Two years later he was the natural choice as the

Egyptian Biologist on the John Murray Expedition, particularly since the ship used was from his own organization.

The Expedition was a major influence in Faouzi's life for it gave him the opportunity, in his own words, for a 'full and wonderful familiarity with oceanography, and fine colleagues, under the direction of the master of marine research in the Indian seas'.

In December 1934, only six months after her return from the John Murray Expedition, the *Mabahiss* left Alexandria once more, this time for a three-month expedition to the Red Sea under the leadership of Dr Cyril Crossland, the Director of the Ghardaqa biological station. This was intended to be a preliminary preparation for a much grander expedition to the Red Sea in 1935/36, and although three of Faouzi's Egyptian colleagues from the John Murray Expedition participated in it, he did not take part himself, perhaps to allow his second-in-command in the Fisheries Research Directorate, Dr Abou Samra, the chance of joining the expedition. Faouzi was, however, a member of the committee established to plan the main Red Sea expedition; in the event this expedition never took place, initially because of the Italo-Abyssinian conflict, then financial problems and, ultimately, the outbreak of the Second World War.

Faouzi continued as Director of Fisheries Research until 1941 when he was appointed Dean of the Faculty of Science and Professor of Zoology in the newly established University of Alexandria. From 1948 to 1952 he was given the task of building up the University's Department of Oceanography with his old John Murray Expedition colleague Abdel Fattah Mohamed as Professor of Physical Oceanography. In 1952 Faouzi was appointed Vice-Rector of the University but continued to teach postgraduate students until his final appointment as Permanent Under-Secretary of State in the new Ministry of Culture took him to Cairo and therefore away from the University for good.

In 1960 Faouzi retired from his official position and entered, as he says, his final career as a humanist! He had already written several books based on his own travels, the first, *Un Sindbad moderne* (1938), being based on his experiences during the John Murray Expedition. From 1961 his writings for a non-scientific readership assumed much greater importance for he began, and continues, to contribute to the weekly supplement of *Al Ahram* on letters, art and humanistic culture. In recent years, selections from these articles have been brought together and republished as five separate books on such diverse topics as 'Great Music' and 'In the Freedom of Thought'. Finally, in further confirmation of Faouzi's breadth of knowledge and interests, he has published a volume on 'the Florentine Renaissance', probably the first of its kind in Arabic.

وزارة التجارة والصناعة

مغفرة فؤاد الاول

للإخاء الماثبة وللمصايد

رحـــــلة

الباخرة المصرية « مباحث »

إلى المحيط الهنـدى مع بعثـة السـير جون مورى

كتاب تذكارى

بقلم

حسـين فوزى

مدير معهد فؤاد الأول للأحياء المائية والمصايد
وعضو بعثة مورى

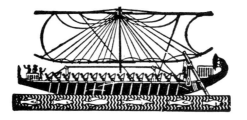

القاهرة

دار الطباعة المصرية

١٩٣٩

FIG. 39. Title page of Hussein Faouzi's own account in Arabic, of the Expedition, published in Cairo in 1939. Opposite: the English translation.

Ministry of Commerce and Industry

———

Faoud I Institute
for Hydrobiology and Fisheries

Cruise of the
Egyptian vessel *Mabahiss*
to the Indian Ocean with the
Sir John Murray Expedition

———

Commemorative book
by
Hussein Faouzi
Director, Faoud I Institute
for Hydrobiology and Fisheries
Member of the Murray Expedition

(Hatsepshut's vessel)

Cairo
Egyptian Printing House
1939

In his earlier research and teaching careers Hussein Faouzi earned the respect of generations of scientists and students with whom he came into contact. Through his newspaper articles he is known to millions more as a traveller, historian and man of letters.

A. L. Rice

Abdel Fattah Mohamed
Chemist

Abdel Fattah Mohamed Ibrahim El-Fiky was born at Mansoura on 28 January 1905. He never used his surname and was always known as Abdel Fattah Mohamed. He received his primary and secondary education at Mansoura, a trading and farming centre which was at the heart of the national movement that led to the 1919 Egyptian revolution and subsequent independence. Like many of his generation, Mohamed was influenced by the social and political revival that took place before and after his entry into the newly established Faculty of Science of the Egyptian University in 1925. Four years later he was among the first batch of graduates, a fact of which he was always proud. These pioneering graduates played a dominant role in developing science in Egypt and filled many of the senior posts in scientific and educational institutions.

Mohamed graduated with a B.Sc. honours degree in chemistry and was soon offered the post of demonstrator in the new Faculty in October 1929, where he obtained his M.Sc. in 1932 as a result of research in physical chemistry.

In 1933 Mohamed was chosen to be the participant representing the Egyptian University on the John Murray Expedition to the Indian Ocean. In preparation for his duties on the *Mabahiss* he was sent during the summer on a mission to Norway to study physical oceanography and to the Marine Laboratory at Plymouth, United Kingdom, where he studied the newly introduced methods of colorimetric determination of nutrient salts in sea-water. There, he also prepared the buffer sets necessary for the colorimetric determination of hydrogen-ion concentration in the Indian Ocean, under L. H. N. Cooper who, during a visit of the writer to Plymouth in 1965, talked of his high esteem for Mohamed's skill in laboratory work, his meticulous precision and scientific honesty.

Mohamed returned to Egypt to board the *Mabahiss* on 3 September 1933 on her way to the Indian Ocean. In this melting pot, Mohamed proved to be a charming companion and a studious worker. Professor Gardiner, FRS, Secretary of the John Murray Expedition, reported that Mohamed 'is a very able man and on the recent cruises in the *Mabahiss* has been a most efficient leader of his section' (*Annual Report of the Director of the Egyptian Education Office*, London, 15 June 1935). In his memoirs Sewell makes special reference to Mohamed, who acted as his companion and guide during his stay in Egypt following the return of the Expedition.

Hussein Faouzi, another Egyptian scientist on board, formed a solid friendship with Mohamed, based on a mutual respect that continued through-out their lives.

Mohamed made news in the Egyptian press and is mentioned in the Sewell and Faouzi memoirs when he fell from the ship into a shark-infested sea; he remembers in his Ph.D. thesis 'the gallant crew of HEMS *Mabahiss* who saved my life when I fell overboard in the early hours of a tropical May morning in 1934'.

Mohamed returned to the University in Cairo after the ship arrived in Alexandria on 25 May 1934, but he was soon sent on a short mission to England in the summer of 1934. He returned to take part in the planning and execution of the Egyptian Expedition to the Red Sea, from December 1934 to February 1935, on which he was the senior Physical and Chemical Oceanographer, and Expedition Leader for two of the four cruises.[1]

Armed with the raw material from these two important expeditions Mohamed went to Europe on a long mission, 1935–39. Here he benefited from one of the Egyptian education system's excellent traditions, which had existed since the nineteenth century, whereby missions abroad were used to gain experience in new branches of science and human knowledge. Under this generous scheme, in addition to obtaining his academic degree, the candidate is offered the chance to gain more theoretical and practical ex-perience. Mohamed's mission led him to the University of Cambridge where he met Professor J. S. Gardiner, FRS, and renewed his acquaintance with his *Mabahiss* colleagues Sewell, Thompson, Gilson and Macan. After Cambridge, Mohamed was sent to work for his Ph.D. at Liverpool Univer-sity with J. Proudman, FRS, Professor of Physical Oceanography, to whom Mohamed was recommended by Gardiner. In Liverpool Mohamed wrote the three volumes of his Ph.D. thesis and participated in cruises in the Irish Sea during the summers of 1936 and 1937.

Mohamed returned to Egypt from the tense political climate of Europe in 1939, having spent two years in the Oceanography Department at Liverpool, nine months in Cambridge, six months at the Tidal Institute in Bidston, United Kingdom, six months at the Institut für Meereskunde of Berlin University, four months at the Marine Laboratory of Plymouth and another four months at the Deutsche Seewarte in Hamburg. Thanks to the generous mission scheme Mohamed had become acquainted with most of the main schools of oceanography in existence in Europe before the war and had forged strong links with these institutions which helped him later to introduce his new Department of Oceanography and its young

1. See S. A. Morcos, 'The Egyptian Expedition to the Red Sea 1934/35', *Deep Sea Research*, Vol. 31 (6-8A), 1984, pp. 599–616.

staff to foreign institutions, particularly the universities of Liverpool and Kiel.

After returning from Europe with his Ph.D., Mohamed was appointed as lecturer in physical chemistry at Cairo University in March 1940.

The war distanced Mohamed still further from oceanography and the oceanographic community abroad. He was seconded as Professor and Head of the Chemistry Department at the Higher Teacher's College in Baghdad, Iraq, from August 1941 to August 1943. His interest in publishing in Arabic encouraged him to write two books on chemistry for secondary schools which were published in 1945 and remained the textbooks selected by the government for secondary schools in Egypt for some years.

After his return from Baghdad, Mohamed was elected Chairman of the Association of Graduates of the Faculty of Science and became the editor-in-chief of its monthly magazine *Risalet Al-Elm* published in Arabic. He resigned as Chairman of the Association in February 1946 but his resignation was not accepted and he was returned by an Extraordinary Assembly on 22 March 1946.

In May 1946 he left Cairo to go to Alexandria University where he was appointed Associate Professor of Physical Chemistry. There he met his senior colleague on the *Mabahiss*, Hussein Faouzi, who was the First Dean of the Faculty of Science and Professor of Zoology at the new University. There they planned to start the Department of Oceanography, a goal which was achieved in 1948, becoming the first such department in any Arab or African university.

In establishing this department in 1948, Mohamed returned to oceanography after an absence of about ten years. He enjoyed lecturing in physical and chemical oceanography and spent his time developing the postgraduate department, which had an average annual enrolment of five students. The writer, who knew Professor Mohamed from his years at Cairo University, was invited by him in 1950 to join the department for what proved to be a long association. Mohamed was appointed Professor of Physical and Chemical Oceanography in 1950 and received a Fulbright Fellowship that enabled him to work at the Scripps Institution of Oceanography from January to June 1951.

Mohamed was Dean of the Faculty of Science from February 1953 to March 1957, when he was appointed Vice-Rector of the University. He continued to occupy this post for eight years until he retired in January 1965 at the age of 60. One of the slogans current in Egypt at that time compared 'men of confidence' with 'men of experience', a reference to the ruler's reliance on those he considered worthy of his trust, as opposed to technocrats. Mohamed was considered to be an efficient and capable technocrat. Although he was Acting Rector of the University from December 1958 to May 1959 and again in 1963/64 owing to the vacancy of the Rector's post, he was not elevated to the rank of University Rector. Twice he had to experience the unpleasant duty of receiving a new University Rector for whom he continued to act as Vice-Rector.

Mohamed occupied a pioneering position and achieved many firsts in the new science of oceanography. He went with the *Mabahiss* to the Gulf of Aqaba forty years after the first Austrian Expedition on *Pola*. There he observed the adiabatic increase of temperature in the deep water of the Gulf for the first time. He also measured phosphate, hydrogen-ion concentration and oxygen and noted, for the first time, the presence of an intermediate layer of minimum oxygen and an intermediate maximum phosphate in the northern Red Sea and its absence in the Gulf. Mohamed described for the first time the exchange of water in the Strait of Tiran between the Gulf and the Red Sea, as well as the circulation of water and origin of bottom water in the northern Red Sea. His cross-sections in the northern Red Sea are among the first, and some of the few available, for this region. His nine-month work in the Indian Ocean contributed significantly to the physical and chemical investigations of the John Murray Expedition. Thompson and Gilson published part of these results, leaving the observations on hydrogen-ion concentration to Mohamed. His studies revealed the conditions which limit the depth of the layers of phytoplanktonic activity in the tropical regions, as well as the origin, character and movement of the Antarctic Intermediate Current and the North Indian Intermediate Current.

When Mohamed finished his thesis in Liverpool, Professor J. Proudman wrote (December 1938): 'When account is taken of Mr Mohamed's practical and theoretical competence and the extent of his knowledge of oceanography, his position in this science is seen to be a very unusual one.' These great expectations were cut short since Mohamed's career, like that of many scientists in developing countries, was the victim of unfavourable conditions. First came his ten years (1939–48) of teaching chemistry in Cairo, Baghdad and Alexandria and his occupation of the chairmanship of the Graduate's Association. His full-time work in the new Department of Oceanography was relatively brief, 1948–53, and was taken up by the activities related to the founding of a new department. From 1953 to his retirement in 1965, Mohamed continued to teach oceanography, but his heavy workload as Dean and Vice-Rector left this accomplished oceanographer little time for research, a fact which he often mentioned with regret.

Immediately after his retirement from Alexandria, Mohamed went to the University of Tripoli, Libya, where he was the Professor of Chemistry in the Faculty of Science. He continued to serve in Libya until his sudden death in Tripoli on 23 September 1967.

Mohamed was survived by his wife Mme Nemat Nassar, who is now working as Director of a Secondary Technical Girls' School in Alexandria, and his daughter Dr Sawsan A. F. Mohamed, Assistant Professor in the Faculty of Pharmacy at the University of Alexandria.

S. A. Morcos

H. C. Gilson
Assistant Chemist

Hugh Cary Gilson was born in 1910 in Birmingham where his father was Headmaster of King Edward's School. He was educated at Winchester College from 1924 to 1929 when he entered Trinity College, Cambridge, to read Natural Sciences, graduating with First Class Honours in the summer of 1933, shortly before the *Mabahiss* sailed.

At Cambridge Gilson was particularly influenced by C. F. A. Pantin, his Director of Studies, who was probably responsible for his taking up the study of the distribution of nitrogenous compounds and their relationship with plankton during the John Murray Expedition.

But it was through the Professor of Zoology, John Stanley Gardiner, that Gilson (and Macan) originally came to be invited to take part in the Expedition. Afterwards, Gilson did some experimental work at the Plymouth laboratory and then returned to Cambridge where, in 1935, he was elected to a three-year Research Fellowship to work up the results obtained from the *Mabahiss*.

Again under the influence of Stanley Gardiner, Gilson led the Percy Sladen Expedition to Lake Titicaca in Peru to investigate the Lake's fauna, flora and chemistry. During his absence in South America he was appointed a Demonstrator in Zoology at Cambridge, a post which he held until after the outbreak of the war.

From 1940 to 1944 Gilson was seconded to the Medical Research Council to help operate, within the Department of Zoology, a freeze-drying plant designed and directed by Dr R. I. N. Greaves to produce dried blood plasma for use in blood transfusions by the Royal Navy.

At the end of the war Gilson was looking for a change from Cambridge and from a department where neither ecology nor field work in general were particularly highly regarded. He was offered the Chair of Zoology at the newly independent University of Southampton, but the Directorship of the Freshwater Biological Association fell vacant in 1946 and Gilson chose the latter, with its opportunities to organize ecological research and field work rather than teaching zoology.

Gilson's interest in freshwater biology had been initially aroused in Cambridge by J. T. Saunders who had, incidentally, a major influence also on Macan. Saunders, along with F. E. Fritsch and W. H. Pearsall, had been a founder of the Freshwater Biological Association, and had run a summer course on hydrobiology which Gilson took over when Saunders left the department to become an administrative officer within the University.

H. C. Gilson

T. T. Macan
Assistant Naturalist

T. T. (Kit) Macan was born in 1910 and passed his youth happily in a world that revolved round dogs, horses and the country sports; the academic world was far away. He was educated at Wellington, from where it was hoped that he would follow in his father's footsteps and join the army but where he realized that he was not cut out to be a military man. A lecture on mosquitoes by J. F. Marshall, founder of the British Mosquito Control Institute, aroused his interest in these insects, and later he discovered that it was possible to make a living studying such creatures. Accordingly, it was at Cambridge, rather than Sandhurst, that his education continued. Christ's College was chosen because the Master had written a book which Macan had been given by his biology master to read during the holidays. This choice was a happy one, for the science tutor at Christ's was J. T. Saunders, one of the founders of the Freshwater Biological Association.

At Cambridge Macan made many friends interested in biology and natural history, among them Hugh Gilson, who was also influenced by Saunders, and Jack Kitching, in later years Professor of Biology at the University of East Anglia. Kitching owned a yacht and a diving helmet with which he made extensive studies of the marine fauna, and Macan was one of those invited to help with his work. In 1931 it was decided to take a break and go cruising, but this project was cut short when, in a gale, the mast broke. An auxiliary engine took the boat to Penzance, where its damaged condition attracted the attention of the local reporter, a man unexpectedly ignorant of the sea and sailing. Consequently, his piece for the local paper, copied in the national dailies, made little sense. It was read by John Stanley Gardiner, Professor of Zoology at Cambridge, who, himself a keen yachtsman, wanted to know what had really happened. Accordingly, early in the autumn term, Kitching having gone down, Macan was invited to Sunday afternoon tea to tell him. Plans for an oceanographic expedition in two years' time were mentioned, although Macan was not officially appointed to the Expedition until June 1933.

Stanley Gardiner's intention was that after the Expedition Macan should work at the Natural History Museum in London on the cores which he had been accumulating since the voyage of the *Challenger*. Macan, with his rural background, showed a lack of enthusiasm and fell into disfavour. The clays collected during the John Murray Expedition were instead worked upon in Cambridge by J. D. H. Wiseman, who transferred to the Natural History Museum in 1936.

Fortunately for Macan, the Freshwater Biological Association, founded in the year when the economic slump started, had by 1934 acquired a little extra money and was offering two new posts. Each post carried a salary of £150 per annum and Macan, who had worked at the FBA laboratory, obtained one of them. His first research study was of the ecology of Corixidae, a family of water-bugs in which each species occupies a distinct habitat ranging from pools near the tops of mountains to brackish pools beside the sea.

In 1941 he found himself in the Royal Army Medical Corps but, thanks to his earlier studies of mosquitoes, as a lieutenant, not as a private, as were five other graduates who later came under his command. Towards the end of the year he was appointed entomologist, with the rank of Major, to a Malaria Field Laboratory which in December 1941 sailed for Iraq and Iran. In Baghdad there was an unexpected but very welcome reunion with Abdel Fatteh Mohamed, at that time teaching in Iraq. After two years the unit moved to India and Burma.

After nearly four years overseas Macan was repatriated and, early in

1946, demobilized. He returned to the Freshwater Biological Association where he found that Hugh Gilson had also turned from the sea to fresh water and was shortly to be appointed Director. Macan embarked on a study of the taxonomy of the nymphs of Ephemeroptera and, this complete, he passed on to the ecology of the nymphs and gradually to more comprehensive surveys of the macrofauna of streams, rivers, tarns and lakes. He published many papers in scientific journals and wrote five books. For fifteen years he was General Secretary of the International Association of Limnology. He retired in 1976 but later that year went to the United States to spend twelve months as Morton Visiting Professor in the University of Ohio at Athens.

T. T. Macan[1]

Four Egyptian officers of the Mabahiss

The origin of today's Egyptian Navy can be traced back to the early nineteenth century when Mohammed Ali, with the help of several European powers, initiated the construction of the naval base at Alexandria. However, its modernization took place only after the First World War, when young boys of 13 were sent to England for seven years of training. This professional training enabled them to assume, later in life, senior positions in the Egyptian Navy and in other services such as the Coast-guard and the Suez Canal Authority. It was from these graduates that the naval officers who served in the John Murray Expedition (Ahmed Badr and Ahmad Sarwat), and in the subsequent Egyptian Expedition to the Red Sea in 1934/35 (Mohamed Shukri, Mohamed Nashid and Faouzi Awad), were recruited. In addition to the four officers covered in the following biographical notes, it should be mentioned that all twenty-four Egyptian crew members who participated in the Expedition, with the exception of the carpenter, were recruited from the Egyptian Coast-guard Service.

In the early 1920s, the young Egyptian students were sent for training in small successive groups to HMS *Worcester*, known as the Nautical Training College, moored off Greenhithe on the River Thames. Photographs of these

---

1. Sadly, before he was able to see this book in print, Kit Macan died at his home in Cumbria on 12 January 1985.

FIG. 40. Officers of the *Mabahiss*. Seated, from left to right: W. J. Griggs, Captain
K. N. MacKenzie, Ahmed Badr. Standing, from left to right: Edward Morcos, Mahmoud
Mokhtar, Ahmad Sarwat, Lloyd Jones.

students at the college appeared in the Egyptian press at that time. The
college presumably had a lasting impact on this generation of naval officers,
bringing them together at such a young age from all parts of Egypt. The
writer has observed the officers reminiscing, with great nostalgia, about
their experiences in those formative years. Therefore at this point it is
worthwhile to provide some information on this remarkable school.

The college, originally called simply the 'Thames Marine Officers
Training Ship', was established in 1862 and financed by subscriptions from
merchants, ship-owners and underwriters.[1] The Admiralty loaned the
college, HMS *Worcester*, a frigate of 1,500 tons which had been built in
1843. This ship was replaced in 1876 by a larger wooden ship of 3,240 tons.

---

1. Commander Gordon Steele, *The Story of the Worcester*, London, Harrap and Co., 1962,
   256 pp.

The keel of this vessel had originally been laid in 1833 in Portsmouth as a sailing-ship-of-the-line (that is, a forerunner of the battleship) and was originally named *Royal Sovereign*. However, in 1839, during construction, her name was changed to *Royal Frederick*. In 1853, while still being built, she was converted to steam, fitted with 500 h.p. engines and launched in 1854. She was finally named the *Frederick William*.

She had a particularly unremarkable career as a naval ship and when loaned to the Worcester Management Committee in 1876, her name was changed yet again to HMS *Worcester*—a common practice in those times when one vessel succeeded another in a particular role.

This second HMS *Worcester* remained in use until 1945, when she was replaced by a ship built specifically for nautical training and launched in 1905 as HMS *Exmouth*. As before, this vessel assumed the name of *Worcester* when she came into use by the Thames Nautical Training College. It is on the second of these *Worcesters* that the Egyptian naval officers were trained.

Since the training college was not directly connected with the Royal Navy, the use of the title 'HMS' is not strictly correct, since such usage is restricted to ships still in commission in the Royal Navy. The college's use of HMS appears to have been originally a mistake, which became accepted by usage over the years until official approval was finally given in 1946.

The writer wishes to express his gratitude to all who helped by providing information which contributed to the biographies of the four Egyptian officers which are presented here. Special thanks are due to the families of the late Ahmad Sarwat and of the late Edward Morcos, to the late Admiral Sami Zaki, to Mr Sherif Ramadan from the Institute of Oceanography and Fisheries in Alexandria, to Mr Mohamed Hussein Taha, retired Chief Engineer of the research vessel *Mabahiss* and to Mr Mostafa El-Naggar from the Egyptian daily *Al-Ahram*. The efforts and interest of the editor of this volume, Tony Rice, in supplying information on the Nautical Training College, HMS *Worcester*, and the South Shields Marine and Technical College, are appreciated.

S. A. Morcos

Junior Lieutenant (*Mulazim Awal*) Ahmed Badr, First Officer

Ahmed Badr was born on 9 December 1909. At the early age of 13, he was sent on a government-sponsored study programme to learn the 'military and merchant naval arts' in England, where he eventually reached the rank of Second Lieutenant in the Royal Navy, having passed all the necessary examinations 'with distinction'. Ahmed Badr then worked with the British Merchant Navy for several years and obtained the Certificate of Second Officer from the United Kingdom Ministry of Transport. During his professional career he sailed extensively on many of the world's oceans and seas, showing distinction in his practical work. He was also noted for his physical prowess.

On 10 May 1929, Badr joined the service of the Egyptian Government, as Sub-Lieutenant, and was promoted to Junior Lieutenant on 1 January 1930. He was then selected from the Egyptian Coast-guard Service to participate in the John Murray Expedition to the Indian Ocean on board the *Mabahiss*. His excellent conduct and active participation in this Expedition, which was acknowledged by the ship's Captain and the Expedition Leader, contributed to his promotion to the rank of Lieutenant (*Yuzbashi*) on 1 June 1934.

In addition to his work as First Officer during the Expedition, he worked with Lieutenant Commander Farquharson as a cartographer, and studied the sea-bed topography using the recently developed and newly installed echo-sounder. He gained considerable experience in the use of this instrument which revolutionized the knowledge of the bathymetry of the Indian Ocean. Badr assumed Farquharson's duties when the latter left the ship for twelve days to study the earth's magnetism in the Maldive Atolls.

Badr returned to Egypt in May 1934 and, six months later, joined the Egyptian Expedition to the Red Sea, 18 December 1934 to 20 February 1935, having in the meantime moved from the Coast-guard Service to the Royal Yachts. This time, he joined the scientific team of the research vessel *Mabahiss* as a cartographer, and his work on the bathymetry of the Red Sea was published in a paper by Badr and Crossland in the reports of the Egyptian Expedition.[1] This was the first detailed study of the northern

1. A. M. Badr and C. Crossland, 'Topography of the Red Sea Floor', in *Reports on the Preliminary Expedition for the Exploration of the Red Sea on the RRS 'Mabahith'* (*December 1934–February 1935*), pp. 13–20, 1939. (Publications of the Marine Biological Station, Ghardaga, 1.)

Red Sea using the newly introduced echo-sounder and, as a result, the Expedition was able to discover many new topographic features.

The first bathymetric chart of the Red Sea had been based mainly on the research vessel *Pola* soundings (1885–96) and the Admiralty charts at the end of the nineteenth century. Only three lines of soundings, representing the routes of submarine cables, appeared along the axis of the Gulf of Suez and the Red Sea. The *Mabahiss* made seven traverses of the northern Red Sea and five of the Gulf of Aqaba. These were the first to be made using an echo-sounder, and were not significantly improved until seventeen years later when, in 1961, the research vessel *Aragonese* made fifty-four traverses and, in 1964, the research vessel *Chain* made another ten.

Among the main features discovered by Badr were Mabahiss Deep I (2,300 m), which lies around latitude 25°20′ N., between Abu-el-Kizan (Daedalus) Reef and the Arabian coast to the north-east, and Mabahiss Deep II (1,829 m), which is the maximum depth of the Gulf of Aqaba. Until then, the greatest depth recorded in the Gulf of Aqaba was 1,287 m, measured by the *Pola* in 1895/96. Badr and Crossland (1939) gave the following account of this discovery:

By making courses transverse to the Gulf of Aqaba, . . . we discovered a trough with a greatest depth of 1,000 fathoms, near the east side of the Gulf, with shelves 200–300 fathoms deep on the west, . . . but the precipice on the east is impressive if it is remembered that it is continued above water by mountains several thousand feet high. The Red Sea is remarkable for its great depth, in proportion to its breadth, yet here we find a nearly equal depth in a gulf less than a tenth of the breadth of the Red Sea. In correspondence with this, the shores are extremely abrupt, the mountains rising sheer from the water. Except in the south, there is no room for the maritime plain which is such a large and constant feature of the Red Sea coast.

After several promotions in rank, Ahmed Badr transferred to the Egyptian Navy, and became a Navy Admiral and General Commander of the Egyptian Royal Navy on 1 July 1948. He held the latter command until his retirement on 6 October 1950. He died in October 1953.

S. A. Morcos

Junior Lieutenant (*Mulazim Awal*) Ahmad Sarwat, Second Officer

Ahmad Sarwat was born in Cairo on 1 January 1910. After obtaining his primary education certificate, he was selected in 1923 by the Ministry of Maritime Transport to study 'military and merchant naval arts' in the United Kingdom. He left on 4 September of that year for England, to attend the Nautical Training College, HMS *Worcester*, moored off Greenhithe in the River Thames.

He completed his studies 'with distinction', but was recognized particularly for his excellent participation in the sporting activities of his college, having been a member of the rugby team during 1924/25. He was a keen yachtsman and was a registered sea scout in Glasgow in 1927. In 1928, he was awarded gold medals for boxing and running in competitions in New Zealand.

Ahmad Sarwat's distinction in studies and experience in England was acknowledged in writing by the Egyptian Ministry of Communication in 1925. He obtained certificates from the Nautical Training College, HMS *Worcester*, in December 1925, from the Royal Navy in June 1926, and a Merchant Navy certificate in April 1929. During the period June 1926 to May 1929, he sailed extensively on many of the world's oceans, then returned to Egypt where he joined the Royal Yachts as a Second Lieutenant in May 1929. In January 1930, he was promoted to Junior Lieutenant and was transferred to the Coast-guard Service in April of that year. During his service, he worked on board the *Mabahiss* between 25 April 1933 and 15 June 1934, and participated as Second Officer in the John Murray Expedition to the Indian Ocean. In recognition of his dedicated work during the Expedition, he was promoted to the rank of Lieutenant (*Yuzbashi*) on 1 June 1934. For the following four years, Sarwat worked on board several naval vessels, then, from 1940 to 1946 was transferred back to the Coast-guard Service. In 1946, he moved to the Egyptian Navy and was sent on a mission to the United Kingdom, to visit some training centres of the British Royal Navy and to acquaint himself with some establishments of the British Merchant Navy. He then assumed various responsibilities including the post of Commander of the Naval College. Several promotions followed until he attained the rank of Admiral in April 1951. He obtained the certificate 'Captain of High Seas' on 20 January 1952 before his early retirement on 15 September 1952, following the Egyptian Revolution of 23 July 1952. His entire service in the Navy had been recognized as exemplary.

Having been a keen sea scout in his early years, Sarwat established the Egyptian Society of Sea Scouts, and became not only a member of its

Council in January 1954, but also the Chairman of its Technical Committee in April 1956. After his retirement from the Navy, between 1963 and 1967, Sarwat assumed the role of Director of the Naval Training Institute.

He was known as a dedicated and admired professor. Many of his students are presently active naval and merchant officers in Egypt and in other Arab and African countries.

Ahmad Sarwat was awarded several medals during his lifetime, from Egypt and from abroad. He died in August 1983, only a few days before the International Symposium celebrating the Fiftieth Anniversary of the Mabahiss/John Murray Expedition, which took place in Alexandria from 3 to 6 September 1983. He is survived by two daughters and two sons. One of his daughters, Zebaida, was a well-known actress in Egypt and the Arab world during the 1960s. His son, Salah El-Din, is a naval officer and Director of the Naval Training Administration.

S. A. Morcos

Junior Lieutenant (*Mulazim Awal*) Mahmoud Mukhtar, Second Engineer

Mahmoud Mukhtar was born in 1908. He studied marine engineering and, in 1929, joined the Coast-guard and Fishery Service as a Second Lieutenant. In 1933, Mukhtar was promoted to Junior Lieutenant and transferred to the *Mabahiss* to participate in the John Murray Expedition between September 1933 and May 1934. He continued working on board the *Mabahiss* after her return in May 1934 and, together with Ahmed Badr, participated in the subsequent Egyptian Expedition to the Red Sea in 1934/35. His experience on the *Mabahiss* earned him a promotion to Chief Engineer of the ship, followed by a promotion to the rank of Lieutenant Commander (*Sagh*) and finally to the rank of Commander (*Bakbashi*). Mahmoud Mukhtar pursued his work as Chief Engineer on board several Egyptian ships until he retired in 1965. He died in 1967.

S. A. Morcos

Junior Lieutenant (*Mulazim Awal*) Edward Morcos, Third Engineer

Edward Morcos was born in 1905 in Assiout, Egypt. He attended primary and secondary schools in Assiout, and studied mechanical and marine engineering at the Marine School of South Shields, United Kingdom, where he received his certificate in 1932.[1] Morcos started his career with the Coast-guard and Fishery Service in Alexandria, and worked as a Second Lieutenant and Engineer on several ships. He was promoted to the rank of Junior Lieutenant, and transferred to the *Mabahiss* where he participated in the John Murray Expedition as Third Engineer. He was then transferred, as Second Engineer, to HEMS *Amira Fawzia* and became its Chief Engineer in 1938. He was promoted to Chief Engineer of the Coast-guard Service and the Egyptian Navy respectively, and finally to the rank of Commodore (*Amiralai*). Edward Morcos died in London in 1962. During his lifetime he was awarded many decorations for his dedicated service. He is survived by his wife, a son, Youssef Morcos, who is at present working as a naval pilot in the harbour of Alexandria, and three daughters.

S. A. Morcos

1. Founded in the 1870s, the Marine School continued as a private organization with its own board of governors until about 1950, when it was taken over by the local authority of South Shields and became the South Shields Marine and Technical College. Then, in September 1984, it merged with another college and became the South Tyneside College.

PART 4

Mabahiss—
the story of the ship

By A. L. Rice

THE need for a substantial research vessel for the Egyptian Fisheries
Service was established during the Directorship of R. S. Wimpenny,
who had taken charge of the service at the end of 1927 on a short-term
contract. Fisheries research in Egypt had been in abeyance since 1923, when
the first Director, Mr G. Paget, had retired. Wimpenny continued the introduction of mullet fry to the great lakes of the Nile Delta, which had
been instigated by Paget, but he also formulated a research programme
directed mainly at the marine fisheries and built up a small but significant
staff of British and Egyptian scientists and local technicians. Such a programme demanded a vessel capable of trawling in deep water and of
carrying out general oceanographic research. Accordingly, funds for such
a ship were included in the Coast-guard and Fisheries Service budget for
1930/31.

The *Mabahiss* (Arabic for 'researches') was built by Swan Hunter and
Wigham Richardson at their Neptune Shipyard on Tyneside, in the United
Kingdom, with Messrs Flannery, Baggalay and Johnson acting as consulting engineers. In his Annual Report for 1930, Wimpenny states that the
vessel was ordered on 14 June and delivered in Egyptian waters by 13
October. This would suggest a remarkably short building period, but it is
clear that the ship was actually ordered in 1929.

In the records of Swan Hunter (now part of British Shipbuilders) the
earliest reference to the *Mabahiss* is in October 1929, when it is assumed
that work in the drawing office began, so that Wimpenny's reference to 14
June must be to an order placed in 1929. The ship was launched on 11
September 1930, underwent trials off Tynemouth on 9 October 1930, and
was delivered to Alexandria later that month.

The ship was built on the lines of a large steam trawler, with an overall
length of 138′, a beam of 23′6″ and a mean draught of 12′6″. Her total
deadweight of 200 tons allowed her to carry enough coal for fifteen days'
steaming at full speed and her single screw, driven by triple expansion
engines, gave her a mean speed of some 11 knots.

Since she was intended to operate entirely in the Mediterranean and Red
Seas, much of the work was expected to be carried out on deck and the
Mabahiss was therefore provided with only a rather small laboratory
amidships. She had accommodation for three scientists in addition to the
total ship's complement of thirty-four officers and men.

The most important item of gear on deck was the steam trawling-winch
placed immediately forward of the bridge. It had a large drum holding
4,000 fathoms (7,300 m) of wire tapering from $1\frac{3}{4}''$ to $1\frac{3}{8}''$ circumference,
and a smaller drum with heavier wire of $2\frac{3}{8}''$ circumference. A small winch
on the bridge was used for obtaining water bottle, plankton net and

FIG. 41. The launch of the *Mabahiss*, 11 September 1930. The vessel was named by H.E. Sesostris Sidarouss Bey, CVO, Egyptian Ambassador to Belgium and the Netherlands (in top hat), who represented the Ambassador to the Court of St James's. He was accompanied by Fuad Mawardy Bey, Deputy Chief Inspecting Engineer for the Egyptian Government, and R. S. Browning Bey, Inspector of Marine Coast-guards and Fisheries Service. (*Photo:* courtesy of Swan Hunter Shipbuilders Ltd.)

bottom grab samples, these gears being worked from special davits on the port and starboard sides and from the foremast derrick. A Lucas steam sounding machine with 3,000 fathoms (5,500 m) of wire was fitted on the small after-deck.

When the *Mabahiss* arrived in Egypt Wimpenny did not have the staff necessary to begin fishery investigations and the vessel was therefore taken over provisionally as a contraband patrol cruiser because, as noted above, the fisheries service was at that time associated with the coast-guard.[1]

1. See S. A. Morcos, 'The Egyptian Expedition to the Red Sea 1934/35', *Deep-Sea Research*, Vol. 31 (6–8A), 1984, pp. 599–616.

FIG. 42. The *Mabahiss* undergoing trials shortly after her launch in 1930.
(*Photo:* courtesy of Swan Hunter Shipbuilders Ltd.)

So began a practice with which the Fisheries Service apparently had to live for some time, for the Annual Report for 1932 states that the *Mabahiss* made a series of short cruises in the Mediterranean during February of that year, but that for the remainder of the time she was used as a patrol vessel.

Wimpenny had left Egypt in December 1931 and had been replaced as Director of Fisheries Research by Hussein Faouzi who ultimately, of course, took part in the John Murray Expedition. Thus, while Faouzi had technically been in charge of the *Mabahiss* for almost two years when the Expedition began, there is every indication that he had been able to use the ship for fisheries research for no more than a few weeks during this period. This conclusion is to some extent supported by Sewell's narrative, and more particularly by some of the rather critical remarks in MacKenzie's journal, which suggest that the ship's crew had had very little experience of the sort of work they were expected to carry out.

During the Expedition the ship's already far from ample accommodation was further strained by the increase of the total complement to forty, that is three more than her intended capacity. Furthermore, the loss of part of the hold to increase her coal-carrying capacity, coupled with the much greater amount of equipment than she would normally have carried, meant that a good deal of gear had to be stored on deck, so that simply moving around the vessel must at times have been a difficult, if not dangerous, undertaking. Sewell graphically describes the cramped working and living conditions which would have been unpleasant in any climate, but which must have been even less tolerable in the high temperatures and humidities experienced in the Indian Ocean.

After her return from the John Murray Expedition in May 1934 the *Mabahiss* was used for a series of four cruises in the Red Sea between 18 December 1934 and 20 February 1935 under the leadership of Dr C. Crossland, Director of the Marine Biological Station at Ghardaga. This was to have been a preliminary expedition in preparation for a much more extensive study of the Red Sea which was to have complemented the John Murray Expedition work in the Indian Ocean. In the event, of course, financial constraints, the Italo-Abyssinian conflict, and ultimately the outbreak of the Second World War prevented this major Red Sea Expedition from taking place. Instead, the *Mabahiss* was used for fisheries and coast-guard duties within Egyptian coastal waters until 1959, when she was transferred from the Coast-guard and Fisheries Service to the Ports and Lights Administration.

For the next six years the ship was used to supply lighthouses and for the inspection of navigation lights in the Red Sea, Gulf of Suez and the western Mediterranean until she was laid up in 1965 in the Western Harbour in Alexandria with the intention of transferring her to the Ministry of Research to be employed as an oceanographic vessel once more.

Mabahiss was already 35 years old and was in need of a major refit, particularly since she had not been docked during the previous five or six years. She still had her largely original wooden bridge and accommodation superstructure and this was replaced with a lighter steel structure by the Ports and Lights Administration at Alexandria shipyard between 1965 and 1968. By this time the hull itself had deteriorated quite badly, with a good deal of corrosion and many of the rivets leaking. As a result, more than 80 tons of steel had to be replaced, including most of the main deck and many of the frames. At the same time the coal storage space was converted into oil tanks for an intended change of fuel, but retaining the original engine.

The financing of these major alterations had always been somewhat uncertain and by 1970 all work was stopped when it became clear that not only were there no funds to complete the refit, but the Ports and Lights Administration would probably not be reimbursed for the considerable investment in the *Mabahiss* which it had already made.

Since that time she has lain untouched in the Western Harbour but has continued to be something of an embarrassment to the Ports and Lights Administration which has had to provide two or three men to inspect her and to tend her security. Finally, in 1983 and as a direct result of the interest in the ship generated by the approach of the fiftieth anniversary of the John Murray Expedition, ownership of the *Mabahiss* was transferred to Alexandria University. While there is now no question of the ship ever putting to sea again as a research vessel, it is hoped that she can be converted into a floating oceanographic museum to illustrate the history of Egyptian marine science in which she played such a prominent part. Unesco has provided a grant towards a feasibility study for her preservation/restoration.

PART 5

The significance of the Expedition[1]

By G. E. R. Deacon[2] and
A. L. Rice

1. Reprinted from *Deep-Sea Research*, Vol. 31 (6–8A), 1984, pp. 573–81, by kind permission of the publisher.
2. After a long and distinguished career in the service of oceanography, Sir George Deacon died on 16 November 1984.

Introduction

THE significance of a major scientific undertaking such as an extensive research cruise can be considered under two main headings. First, what might be termed the political implications, affecting institutions and the availability of funding for particular areas of research, or the direction taken by the careers of individuals; these effects are essentially relatively short-term, although the repercussions may be long lasting. Second, the scientific results, usually embodied in the expedition reports or in independent publications, tend to be rather less ephemeral and may become important decades after their appearance. Such a separation is by no means clear, but the extremes are readily identifiable.

For example, in the case of the most famous of all oceanographic expeditions, that of HMS *Challenger*, at least some of the political effects are obvious. Overseas, it encouraged several nations to mount their own expeditions so that there was a burgeoning of deep-sea research in the 1880s and 1890s (see Yonge, 1972). At home, the results were more equivocal. Two of the *Challenger* scientists (Buchanan and Murray) were established by the expedition into marine careers in which they became increasingly influential. In Murray's case the expedition also led to the acquisition of considerable personal wealth (Burstyn, 1975) and, through this, to the funding of oceanographic projects such as the Michael Sars Expedition (Murray and Hjort, 1912) and, of course, the John Murray Expedition itself. But the British Government, having found itself funding the first example of 'big science' (Burstyn, 1968), seemed reluctant to become re-involved in deep-sea work; it did not do so, in any major way, for almost half a century, though the official 'memory' of the financial wrangles which surrounded the Challenger Expedition, particularly the publication of the Reports, can hardly have lasted much beyond the turn of the century.

The scientific results were clearly of considerable immediate significance since they answered many of the current questions about oceanic biology, chemistry, physics and geology—and, of course, posed many more. In both cases they profoundly influenced the direction of oceanographic research in the decades following the expedition. A hundred years on, the *Challenger* results are largely of historical interest, though in some areas, such as systematic zoology which occupied the bulk of the scientific reports, they have a lasting value, while changing concepts may even now lead to reinterpretation of the results which may consequently assume an unexpected new significance (see, for instance, Rice, 1983). Although the John Murray/ Mabahiss Expedition does not compare with that of HMS *Challenger* in geographical extent, duration, aims, achievements or indeed costs, its significance and influence can be considered under the same headings.

Political significance of the John Murray Expedition

The Expedition seems to have had little or no influence on subsequent events in the United Kingdom, except at the level of the individual scientist. Production of the main scientific reports, published by the British Museum (Natural History) between 1935 and 1967, would have occupied the authors for long periods and may have influenced their subsequent work. In some cases the Expedition may have significantly influenced whole careers. J. D. H. Wiseman, for instance, moved from Cambridge to the Natural History Museum in 1936 when he was appointed Assistant Keeper specifically to work on the sea-floor samples collected from the *Mabahiss*. He retired from the museum in 1972, after a distinguished career in marine geology which may have taken a quite different direction had it not been for the John Murray Expedition.

The careers of the British scientists who were on the *Mabahiss* seem to have been hardly affected by their participation. For Sewell it was too late for such an effect since he had retired from his long career in India before the Expedition began, though writing his own contributions to the scientific reports and editing the manuscripts of others must have occupied much of his time during the 1930s and 1940s.

Farquharson was already an established naval surveying officer for whom the cruise was not a particularly unusual experience. Nevertheless, the efficiency with which he carried out his duties during the Expedition would have done him no harm in the eyes of his superiors in the Royal Navy and, later, when he moved to the Canadian Hydrographic Service and then to the Bedford Institute.

Thompson's career continued in oceanography after the Expedition, with almost thirty years as a teacher of the subject at Yale University. After the *Mabahiss* experience Thompson never again worked on truly deep-ocean subjects, but it is possible that his participation in the John Murray Expedition would have had a greater influence if he had written up his results in more detail, as Sewell hoped.

The careers of the two youngest of the British scientists, Gilson and Macan, were even less affected by their participation in the cruise, for after they had written their respective parts of the scientific reports both turned away from oceanography and moved into freshwater science.

The situation in Egypt was quite different. No deep-sea oceanographic tradition existed, and the limited marine research being carried out during the 1920s was directed specifically at commercial fisheries, with key positions occupied by British rather than Egyptian scientists (see Wimpenny, 1934). By the time the John Murray Expedition began, all the foreign scientists had left, with the exception of Dr C. Crossland who continued to head the Ghardaqa laboratory, and their duties had been taken over by Egyptians. Consequently, the opportunity to take part in a major expedition so early in the new regime was very important and the return of the John Murray Expedition was greeted in Egypt with great enthusiasm. For example, in a letter to the *Nautical Magazine* from Lieutenant F. Awad, Royal Egyptian Navy, written in 1936, the cruise was referred to as one 'which will remain in history as second only to that of the research ship *Challenger*'. Awad's enthusiasm was understandable, if greatly overstated, for the Expedition had certainly thrust Egypt into the oceanographic limelight at a time when deep-sea research was generally going through a relatively unfashionable period.

It was also a pioneering enterprise in international co-operation. There was a long tradition of international co-ordination of national contributions, especially in fisheries research (see for instance, Went, 1972), but it was a considerable advance to have scientists from different countries working together at sea and continuing to work in friendly co-operation after the ship's return, and the experience gave the self-confidence of the Egyptian authorities a considerable boost.

During the early preparations for the John Murray Expedition, when it was still intended to use the *George Bligh*, the Egyptians had been asked to conduct a simultaneous expedition in the Red Sea but had declined because they felt that they did not have sufficient expertise. After having had Egyptian officers and scientists working alongside British counterparts on the *Mabahiss* they readily agreed to undertake their own major investigation. A three-month preliminary cruise was conducted in 1934/35, but the Italo-Abyssinian conflict, and subsequently the Second World War, prevented the main expedition from ever taking place (Morcos, 1984). No significant developments in Egyptian oceanography therefore took place until the late 1940s, particularly with the establishment of the Department of Oceanography at the newly opened University of Alexandria, the first such department in any Arab country or, indeed, in any country bordering on the Arabian Sea, and the growth of what is now the Egyptian Institute of Oceanography and Fisheries.

The significance of the John Murray Expedition in these developments, separated as they were by almost fifteen years, is not clear. At the time, the Expedition certainly generated considerable local interest, even at the very highest levels, but the tangible benefits to Egyptian oceanographers were not obvious. For instance, apart from the short Red Sea cruise, the fisheries scientists in Alexandria, for whose use the *Mabahiss* had principally been purchased, had great difficulty in the years following the Expedition in wresting the ship from the Coast-guard Service to which she technically belonged.

The connection between the Expedition and the later developments is more apparent at the personal level, since the Egyptian scientists on the *Mabahiss* each played key roles, Hussein Faouzi being given the task of building up the Department of Oceanography in its early years and Abdel Fattah Mohamed being the first Professor of Physical and Chemical Oceanography.

Significance of the scientific results

Topography and seafloor geology

At the time the *Mabahiss* sailed from Alexandria the Arabian Sea was certainly, as Stanley Gardiner (1933) wrote, 'one of the least known of oceanic areas'. While the continental coastal waters and the shallow regions around the major island groups had been reasonably well surveyed because of their navigational importance, very few soundings were available in the deeper, mid-ocean regions. This is not surprising, since the area had been missed by most previous oceanographic expeditions which might have been expected to devote the necessary time and effort to obtaining vertical wire soundings, while the comparatively new technique of echo-sounding was only just becoming routinely used by survey vessels. By far the most important of the very few echo-sounding runs in the region was that of the *Dana* between Colombo and the Seychelles in 1930. In the region of 1° N. the *Dana* had crossed a major ridge, named the Carlsberg Ridge by Schmidt (1932), who suggested that it might run from the Chagos group to Socotra. Otherwise, apart from some indications of major irregularities in the northern parts, virtually nothing was known of the sea-bed topography.

By the time the *Mabahiss* returned she had obtained continuous echo-sounder records for the greater part of her 22,000-mile track, so that Farquharson's (1936) bathymetric charts contain all the major topographical features of the region.

This was no mean achievement, for the 'Acadia' Admiralty Recording Echo-sounder, manufactured by Henry Hughes & Son Ltd, was a very crude machine by modern standards and it was remarkable that first Tyler, the Hughes engineer who accompanied the ship as far as Aden, and then Farquharson alone, were able to keep it going for 90 per cent of the time. The hammer and its valves and the hydrophone were necessarily fitted in cramped working spaces near the bottom of the ship, while the water tank and wick which moistened the starch iodide paper in the recorder, and the heater which afterwards dried it, were not ideal adjuncts to a box of what would now seem to be very primitive electronics. In fact, the sounder gave very little trouble, the loss of time being mainly due to failure of the transmitter solenoids because of damage to the insulation of the leads caused by vibration from the hammer. The solenoids were repaired by the Eastern Telegraph Company in the Seychelles, while the same company replaced some damaged resistances in Aden. Otherwise, most of the system worked very well, although a spare transmitter had to be fitted when the original cracked due to metal fatigue, and the amplifier caused some problems to-wards the end of the cruise. Farquharson's efforts were well worth the trouble, for apart from the general improvement in knowledge of the bathymetry of the Arabian Sea and the Gulfs of Aden and Oman, the echo-sounder records produced three major discoveries of which the significance has become apparent only since the development of the theory of plate-tectonics and sea-floor spreading in the 1960s (see Girdler, 1984).

The first of these was the discovery of a series of north-east to south-west trending ridges in the Gulf of Aden which are now recognized as transform faults between the African and Arabian plates.

The second major advance was the further mapping of the Carlsberg Ridge, confirming Schmidt's guess that it extended towards Socotra and demonstrating its double nature with an axial valley now known to be typical of divergent plate boundaries.[1]

Finally, during Cruise 4 from Karachi to Bombay, a zig-zag track along the Makran coast revealed a series of gullies and ridges parallel to the coastline which are now recognized as resulting from 'tectonic folding of sediments as they are scraped off a subducting oceanic plate' (White, 1984).

None of these discoveries, of course, received the modern interpretation at the time for, as Girdler points out, in the 1930s the idea of Continental Drift and horizontal movements generally were very unfashionable among most geologists. Instead, the earth was thought to be contracting and all

---

1 This ridge, the most impressive feature recorded by the *Mabahiss*, was to have been named after the Expedition's benefactor. When it was realized that it had already been named after the Dana Expedition's sponsor, the name Murray Ridge was applied to the much less dramatic feature off the mouth of the Gulf of Oman and now known to be the northward extension of the Owen Fracture Zone (see Sewell, 1934*b*, p. 686).

surface features were considered to have been produced by the resulting compression and vertical movements. In the first public announcement of the Expedition in *The Times* on 2 August 1932, a mention of the hypothetical continent of Lemuria, supposed to lie submerged to the west of India, resulted in several subsequent newspaper articles stressing that the Expedition was searching for a lost continent. This was not too far from the truth, for Sewell (1934*a*) suggested that the gully along the Makran coast might represent the sunken bed of a river, perhaps the Indus, and when basalt rock fragments were obtained from the Carlsberg Ridge and from the basin to the north-east of it, he expected them to resemble the basalts of the Deccan Trap in India and to represent a submerged outflow from it. However, Wiseman's (1937) subsequent analysis of these rocks, the first comprehensive one of a basalt from a mid-oceanic ridge, revealed that they were quite different from Deccan Trap samples, the oceanic basalts having a much higher sodium content and lower levels of iron and potassium. In attempting to summarize the implications of the John Murray results, together with the available seismological and gravity data, Wiseman and Sewell (1937) concluded: 'There is little or no indication that any older continental mass or land isthmus such as the hypothetical continent of Gondwanaland or the isthmus of Lemuria, ever existed except in the granite mass of the Seychelles and perhaps the corresponding granites of Socotra and the Kuria Muria Islands. . . .'

Of much greater interest, however, are the remarkable insights shown by Wiseman and Sewell (see also Girdler, 1984), particularly in pointing out the similarities and connection between the ridges in the Arabian Sea and the East African Rift system based on topography and also on the seismicity maps that had recently been published by Heck (1935). Their discussion consequently contains the germ of the concept of a world rift system which was eventually developed in the 1950s and which is fundamental to modern ideas of sea-floor spreading and plate tectonics.

Physical and chemical oceanography

The main physical oceanographic results of the Expedition addressed two very different types of problem: first, the very specific question of the pattern of water flow between the Red Sea and the Gulf of Aden through the Straits of Bab-el-Mandab; and second, the much more diffuse question of the general circulation within the Arabian Sea.

A series of five stations in the neighbourhood of the Straits were occupied by the *Mabahiss* in September 1933, that is at the end of the summer period when the wind blows from the north-north-west, and again in May 1934, at the end of the winter during which the wind blows from the south-south-east.

Most of the earlier observations of the currents in the Straits, made during the winter period, had indicated a surface flow into the Red Sea and a deep current into the Gulf of Aden. The *Mabahiss* observations in May agreed with these, but those made in September revealed a quite different three-tier system with a very warm surface current and a highly saline near bottom current flowing into the Gulf and an intermediate low-salinity, low-temperature flow in the opposite direction. In reporting these results both Sewell (1934*a*, 1934*b*) and Thompson (1939) seem to have been unaware that a similar three-layer situation had been reported in 1931 by Vercelli from Italian observations made in July 1929 (see Mohamed, 1940). Thus, although the *Mabahiss* observations were not so novel as was at first thought, they added significantly to knowledge of the water masses on either side of the straits and indicated the most fruitful timing of future observations, including the need to investigate the tidal effects. They also clearly demonstrated that the seasonal changes in wind strength and direction are the main factors determining the current regime within the Straits.

Prior to the John Murray Expedition the available data on the general circulation in the Indian Ocean had been reviewed by Möller (1929) who recognized four main layers—the nomenclature for which was based on that used for the Atlantic circulation, with which Schott (1926) had demonstrated that the Indian Ocean circulation was closely analogous. According to Möller a warm, saline upper layer, generally a few hundreds of metres thick, was underlain by an intermediate layer of cooler and less saline water of Antarctic origin. Beneath this was a warm and highly saline layer, the north Indian deep water, which was formed in the Arabian Sea and contributed to by the high salinity mid-depth outflows from the Red Sea and the Persian Gulf. Finally, a cold and low-salinity water mass, the Antarctic bottom water, crept northward but was hardly distinguishable north of the equator.

Subsequent data from the *Dana* (1929/30) and from the *Snellius* (1929) led Thomsen (1933) to challenge Möller's claim that deep high-salinity water in the southern Indian Ocean was continuous with the north Indian deep water. From observations from *Discovery II* in 1935, Clowes and Deacon (1935) suggested that the north Indian deep water could be detected by its high salinity as far as 20° S., and that it could be found farther south as a tongue of poorly oxygenated water sandwiched between the Antarctic intermediate water and eastward-flowing Atlantic deep water which has a much higher oxygen content and which had not figured in Möller's scheme.

This is roughly the situation as accepted today for the deep circulation of the Indian Ocean as summarized by Wyrtki (1973) although he terms the high-salinity, low-oxygen water originating in the Arabian Sea the North Indian intermediate water. The observations made during the John Murray Expedition added greatly to the available data from the north-western Indian Ocean, but made little difference to the interpretations of the time. Mohamed's (1940) study of the *Mabahiss* pH observations generally substantiated earlier conclusions about the nature and origin of the Antarctic intermediate and bottom waters, but led him to suggest that Red Sea water contributed little to the North Indian intermediate water (Möller's 'deep' water), a conclusion which would not be accepted today (see Wyrtki, 1973; Swallow, 1984).

Sewell (1934*a*, 1934*b*) summarized the results of the Expedition, including those from the hydrographic observations, in two brief articles published in *Nature*. The pH observations were the subject of the extensive report by Mohamed referred to above, while the chemical determinations, and particularly those relevant to the nitrogen cycle, were dealt with by Gilson (1937). However, apart from Thompson's report (1939) on the general hydrography of the Red Sea, the salinity and temperature observations were never adequately worked up. This was apparently due to Thompson's great reluctance to 'put pen to paper' (see biographical note, page 278). It is intriguing to speculate on whether the John Murray Expedition would have had a greater impact on the development of knowledge of the physical oceanography of the Arabian Sea if Sewell had managed to encourage Thompson to write up the results!

Biological oceanography

There is no doubt that the main objective of the John Murray Expedition was the study of the biology of the Arabian Sea, and particularly of the bottom-living animals which could be collected in trawls and dredges. Although the Expedition's hydrographic work had the independent objective of characterizing the water masses and their circulation, it was also expected that these observations would be correlated with the biological conditions encountered (see Thompson and Gilson, 1937).

Papers based on the biological collections occupy eight of the eleven volumes of the Expedition Scientific Reports, and 85 per cent of the 8,500 pages. These statistics, however, should not be taken as an indication of the relative significance of the biological and non-biological findings of the Expedition, for many of these Reports contain a great deal of necessary, but rather tedious, taxonomic detail. This was inevitable since, apart from the samples obtained by the Indian Marine Survey vessels *Investigator I* and

Investigator II between 1885 and 1925, no extensive collections of the deep-sea fauna of the Arabian Sea had been made prior to the John Murray Expedition. Consequently, many of the specimens retrieved in the *Mabahiss* deep-sea samples were of undescribed species (see Sewell, 1952) and the collection as a whole, housed mainly in the British Museum (Natural History) in London, is still one of the most important from the region from a taxonomic and zoogeographic point of view. Moreover, several of the biological reports deal with material other than that collected from the *Mabahiss* and include discussions of taxonomy, comparative functional morphology and zoogeography which give them a much more general significance than would have been the case if they had been straightforward taxonomic catalogues of the John Murray Expedition samples alone. For example, Sewell's reports (1947a, 1947b) on the taxonomy and zoogeography of the planktonic copepods, based mainly on the relatively small number of mid-water samples taken during the Expedition, are classics of their kind. Similarly, the review of the sepiid cephalopods by Adam and Rees (1966) is a comprehensive taxonomic treatment of the whole family, while the final volume published, Knudsen's account (1967) of the deep-sea bivalves, is an important summary of knowledge of this group in the region and includes the study of material collected both before and after the John Murray Expedition.

However, of much wider potential significance were the more general observations on the distribution of the benthic fauna and of the physical and chemical factors affecting it. The most dramatic and unexpected discovery of the cruise was undoubtedly the more or less azoic area of the sea floor extending from about 100 metres to 1,300 metres depth off the coast of Arabia and somewhat deeper in the Gulf of Oman. In several of the samples taken in this zone, and particularly in the neighbourhood of Ras el Hadd, the mud brought up in the trawls and dredges smelt strongly of hydrogen sulphide and a hastily improvised assay technique revealed almost 30 mg H_2S/l in the interstitial water (Mohamed, 1940). Similar conditions had been found in the Black Sea and in some enclosed fjords, but this was the first record in the open sea. Hydrogen sulphide found in the bottom muds of several of the lagoons of the Maldive Archipelago was thought to be due to the decomposition of abundant organic matter derived from the vegetation of the islands. No explanation for the open sea observations was offered, however, other than that 'the sterility of the area must be attributed either to some harmful character of the bottom deposit or else to some seasonal change in the general conditions of the deep water'. At least part of the answer became apparent from the work on mid-water chemistry by Mohamed, and particularly by Gilson.

Gilson's particular responsibility during the cruise was the investigation of the nitrogen cycle which involved the study of the distribution of nitrogenous compounds in the water column in relation to the phytoplankton, and some laboratory work at the Plymouth Laboratory after the Expedition. The resulting report (Gilson, 1937) is an excellent summary of the state of knowledge of phytoplankton ecology which, during the 1920s and 1930s, was developing rapidly.

At the turn of the century Brandt had developed his theory that the growth of phytoplankton was controlled by the availability of nutrients. He believed that nitrate supplies to the phytoplankton came entirely from the land and that this explained the richness of inshore waters compared with oceanic regions. The control of the availability of nitrate to the phytoplankton was attributed by Brandt to the activities of nitrate-reducing bacteria, which prevented the nitrates from reaching lethal levels in the sea.

No significant progress in extending and refining Brandt's ideas was made until Atkins and Harvey improved the analytical techniques for phosphates and nitrates at Plymouth in the mid-1920s and later, together with Cooper, began to examine the annual cycle of nutrient levels in the English Channel and adjacent regions. Thompson had spent some weeks at the Plymouth laboratory specifically to familiarize himself with the latest analytical techniques and the John Murray Expedition provided an early opportunity to apply them to a tropical ocean.

Taking advantage of these techniques, Gilson made a number of important contributions and observations, many of which have been largely ignored by later workers. First, he derived a workable relationship between Marshall and Orr's (1928) recently defined 'compensation point', the depth at which oxygen produced by photosynthesis just balances that consumed by phytoplankton respiration, and Secchi disc determinations of the opacity of the water column. The general validity of the compensation point calculated in this way seemed to be confirmed by the fact that this depth corresponded closely in most of the John Murray stations with the lower limit of the layer depleted of nutrients. However, in several of the Gulf of Aden stations there was a marked thermocline well above the computed compensation depth, with the nutrient deficient and high oxygen layer restricted to the zone above the discontinuity. These results, and others, did much to confirm earlier work indicating the importance of thermal stratification of the water column in controlling primary productivity.

Gilson found that the oxygen profile in the euphotic zone often showed a peak well below the surface, indicating inhibition of photosynthesis by high light intensities and agreeing with Marshall and Orr's (1928) observations. Moreover, this oxygen peak was usually rather higher in the water column than the layer of maximum abundance of phytoplankton cells as determined by net catches so that, as Gilson wrote (1937, p. 38), 'The total algal population is not necessarily a true measure of the productivity, if we define productivity as the rate of carbon assimilation and cell increase.' He had, incidentally, no direct means of measuring primary productivity, but obtained what he called 'the roughest of approximations' to a general figure for the Arabian Sea as a whole. This was computed from the observed general deepening of the compensation point from late September to late February and the change in nitrate levels (used by the phytoplankton) in this same period. Using Cooper's (1933) recently published information that nitrogen represented 0.5 per cent of the wet weight of phytoplankton, Gilson calculated a production rate of 14.4 g wet wt/m^2/day, though he felt that this was too low for the upwelling regions and too high for most of the Arabian Sea. Assuming that carbon represents about 3 per cent of phytoplankton wet weight, Gilson's figure would be roughly equivalent to 500 mgC/m^2/day, which is not very different from modern estimates (see Qasim, 1982; Krey, 1973).

In his main work, on the nitrogen cycle, Gilson made particularly important observations on the nitrite concentrations. He noted that almost all of the John Murray Expedition stations showed a high level of nitrite in a narrow zone at the base of the nutrient-depleted surface layer, a phenomenon which had already been observed and has been widely found subsequently in oceanic areas. Gilson suggested that this primary nitrite maximum was the result of the activity of nitrate-reducing bacteria in the special conditions occurring in this zone where ample nitrate occurs together with abundant organic matter, providing an easily oxidized energy source. This explanation had already been suggested by Rakestraw (1933), but studies in the late 1930s and much more recently (see Raymont, 1980, p. 313) indicate that this nitrite peak is due to bacterial oxidation of ammonia released from dead phytoplankton cells, rather than to denitrification, or to the direct release of nitrite by phytoplankton.

Gilson would have been more in line with modern thinking if he had applied the same explanation for the secondary nitrite maximum at depths below about 150 metres at several stations, particularly in the north-eastern Arabian Sea, off the Makran coast and off the coast of Arabia. This was the first record of such secondary maxima which are now known from a number of other regions including the eastern tropical Pacific. They are restricted to water bodies with very low levels of oxygen and are thought to be due to the action of denitrifying bacteria (Raymont, 1980). Curiously, Gilson (1937, p. 65) made the point that bacteria known to be capable of reducing nitrate to nitrite required low levels of oxygen, as found at those stations where the secondary nitrite maxima were encountered, but he did not go on to suggest such denitrification as an explanation. He did, however, point out that 'the fact that these stations lie in the neighbourhood of the "dead areas" described elsewhere in these reports . . . is suggestive, but the connection cannot be regarded as established'.

Thus, these azoic regions were found where water with a high nitrite and, much more to the point, very low dissolved oxygen content, Wyrtki's (1973) north Indian intermediate water, impinges on the sea-bed. The reason for the deep oxygen minimum layer in the Arabian Sea and elsewhere is the result of the balance between consumption by the oxidation of abundant organic matter beneath regions of high primary productivity and re-plenishment by advection and mixing with other water masses, an explanation clearly stated by Sewell and Fage (1948). In the Arabian Sea the situation seems to be exacerbated by the fact that the replenishing water flowing northward into the area at intermediate depths already has a depleted oxygen content (Swallow, 1984). But the connection between the low oxygen content of the overlying water, producing inhospitable anoxic benthic conditions, and the absence of megabenthic organisms, seems not to have been made at the time, resulting in Sewell's (1934a) curiously non-committal explanation of the azoic zones quoted above. The reasons for this failure seem to be twofold. First, the mid-water hauls made during the Expedition revealed fairly abundant pelagic life in the oxygen minimum layer (see Sewell, 1947a; Sewell and Fage, 1948) clearly showing 'that this water is not *per se* responsible for the absence of life' (Sewell, 1934a). Second, and perhaps even more important, is the fact that although Mohamed (1940, p. 191) emphasized the correspondence between the low dissolved oxygen levels and his low pH levels, the details of the oxygen profiles obtained in the Arabian Sea and the Gulf of Oman, like the temperature and salinity sections, were never published. If they had been, Sewell would perhaps have realized that the overlying water in the azoic regions was, indeed, responsible for the absence of life.

Conclusion

The answer to the question: Was the John Murray/Mabahiss Expedition particularly significant? must be 'Yes'. But such an answer is subject to some important qualifications. First, its 'political' implications were minimal in the United Kingdom, but considerable in Egypt. Second, the scientific results, which might have been expected to have had a wider and longer-lasting impact, had remarkably little effect at the time and their potential importance has become apparent only in retrospect. The reasons are undoubtedly complex, but the following factors each surely played a part.

First, the conceptual framework necessary for an appreciation of the significance of the results on sea-floor topography and geology did not exist in the 1930s and was not to materialize for at least a further two decades. Second, many of the results, though published, seem to have escaped the notice of later workers. Gilson's (1937) excellent report on the nitrogen cycle, for instance, does not receive a single mention in the volume on the biology of the Indian Ocean edited by Zeitzschel (1973), and only a single reference in Raymont (1980). Most of the results, of course, appeared in the Scientific Reports of the Expedition rather than in conventional scientific journals and may therefore have failed to reach as wide a readership as they might otherwise have done. On the other hand, the results of many other expeditions were published in much the same way but nevertheless entered the literature adequately. Perhaps the war was to blame for this, as for many other things. In the excitement of the post-war boom in marine research there was certainly a tendency to start afresh in many areas and to ignore, albeit unintentionally, the older literature. The earlier John Murray Reports were perhaps among the casualties. Finally, and most regrettably, some of the potentially most important results were never published. For this there is no obvious explanation other than lack of time or motivation, which most of us use to excuse our failure to produce. John Murray, who wrote 1,600 pages of the *Challenger* Reports and co-authored as much again, would have found this unforgivable!

References

ADAM, W.; REES, W. J. 1966. A Review of the Cephalopod Family Sepiidae. *Scientific Reports. The John Murray Expedition 1933–34*, Vol. II, No. 1, pp. 1–165.

BURSTYN, H. L. 1968. Science and Government in the Nineteenth Century: The *Challenger* Expedition and its Report. *Bulletin de l'Institut océanographique de Monaco*, Special Issue 2, pp. 603–13.

——. 1975. Science Pays Off: Sir John Murray and the Christmas Island Phosphate Industry, 1886–1914. *Social Studies of Science*, Vol. 5, pp. 5–34.

CLOWES, A. J.; DEACON, G. E. R. 1935. The Deep-water Circulation of the Indian Ocean. *Nature* (London), Vol. 136, pp. 936–8.

COOPER, L. H. N. 1933. Chemical Constituents of Biological Importance in the English Channel, November 1930 to January 1932. Part II, Hydrogen Ion Concentration, Excess Base, Carbon Dioxide and Oxygen. *Journal of the Marine Biological Association of the United Kingdom*, Vol. 18, pp. 729–54.

FARQUHARSON, W. I. 1936. Topography, with an Appendix on Magnetic Observations. *Scientific Reports. The John Murray Expedition 1933–34*, Vol. 1, No. 2, pp. 43–61.

GILSON, H. C. 1937. Chemical and Physical Investigations. The Nitrogen Cycle. *Scientific Reports. The John Murray Expedition 1933–34*, Vol. 2, No. 2, pp. 21–81.

GIRDLER, R. W. 1984. The Evolution of the Gulf of Aden and Red Sea in Space and Time. *Deep-Sea Research*, Vol. 31 (6–8A), pp. 747–62.

GARDINER, J. S. 1933. The John Murray Expedition to the Indian Ocean. *Geographical Journal*, Vol. 81, pp. 570–3.

HECK, N. H. 1935. A New Map of Earthquake Distribution. *Geographical Review*, Vol. 25, pp. 125–30.

KNUDSEN, J. 1967. Deep-sea Bivalvia. *Scientific Reports. The John Murray Expedition 1933–34*, Vol. 11, No. 3, pp. 235–346.

KREY, J. 1973. Primary Productivity in the Indian Ocean, I. In: B. Zeitschel (ed.), *The Biology of the Indian Ocean*, pp. 115–26. New York, Springer Verlag.

MARSHALL, S. M.; ORR, A. P. 1928. The Photosynthesis of Diatom Cultures in the Sea. *Journal of the Marine Biological Association of the United Kingdom*, Vol. 15, pp. 321–60.

MOHAMED, A. F. 1940. Chemical and Physical Investigations. The Distribution of Hydrogen-ion Concentration in the North-western Indian Ocean and Adjacent Waters. *Scientific Reports. The John Murray Expedition 1933–34*, Vol. 2, No. 5, pp. 121–202.

MÖLLER, L. 1929. Die Zirkulation des Indischen Ozeans. *Veröffentlichungen des Instituts für Meereskunde Universität Berlin*, Series A, Vol. LVII, No. 21, pp. 1–48.

MORCOSS, S. A. 1984. The Egyptian Expedition to the Red Sea 1934/35. *Deep-Sea Research*, Vol. 31 (6-8A), pp. 599–616.

MURRAY, J.; HJORT, J. 1912. *The Depths of the Ocean*. London, Macmillan, 821 pp.

Qasim, S. Z. 1982. Oceanography of the Northern Arabian Sea. *Deep-Sea Research*, Vol. 29, pp. 1041–68.

Rakestraw, N. W. 1933. Studies on the Biology and Chemistry of the Gulf of Maine, I. The Chemistry of the Waters of the Gulf of Maine in August, 1932. *Biological Bulletin. Marine Biological Laboratory, Woods Hole*, Vol. 64, pp. 149–58.

Raymont, J. E. G. 1980. *Plankton Productivity in the Oceans.* Vol. 1—*Phytoplankton*. 2nd ed. Oxford, Pergamon. 489 pp.

Rice, A. L. 1983. Thomas Henry Huxley and the Strange Case of *Bathybius haeckelii*: A Possible Alternative Explanation. *Archives for Natural History*, Vol. 2, pp. 169–80.

Schmidt, J. 1932. *Dana's Togt Omkring Jorden, 1928–1930.* Copenhagen, Gyldendalske Boghandel Nordisk Forlage. 255 pp.

Schott, G. 1926. Die Tiefwasserbewegungen des Indischen Ozeans. *Annalen de Hydrographie und Maritimen Meteorologie (Deutsche Seewarte)* (Hamburg), Vol. 12, pp. 417–31.

Sewell, R. B. S. 1934a. The John Murray Expedition to the Arabian Sea. *Nature* (London), No. 133, pp. 86–9.

——. 1934b. The John Murray Expedition to the Arabian Sea. *Nature* (London), Vol. 134, pp. 685—8.

——. 1947a. The Free-swimming Planktonic Copepoda. *Scientific Reports. The John Murray Expedition 1933–34*, Vol. 8, No. 1, pp. 1–303.

——. 1947b. The Free-swimming Planktonic Copepoda. Geographical Distribution. *Scientific Reports. The John Murray Expedition 1933–34*, Vol. 8, No. 3, pp. 317–592.

Sewell, R. B. S.; Fage, L. 1948. Minimum Oxygen Layer in the Ocean. *Nature* (London), Vol. 162, p. 4129.

Swallow, J. C. 1984. Some Aspects of the Physical Oceanography of the Indian Ocean. *Deep-Sea Research*, Vol. 31 (6–8A), pp. 639–50.

Thompson, E. F. 1939. The Exchange of Water between the Red Sea and the Gulf of Aden over the 'Sill'. *Scientific Reports. The John Murray Expedition 1933–34*, Vol. 2, No. 4, pp. 105–19.

Thompson, E. F.; Gilson, H. C. 1937. Chemical and Physical Investigations. Introduction. *Scientific Reports. The John Murray Expedition 1933–34*, Vol. 2, No. 2, pp. 15–20.

Thomsen, H. 1933. The Circulation in the Depths of the Indian Ocean. *Journal du Conseil Permanent International pour l'Exploration de la Mer*, Vol. 8, pp. 315–17.

Went, A. E. J. 1972. Seventy Years Agrowing. A History of the International Council for the Exploration of the Sea, 1902–1972. *Rapport et procès-verbaux des réunions du Conseil Permanent International pour l'Exploration de la Mer*, Vol. 165, pp. 1–252.

White, R. S. 1984. Active and Passive Plate Boundaries around the Gulf of Oman, North-west Indian Ocean. *Deep-Sea Research*, Vol. 31 (6–8A), pp. 731–45.

WIMPENNY, R. S. 1934. The Fisheries of Egypt. *Science Progress* (London), Vol. 114, pp. 210–27.

WISEMAN, J. D. H. 1937. Basalts from the Carlsberg Ridge, Indian Ocean. *Scientific Reports. The John Murray Expedition 1933–34*, Vol. 3, No. 1, pp. 1–30.

WISEMAN, J. D. H.; SEWELL, R. B. S. 1937. The Floor of the Arabian Sea. *Geological Magazine*, pp. 219–30.

WYRTKI, K. 1973. Physical Oceanography of the Indian Ocean. In: B. Zeitschel (ed.), *Ecological Studies, Analysis and Synthesis*, Vol. 3, pp. 18–36. New York, Springer Verlag.

YONGE, C. M. 1972. The Inception and Significance of the *Challenger* Expedition. *Proceedings of the Royal Society of Edinburgh*, Series B, Vol. 72, pp. 1–13.

ZEITZSCHEL, B. 1973. *The Biology of the Indian Ocean.* New York, Springer Verlag. 549 pp.

APPENDIX

John Murray Expedition Scientific Reports,
published by the British Museum (Natural History),
1935–67

Vol 1.

No. 1. R. B. S. Sewell, 'Introduction and List of Stations', pp. 1–41, 23 November 1935.

No. 2. W. I. Farquharson, 'Topography, with an Appendix on Magnetic Observations', pp. 43–61, 27 June 1936.

No. 3. R. B. S. Sewell, 'An Account of Addu Atoll', pp. 63–93, 27 June 1936.

No. 4. E. A. Glennie, 'A Report on the Values of Gravity in the Maldive and Laccadive Islands', pp. 95–107, 27 June 1936.

No. 5. R. B. S. Sewell, 'An Account of Horsborough or Goifurfehendu Atoll', pp. 109–25, 27 June 1936.

Vol. 2.

No. 1. J. Paton, 'Report on the Meteorological Observations', pp. 1–14, 24 October 1936.

No. 2. E. F. Thompson and H. C. Gilson, 'Chemical and Physical Investigations. Introduction, pp. 15–20; H. C. Gilson, 'The Nitrogen Cycle', pp. 21–81, 27 November 1937.

No. 3. E. F. Thompson, 'The General Hydrography of the Red Sea', pp. 83–103, 25 November 1939.

No. 4. E. F. Thompson, 'The Exchange of Water between the Red Sea and the Gulf of Aden over the "Sill" ', pp. 105–19, 25 November 1939.

No. 5. A. F. Mohamed, 'The Distribution of Hydrogen-ion Concentration in the North-western Indian Ocean and Adjacent Waters', pp. 121–202, 24 May 1940.

Vol. 3.

No. 1. J. D. H. Wiseman, 'Basalts from the Carlsberg Ridge, Indian Ocean', pp. 1–30, 23 July 1937.

No. 2. H. G. Stubbings, 'The Marine Deposits of the Arabian Sea', pp. 31–158, 22 July 1939.

No. 3. H. G. Stubbings, 'Stratification of Biological Remains in Marine Deposits', pp. 159–92, 24 November 1939.

No. 4. J. D. H. Wiseman and H. Bennett, 'The Distribution of Organic Carbon and Nitrogen in Sediments from the Arabian Sea', pp. 193–221, 23 March 1940.

Vol. 4.

No. 1. H. G. Stubbings, 'Cirripedia', pp. 1–70, 24 October 1936.

No. 2. A. D. Imms, 'On a New Species of *Halobates*, a Genus of Pelagic Hemiptera', pp. 71–8, 24 October 1936.

No. 3. J. F. G. Wheeler, 'Nemertea', pp. 79–86, 1 January 1937.

No. 4. A. H. Clark, 'Crinoidea', pp. 87–108, 1 January 1937.

No. 5. S. J. Hickson, 'Pennatulacea', pp. 109–30, 5 April 1937.

No. 6. K. H. Barnard, 'Amphipoda', pp. 131–201, 5 April 1937.

No. 7. G. Stiasny, 'Scyphomedusae', pp. 203–42, 24 April 1937.

No. 8. C. C. A. Munro, 'Polychaeta', pp. 243–321, 26 June 1937.

No. 9. T. T. Macan, 'Asteroidea', pp. 323–435, 26 March 1938.

Vol. 5.

No. 1. H. G. Stubbings, 'Phyllirhoidae', pp. 1–14, 27 November 1937.

No. 2. H. G. Stubbings, 'Pteropoda', pp. 15–33, 26 March 1938.

No. 3. M. M. Ramadan, 'Crustacea: Penaeidae', pp. 35–76, 26 March 1938.

No. 4. N. B. Eales, 'A Systematic and Anatomical Account of the Opisthobranchia,' pp. 77–122, 16 April 1938.

No. 5. M. M. Ramadan, 'Astacura and Palinura', pp. 123–45, 26 February 1938.

No. 6. W. T. Calman, 'Pycnogonida', pp. 147–66, 26 February 1938.

No. 7. J. Stanley Gardiner and P. Waugh, 'Flabellia and Turbinolid Corals', pp. 167–202, 23 July 1938.

No. 8. W. M. Tattersall, 'Euphausiacea and Mysidacea of the John Murray Expedition to the Indian Ocean', pp. 203–46, 25 March 1939.

No. 9. K. A. Pyefinch, 'Ascothoracica (Crustacea, Cirripedia)', pp. 247–62, 22 July 1939.

Vol. 6.

No. 1. T. Mortensen, 'Report on the Echinoidea of the John Murray Expedition', pp. 1–28, 28 October 1939.

No. 2. H. L. Clark, 'Ophiuroidea', pp. 29–136, 28 October 1939.

No. 3. B. Chopra, 'Stomatopoda', pp. 137–81, 28 October 1939.

No. 4. W. T. Calman, 'Crustacea: Carida', pp. 183–224, 22 July 1939.

No. 5. J. Stanley Gardiner and P. Waugh, 'Madreporaria Excluding Flabellidae and Turbinolidae', pp. 225–42, 28 October 1939. J. Stanley Gardiner, 'The Ecology of Solitary Corals', pp. 243–50, 28 October 1939.

No. 6. G. E. H. Foxon, 'Stomatopod larvae', pp. 251–66, 28 October 1939.

No. 7. S. J. Hickson, 'The Gorgonacea with Notes on Two Species of Pennatulacea', pp. 267–317, 23 February 1940.

No. 8. H. G. Cannon, 'Ostracoda', pp. 319–25, 22 June 1940.

Vol. 7.

No. 1. J. R. Norman, 'Fishes', pp. 1–116, 25 October 1939.

No. 2. R. B. S. Sewell, 'Copepoda, Harpacticoida', pp. 117–382, 9 March 1940.

No. 3. H. G. Stubbings, 'Cirripedia', pp. 383–99, 9 March 1940.

No. 4. A. C. Stephen, 'Sipunculids and Echiurids,' pp. 401–9, 24 October 1941.

No. 5. E. F. Thompson, 'Paguridae and Caenobitidae', pp. 411–26, 25 June 1943.

Vol. 8.

No. 1. R. B. S. Sewell, 'The Free-swimming Planktonic Copepoda', pp. 1–303, 20 March 1947.

No. 2. H. Broch, 'Stylasteridae', pp. 305–16, 20 March 1947.

No. 3. R. B. S. Sewell, 'The Free-swimming Planktonic Copepoda. Geographical Distribution', pp. 317–592, 28 September 1948.

Vol. 9.

No. 1. T. Mortensen, 'Report on the Echinoidea of the John Murray Expedition, Part II', pp. 1–16, 26 June 1948.

No. 2. R. B. S. Sewell, 'The Littoral and Semi-parasitic Cyclopoida, the Monstrilloida and Notodelphyoida', pp. 17–199, 28 March 1949.

No. 3. I. Gordon, 'Crustacea: Dromiacea. Part I. Systematic Account of the Dromiacea Collected by the John Murray Expedition. Part II. The Morphology of the Spermatheca in Certain Dromiacea', pp. 201–53, 31 January 1950.

No. 4. R. B. S. Sewell, 'The Epibionts and Parasites of the Planktonic Copepoda of the Arabian Sea', pp. 255–394, 20 July 1951.

No. 5. L. M. Newton, 'Marine Algae', pp. 395–420, 24 March 1953.

Vol. 10.

No. 1. R. B. S. Sewell, 'The Pelagic Tunicata', pp. 1–90, 27 November 1953.

No. 2. N. H. Ludbrook, 'Scaphopoda', pp. 91–120, 29 January 1954.

No. 3. J. E. Webb, 'Cephalochordata', pp. 121–8, 29 January 1957.

No. 4. P. Knott, 'The Sessile Tunicata', pp. 129–49, 17 May 1957.

No. 5. M. Burton, 'Sponges', pp. 151–281, 24 November 1959.

No. 6. H. M. Muir-Wood, 'Report on the Brachiopoda of the John Murray Expedition', pp. 283–318, 24 November 1959.

No. 7. N. M. Tirmizi, 'Crustacea: Penaeidae, Part II. Series Benthesicymae', pp. 319–83, 29 January 1960.

No. 8. N. M. Tirmizi, 'Crustacea: Chirostylidae (Galatheidae)', pp. 385–415, 30 December 1964.

Vol. 11.

No. 1. W. Adam and W. J. Rees, 'A Review of the Cephalopod Family Sepiidae', pp. 1–65, 1 April 1966.

No. 2. N. M. Tirmizi, 'Crustacea: Galatheidae', pp. 167–234, 3 May 1966.

No. 3. J. Knudsen, 'Deep-sea Bivalvia', pp. 235–346, 19 May 1967.

INDEX

Abd al Kuri (island of Socotra group), 101, 246

Abu Zanima (Abu Zenima, Sinae), 78

Acadia echo-sounder, 62, 312

Accidents
  Abdul Ghani, ship's carpenter, injured foot, 257
  Mohamed overboard, 256
  un-named crew member, injured hand, 253

Accommodation, 79–82

Accumulator, 66

Acropora, see Corals

Aden, 95, 97, 109, 111, 256, 259

Addu Atoll, Maldives, 210, 214, 220

Ahmed Fuad Bey, Director General, Egyptian Marine, 39, 44, 264

Al Ahram, 281

Albani, Mr, Coast Guard Service, Alexandria, 264

Alcock, A., Surgeon Naturalist, *Investigator*, 253

Aldabra Atoll, 196

Alexander Agassiz Medal, endowed by Sir John Murray, 22

Alexandria, University of, 13

Allen, J., Director, Marine Biological Laboratory, Plymouth, 22

Alula-Fartak ridge, 107

Amphipods (crustaceans), 168

Antennarius (fish), 115

Anthropological Survey of India, 272

Arca (mollusc), 122

Ari Atoll, Maldives, 230

Atolla (jelly-fish), 95, 102, 251

Aurelia (jelly-fish), 101, 122, 164, 190, 198, 239

Axial valley, 313

Azoic zones, 126–8, 138–9, 143, 149–52, 239, 249–50, 250, 252 317

Bab-el-Mandab, Straits of, 88, 259, 314

BANZARE (British, Australian and New Zealand Antarctic Research Expedition), 27, 275

Bacteria, 149, 154

Baghdad, 286, 290

Baillie sounding rod, 66

Balistes (fish), 102

Baluchistan, 135, 136

Bangham, D. H., Dean of Faculty of Science, Cairo University, 38

Baringtonia (tree), 214

Basalts, 200

Beaufort, HMS, 277

Bedford Institute of Oceanography, Halifax, N.S., Canada, 278

Benthosaurus (fish), 243

Berbera (Somalia), 259

Beröe (ctenophore or sea-gooseberry), 113

Bibby Line, 235

Bigelow bottom sampler, 68

Bioluminescence, 158, 161, 162, 198
Bird Island, Seychelles, 195
Birgus (giant robber crab), 185
Bivalves (molluscs), 248, 261
Blue Funnel Line, 274
Bolinia (ctenophore or sea-gooseberry), 114
Bombay, 151–4, 234
Bombay Natural History Society, 153
Bonito (tuna), 243
Botanical Gardens, Peredenya, Ceylon, 204
Bottom sampler, Bigelow, 68
Brabourne, Lord, Governor of Bombay, 153
Brachiopods, 229
Brandt, K., 318
Bremner, Political Agent, Muscat, 142
Bridge of Allan, Scotland, 19
Bristol Hotel, Colombo, 203
British India (B.I.), 41
British Mosquito Control Institute, 289
British Museum (Natural History), 13–14, 24, 40, 290, 317
Britannia, SS, 132
Brodie, Captain, BISS *Karanja*, 246
Brooke-Smith, Captain, Meteorological Department, Air Ministry, 42
Buccinum (mollusc), 90
Buddha, Temple of the Sacred Tooth, Kandy, 204
Bulldog, HMS, 35
Bushey Island, Addu Atoll, 211

Cairo, 217, 221, 264
Cairo, University of, 221, 264
Calman, W. T., Keeper of Zoology, British Museum (Natural History), 22, 24, 40
Canadian Hydrographic Service, 278
Cape Comorin, 234
Cape Gardafui, Somalia, 98, 100–2, 181, 190, 215, 243, 244, 245
Caranx (fish), 105, 109, 116, 122, 161, 164, 195
Carcharias, 86, 164, 242, *see also* Sharks

Cardium (mollusc), 122
Carlsberg Ridge, 199, 201, 240, 243, 313, 314
Caryophyllia (solitary coral), 251
Casino Palace Hotel, Port Said, 263
Central Fisheries Research Institute, India, 272
Centrostephanus (sea-urchin), 229
Ceratium (diatom), 99
Ceylon, 203
Chagos Archipelago, 209, 215, 240
Chaki Chaki Creek, Pemba Island, 178
Challenger, HMS, 35, 36, 162, 184, 199
Chiton (mollusc), 90, 190
Christmas, 166, 167
Christmas Island, 20 et seq.
Christmas Island Phosphate Company, 21 et seq.
Chumbi Island, Zanzibar, 184, 189
City Line, 275
City of Dieppe, SS, 276
City of Valencia, SS, 275
Clive, RIMS, 153
Coburg, Ontario, 19
Cochin, India, 234
Cocos and Keeling Islands, 21
Coeloria (coral), 190
Colaba Point, Bombay, 152
Collins, Lt-Cdr R., RIM, 209
Colombo, 204, 205–6, 210, 232, 234, 237, 238
Comorin, Cape, India, 234
Compensation point, 318
Cooper, L. N. H., 318–19
Corals, 79, 91, 115, 119, 211, 223, 226, 229, 261
Corixidae, 290
Cornwall, HMS, 98
Coryphaena (fish), 116, 161
Crepidula (mollusc), 144
Crinoids (sea-lilies), 101, 229
Crossland, C., 70, 311
Cucumaria (sea cucumber or holothurian), 122
Currents, Straits of Bab-el-Mandab, 88, 314

Cyclothone (fish), 95, 162
Cymodocea (turtle-grass), 175

Dana, Royal Danish Research Ship, 24, 37, 199, 315
Davis, Captain J. K., 275
Decapod shrimps, 87, 94, 150, 178, 181, 228
Deccan Trap, India, 314
Deep circulation, Indian Ocean, 315
Denitrification, 319
Depth from thermometers, 60–2
Dicerobatis (giant-ray), 168
Difuri Island, Fadiffolu Atoll, Maldives, 220
Diodon (fish), 115
Discoloration of water, 128, 169, 217, 254, 260
Discovery, RRS, 25, 37, 40, 275
Dolphins, *see* Porpoises
Dostia (mollusc), 91
Double Peak Island, 90
Douglas, Sir H. P., Hydrographer to the Admiralty, 40
Dredge, Salpa, 54
Dredge, triangular, 54
Driver sounding tube, 66
Dubal Dibbah (Arabian village), 145
Duendes, SS, 274

Eastern Telegraph Company, 197
Echeneis (fish), 239
Echinoids (sea-urchins), 102, 106, 200, 248, 254, 261
Echo-sounder, 62, 64
Echo-sounder, amplifier fault, 206
Echo-sounder, cracked transmitter, 209
Edgell, Captain J. A., hydrographer, 26
Edinburgh, University of, 19
Effingham, HMS, East India Squadron, 234
Egeria, HMS, 20
El Amira Fawzia, HEMS, 44
Elephant Back Rock, Somalia, 104, 247
Elephants, Kandy, 204
El-Filey, *see* Mohamed
Ellerman City Line, 41

Elliot and Garrood, 49
Encephaloides (spider crab), 127
English Coaling Co. Ltd, 41
Enterprise, HMS, 263
Ephemeroptera, 291
Euphorbia, 190

Fadiffolu Atoll, Maldives, 219–20, 231
Fantome, HMS, 276
Faouzi, Hussein, 280–1
Farquharson, W. I., 276–8
Favia, *see* Corals
Fazan, Mr, Political Resident, Mombasa, 171
Fehendu Island, Horsburgh Atoll, Maldives, 224
Fireworks, 222
Flannery, Baggaly & Johnson, Ltd, 301
Flying Fish, HMS, 167, 168, 169, 195, 213, 219, 238, 240, 242, 243
Fuad, King, 37, 44, 101, 266; *see also* King Fuad Bank
Fouling of hull, 169, 194
Freshwater Biological Association, 289, 290, 291
Fumigation, 203

Galle Face Hotel, Colombo, 204
Gan Island, Addu Atoll, 210, 211
Gardaga, *see* Hurgada
Gardafui, Cape, Somalia, *see* Cape Gardafui
Garden of Eden, 131
Gardiner, J. Stanley, 30, 31, 37, 40, 225, 232
Geodetic observations, 219, 230
George Bligh, FRV, 37
Ghardaga, *see* Hurgada
Ghubbet Binna bay, Somalia, 100
Giant robber crab (*Birgus*), 185, 190, 196
Gilson, H. C., 14, 288–9, 317–20
Glennie, E. A., Survey of India, 41, 205, 211–14, 223, 231–4, 238
Globigerina (foraminiferan), 99, 129, 159, 160, 169, 186, 228, 229, 239, 240, 242

Golden Cape, SS, 275

Gondwanaland, 314

Gonodactylus (stomatopod), 190

Grand Oriental Hotel, Colombo, 203

Grab, Petersen, 71

Great Hanish Island, *see* Hanish Island

Greaves, R. I. N., 289

Gulf of Aden, 246, 249, 254, 259

Gulf of Aqaba, 295

Gulf of Cambay, 152

Gulf of Oman, 142 et seq., 150, 239

Gulf of Suez, 76

Gulf of Tajura, 131, 260

Haddummat, Atoll, Chagos Group, 215

Haffkine Institute, Parel, 153

Halaniya Island, Khorya Morya group, 116, 120

Hall & Co., 41, 44

Halogens, 62

Hamdi, Bey, Coast Guard Official, Ismailia, 262, 263

Hanish Island, 77, 89, 91

Harvey phytoplankton net, 58

Hawkins, HMS, 235

Heratera Island, Addu Atoll, 211, 212

Herdman, H., 40

Hermit crabs, 88

Hogg, Mr, partner, MacKinnon, MacKenzie & Co. Ltd, 153–4

Holothuria (sea-cucumber), 212

Holothurians (sea-cucumbers), 91, 122, 129, 148, 176, 212, 248

Horsburgh Atoll, Maldives, 223, 224, 230

Horst, SS, 231–3

Howard, Mr, Port Health Officer, Karachi, 132

Hughes and Co., 62

Hurgada (Ghardaga), 77, 79

Hyalonema (sponge), 253

Hydrocyanic acid gas (fumigation), 203

Hydrogen sulphide, 126–8, 149–52, 213, 216, 220, 221, 224, 230, 252, 317

Hydrographic Department, Admiralty, 276–8

Hydroids, 260

IOF (Institute of Oceanography and Fisheries), 13

Ianthina (pelagic mollusc), 122

Illnesses
    Chief Engineer Griggs, 97
    influenza, 161
    Macan, 182–3, 191
    Captain MacKenzie, 203, 223, 256, 259

Imperial Institute of Science, Bombay, 154

Indian Medical Service, 256

Indian Museum, Calcutta, 253

Institut für Meereskunde, Berlin University, 285

Institute of Oceanography and Fisheries, Alexandria, *see* IOF

International Association of Limnology, 291

Investigator, RIMS, 36, 42, 107, 109, 132, 140, 184, 199, 234, 249, 253

Ipnops (fish), 184

Iron sulphide, 160

Jelly-fish, 84, 95, 101, 102, 121, 148, 168, 190, 239, 251–2

Jezirat Halaniya Island, *see* Halaniya

Joe Chamberlain fish, 199

Kaiser-i-Hind, SS, 41, 43

Kandy, Ceylon, 203

Karanja, BISS, 246

Karachi, 130–2, 135, 194

Karachi Plateau, 130

Kardiva Channel, Maldives, 199, 202, 221, 225, 227, 231, 237

Kellett, HMS, 276

Kemp, S. W., Director, *Discovery* investigations, 26

Khedivial Mail Co. Ltd, 44

Khor Fakkan (Arabian village), 146
Khorya Morya Islands, 116; *see also*
    Kuria Muria Islands
Kilindini, 170
Kingaje Bay, 187
King Fuad Bank, 230, 237, 266
Kitching, J., 290
Kolumadulu Atoll, Maldives, 213, 215
Koshani Island, Pemba, 190
Koubbeh Palace, Cairo, 266
Krakatoa, 172
Kuria Muria Islands, 114, 314

Laccadive-Maldive ridge, 233
Laccadive Sea, 203
Laganum (echinoid or sea-urchin), 254
Lanier, Captain, Acting Port Officer
    and Pilot, Mahé, 196
Lawrence, RIMS, 153
Lemuria, 314
Lepas (barnacle), 102
Leptocephali (eel larvae), 88
Lightning, HMS, 36
Light organs, 198
Lithothamnion (coralline alga), 90, 119,
    122, 217
Livingstone, D., 176
Lloyd Jones, J., 28
London, Midland & Scottish Railway
    Company (LMS), 276
Lophelia, *see* Corals
Lophohelia (coral), 251
Lucas sounding machine, 66

Mabahiss, HEMS, 299–305
Macan, T. T., 14, 289–91
MacDonald, Captain, Ellerman-City
    Line, 41
MacElderry, Mr, Chief Secretary,
    British Residency, Zanzibar, 176
MacKenzie, Captain K. N., 14, 274–6
MacKinnon, MacKenzie & Co., 42,
    153
Maclear, Captain J. F. L. P., 20
Macrurus (fish), 198–9
Madras, 203
Magnetic observations, 219, 232

Mahé Island, Seychelles, 195
Malacosteus (fish), 199
Malaria, *see* Illnesses
Maldive Archipelago, 199, 202, 209,
    215, 237
Maldive ridge, 209, 228
Maldives representative, Ceylon, 205
Maldives, Sultan of, 202
Malé, Maldives, 202
Manganese nodules, 238–9
Mangroves, 196
Manza Bay, 180
Marine Survey of India, 234
Marriott, Captain, RN, 26
Mashobra, SS, 75
Matthews, D. J., 26
Mawson, Sir Douglas, 40
Medical Research Council, 288
Menai Bay, Zanzibar, 185
Meteorological observations, 59–60
Meteorological Office, 29
Michael Sars Expedition, 22
Midu-Huludu, Addu Atoll, 212
Minikoi, Maldives, 231
Minister of Public Instruction, Egypt,
    266
Mkoani Channel, Pemba Island, 188
Mkokotoni Bay, Zanzibar, 177
Modasa, SS, 209
Mohamed, Abdel Fattah, 284–8
Mombasa, 145, 170–2
Monagym, HEMS, 78
Monsoon, 163, 193, 197
Mud line, 177
Mulakadu Island, Addu Atoll, 211
Mulaku Atoll, Maldives, 216
Mullet, 88
Munro Bros, 41, 50, 109
Muona Buona Lighthouse, 190
Murex (mollusc), 76
Murray, John Challenger, 24, 37, 264,
    266
Murray, Thomas Henderson, 22, 266
Murray Ridge, 130, 135
Murray, Sir John, 19 et seq., 37, 201,
    239
Muscat, 140–3, 179

Muscat, Sultan of, 120
Muttrah, Muscat, 142

Nairobi, 172
Narbadda, River, 152
Naucrates (fish), 234
Nares, Captain G. S., 20
Negretti & Zambra, 41
Nitrite, 319
Nitrogen cycle, 319
Noctilua (dinoflagellate), 125, 128

Oman, *see* Gulf of
Ophiuroids (brittle stars), 91, 124, 129,
    181, 253
Orca (killer whale), 249
Ormonde, HMS, 276
Orontes, SS, 98
Owen Fracture Zone, 313
Oxygen, dissolved, 62

P. & O. Co., 41, 111
Pantin, C. F. A., 273, 288
Paralomis (anomuran crab), 128
Pathan, RIMS, 153
Pearsall, W. H., 289
Pegea (salp), 121, 128, 143
Pelagia (jelly-fish), 101, 144, 168,
    239
Pelham Aldrich, Captain, HMS *Egeria*,
    20
Pemba Island, 176, 178, 179, 188
Pendulum observations, 205, 211, 232
Penzance, HMS, 98
Percy Sladen Expedition to Lake
    Titicaca, 288
Peredenya, Ceylon, 204
Perim Coal Company, 92
Perim Island, 77, 92, 232, 260
Periphylla (jelly-fish), 95, 102, 251
Persia, 143, 144, 145
Petersen grab, 71, 75
pH, 62
Phipson, Port Health Officer, Aden,
    98, 256
Phormosoma (sea-urchin), 200
Phosphorescence, 158, 162

Phytoplankton net, Harvey, 58, 186
Pyrazus (mollusc), 212
Pirogues, native canoes, Mahé, 195
Pirula (mollusc), 144
Plankton, 88
Plankton nets, 57, 58
Plate tectonics, 314
Pola, RV, 295
Polychaets (worms), 248, 260, 261
Porcupine, HMS, 36
Porpita (coelenterate), 112–13, 164
Porpoises, 78, 88, 98, 109, 116, 148,
    163, 199, 202–3, 234, 238, 244,
    254
Port Said, 38, 42, 75, 267
Port Tewfig, Suez, 76, 78, 261
Port Victoria, Mahé, Seychelles, 195
Ports and Lights Administration,
    Egypt, 304
Portuguese ownership of South Malé,
    Maldives, 218
Pottery, 179
Prashad, Baini, Zoological Survey of
    India, 42, 144
Prater, Mr, Bombay Natural History
    Society, 153
Prawns, *see* Decapod shrimps
Pretorian, SS, 274
Priestman Bros, 41, 71, 75
Prince of Wales Museum, Bombay,
    153
Promotions of crew members, 263
Proudman, Professor J., 287
Psychrometer, Asman, 86
Pteropods, 88, 261
Puerulus (lobster), 255
Pumice, 172
Putali Island, Addu Atoll, 212
Pycnogonids (sea-spiders), 91
Pyrosoma (salp), 161, 198, 250, 251

Radiolarians, 169
Ramadan, 161
Rankine, Sir Richard, British Resident,
    Zanzibar, 176
Ranpura, SS, 267
Ras al Hadd, Oman, 127, 130, 250

Ras Ali Bash Kil promontory, Somalia, 100

Ras al Khabba promontory, Arabia, 150

Ras Alula, Somalia, 98

Ras Fartik (Ras Fartak, South Yemen), 98

Ras Madraka, Oman, 118, 120, 121

Ras Sukhra, Oman, 119

Rattray J., Commander, RIM, 131

Red clay, 239

Red Sea, 260–2

Renard, Abbé, 20

Rey, Mr, Hall & Co., 44

Rhineodon (whale shark), 249

Rhizosolenia (diatom), 93

Rift Valley, East African, 314

Robber crab, *see* Giant robber crab

Rolleston, Mr, District Officer, Pemba Island, 189

Ross, George Clunies, 21

Rostellaria (mollusc), 127, 139, 144

Royal Indian Marine Dockyard, Bombay, 154

Royal Naval College, Dartmouth, 276

Royal Society, Sewell's fellowship, 205

Sagitta (arrow-worm), 99

Salama Bey, Acting Director, Coast-Guard Administration, 39, 264

Salinity, 62

Salisbury, Lord, British Prime Minister, 21

Salpa, 88, 142

Salps, 88, 121, 128, 142–3, 162, 250

Sanderson, Commander, Marine Survey of India, 234

Sargasso weed, 102, 109, 246, 254, 260

Saunders, J. T., 289

Schmidt, J., 25, 312–13

Sea-cucumber, *see* Holothurians

Sea snake, 145

Secchi disk, 58, 186

Setarches (fish), 181

Sewell, R. B. Seymour, 13, 271–3

Seychelles Bank, 195–6

Seychelles Islands, 195–7

Seymour Sewell, *see* Sewell

Sharks, 86, 91, 113, 164, 202, 221, 239, 243, 245

Shearwaters, 244

Siphonophores, 88

Snapper lead, 70

Socotra current, 99, 102, 107

Socotra Island, 100, 194, 240, 243, 246

Soda Island, Khorya Morya group, 116

Sokhay, Colonel, Director, Haffkine Institute, 154

Sollum, HEMS, 264

Somers, Captain, Assistant Port Officer, Zanzibar, 189

Sorbonne, Paris, 280

Sounding machine, Lucas, 66

Sounding rod, Baillie, 66

Sounding tube, Driver, 66

South Malé Atoll, Maldives, 217–19

South Malosmadulu Atoll, Maldives, 223, 230, 238

Spence, Sir Reginald, Bombay Natural History Society, 153

Spurrier, Dr, Curator, Zanzibar Museum, 176

Squilla, 253; *see also* Stomatopods

Stanley, Sir Henry Morton, 176

Stirling, Scotland, 19

Stomatopods (mantis or locust shrimps), 89, 190, 253

Stork, HMS, 277

Stubbs, Sir Edward, Governor of Ceylon, 205

Subduction, 313

Suez, 77, 78

Suez Canal, 76

Sultan of South Malé, Maldives, 217–19

Sultan's Island, South Malé, Maldives, 217–19

Superphosphate, 20

Survey of India, 205

Swan Hunter and Wigham Richardson, 301

Swimming crab, 260

Sword-fish, 102, 262

Synapta (holothurian), 212

Tait, P. G., Professor of Physics,
    University of Edinburgh, 19
Taj Hotel, Bombay, 153
Tajura, *see* Gulf of Tajura
Tanga, 181
Tapti, River, 152
Tate Regan, C., 24
Taxonomic results, 317
Taylor, F., Contractor, Colombo, 235
Taylor, G. I., 24
Taylor, Odin, Chief Engineer, Sukkur
    Barrage, 131
Telegraph Construction and
    Maintenance Co., 41
Temple of the Sacred Tooth, Kandy,
    Ceylon, 204
The Man Who Never Was, film
    involving Farquharson, 277
Thermograph, recording, 60
Thompson, Sir Charles Wyville, 19,
    36
Thomson, E. F., 278–80
Thurson, SS, 41
Timarafuri Island, Kolumadulu Atoll,
    Maldives, 214
Tiwi, near Mombasa, 171
Toddu Island, Maldives, 227, 230
Tombasi, Mr, Resident of Karachi, and
    giant ray, 168
Toulouse, 280
Tourky, Dr, University of Cairo, 42
Transform faults, 313
Trawls
    Agassiz, 51
    Monegasque, 53
    otter, 50
Trichaster (ophiuroid), 253, 254
Trichodesmium (alga), 93, 99, 125,
    217
Tripoli, University of, Libya, 288
Tubipora, *see* Corals

Turtle, 131

Unesco, 7, 13
Union Castle Line, 274

Victoria (Italian ship), 98
Virgularia (sea-pen), 94, 188
Violin, Faouzi playing for Sultan of
    South Malé, 219

Wadge Bank, 234
Wait, Mr, Acting Chief Secretary to
    the Ceylon Government, 205
Wallich, George Charles, 35
Wallich, Nathaniel, 35
Walsh, Dr, Administrator, Mahé, 196
Water bottles
    Eckman reversing, 60
    Nansen-Pettersson insulating, 60
Wells Pasha, Admiral, RN, Head of
    the Egyptian Ports and Lights
    Department, 39, 264
Westcott & Laurance, 41
Whales, 106, 164, 176, 249
Whale-sharks, *see* *Rhineodon*
Wharton, Captain W. J. L.,
    Hydrographer, 20
William Scoresby, RRS, 37
Wimpenny, R. S., 280, 301
Winch, hydrographic, 49
Winch, trawling, 68 et seq.
Wire, hydrographic, 49, 240
Wire, trawl, 48
Wiringilli Island, Addu Atoll, 210–11
Wiseman, J. D. H., 290, 314

Zanzibar, 175–6, 178, 184
Zanzibar Museum, 176
Zanzibar, Sultan of, 175, 176, 190
Zoogeography, 273, 317
Zoological Survey of India, 24, 189,
    271–2
Zukhiar Island, 87, 89